Praise for *Witch*

"In this rewarding book Robin Briggs repeatedly reminds us of what is perhaps the most dumbfounding aspect of the ghastly witch-trials of the early modern period: the simple, now all-but-unassimilable fact that they were carried out in good faith."
—*The Sunday Times*

"Robin Briggs writes with a combination of accessibility, narrative flair, and the expansive painstaking knowledge of a rigorously thorough, professional historian. He has written a popular yet scholarly analysis of witchcraft that dispels long-standing misconceptions held by specialists and a public keenly interested in the subject." —*Houston Chronicle*

"His arguments are persuasive." —Jeanette Winterson

"A masterly history of witch-hunts." —*Sunday Telegraph*

"An impressively researched cross-cultural exploration of a disturbing phenomenon in European history. . . . The circumstances surrounding the decline of a belief in witchcraft reserve an additional volume from this able researcher and deft writer."
—*Kirkus Reviews*

"This book covers in great detail the myths and folklore that surround witchcraft and the way in which neighbors of alleged witches blamed all their ill fortune on these individuals."
—*Manchester Evening News*

"Recommended reading . . . a fascinating study of the social and cultural context of European witchcraft."
—*USA Today*

PENGUIN BOOKS

WITCHES & NEIGHBORS

Robin Briggs is a senior research fellow of All Souls College and a university lecturer in modern history at Oxford. Educated at Balliol College, Oxford, he has been at All Souls since his election as a prize fellow in 1964.

WITCHES

&

NEIGHBORS

The Social and Cultural Context of
European Witchcraft

ROBIN BRIGGS

PENGUIN BOOKS

PENGUIN BOOKS
Published by the Penguin Group
Penguin Putnam Inc., 375 Hudson Street,
New York, New York 10014, U.S.A.
Penguin Books Ltd, 27 Wrights Lane, London W8 5TZ, England
Penguin Books Australia Ltd, Ringwood, Victoria, Australia
Penguin Books Canada Ltd, 10 Alcorn Avenue,
Toronto, Ontario, Canada M4V 3B2
Penguin Books (N.Z.) Ltd, 182–190 Wairau Road,
Auckland 10, New Zealand

Penguin Books Ltd, Registered Offices:
Harmondsworth, Middlesex, England

First published in Great Britain by HarperCollins Publishers, 1996
First published in the United States of America by Viking Penguin,
a division of Penguin Books USA Inc. 1996
Published in Penguin Books 1998

1 3 5 7 9 10 8 6 4 2

Illustrations from "The Beggars" series by Jacques Callot.
Courtesy of the Musée Lorrain, Nancy, France.
Photographs by Rémi Songeur.

THE LIBRARY OF CONGRESS HAS CATALOGUED THE VIKING HARDCOVER AS FOLLOWS:
Briggs, Robin.
Witches & neighbors: the social and cultural context
of European witchcraft / Robin Briggs.
Briggs, Robin.
p.   cm.
Includes bibliographical references and index.
ISBN 0-670-83589-7 (hc.)
ISBN 0 14 01.4438 2 (pbk.)
I. Title.   II. Title: Witches and neighbors.
BF1584.E9B75   1996
133.4′3′094—dc20   96–25843

Printed in the United States of America
Set in Linotron Garamond No. 3

FOR BRIDGET AND CHRISTOPHER HILL

Contents

MAPS

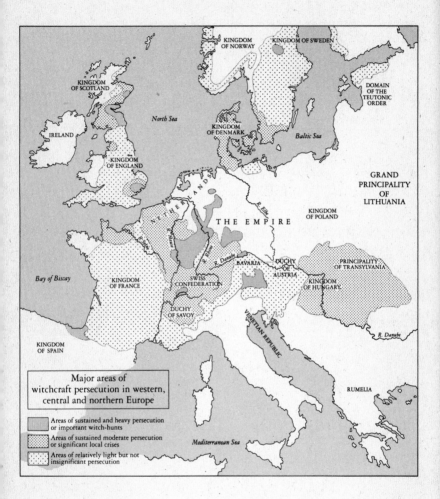

KINGDOM OF NORWAY
KINGDOM OF SWEDEN
KINGDOM OF SCOTLAND
DOMAIN OF THE TEUTONIC ORDER
IRELAND
North Sea
KINGDOM OF DENMARK
Baltic Sea
KINGDOM OF ENGLAND
GRAND PRINCIPALITY OF LITHUANIA
NETHERLANDS
THE EMPIRE
R. Elbe
KINGDOM OF POLAND
R. Rhine
Bay of Biscay
R. Rhine
R. Danube
BAVARIA
DUCHY OF AUSTRIA
PRINCIPALITY OF TRANSYLVANIA
KINGDOM OF FRANCE
SWISS CONFEDERATION
KINGDOM OF HUNGARY
DUCHY OF SAVOY
VENETIAN REPUBLIC
R. Danube
KINGDOM OF SPAIN
RUMELIA
Mediterranean Sea

Major areas of witchcraft persecution in western, central and northern Europe

Areas of sustained and heavy persecution or important witch-hunts

Areas of sustained moderate persecution or significant local crises

Areas of relatively light but not insignificant persecution

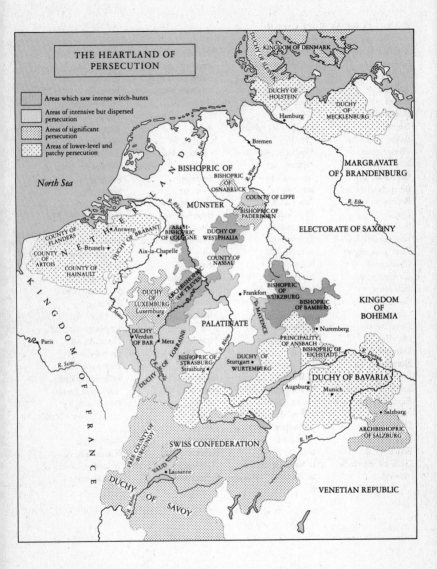

THE HEARTLAND OF
PERSECUTION

Areas which saw intense witch-hunts

Areas of intensive but dispersed
persecution

Areas of significant
persecution

Areas of lower-level and
patchy persecution

North Sea

KINGDOM OF DENMARK

DUCHY OF SLESVIG

DUCHY OF
HOLSTEIN

DUCHY
OF
MECKLENBURG

Hamburg

Bremen

MARGRAVATE
OF BRANDENBURG

BISHOPRIC OF
OSNABRÜCK

R. Ems

R. Weser

R. Elbe

BISHOPRIC OF

COUNTY OF LIPPE

MÜNSTER

BISHOPRIC OF
PADERBORN

ELECTORATE OF SAXONY

COUNTY OF
FLANDERS

Antwerp

N E T H E R L A N D S

DUCHY OF BRABANT

ARCH-
BISHOPRIC
OF COLOGNE

DUCHY OF
WESTPHALIA

R. Rhine

Brussels

COUNTY OF
ARTOIS

Aix-la-Chapelle

COUNTY OF
HAINAULT

COUNTY OF
NASSAU

KINGDOM

DUCHY
OF
LUXEMBURG

ARCHBISHOPRIC
OF TREVES

Luxemburg

R. Meuse

BISHOPRIC
OF WÜRZBURG

Frankfort

BISHOPRIC
OF BAMBERG

KINGDOM
OF
BOHEMIA

R. Danube

PALATINATE

DUCHY
OF BAR

Verdun

Metz

PRINCIPALITY
OF ANSBACH

Nuremberg

BISHOPRIC OF
EICHSTÄDT

O F

Paris

R. Seine

DUCHY OF LORRAINE

R. Moselle

R. Rhine

BISHOPRIC OF
STRASBURG

Strasburg

DUCHY OF
WÜRTEMBERG

Stuttgart

DUCHY OF BAVARIA

F R A N C E

Augsburg

Munich

Salzburg

ARCHBISHOPRIC
OF SALZBURG

FREE COUNTY OF
BURGUNDY

SWISS CONFEDERATION

R. Inn

VAUD

Lausanne

VENETIAN REPUBLIC

DUCHY
OF
SAVOY

KEY TO PLACE-NAMES

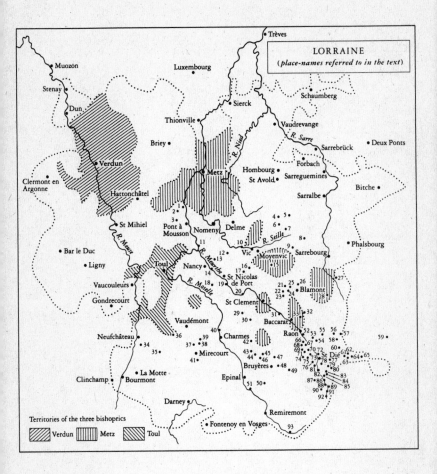

LORRAINE
(*place-names referred to in the text*)

Trèves

Muozon

Luxembourg

Stenay

Schaumberg

Dun

Sierck

Thionville

Vaudrevange

R. Nied

R. Sarre

Briey

Sarrebrück

Deux Ponts

Verdun

Metz

Hombourg

Forbach

Clermont en Argonne

Hattonchâtel

St Avold

Sarreguemines

Bitche

Sarralbe

2

3

Pont à Mousson

Nomeny

Delme

4 5

6

7

St Mihiel

R. Meuse

11

10

Vic

R. Seille

8

9

Sarrebourg

Phalsbourg

Bar le Duc

12

Moyenvic

13

Ligny

R. Meurthe

13

14

Toul

Nancy

16

17

St Nicolas de Port

21 25 26

22 24

Blamont

27

Vaucouleurs

R. Moselle

18

19

23

28

Gondrecourt

20

St Clement

29

30

31 32

33

Vaudémont

Baccarat

36

40

Charmes

Raon

52 53 55 56

54 58 57

Neufchâteau

39

37 38

42

66 67 60

68 69 70 72

St Dié

61 62

34

Mirecourt

43

44

45 47

46

74 75 73 77 79

80

63

64 65

35

41

Bruyères

48

76 81

49

82

83

Clinchamp

La Motte Bourmont

Epinal

87 86 84 85

90 89

88 91

Darney

51 50

92

Remiremont

93

Fontenoy en Vosges

Territories of the three bishoprics

Verdun   Metz   Toul

Preface

Like most books, this one could not have been written without help from many people; too many, in fact, for it to be possible to thank them all by name. The support of institutions has also been invaluable, above all that of All Souls College. Both the archival research and the writing would have taken far longer but for the special opportunities and freedom I have been given. Working in foreign archives is an expensive business, and I have received generous grants from my college, the Oxford Modern History Faculty, and the British Academy. The staff of the Departmental Archives at Nancy have shown enormous patience and efficiency over the years, for which I am particularly grateful; working there has always been a special pleasure. An additional reason for this has been the kindly interest taken in my work by two eminent local historians, Guy Cabourdin and Jean Coudert.

However gloomy their subject matter, historians of witchcraft are a friendly group, always ready to exchange material and ideas. Various conferences and less formal meetings have allowed me to learn from many people. Among those who have been particularly helpful over the years I must single out Alfred Soman, Stuart Clark, Lyndal Roper, David Harley and Jim Sharpe, but there have been many others. Caroline Oates generously allowed me to read her unpublished thesis. I have enjoyed many stimulating conversations with my one-time pupil and present colleague Scott Mandelbrote and with Miri Rubin of Pembroke College. Numerous invitations to give lectures and seminar papers have allowed me to try out my ideas in front of some very lively audiences.

The genesis of this book goes back to a conversation with Julia Segal, although I fear it is not quite the lively short essay she had in mind; her interest and encouragement were vital at that point. Since then the project has taken shape with the aid of my literary agent Felicity Bryan, Stuart Proffitt of Harper-Collins and Peter Mayer of Viking Penguin, who have all kept me up to the mark in a most tactful manner. I owe a special debt to my editor Philip Gwyn Jones for his attentive reading of the text, and for many suggestions I have gladly followed. His work has been followed up by meticulous copy editing from Toby Mundy, for which I am very grateful. Above all, however, I must thank my wife Daphne, who has helped me in every possible way. Without her input, both intellectual and practical, the book would have taken much longer and lacked some important dimensions. For whatever is still wrong with it, the responsibility is of course my own.

The dedication acknowledges a very special debt, of the type that can hardly be repaid. Ever since my undergraduate days at Balliol College I have benefited more than I can say from the kindness and inspiration given by Bridget and Christopher Hill. They have been the warmest and best of friends, and this is some token of my gratitude. I hope that a book which is much concerned with the lives of ordinary people and of women in the past will have a particular appeal for two historians who have written so illuminatingly on these matters.

INTRODUCTION

WITCHES HAVE HAUNTED the human imagination with remarkable persistence. Destructive and malicious figures, they have always represented the opposite of all positive values. The witch is an incarnation of the 'other', a human being who has betrayed his or her natural allegiances to become an agent of evil. Belief in such persons and such conduct has been general across both time and space. Very few known human societies appear to have been completely free from it. Some African pastoral tribes with a peculiarly nomadic lifestyle seemed to be among these rare exceptions; their response to social conflict was to move on and if necessary to split into new groupings. As soon as they changed to a more sedentary existence, however, accusations of witchcraft started to proliferate among them, because their traditional methods for defusing conflict were no longer available. As this example suggests, exceptions to the rule are in fact so rare that one must start from the assumption that any given society will possess such beliefs. The obvious exceptions are the industrialized societies of the modern Western world, in which belief in witchcraft is generally stigmatized as a sign of primitivism. As with many such attitudes, this one is none too firmly based in either superior practice or greater understanding. The presence in the West of considerable pockets of residual belief in witchcraft is perhaps the least of the objections to this view. One might also doubt whether we are really more tolerant towards those identified as deviants, or indeed to minority groups more generally. If we in the industrialized world mostly take witchcraft less seriously than our ancestors did, this arguably owes more to social changes than to any massive spread of Enlightenment values.

Such social changes have much to do with the decline of neighbourhood and the associated rise of national and bureaucratic power structures as dominating forces in our lives. There is a sense in which many people now deal with social conflict as the African nomads did; they move on or find new groups to associate with. Large and amorphous communities allow such freedoms, while we rarely perceive neighbours as direct competitors. It is therefore hard for us to understand the ways village and small-town societies used to work, when their members were far less mobile and interacted in a much closer fashion at many levels. For good or ill, people could not easily escape one another, something which played a vital role in breeding charges of witchcraft. This was the case because the core of the belief lay in the notion that witches had peculiar powers to harm their neighbours and the community at large. Not only were they the enemy within, they were individuals whom their supposed victims knew all too well, whose reputations were built up over many years by an insidious process of rumour and gossip. In calling this book *Witches & Neighbours* I have deliberately placed the emphasis on this social context, whose detailed workings will be discussed at some length.

Witchcraft cannot, however, be explained in purely social terms. There is also a cultural context, albeit of a very broad kind. Here too it is worth thinking about the reasons for the decline of belief in witchcraft. Religious ideas no longer dominate our world because the Christian churches have abandoned their old pretensions that they can offer various means of explanation, prediction and control in the natural world; the rise of modern science has rendered such claims untenable by mainstream churches so that they only survive amongst fringe groups of fundamentalists. Good and evil, God and the Devil – it is not only the words but the concepts which are mutually dependent. If witches had power, this was because the world was thought to be full of hidden and potent forces that ultimately referred back to the two great antagonists. In order to harm other people, the witch was therefore normally supposed to be in contact with some external source of power, located in the world of spirits, demons and devils. Religion, magic and witchcraft have thus been inextricably linked throughout human history. As enemies of society, witches have also been believed to form a furtive and conspiratorial anti-society. To this end they have allegedly flown by night to meetings where orgiastic, blasphemous or cannibalistic rituals symbolize their defection from social and personal virtue. While these more elaborate beliefs do vary considerably in different cultures, none of them appears to be culture-specific; they all belong to the general syndrome of witchcraft. Similar fantasies reappear in very different local contexts, although each combination is subtly different.

Witchcraft is therefore culturally constructed in a specific sense, for it depends on certain views about the natural world and the ways it operates. A third type of context must be considered as well, for there are overwhelming reasons to believe that it is also psychologically constructed. So pervasive a belief must respond to deep human needs or anxieties. At one level it is a simple attempt to explain misfortune, which in turn may offer the hope this can be reversed. It also seems to incorporate elements of our shared fantasy life, to articulate some of our deepest fears and to express our latent suspicions of other people. There may be a very real sense in which societies which abandon belief in witchcraft or diabolical power feel deprived in consequence and need to develop alternative demonologies. Nostalgia for traditional witchcraft beliefs is a rather different phenomenon that appears to have become endemic in modern Western culture. Goya produced terrifying pictures of witches in whom he did not believe; now the cinema's capacity to fake the supernatural has encouraged a genre of horror movies which exploits every past stereotype. Witches are everywhere in modern children's literature. Sometimes they retain their old character, representing evil in its most virulent form, but more often they have become either harmless tricksters or repositories of ancient wisdom. Such trends remind us how easily the pliable figure of the witch can be manipulated to fit the spirit of each age.

The extreme case of such manipulation is found in the modern pseudo-religion of witchcraft. Although this syncretic construct does cobble together elements of genuine pagan belief and ritual, much of it appears to rest on a false genealogy. Its adepts commonly assert that the witches persecuted in medieval and early modern Europe were genuine dissidents who followed a pre-Christian natural religion and used a range of herbal and occult medical techniques. This picture has just enough marginal plausibility to be hard to refute completely, yet it is almost wholly wrong. The witches of the past were not adherents of surviving pagan cults or guardians of secret knowledge. Most popular accounts of the matter repeat a series of misconceptions, which threaten to become conventional wisdom. It is dangerously easy for writers who do not know either the sources or the specialized literature to pick up details, then exaggerate their significance or otherwise misinterpret them. For example, we shall see that although some of those accused of witchcraft were magical healers whose activities were condemned by the church, there was nothing knowingly pagan in their mixture of animist and Christian belief. They became deviants because others identified them as such, not through any conscious intent. In any case they only formed a small minority of the persecuted, most of whom had done no more than find themselves at odds with their neighbours. This pattern, long familiar to social anthropologists, is exactly what one would naturally expect to find in Europe. It has taken a series of ingenious historical errors to obscure some rather obvious truths. Since many people plainly want to believe in these errors, it seems unlikely that the resulting fog of disinformation will ever be properly dispersed.

At the risk of disappointing many people in search of sensational discoveries or retrospective legitimation, one simple point must be made. Historical European witchcraft is quite simply a fiction, in the sense that there is no evidence that witches existed, still less that they celebrated black masses or worshipped strange gods. There were plenty of individuals who dabbled in the occult, in search of wealth, power or revenge, but none of these thought themselves members of a satanic sect. The fact that clerics often tried to lump different kinds of behaviour together under the heading of diabolism should not lead us to follow suit. We need to distinguish scrupulously between forms of conduct and the various contemporary perceptions of them, as we do between types of alleged witches. As these remarks will have suggested, the belief system that made witchcraft credible was both widespread and complex. This book sets out to show how it related to reality and how far it pervaded the mental and social worlds of our ancestors. My concern is as much to reconstruct a way of thinking and living as to offer explanations for the great persecutions of the sixteenth and seventeenth centuries.

It is understandable that nearly all previous historians have made the persecution their main subject, since the idea of the witch-hunt has been so prevalent. In addition, the sources are essentially records of the legal processes by which some of the suspects met their fate. Even so, too many of these historians have thought they could find a single hidden reason for this sad episode in the European past. The persecution is almost always interpreted as a cover for some other hidden purpose, whether it be state-building, the imposition of patriarchy or religious bigotry. Although these explanations usually possess some genuine value, they always break down if they are applied in too mechanical or sweeping a fashion. The notion of a single primary reason behind these events is an obvious misfit, since on close investigation the causes turn out to be dauntingly complex. In fact the persecution is a classic example of multiple causation, which varied considerably across both time and space during its relatively brief existence. As a result, sweeping generalizations about it are either false or so banal as to lack any analytical power. My approach is rather different, for the main focus is on the lives and beliefs of the ordinary people who were at once the victims and the principal instigators of most prosecutions. Explanations need to start at this level, with an analysis of the climate in which beliefs flourished. Furthermore, my main purpose is to explore these structures, with their multiple ramifications. While the persecution must be a constant theme of this book, I do not see it as the central one. In the end I hope this oblique approach actually makes it much easier to place witch-hunting in perspective and to understand its contingent nature.

A degree of concentration on the persecution is inevitable, since without it we would know relatively little about the much more enduring phenomenon of local belief in witchcraft. Scattered references stretching back to the early Middle Ages, the writings of nineteenth-century folklorists and novelists and the work of recent social anthropologists working in rural Europe all attest to this longevity. They can, however, only give us a very partial view, because they are either too fragmented or too late in time. The great bulk of our information comes from the surviving trials of witches and from the writings of contemporary reporters and commentators. Despite its abundance, this material too demands great caution on the part of its interpreters. We cannot simply assume that such moments of extreme tension and catharsis are typical, any more than we should believe that the experience of one region can stand for all. For example, there is some reason to think that persecution began when popular anxiety about witchcraft was at a relatively low level and only became endemic in a period of grave social and economic dislocation. The experience of persecution probably heightened anxiety among the general population further, leading to threats of epidemic witch-hunting just as elite opinion was moving decisively against such action. None of this can be proven, or is ever likely to be; it remains a plausible hypothesis to be judged as much by its inner coherence as its relation to the known facts.

Witchcraft is also rendered slippery by its status as a logical and linguistic construct whose boundaries are both arbitrary and insecure. This difficulty already presented itself in relation to the various Biblical references; what did the Hebrew and Greek terms translated as 'witch' really mean? More recently the term 'witch-hunt' has entered the language to express the idea of a paranoid search for hidden deviants. A subtle distortion is threatened here, for witches are thereby assimilated to persecuted minorities in a more general sense. While there are clearly very important parallels between the labelling and scapegoating processes involved and the construction of stereotypes, it is vital to understand that they vary significantly case by case. However fruitful a comparison between Senator Joseph McCarthy and the East Anglian 'witchfinder general' Matthew Hopkins may prove, it must be informed by a sense of their profound differences. When Arthur Miller used the Salem trials in *The Crucible* to write a parable on McCarthyism, the result was a gripping play which did considerable violence to the historical reality.

Miller's historical error was a venial one, for the central tension in his play between theocracy and personal liberty really did exist in New England, although it does not explain the Salem outbreak in quite the ways he thought. There is much less excuse for the widely drawn parallel between the Nazi Holocaust and the persecution of witches. There are points in common here – among them the projection of evil onto others and accusations of ritual magic and child murder – but genocide is radically different from the search for hidden inner enemies. One of the most misleading ideas about the witchcraft persecution is that it was inspired and manipulated by the ruling elites for their own cynical purposes. This is precisely the image that the Holocaust comparison throws up, in combination with a huge exaggeration of the numbers involved. On the wilder shores of the feminist and witch-cult movements a potent myth has become established, to the effect that 9 million women were burned as witches in Europe; gendercide rather than genocide. This is an overestimate by a factor of up to 200, for the most reasonable modern estimates suggest perhaps 100,000 trials between 1450 and 1750, with something between 40,000 and 50,000 executions, of which 20 to 25 per cent were of men.

These figures are chilling enough, but they have to be set in the context of what was probably the harshest period of capital punishments in European history. With few exceptions European criminal courts showed notable restraint and caution in dealing with witchcraft suspects, who often displayed a remarkable willingness to confess impossible acts. In most areas executions had virtually stopped long before it was respectable to deny that there were such figures as witches. Nor did ordinary people normally rush to prosecute neighbours whom they suspected of damaging them by maleficent witchcraft; it often took fifteen or twenty years of accumulated incidents before they would act. If these remarks surprise most readers, this illustrates an alarming general failure in our understanding. Common assumptions about the subject tend to have one very marked feature in common, which is that they are hopelessly wrong. It is no real surprise to find that general textbooks on the early modern period, often written by excellent historians, usually offer only a mixture of half-truths and errors, if they dare to write about witchcraft at all.

This curious situation must in part reflect the dangers of growing specialization in historical studies, since the last thirty years have seen numerous admirable books and articles on the history of witchcraft. It has often been suggested that the subject has received too much attention; certainly there can be few major archives which remain unexplored. For the first time it has become possible to build up a regional map showing the situation across most of Europe in some detail. While this represents an enormous advance in knowledge, the gains have been much less obvious in interpretative terms. The more we know, and the more ingenious and subtle local analyses emerge, the harder it apparently becomes to give coherent answers to many large questions. Similar remarks could be made about many other areas of study both within and outside history, which implies that there is a general intellectual problem here. The whole tendency of post-Enlightenment thought in the West has been to divide in order to understand and to apply a cognitive method based on the rigorous testing of all hypotheses. Such trends have long since taken the natural sciences beyond the full comprehension of outsiders, a situation most people accept with apparent equanimity. We 'know' science works because its practical applications structure our whole lives, and we accord it much of the awe and respect once reserved for religious systems.

History, even more than the social sciences, is in a very different situation. Although most of its production may be internal, in the sense that it is only read by other historians, this work must ultimately be communicable to a wider public to have any real impact. In the world of the sound-bite and the quick fix it is hard to get much attention for the message that the past was almost as complex as the present and that reconstructing it requires as much patience as rebuilding a Greek vase from the surviving fragments. When dealing with a subject like witchcraft the difficulties are in some respects even greater, because it merges into many neighbouring areas. Witchcraft was not an objective reality but a set of interpretations, something which went on in the mind. Even as a crime it was 'transparent', with a hole at the centre, since witches did not actually do most of the things alleged against them. In consequence it drew to itself a great range of conflicts and can only be explained properly in the context of the whole society within which it existed. This is a principle, already well understood by social anthropologists, which historians have been slow to accept.

The challenge of making historical witchcraft comprehensible is therefore a formidable one and this book will not offer any easy answers. Yet there is something important to be said on the other side. The subject is enormously attractive, because it allows us privileged access into the world of ordinary people in the past. We hear them talking about their everyday lives, their hopes and fears, their families. It is the kind of fault-line which provides unique opportunities for understanding their society, a hotly disputed boundary zone where categories, practices and beliefs either clashed or failed to work properly. In these respects the legal persecution is only part of something much larger and more enduring. We have to start from the records of persecution but the first thing to reconstruct is the history of witchcraft in this broader sense. Only when we understand how the system functioned at the base will we be able to make much sense of its relationship to higher authority. There is a further advantage to this approach, for paradoxically it is at this local level that it is easiest to generalize across much of Europe.

A truly comprehensive analysis of European witchcraft would require not only several large volumes but also several lifetimes of study. The secondary literature on the subject is very large and continues to expand. Some massive archives (often in appalling handwriting) still await the really detailed scrutiny which should unlock their secrets. Faced with this daunting prospect I have adopted a deliberately primitive approach, in the sense of simply writing down what I believe to be the essential truths about the phenomenon. In the process I have rarely stopped to indicate the complexity of the historiography or to engage in formal arguments designed to refute or qualify the views of other historians. Since the endnotes have been restricted to the barest indications of source material for quotations and factual statements, many of my intellectual debts have gone unacknowledged. Like most historians I am something of an intellectual magpie, picking up ideas where they catch my fancy, then forgetting their exact provenance, so it would have been impossible for me to give credit everywhere it is due in any case. Those who know the literature, however, will recognise both how much I have borrowed from others and how controversial many of my claims must be. Anyone who proceeds like this is bound to feel like a hermit crab who has rashly – or even suicidally – abandoned his shell. My reason for proceeding in this eccentric fashion is that I believe the only way to match up to the challenge of this enormous subject is to take proportionately large risks. It is simply not worth trying to write a 'safe' book about witchcraft. We would all like to be infallible, but since all previous attempts in this vein have been littered with errors, I am under no illusions that I shall have avoided the innumerable pitfalls.

A little more should be said about geographical range. I have been able to draw on secondary works, sometimes also printed documents, which relate to a large part of Western, Northern, and Central Europe. More specifically, the areas concerned include France, England, Scotland, the Low Countries, Scandinavia, parts of Germany and the smaller states between France and the Empire (Luxembourg, Lorraine, Switzerland, and Savoy). Southern Europe is less well covered, since available information on Italy and Spain tends to be limited to certain regions that may be atypical, such as Venice and the Basque country. The English colonists took their witchcraft beliefs across the Atlantic and some of the most exciting work on witchcraft concerns New England. In this respect the Old and the New World are very close, and I have felt able to incorporate material from New England without any sense of strain. My own research work has involved the close study of nearly 400 trials from Lorraine, which naturally play a considerable role in this study. Much the greater number of my detailed examples come from this source, simply because few other scholars have so far been interested in quite the same issues, or found material bearing on them. Nevertheless, I believe it to be true that the Lorraine material fits remarkably well with the vast majority of detailed studies on other regions, so that one is recognizably dealing with very similar phenomena. The differences seem far less impressive than the likenesses, particularly at the village level (which is my primary concern). This is not the only problem with examples. However many citations one piles up, there are insoluble difficulties in proving most of one's claims by such means. Too much depends on interpretation for claims about typicality to be at all safe; attempts to classify beliefs and social conduct rapidly founder on the immense diversity of human behaviour, while massive losses of records often make promising comparisons impossible.

Another difficulty with specific examples relates to the structural characteristics of both witchcraft trials and witchcraft itself. Essentially, what we have is an overlapping set of narratives, which might be envisaged as comprising a mosaic, that contain both smaller and larger patterns. They vary from tiny sequences of events taking place within a day or less to evolutions over decades or centuries. The briefest time spans are usually those invoked by witnesses or represented by the trial itself. Then there are the life histories of the accused, complete with imaginary narratives of their seduction and subservience to the devil. At the more general level, the historian must provide accounts of intense local persecutions, regional or national characteristics and changing ideologies. Fitting these together to form an analytical structure is fiendishly difficult because they constantly threaten to interrupt one another. The reader will find that the same themes recur in different chapters, with a certain degree of inevitable repetition; this is a problem for which I have been unable to find a tidy solution. A related danger is that when using precise examples one will lose any sense of the narrative frame, because a single detail is picked out to suit the argument. I have tried to counteract this by mixing in some longer citations; it will be obvious that many of these illustrate points which are discussed elsewhere in the book, while I hope that they will give a better 'feel' of the type of evidence one is dealing with.

Those who know anything about the existing literature will have been startled by an implicit premise in much of what has just been said. Most Anglo-American historians have stated or assumed that British, and notably English, witchcraft must be sharply distinguished from that found on the Continent. It has been supposed that there was a major contrast between a Continental persecution directed by the elites and an English persecution which originated among the ordinary people. In addition, the first allegedly concentrated on relations between witches and the Devil, whereas the focus of the second was on the harm done to others. This view involves serious misunderstandings that have vitiated several attempts to develop a general interpretation of the subject. In most cases the Continental persecutions were just as firmly founded in local opinion about *maleficium* (harm by occult means) as those on the other side of the Channel. While there are differences, as we would expect, they are of much subtler kinds. Some of them will emerge more clearly in the course of the book; for the moment it is sufficient to make the point in these general terms.

Generalizations which involve an area of this size are bound to be untrustworthy. I have made the working assumption that certain features of life were broadly similar everywhere, while trying to remain alive to the oversimplifications this must necessarily create. At other times, when differences in local experience are very revealing, these are highlighted. The reader should bear in mind that there is no such thing as a typical village; gradations on the scales between concentrated and dispersed habitat, cereal and pastoral economies, partible inheritance (equal sharing between children) and primogeniture (eldest child takes virtually all) are only some of the most important variables. Nor is it easy to say that there were typical peasants, judges, clerics and others. In every case we need to think of people placed somewhere along a spectrum rather than forming one group. Europeans certainly did not all think alike, although most of them shared certain basic attitudes. The historian has to describe trends or tendencies, without pretending to impose a false homogeneity on the past. Witches themselves were a very heterogeneous lot. Although the study of many trials makes the historian familiar with certain stereotypes, hardly any of these seem to apply to more than a small minority of cases. The obvious exceptions are those broad categories of quarrels linked to misfortunes and supposed associations with the devil, which are really no more than the defining features of witchcraft in the first place. I shall attempt to show that at a deeper level there are psychological and social features common to most if not all cases, but these are not obvious at a first glance.

All this said, the one sensible path forward is through a close look at the evidence, assuming that it has something to tell us about past realities. Just as the only way to know a landscape properly is to cover it on foot and keep one's eyes open, so societies must be patiently scanned, not summed up in easy phrases or classified in simple boxes. When we take this road, witchcraft becomes comprehensible in rather different terms. It no longer seems a strange aberration, calling for some very special explanation, but an integral part of past European society. Why many people were persecuted as witches then becomes a related but separable question, as does the less commonly recognized problem of why many others were not.

CHAPTER I

MYTHS OF
THE PERFECT WITCH

A *witch confesses*

IN JULY 1596 THE *PRÉVÔT* (the local administrator and law enforce-ment officer) of the small Lorraine town of Charmes reported the arrest of Barbe, wife of Jean Mallebarbe. This old woman of about sixty had fled Charmes some months earlier after being called witch in public, just as legal proceedings were being started against her. She evidently hoped that feelings would have calmed down in her absence, particularly since the old *prévôt* who had been very hostile to her had just died. When she found this was not the case, Barbe plainly wanted to get the inevitable over as quickly as possible – she even tried in vain to hang herself in prison, then asked to be put to death without being tortured. Few of the thousands of people executed as witches can have been more eager to please, or to confirm the beliefs of their persecutors. Her original confession had been simple and to a degree self-exculpatory. She and her husband of some twenty-seven years had always been day-labourers; more recently they had been forced to sell some small plots of land and, being left with only a house and garden, were increasingly dependent on charity (the husband was said to be old and crippled). Six months earlier Barbe, angry after a beating from her husband, had been seduced by 'master Percy', as the Devil was often named in Lorraine, who promised her 'money in abundance'. The Devil gave her two sacks of powder, but she threw these in a stream, and had done no-one any harm. The judges were unimpressed, for they knew there were plenty of witnesses who thought they had suffered very real harm at her hands. They threatened Barbe with torture, beginning a process which over the next two weeks (ending with a session when she was lightly racked) would see her story become steadily more elaborate. Although to our eyes this was a parody of justice, with relentless pressure applied to a defenceless old woman, it was also, in its way, a negotiation. The questions indicated the kind of answers required, but the details were supplied by the accused, drawing on a common stock of stereotypes.

Barbe's culpability grew, until she was admitting to at least twenty years in the Devil's service. Early admissions to killing the cows of men against whom she had grievances, and a horse at each of three houses where she was refused alms, did not satisfy the court. The accused was pressed to admit that she had harmed people, responding with a story about how she had killed her neighbour Claudon Basle, with whom she had quarrelled, and who had called her an 'old bigot and witch'. Barbe's revenge was to throw powder down her neck, inflicting an illness which killed Basle 18 months later; Barbe had not wished to cure Claudon, who had never asked her to do so anyway. The imminent prospect of torture drew out a new series of confessions to crimes against those who had offended her. Some had been given lingering illnesses, so that their limbs were twisted and they became permanently crippled, while others were killed. Among these was a servant she met in the woods with a cart and horses; after he refused her some bread she heard the crows by the track calling to her 'kill him, and break the necks of his horses', advice she duly followed. She had been changed into the form of a cat by her master, so that she could try to strangle the wife of Claude Hullon, after he had accused her of causing a fog on the lake. When she found she did not have the power to carry out this plan she still terrified the victim by speaking to her, then attacking her in her cat-form. After Laurent Rouille called her 'old witch' and accused her of stealing wood from his barn she wanted to kill him too, but a wind had come in her ear telling her she had no power over him, so she had to be content with killing an ox and two cows. The torture produced a final batch of admissions of using her powder to kill men, women and children after she was refused alms. Barbe knew she must name accomplices she had seen at the sabbat, where witches met, so identified three other women, two of whom were quickly arrested and tried after she maintained her accusations against them to the last.

Like many other witches, Barbe claimed she had simply been unable to escape the clutches of the Devil once she took the fatal decision to enter his service. On the other hand, she was not completely subservient to him. When the *receveur* of Charmes, meeting her by chance on the road, called her an old witch, Percy urged her to avenge herself – but she remembered that he was often charitable to her and would not harm him despite beatings from her angry master. She suffered similar attacks at the sabbat, when she resisted plans to harm the crops, because of the prospect of dearth and hardship for the poor. When one male witch (recently executed nearby) wanted to cause a hailstorm, she accused him of hoping to raise the price of the grain he had in store, only to be kicked in the backside by Percy and propelled an incredible distance. Asked if the Devil spoke to them gently, she replied 'ho, what gentleness, seeing that when he commanded us to cause harm and we did not want to obey his wishes, he would beat us thoroughly'. With no more than the minimum of suggestion from her judges, whose questions are carefully recorded, Barbe was able to produce an extensive confession that included just about every stereotypical feature of general beliefs about witches. Unlike most other accused, she had not heard the specific charges against her because she had started to confess before the witnesses had been summoned. Her widespread anger and malevolence was something she either recalled or invented without specific prompting. Witnesses only entered the proceedings at the final stage, to confirm some of the quarrels and deaths she had already reported.[1]

'La Mallebarbe' cannot be regarded as 'typical', any more than any other individual witch. As we shall see, many different types of people were accused, while the charges might vary widely. Nevertheless, her pathetic story of deprivation, insults and resentment was a familiar one across most of Europe during the hard decades of the late sixteenth and early seventeenth centuries. These, rather than grand theories about diabolical conspiracies, were the common currency of witchcraft as it was actually experienced and punished. They were stories anyone could tell, drawing on a great reservoir of shared beliefs and fantasies, endlessly recycled as part of everyday experience. Those who accused their neighbours could easily become suspects in their own turn, caught up in the same remorseless machinery of local conflicts and rumours. Even when reading the actual documents, it can be hard to believe that such trials really happened, that real people, flesh, blood and bone, were subjected to appalling cruelties in order to convict them of an impossible crime. If torture was barely used in this case it was only because the accused was already so frightened that she confessed without direct coercion. On 6 August 1596 Barbe was bound to the stake at Charmes, allowed to feel the fire, then strangled before her body was burned to ashes. The two other old women with whom she used to go begging and whom she had denounced as accomplices, Claudon la Romaine and Chesnon la Triffatte, followed her to the stake on 3 September of the same year. The sceptical English gentleman Reginald Scot had written angrily a decade earlier, with reference to a scabrous passage in the early witch-hunting manual the *Malleus Maleficarum*, 'These are no jests, for they be written by them that were and are judges upon the lives and deaths of those persons'.[2] Elsewhere he had asked 'whether the evidence be not frivolous, and whether the proofs brought against them [the witches] be not incredible, consisting of guesses, presumptions, and impossibilities contrary to reason, scripture, and nature'.[3] Indeed they were, but we have to go beyond indignation and horror to understand why just about everyone believed in witches and their power and why, within their own thought systems, it was neither irrational nor absurd for them to do so.

The witch-figure

Modern ideas of the witch have been simplified to the point of caricature. It is easy to depict a witch with a few strokes of the pen or a crude silhouette; the least talented mime needs no more than a hat. A fascinating collection of descriptions from modern Newfoundland includes the following quite typical portrait of the witch as

> a creature with long, straight hair, a very sharp nose, and long slender fingers. She has a big mouth with pointed teeth. She dresses in black. Her dress is black and she wears a pointed black felt hat on her head. A witch usually sails through the air on a long broom and is always accompanied by a fierce-looking cat.[4]

The crude woodcuts which accompanied early witchcraft pamphlets are very similar, although contemporaries would have seen nothing odd about the dress or the hat, which were the normal attire of older women. In 1584 Reginald Scot described the Kentish suspects he knew as 'women which be commonly old, lame, blear-eyed, pale, foul, and full of wrinkles'; they were also 'lean and deformed, showing melancholy in their faces to the horror of all that see them'.[5] One of the Pendle Forest witches tried at Lancaster in 1612, Anne Whittle alias Chattox, 'was a very old, withered, spent and decrepit creature, her sight almost gone . . . Her lips ever chattering and walking: but no man knew what'.[6] Around 1600, therefore, this image was already in existence in most essentials; a few decades later, in 1646, another critic of the persecution, the Hertfordshire minister John Gaule, deplored the fact that during the current witch hunt in the eastern counties

> Every old woman with a wrinkled face, a furred brow, a hairy lip, a gobber tooth, a squint eye, a squeaking voice, or a scolding tongue, having a rugged coat on her back, a skull-cap on her head, a spindle in her hand, and a dog or cat by her side, is not only suspected but pronounced for a witch.[7]

This familiar portrait is nevertheless highly misleading as a guide to the people persecutors thought they had to deal with. It was the small group of sceptical writers on witchcraft, notably Johann Weyer and Scot, who picked on the fact that many of the accused were pathetic old women whom their neighbours found obnoxious. Their aim was to ridicule the extravagant claims made for this secret resistance movement recruited by the Devil, whose chief accomplishment was apparently to kill a few cows and impede the making of butter or beer. There is good reason to think that this line of argument proved very effective among their educated contemporaries but believers in witchcraft saw the matter differently.

Those writers who pleaded for greater severity were usually careful to avoid any suggestion that witches could be typecast in such a facile manner. It took a very naive demonologist like Nicolas Remy in Lorraine, to describe his enemies as a 'vile rabble' composed primarily of beggars.[8] In any case he also noticed the claims, often found in the trials he used, that there were many rich people at the sabbats.[9] The typical approach was to stress the seriousness of the diabolical fifth column, the secrecy with which it operated and its closeness to the centres of political and social power. Even those such as Jean Bodin, who asserted (quite wrongly) that almost all witches were women, still made much of the minority of powerful male figures among them. The Catholic zealots of the Holy League, who sought to overthrow King Henri III of France, circulated pamphlets claiming to have found evidence that he was a witch himself. It was easier to argue that the Devil was successful up to the highest level because a number of early trials had been political set-ups directed at powerful individuals. The demonologists, who openly plagiarized one another, made repeated reference to these cases. Fantasies about satanic conspiracies on a national or international scale could gather around the occasional elite victim, like Louis Gaufridy (a priest from

Aix-en-Provence burned in 1611). Two years later the exorcists who had 'unmasked' him had moved on to extract tales from possessed nuns in the Spanish Netherlands who described how Gaufridy presided as prince at great sabbats.[10]

Early pictures of witches convey the same message. Old hags are usually present among them, but they mix with nubile young women, men and children. Witchcraft was neither gender nor age specific for these artists, any more than it was confined to one social class. In reality members of the elite were rarely brought to trial, outside such exceptional pandemics as afflicted the German prince-bishoprics of Bamberg, Trier, and Würzburg. Nevertheless, there were enough scattered cases and, no doubt, more extensive rumours, to keep the notion of hidden satanists in high places alive well into the seventeenth century. A high proportion of those concerned were men, with clerics prominent among them. The exceptional rarity of men among those accused in England, coupled with misogynistic statements by various demonologists, has encouraged an uncritical belief that nearly all the accused were women. In many parts of Europe men comprised 20 or 25 per cent of those charged; in some, including large areas of France, they actually formed a majority. There does seem to have been a widespread conviction that women were specially vulnerable to the wiles of the Devil, so that most confessing witches said they were more numerous at the sabbat; however, a fair number insisted there was parity of the sexes, or even a preponderance of men.

For persecutors and general populace alike then, the stereotype of the old woman as witch had no more than a marginal purchase on their minds. Some old women who found themselves accused complained of their special vulnerability, and where statistics are available they bear this out to an extent, in that older women and widows are heavily over-represented among the sample. One of these, Marion le Masson, gave another woman some money to buy medicine from the apothecary, then said 'poor old women, like herself, no longer dared to provide remedies, since when they did so for an illness, immediately people said they were evil people, so there was no need for her to reveal what she had told her'.[11] Despite this poignant evidence, the statistics need careful handling; we have to remember that many of those who came to court had been suspected for ten, fifteen or twenty years. Therefore their reputations very often went back to middle life or earlier, while relatively few first attracted suspicion as elderly crones. This is not a conclusive argument, for we have no way of telling how widespread or intense such suspicions were; the high level of defamation cases suggests that potentially dangerous accusations may have flown about pretty thickly in village society. One must also allow for a degree of retrospective reinterpretation by witnesses who had an obvious interest in exaggerating past events. In numerous cases, however, suspects confirmed such claims at a stage when they were still asserting their innocence, sometimes giving a specific explanation for the start of their problems. Colatte Bertrand knew that when Claudon Jean Remy had lost some honey fifteen years earlier, he had been to the *devin* at Orbey to find the thief, whereupon she was named, with the additional claim that she was a witch. Remy had told others, but when she and her husband wanted to take him to court no-one would testify to this.[12] In general my impression is that alleged lengths of reputation are more accurate than not, although it is hard to see how this could be proven.

The popular image of the witch was that of a person motivated by ill-will and spite who lacked the proper sense of neighbourhood and community. Suspects were often alleged to have shown themselves resentful in their dealings with others and unwilling to accept delays or excuses in small matters. There seems little doubt that some of them were notoriously quarrelsome, although it is less clear whether this carried any *necessary* imputation of witchcraft. Indeed, to some extent such behaviour must have been as much the result as the cause of reputations, for there could hardly have been a more effective way of damaging communal or personal relationships than calling a neighbour a witch. There is a strong impression when studying larger groups of trials that such personal characteristics were commonly brought into play to reinforce suspicions which began for other reasons. Those who conciliated others were liable to find themselves described, like Marguitte Laurent, as 'fine and crafty, careful not to quarrel with people or threaten them', while a failure to react was readily interpreted as betraying vengefulness.[13] A particularly damaging charge was that the accused had talked of concealing anger until the moment for revenge had come. Jehenne la Moictresse was alleged to have told another woman that she should imitate her practice of giving no sign when angry, while Mengeotte Lausson claimed that when she had been angered she remembered it seven years later, without giving any sign. Mengeon Clement Thiriat told Helenne Thomas as they were carting hay, 'that she did not yet know what it was to live in the world, and it was necessary to put on the best and finest appearances with those one hated the most'.[14] The commonest of all remarks attributed to witches were those on the lines of 'you will repent' or 'you had better watch out', much of whose meaning depended on the context in which they were made. In many cases it was also said that the accused had taken no notice or pretended not to hear, when called a witch in public. In theory the proper response was to seek damages for slander, but suspects must have been very reluctant to embitter relationships further by such action.

Popular descriptions of witches do not therefore give any very certain guide to the reasons why they were identified; they are simply too flexible and circumstantial. Close analysis of the trials reveals why this was bound to be the case. There was no single or dominant reason why individuals fell under suspicion, while reputations were built up piecemeal over time and could incorporate very disparate elements. In consequence, supposed witches were a very heterogeneous group, even in the broadest terms. They were more often poor than rich, old rather than young and female rather than male, but there were quite numerous exceptions to all these tendencies. At any one time a particular community probably had a small group of strong suspects, with a much looser periphery of marginal ones; the latter were probably only known to individual families or close neighbours, and were not yet the subject of general village gossip. The multiple ways in which these processes worked will form the subject of future chapters. These will also explore the many ambiguities of the position. For other members of the community, the witch appears to have alternated between being a terrifying enemy who could bring ruin or death and a pathetic figure to be despised and insulted.

One very powerful link did unite many of the accused; that of family and heredity. The idea that a 'race' was either sound or tainted was much employed, both in self-defence and in accusations. To be the child of a convicted or reputed witch was inherently dangerous; in one pathetic case in Lorraine a young couple were both accused, and it emerged that they had decided to marry after attending the execution at the stake of their respective parents, 'so that they would have nothing to reproach one another with'.[15] There are signs that as persecution became established in some areas this element was progressively strengthened, with a growing proportion of victims having such antecedents. How far this was just a natural statistical outcome of the situation is harder to determine; here we still lack good comparative information for different regions. The possibility remains open that in areas of endemic persecution this tended to concentrate increasingly on a self-defining group of 'witchcraft families'. It is also unclear how far the popular ideas on the subject implied some kind of congenital weakness, as opposed to the notion that parents might deliberately initiate their children as witches. Judges certainly showed considerable interest in the latter possibility, but it is less obvious in the testimony of witnesses. Confessing second-generation witches, who quite often blamed their parents for their initial seduction, are probably best seen as trying to displace responsibility rather than as expressing general beliefs.

The diabolical pact

Everyone seems to have known how the Devil carried out his seductions. Once witches decided to confess they told similar stories, with very little prompting, which rarely changed much over time. The Devil normally appeared unbidden to someone who was in a receptive psychological state. This might involve anger against relatives or neighbours, despair caused by poverty or hunger, or anxiety at being called a witch. He offered consoling words, a gift of money and assurances that his followers would not want for anything. He might also promise that they would have power to avenge their wrongs, often providing a powder with which such revenge could be effected. Once the prospective recruit agreed to renounce God and take the Devil for master, the latter gave symbolic force to the change of allegiance. This normally meant touching the new witch to impose the mark, leaving either a visible blemish on the skin or an insensible place. At the same time the chrism given at baptism was supposedly removed. With women the Devil then took possession of them sexually, an experience they often described in vivid terms as a virtual rape, made more unpleasant by the glacial coldness of his penis. Any remaining illusions were shattered when the money turned out to be leaves or horse-dung, at which point the witches knew they had been cheated. Men occasionally produced their own version of the sexual element, with the Devil taking female form, but this got the symbolism so obviously wrong that it never became general.

Individual confessions often left out parts of this scenario, partly because judges do not seem to have pressed the accused very hard on details, but it is usually visible as a whole beneath briefer accounts. It formed the first stage in a narrative of apostasy from both community and Christian church, which continued with attendance at the witches' sabbat and malicious action against crops, animals and people. Once the witch had been lured into this disastrous error there was thought to be no way back. A handful of the accused claimed they had made some attempt to reintegrate themselves within the church, but all had apparently found this impossible. Catherine Charpentier tried to take advantage of the special terms available to penitents during the Jubilee of 1602 by confessing her apostasy to a friar at St Nicolas. He made her promise to abandon the Devil, then absolved her, after which she felt the Devil leave her. She was also to carry holy bread and candle wax with her, then make a full confession to her own *curé* the following Easter, with three-monthly confessions thereafter. Unfortunately, although at the outset she was determined to comply, 'once she was at home and the time arrived to make her confession to the *curé*, the shame of revealing herself to him, together with her fear that he would expose and defame her, overcame her to such an extent that she did not say a word to the *curé*'. The Devil saw his opportunity, duly appearing to reclaim her allegiance.[16] There is a contrast here with the folk-tales in which the Devil was often deceived or outwitted; the difference is of course that the witches' narratives had to conform to the logic of their own situation. That logic also produced a strange internal imbalance, for the stories were at once psychologically acute and preposterous. The state of mind which rendered the witch vulnerable was highly convincing, conveying just that condition of being overwhelmed by emotion which leads people to foolish and passionate actions. On the other hand, the Devil's mendacity was so blatant and his identity so obvious, that it was hard to see how anyone could fail to spot the trap.

Many accounts of the pact are patently about the witch, with the Devil as a conventional villain acting a predetermined part. When Catherine la Rondelatte was being interrogated in 1608 she suddenly began to confess, saying:

I am a witch. Ten years ago last St Laurence's day I was coming back from visiting my sister Barbon at Magnieres, walking alone through the woods all dreaming and thoughtful that I had been so long a childless widow, and that my relatives discouraged me from remarrying, which I would have liked to do. When I arrived at the place of the round oak in the middle of the woods I was astonished and very frightened by the sight of a great black man who appeared to me. At first he said to me 'Poor woman, you are very thoughtful', and although I quickly recommended myself to St Nicolas he then suddenly threw me down, had intercourse with me, and at the same time pinched me roughly on the forehead. After this he said 'You are mine. Have no regret; I will make you a lady and give you great wealth.'

I knew in the same hour it was the evil spirit, but could not retract because he had instantly made me renounce God, chrism, and baptism, promising to serve him. He gave me a stick, saying that if I bore hatred to anyone, I could avenge myself by touching them or their animals with the stick, then disappeared, saying I would soon see him again, and his name was Percy.

The widow's loneliness is vividly conveyed here, in comparison with the almost perfunctory depiction of the Devil.[17] A similar picture emerges from the account given by Franceatte Charier:

At a time when some executions were already taking place locally, she was extremely angry and miserable because her husband did her much harm, while she saw herself reduced to poverty; desolated as she was by this situation, one day behind their house she was overcome by several evil thoughts which blew into her ears, and at that moment she saw a man of middling size dressed in black climb down from a tree . . .

Although she twice resisted his 'honeyed words', the third time she yielded. The Devil's money turned out to be grass and leaves, while after using the powder a few times she felt such regret at being 'so miserably abused and deceived, as well as fearing to be discovered by the villagers, especially her husband', that she threw all the powders in the fire.[18] Whereas most Lorraine witches served devils called Persin or Napnel, the crippled beggar-woman Mengeotte Gascon was approached by a man in black who said his name was Pensée de Femme. A devil who embodied women's secret thoughts in his very name was a superb expression of the inner logic of the situation; he told Mengeotte:

that he gave her power over all those who did her harm, and towards whom she bore any hatred, so that by striking them with her hand she could make them die or sicken as she wished, while she could heal them if she wished, that she should have no worry about this, giving her some powder to use if she wished or the power simply to touch them with her hand.[19]

The power to hurt and (sometimes) to heal was the part of the offer which was invariably represented as genuine, as distinct from the deceitful promises of riches. It was possible for the basic premises of the conventional story to be challenged, as when Nicolas Claudon made a very rash entry into the conversation at the mill of Chastay. When he was on trial several years later there were two witnesses to this, one of whom deposed:

> it happened that talk turned to the *devineresse* of the village of Bouray who had been executed for the crime of witchcraft, and how one day she had received money from the Devil, which when she got home turned out to be leaves or horse-dung, to which the accused replied that it was just as good money as any other, and that the officers were too shrewd to say in the record that it was good, otherwise everyone would want to be a witch.[20]

An aberrant case of this kind does reveal something of the elaborate cultural interchanges which must constantly have taken place. It is mistaken to think of simple oppositions between popular and learned culture, which are really no more than abstractions invented by historians to describe a much more complex reality. Judges, clerics and peasants shared much of their cultural experience, while their ideas were always interacting. The diabolical pact was a very ancient story that all concerned were readily able to manipulate. The narratives combined elements of folklore and official demonology, which were fitted around social and psychological determinants. The Devil stood for the temptation to reject the normal constraints and obligations which regulated personal relations. In a society where communal norms were so coercive and privacy so elusive, the related stresses must have been peculiarly intense. The fantasy of the pact brought together an inner drama experienced by individuals with the judges' requirements for clear cut offences. As the ultimate treason against God and man it could be held to justify an automatic death sentence, even the bending of normal rules of procedure. For the theorists of witchcraft the pact led into elaborate questions about the relevance and force of the mutual contract involved. This was one of the points at which they tended to tie themselves in logical knots over where responsibility ultimately lay, providing a good opportunity for sceptical critics, but these disputes between experts had little resonance at popular level.

It has often been said that England constitutes the great exception, the land without the diabolical pact. It is certainly true that in English law it was only the Jacobean Witchcraft Act of 1604 that made the pact itself a capital offence, and that in practice the harm done to others was almost always the main charge. Until the 1604 Act, first offenders who had not caused the deaths of persons were only liable to a year's imprisonment, implying that there was nothing irredeemable about their offence. There does therefore seem to have been a difference in elite views as between England and Europe, although it would be dangerous to make too much of this. Most Continental trials were also primarily concerned with *maleficium*, fear of which provided their main driving force. English witchcraft narratives, however, are much closer to the standard pattern in their form, despite striking peculiarities of detail. The animal familiars or imps which appear in almost every well documented case quite clearly performed the role of the Devil. The witch made an effective compact with them; she usually allowed them to suck her blood and was supposed to have special teats for this purpose. These last took the place of the diabolical mark, becoming the object of regular searches by special juries of local midwives and matrons.

In one of the very first English trials the nature and functions of the familiar emerge with great clarity. Elizabeth Francis of Hatfield Peverel admitted in 1566 that her grandmother had

> counselled her to renounce God and His word, and to give of her blood to Satan (as she termed it) which she delivered [to] her in the likeness of a white spotted cat, and taught her to feed the said cat with bread and milk, and she did so. Also she taught her to call it by the name of Satan, and to keep it in a basket.
>
> When this mother Eve had given her the cat Satan, then this Elizabeth desired first of the said cat (calling it Satan) that she might be rich, and have goods, and he promised her she should, asking her what she would have, and she said 'Sheep' (for this cat spoke to her, as she confessed, in a strange hollow voice, but such as she understood by use) and this cat forthwith brought sheep into her pasture to the number of 18, black and white, which continued with her a time, but in the end did all wear away, she knew not how.
>
> Item: when she had gotten these sheep, she desired to have one Andrew Byles to her husband, which was a man of some wealth, and the cat did promise that she should, but he said she must first consent that this Andrew should abuse her, and so she did.
>
> And after, when this Andrew had thus abused her, he would not marry her, wherefore she willed Satan to waste his goods, which he forthwith

did; and yet not being contented with this, she willed him to touch his body, which he forthwith did, whereof he died.

Item: that every time he did anything for her, she said that he required a drop of blood, which she gave him by pricking herself, sometime in one place and then in another, and where she pricked herself there remained a red spot which was still to be seen.[21]

It would hardly be possible to make the devilish nature of the familiar more explicit than by calling it Satan, while the blood gives vivid expression to the idea of an implicit pact. If the cat could not plausibly have sexual intercourse with the witch, he could incite her to fornication with others. Just like the Continental devils, most importantly of all, the cat was the container or cipher for the witch's own desires and anger.

Elizabeth Francis was seduced by her grandmother rather than directly by her familiar, but another confession from the same pamphlet has Joan Waterhouse asking her mother's familiar, Satan, to harm another girl. She offered him a red cock, to which he replied 'No, but thou shalt give me thy body and soul'.[22] At another Chelmsford trial two decades later, Joan Prentice of Sible Hedingham reported how the Devil appeared to her 'in the shape and proportion of a dunnish coloured ferret, having fiery eyes', and said, 'Joan Prentice, give me thy soul'. He eventually settled for some of her blood, after which he would come when called, suck blood from her cheek, and perform 'any mischief she willed' against her neighbours.[23] Thus, far from going against the central stereotype the English cases show how an independent folkloric tradition could be moulded into the same patterns. Gradually the idea of personal appearances by the Devil in the form of a man was blended into it, beginning with the Lancashire witches of 1612. Elizabeth Southerns told how she had been approached by 'a spirit or devil in the shape of a boy' who said 'that if she would give him her soul, she should have anything that she would request'. The spirit, called Tibb, also took the forms of a brown dog and a cat at different times, while the devil who appeared to Anne Whittle in the form of a man was accompanied by 'a thing in the likeness of a spotted bitch'.[24] This kind of shapeshifting was also quite common, for both devils and witches, in Continental trials. Cats and dogs were often seen as diabolical by neighbours elsewhere in Europe, although the idea of suckling them does not appear; some Continental witches were accused of keeping toads as familiars. In certain respects the English familiars, always found about the witch's house, were a more pervasive satanic influence than the human manifestations of the Devil, who were much less omnipresent.

Such variations around standard themes could be illustrated at much greater length. They demonstrate how readily witchcraft beliefs could incorporate a disparate collection of folkloric elements and demonological theories, with the trials themselves and the books and pamphlets to which they gave rise helping to generate or modify the content over time. In essence, however, the message of the stories did not change significantly over time and space. Their themes evoked a mythical world, in which the tensions of personal and communal life were personified in the Devil and his agents. It was therefore entirely natural that these narratives should revolve around a common structural core. Although we can never hope to reconstruct the precise ways in which individual or local versions combined the different elements, it is not clear this information would be much help in any case. Specific origins are less important than the process itself, whose outlines are perfectly clear. Apart from a few extreme sceptics, the great majority of people believed that there was a diabolical anti-world in which normal polarities were reversed and of which human beings had only very partial glimpses. Suspects were thus free to elaborate their accounts in the fashion already described; the trials were the crucible in which a range of new alloys could be forged.

The witches' sabbat

In many accounts the pact was followed by the sabbat; either immediately after the seduction or within a few days, the Devil would lead the new witch to a meeting with others. This too was a notably malleable set of ideas, which formed part of the same narrative and overlapped with other elements in it. In the peculiarly highly coloured version of the sabbat described by Basque witches, called the *aquelarre*, the themes of heredity and the pact were incorporated into the witches' meetings. Here the accused regularly explained that they had been taken along by their parents when they were children, paid homage to the Devil and worked their way up from the status of novices to become senior witches. When the witches themselves were so active in recruiting, the Devil could evidently be spared the task of going around tempting individuals to join his forces. It is impossible to determine how far these confessions sprang from an exceptionally rich local folklore and how far they were generated by a very active group of clerical and lay persecutors. Certainly the witchcraft panic in both French and Spanish Navarre in 1609–11 produced some of the most sensational testimony about the sabbat, whose influence has been remarkably durable. The French judge Pierre de Lancre was largely responsible for this, for he wrote the statements up in a suitably lurid fashion. In a famous purple passage he described the purposes of those attending the sabbat as being

> to dance indecently, to banquet filthily, to couple diabolically, to sodomize execrably, to blaspheme scandalously, to pursue brutally every horrible, dirty and unnatural desire, to hold as precious toads, vipers, lizards and all sorts of poisons; to love a vile-smelling goat, to caress him lovingly, to press against and copulate with him horribly and shamelessly.[25]

The idea of secret meetings where orgies take place and evil is planned must be one of the oldest and most basic human fantasies. Charges of nocturnal conspiracy, black magic, child murder, orgiastic sexuality and perverted ritual were nothing new in Europe when they were applied to witches. They had been used against early Christians and then against heretics, Jews and lepers. In the fourteenth century they were made against popes, bishops and the great Crusading order of the Knights Templar. The stereotype is obvious; it consisted of inverting all the positive values of society, adding a lot of lurid detail (often borrowed from earlier allegations), then throwing the resulting bucket of filth over the selected victims. A kind of scholarly pornography was generated, while the use of torture secured the required confessions. It was also in the fourteenth century that humble people started to be convicted for witchcraft, at first in very small numbers; initially they were simply charged with causing harm to their neighbours by occult means, with no mention of devil-worship. This was quickly added to, however, drawing on a range of popular beliefs about nocturnal activities, mostly ascribed to women. Some were negative; stories of cannibalistic women who flew by night, killing and eating children in particular. Others were positive, concerning various forms of guardian spirits who were dangerous if not treated with respect, but essentially acted as protectors of people, animals and crops. The stories of the sabbat represented a fusion between the persecuting stereotypes elaborated by clerics and judges and the various older folkloric traditions of the peasantry.

This fusion can be dated, apparently with great precision, to around 1428–9, in the Valais region of southern Switzerland and in northern Italy. A Lucerne chronicler, writing a few years later, gave a classic description of the witches' sabbat in his account of the Swiss trials, while the case of Matteuccia Francisci at Todi in 1428 includes an actual confession in what was to become the standard form.[26] From then on a growing number of witches confessed, usually under torture, that they had attended the sabbat and many named others they had seen there. This date is probably misleading, however. Two trials from different places in the same year are really an embarrassment to the historian, for they suggest the stereotype was already quite well established in the Alpine regions. We know from a work by the Dominican John Nider, written between 1435 and 1437, that around the turn of the fourteenth and fifteenth centuries the Bernese judge Peter von Greyerz and the inquisitor of Evian were trying numerous witches, some of whom admitted having been at ceremonies where they did homage to the Devil and used the bodies of murdered children for magical purposes. Some elements of the classic sabbat are missing, but it sounds very much as if the notions were taking shape.[27] Around the same time we have some clear evidence of clerical concern about widespread deviations in both the western and the eastern Alps. In one instance a papal Bull of 1409 links together Jews fleeing persecution, Waldensian heretics and witch-craft practices, and instructs an inquisitor to deal with them.[28] Here we do seem to have precisely the combination of factors needed to produce the final lethal mixture that was clearly operating twenty years later.

There is a serious problem with evidence, for trial records are rare for this early period and accounts at second hand can never be fully trusted. In addition, as we ought to know from modern experience, documents purporting to record interrogations need to be treated with great caution. Judges did not necessarily record when they used torture, or the leading questions which were part of their normal technique. This makes it impossible to reconstruct the precise operations involved at this crucial stage, so the evolution of the full-blown sabbat myth seems likely to remain hidden from us to some degree. On the other hand, there is a sharp discontinuity in surviving records around the pivotal period of the first third of the fifteenth century; after this, references to the sabbat become quite commonplace in Alpine trials and start cropping up else-where. There were trials involving twenty-five to thirty people at Metz in 1456 and Arras in 1459 where detailed stories were extracted under torture.[29] Like the pact, the sabbat evidently represented a fusion of learned and popular ideas mediated through inquisitors, secular judges and the accused themselves. A conspiracy theory of this kind offered the potential for large-scale witch-hunting; it might even be thought to demand urgent action by the authorities. Historians have often assumed that it was the elaborated myth of the sabbat which underlay the great persecution, which was fundamentally a search for these secret devil-worshippers. This is a natural inference, but it would seem to be a half-truth at best.

Once the mechanism was in place, it could have been expected to generate a steadily increasing flow of cases. The belief in witchcraft was plainly widespread in Europe, leaving the way open for persecution to feed on itself. Each witch who came to trial might be tortured, then denounce several others seen at the sabbat, in a kind of infernal, elaborate domino effect. Although there does seem to have been a small peak of trials in the 1480s, it was not until the late sixteenth century that denunciations came to function widely in this way. In fact it looks as if the idea of the sabbat was slow to spread from its Alpine origins. The great early witch-hunter's manual of 1486, the *Malleus Maleficarum*, hardly mentions the sabbat; although the authors are evidently quite well aware of the idea that witches meet in assemblies, the rigid scholastic format of the work somehow prevents them putting any emphasis on this. When Bodin wrote his *Démonomanie des Sorciers* in 1580 he felt it necessary to offer extensive proofs that witches really were transported to the sabbat, while commenting angrily on the way some judges and others ridiculed the whole notion.[30] It can in fact be argued that the idea of the sabbat discouraged the elites from taking witchcraft seriously, because it was thought too implausible and too much tainted by popular credulity. In other words, for the better part of a century the destructive potential of the belief in groups of night witches failed to operate as might have been expected. Furthermore, even in the peak decades of persecution the role of the sabbat remains very ambiguous.

When trials did multiply, notably from the 1580s, there were numerous areas of Europe where the full-blown version of the sabbat was very slow to emerge from the trials or indeed never did so. Around this time the early critics of witch-hunting, such as Weyer and Scot, were already raising the question of whether such confessions did not merely demonstrate that their makers must be deluded. This was simply a more vigorous expression of long-standing uncertainties, for, in what may well have been the first formal discussion of the new crime of diabolical witchcraft, John Nider seemed to imply that the sabbat was some kind of diabolical illusion. Some later advocates of persecution would follow him on this specific point, which can also be found in such classic early texts as the ninth-century canon *Episcopi*. Even at the level of illiterate peasants making such confessions, the question of reality and illusion sometimes came to the fore. Barbe la Grosse Gorge gave a positive answer when asked if she had been to the sabbat but said she had seen no-one there because 'all that one can say about it is no more than dreams and illusions'.[31] Mingling the worlds of reality and dreams in this way gave witchcraft ideas great flexibility, yet at the same time exposed them to attack. Another idea shared by intellectuals and ordinary suspects was that some kind of substitution took place when the witch went to the sabbat; either their body stayed behind in bed, or a diabolical illusion took its place. Evasive reasoning of this kind, all too common, was really a sign of weakness faced with the implausibilities of the standard myth. In Spanish Navarre the sceptical Inquisitor Alonso de Salazar y Frias was quick to point out that if this were the case it was impossible to prove either innocence or guilt. Accusations based on sightings at the *aquelarre* might be based on personal malice or deception by the Devil, and were inherently untrustworthy. As he put it:

> Let us suppose that one was willing to give credence to all this, and to believe that the Devil is able to make persons present when they are not, and make others invisible when they pass before people who would certainly recognize them, with the result that nobody can be sure that he or she who is present is any more real than he or she who is with the witches; then surely one could conceive another explanation far more readily: the Devil only deludes those 'invisible' ones, or those who think that they have been absent, without this ever happening, in order that the deceived person should speak in good faith and find acceptance for these and similar lies, and consequently also be believed when he says that he has seen other people at his *aquelarre* whom he subsequently denounces. Thus immediately and without any effort the Devil leaves the village in an uproar [and] those unjustly incriminated exposed to condemnation.[32]

This was an extreme case, for such critical rationalism was largely confined to experienced and sophisticated judges. Salazar's two fellow Inquisitors in the local tribunal at Logroño were outraged by his views, but he had the backing of the Grand Inquisitor himself, and the central authority of the Spanish Inquisition, the *Suprema*, had adopted his position. Although earlier Inquisitors in the Alps and the Rhineland may have helped to create the myth of the sabbat, the highly professional courts of the Spanish and Italian Inquisitions were among the earliest to reject it. The elite judges of the *parlement* of Paris, a prestigious court whose appellate jurisdiction covered half of France, also adopted a highly nuanced position, based on similar doubts about the quality and reliability of the evidence. Bodin was quite right, from his point of view, to grumble about this, as was de Lancre in his complaints about his colleagues in Bordeaux. In the 1580s an ex-councillor in the same *parlement* of Bordeaux, Michel de Montaigne, had remarked, 'it is putting a very high price on one's conjectures to have a man roasted alive because of them'. In an obvious sideswipe at Bodin he had begun this section of his superb essay 'On Cripples' with the comment 'The witches of my neighbourhood are in mortal danger every time some new author comes along and attests to the reality of their visions.'[33] The danger was real, but far better controlled by a kind of mitigated elite scepticism than he feared. By an irony which would have delighted Montaigne, the extravagant claims made for the sabbat probably did more to discredit and limit the great persecution than they did to forward it, at least from the beginning of the seventeenth century. There is another side to the picture, however. For over a century, widely divergent views on the sabbat apparently coexisted in Europe, and some of the most violent witch-hunts were built around these excited fantasies. This was the case in numerous German cities and principalities, as it was in the belated Swedish pandemic around 1670. The fact that only a small fraction of Europe was ever seriously affected does not detract from the horror of these events, which have done much to fix the stereotype of the witch-hunt for later generations.

Among the elites the sabbat often demonstrated a remarkable capacity for polarizing opinion. In the Spanish Netherlands during the years 1613–15 a violent controversy raged about allegations made by groups of nuns supposedly possessed by the Devil. A sceptical party led by local clerics and backed by the papal Nuncio confronted other clerics and at least one powerful member of the ruling Council. The matter went as far as the Pope himself, who supported the sceptics, a decision which produced a bitter complaint from one of the opposing party that 'in Rome they know nothing about this business of witchcraft'.[34] These cases belong to a rather special group, in which 'possessed' members of female religious houses levelled charges against male priests. This was turning the tables with a vengeance and one may reasonably suspect that this inversion of the sexual and ecclesiastical hierarchy had something to do with the strong negative reactions of many observers. This cannot be a general explanation, however, because some possession cases did not follow this model. Many involved accusations by adolescents or children, who were sometimes detected counterfeiting their symptoms; others had an obvious religious or political motivation. It was not surprising that they became discredited, doing much to damage the wider fantasies of satanic conspiracies in the process.

The complex relationships between the sabbat myth and persecution are not the whole of the story. What was the meaning of these notions for ordinary people? Carlo Ginzburg has suggested that there was a distinct set of folk beliefs, going back far into the past, which can be detected beneath the Inquisitorial veneer. He argues that the Sabbat brought together various popular myths about a journey to the land of the dead and back and was associated with the idea that those recently dead were hostile and dangerous to the living.[35] This ingenious interpretation has not found much support among other historians; in any case it does not seem to be very helpful in relation to the situation during the sixteenth and seventeenth centuries. Whatever the origins of the belief system, by this time it had developed an internal logic which related it to a nexus of ideas about witchcraft rather than those about dead ancestors. Although the way in which rather different traditions were appropriated is a valid topic for study and speculation, this is largely incidental to an understanding of the symbolic function of the sabbat as a diabolical festival.

The view of the sabbat proposed by Margaret Murray in *The Witch-Cult in Western Europe* (1921) and then repeated in her *Encyclopaedia Britannica* article on witchcraft remains enormously influential, although conclusive refutations have been appearing ever since that time.[36] Murray argued that witches were really worshippers of the ancient pagan cult of Diana and that the sabbat was a traditional fertility rite. Apart from the banal point that certain pagan traditions had survived into Christian Europe, this is complete nonsense, based on systematic misrepresentation of the source material. Murray deleted all the fantastic elements of flying, shape-changing and so forth to give the impression that the underlying reality was one of cosy local meetings that could be easily explained in rational terms. She also used fanciful combinations of the numbers given in some trials to claim that witches were organized in covens of thirteen, aided by the natural tendency of confessing witches to use a dozen as a round number. There is no good evidence that a single coven existed or that witches ever participated in a sabbat of any kind. The natural conclusion from the documentary sources is that the whole myth of the sabbat was a fabrication from beginning to end. Falsification of the sources is perhaps the ultimate historical crime, but theories of this kind are also intellectually very weak. The fundamental defect of the Murrayite approach is its desperate literal-mindedness, which includes a refusal to accept that fantasy is a genuine experience. Any attempt to explain the stories in purely 'realistic' terms can only lead to a gross distortion of their meanings and a complete misunderstanding of the way they were produced.

Like other myths of its type, the sabbat worked on the basic principle of inversion; it presented a mirror image of the Christian world in which people actually lived. Familiar practices and relationships remained quite recognizable, but in distorted or parodic forms.[37] This at least seems to be true wherever one looks. It is difficult to write with any certainty about the many variations in detail found over time and space because most historians have been curiously uninterested in such matters. They have generally been content to cite examples of typical confessions, without attempting much in the way of analysis or comparison. As a result, my attempt to penetrate beneath the surface has to be built around the one large body of data readily available to me, the manuscript records of some 300 confessions from the duchy of Lorraine. This was an independent state, sandwiched uneasily between France and the Holy Roman Empire, that saw a high level of small-scale persecution, very largely rural. There are some peculiarities in the Lorraine material, as one might expect, but these can be fairly easily recognized and do not really affect its validity as an example of how the sabbat was integrated into the wider phenomenon of witchcraft.

The sabbat in Lorraine

Almost all Lorraine witches admitted they had been to the sabbat, once they had decided to confess. This was the third and last part of the classic disclosure, following the pact and the *maléfices*. Once they had decided to confess, few made any difficulty on this point; they were much more likely to deny *maleficium* or claim they could not identify accomplices. Their implicit attitude is that expressed by Jacotte Colin, who told the *prévôt* of Arches 'I'll readily speak your wine' – meaning she would say what he wanted.[38] On the other hand, few of them said much about the sabbat; the detailed descriptions come from a small minority of cases, less than 10 per cent of the whole. In these rare instances the accused were clearly doing more than respond to prompting by the judges; their accounts have too individual a character to be explained in that way. This does not mean that there is anything really aberrant about the longer statements in terms of their content. I do not think any reader would doubt that we are in the presence of a coherent body of folklore, with certain local variations. The most striking differences are found on the linguistic frontier, which makes very good sense. The main reason why there are so few elaborate accounts is simply that the judges, less salacious or inquisitive than legend would suppose, did not ask for them. Questions about the sabbat were usually brief and formal; only if the accused was loquacious were they pursued with any determination. Even in these cases the judges rarely did much to guide the answers. The only detail on which they insisted with any determination was in obtaining the names of the others who had been seen there.

Scattered trials in Lorraine date back to the 1450s, but full trial documents are only available much later. Two early confessions from 1553 and 1561 include brief accounts of the sabbat that show that the beliefs were already quite familiar before the major persecution began – here as elsewhere trials were run until the 1580s. When Marguerite Valtrin was asked what she did after her master Pantoufle took her to the sabbat, she replied 'some danced, others played and did marvellous things, and when they left their masters gave them powder to kill people and animals, inciting them to do this'.[39] La Grosse Alison described how she had killed a small child, whose corpse she later dug up from the grave and took to be eaten at the next sabbat.[40] This is in fact a most unusual element in Lorraine confessions, which normally just describe a banquet at which the meat was unpleasant and unsalted. When the flesh was identified it was most commonly said to be that of small birds. Over nearly a century the accounts do not change in any obvious way; there is no sign of any evolution in popular beliefs about the sabbat. Petty deviations from the norm were themselves normal, but unlike genetic mutations did not generate distinct new strains.

The norm itself is very clear. Witches went to the sabbat under orders, often carried by their master or on a broom, even when it was so close that these methods of transport were gratuitous. Sometimes they returned on foot, which emphasized how the outward journey by air was a detail intended to stress the abnormality of the whole affair. Symbolically it expressed the extraordinary character and difficulty of transfer between the normal world and another opposed anti-world. Night flying could also explain large meetings of witches coming from long distances, but such big gatherings were rare events which appeared in few confessions. In a parody of a village festival the witches danced back to back, consumed horrible food and made hail, frosts or caterpillars which damaged their own crops. Sexuality and cannibalism were only mentioned in a handful of cases. This was an anti-fertility rite conducted on the familiar principle of inversion. Many accounts had the participants concealing their identity by wearing masks, aided by the fact it was night. A more obsessive secrecy was suggested by Claudon Bregeat, who explained;

> there were only some musicians who played the flute on some wooden sticks like whistles, while nobody said a word, and the tunes and songs were unknown to her. At the centre of the dance there was someone who kept watch on the dancers, and as soon as they saw anyone looking at the others they pushed them, by which means they were prevented from getting a look at others, or turning to the side, so that there was no way of recognizing one another for this reason, as well as the darkness and the fact that everyone had masks of sailcloth or linen, even headdresses or hats pulled down low over their faces . . .[41]

Nearly all the standard features of the sabbat could be reinverted – in the odd aberrant confession the witches even enjoyed a good meal or went by day. These symbolic constituents were apparently not very firmly grasped by a significant minority of those who confessed. Although the idea that witches held secret meetings was well established in popular folklore, the formal structures of inversion seem to have been rather insecurely attached to this central theme.

The really constant element in the confessions is harming the crops, occasionally omitted but never reversed. Just as the main purpose of most communal Christian rites was to protect the crops and encourage fertility, so the diabolical festivals sought to destroy them. This fundamental inversion was never misunderstood. That this was the primary meaning of the sabbat is emphasized by the numerous accounts of disputes between rich and poor witches over such plans. Catherine Charpentier claimed that the rich 'who said that they still had enough grain in store, wished and suggested that they should make hail and destroy the grain and the other fruits of the earth. As for her, she had never wished to agree, because of her fear of being in want, knowing as she did the poverty of her husband, also, she had several times been beaten by her said master Persin, who supported the wishes of the others'.[42] This is a very common theme recounted by the witches, one which plainly expressed the basic social divisions of the local community. High prices meant desperate times for the poor but profits for those with a surplus of grain to sell, who were also likely to take advantage to increase their land holdings. Here inversion normally stopped in the fantasies, for only in a few cases did the rich not get their way at the sabbat as they did in the real world. Occasionally the poor won the argument; more often they managed to sabotage the hail-making in some way – perhaps by upsetting the pot being used – at the price of a beating from the Devil.

In fact the sabbat was hierarchical in a depressingly conventional fashion. If there were several devils present they had their ranks, while the rich (or occasionally the young) witches took precedence over the majority who were old and poor. Jean Caillerey grumbled that

> there was a devil there, whose name he did not know, assisted by several other devils, who commanded all the others. He saw easily that his own master Houbelot was only the servant of the others, while for his own part because he was poor he was always at the rear, and only got the left-overs.[43]

For her part, Didielle Simmonel voiced what sounds like a proto-feminist complaint:

> She said further that each year at the general sabbat their master Persin chose one among them as mayor and another as dean, who commanded the other witches for the whole year, these being obliged to obey them . . . adding that at these sabbats these officers were always seated closest to their master Persin, and made reports to him on those who had not been willing to obey.
>
> To make the hail, they beat water with small white batons which their master Persin gave them, then a cloud full of hail suddenly rose in the air, and was guided by the said officers, who rose in the air first, followed

by the other male witches. Meanwhile she and the other women remained on the spot, and did the cooking while they waited for the men to return for the banquet.[44]

In the accounts of such officers being chosen they were almost always men who were also named as leading witches by others. Here was another area where normal hierarchies – this time those of gender – were transferred to the sabbat without being inverted.

How were ideas about the sabbat maintained and spread? We can never know with certainty, but their persistence into recent folklore is suggestive. There are many references to the *veillées* – winter evening meetings for spinning, storytelling and flirtation – in the trials; none mention the telling of witchcraft stories explicitly, but all the more recent evidence suggests they are a staple of such gatherings. That the notion was in common parlance is plain from evidence given in the trials themselves, quite apart from the confessions. A year before her arrest, Jeanne le Schrempt talked of how 'the witches of Guermange had said that when they were at the sabbat the rich drank from silver cups and the poor from glasses, that there was one of them who arrived at the lake of Lindre in a carriage, whose master always went in front, having a horsetail for a beard'.[45] A witness against Mongeatte de la Woeuvre had been told stories by the daughter of the accused about how witches killed babies in their cradles when their mothers were not looking, then dug up the bodies to make powder.[46] Anything odd which happened in connection with a storm would be remembered for future use. Jacquotte Tixerand blamed her reputation on such an incident, for 'the people had a bad opinion of her on one occasion, when she returned from the spring with her daughter without having been wetted, at the time of the great hailstorm which spoiled all the crops at Amance about three years earlier, but they did her great wrong'.[47] Those who happened to get caught in a mountain storm and were seen coming back drenched might also give rise to talk behind their backs, as in the case of Jehenne Stablo, when the boys 'started to say among themselves it was certain she was coming back from the sabbat'.[48] There is abundant evidence in the trials of such talk among children and adolescents, either in social gatherings or while they were keeping the animals, while a very large number of the elaborated stories (in proportion to their numbers among the accused) came from these young people. Apart from those who made such confessions, there are a significant number of other cases where children made themselves seem important or perhaps took their revenge with tales about the sabbat, only to send one or both of their parents to the stake.

Ideas about the sabbat were also perpetuated through the trials themselves. It was routine practice to read out the confessions of the accused at their execution, itself a well-attended public event. When Mengeatte des Woirelz retracted her confessions to escape with banishment, she combined this element with a vivid picture of the pressures she had felt. She explained in connection with her statements about the sabbat that

> tired of being in prison, and of the pain of the torture, joined with the fear of the evil reputation she had been falsely given in the town, she had chosen to die rather than live in such anguish. She had reckoned that in saying what she did to us, copying the confession of a woman executed at Creny, and the suspicions held by various witnesses used against her, we would have enough reason to put her to death.

When the judges objected that this amounted to 'self-murder', she replied 'that the desire for death had led her to do this'.[49] In a similar fashion, Barbelline Chaperey said

> that she had confessed more than she had committed or done, but this was because she was under torture, and that she had not reckoned there would be so many people hostile to her, after thinking about which, she had been led to make such confessions.

Although she persisted in some essential confessions, she withdrew what she had said about the sabbat, saying 'she had learned this from the trials of other witches who had already confessed'.[50]

As already suggested, there was some awareness of possible confusion between dreams and reality. Jean de Socourt claimed 'it is all abuse and trickery, and most commonly when they think they are there they do not budge from their beds'.[51] The judges themselves asked Jeanne Martin if witches were really present at the sabbat 'in their real form, or if it is only in dreams or imagination'. She did not take the opportunity to reply, beyond saying she sometimes went in the form of a cat.[52] I think any modern reader must be struck by the extraordinarily dream-like quality of the longer stories told by some of the accused and wonder how far their authors constructed these fantasies around a dream-life whose basis lay in local folklore and local events. In the sphere of fantasy this may have allowed the downtrodden to express their resentments through a fantasy life in which they acquired a degree of power over the oppressive society in which they lived. Nicolas Raimbault was a poor herdsman who was sometimes reduced to stealing grain or wood, but when he went to the sabbat,

> there were many others dancing to the sound of an oboe, so he did the same, choosing a young woman or girl whom he took to dance with the others, and because she was attractive she was the only one he danced with on that occasion; then they had a banquet with a great feast, but there was only boiled meat and some wine he did not find very good. Among his accomplices some were more qualified than the others, the great – who seemed to him to be gentlemen – being more cherished and favoured than the small, and as they banqueted some proposed to make hail to spoil the wheat, the others to cause insects and flies to attack the vegetables. But the poor opposed this, especially the proposal to destroy the wheat, preferring that it should be the oats. Nevertheless the rich were the masters, so that after they had beaten the water of a spring, and the stream next to it, with sticks which were in small sections, a great mist came up with a cloud and hail which did some damage to the wheat beyond Leintrey; and when one of the accomplices did not beat the water as much as the others their masters struck them like a sergeant in the army.

On another occasion he was taken to a place where

> there were a few people, more men than women, who were beating the water in the spring, and finding his stick, which was larger than before and of red wood, all ready, he beat the water with them. But immediately his accomplices went up in the air on horseback, since the cloud was already made and starting to drop its contents, which caused some hail which fell slightly on the wheat at Autrepierre and Amenoncourt, but the greater part fell on the hilltops, and when he saw his accomplices going up in the air he was so astonished he said Jesus Maria, for which reason he found himself alone and obliged to return home on foot.

He was taken to yet another sabbat when his master found him cutting wood, then had him mount behind him on his horse to go to the woods, where this time they found more women than men:

> A great whirlwind came up, and his master cried out to him to touch inside it, which taught him to do as the others did, that is to say to pull

up the oaks (as it seemed to them), and he admitted that when he pushed an oak it fell down, and his master made his horse jump over the top of the oaks which he levelled to the ground, as it also seemed to him, and all this was done for the purpose of destroying the acorn crop . . .[53]

Only a handful of the accused managed to invent anything as exciting as this (and one wonders if Raimbault was a village storyteller). The theme of the illusion which vanished at the name of Jesus was a familiar one, however, which appeared in other confessions. The dispute between poor and rich is also a routine feature, in this case with the poor wanting to spoil the oats because these were primarily food for animals, especially horses, so their loss would mainly affect the rich.

It is a psychoanalytic commonplace that fantasies of omnipotence never satisfy. Certainly the sabbat appears as a deeply unsatisfactory experience for nearly all participants from their own accounts – Raimbault is not really typical here, although there were plenty of negative features even in his story. It is characteristic that this should be least apparent in the case of some of the children; in Lorraine four of them made long confessions that suggest that for them dreams and fantasies could be a form of comfort. The Devil they met may have been harsh and terrifying, but he also offered excitement and adventure. The experience was more like attending a blackly comic horror movie than being part of the grim punitive world commonly evoked by the adults, even when Demenge Masson described how his friend Pierron hid in order to escape the duty of kissing the Devil's backside. As so often, the Devil involved did not seem particularly quick-witted to be so easily deceived. The infernal kiss apart, he seems to have set out to give the two boys an adventure as they rode in the air with him on his black horse to the sabbat, where he found the two prettiest girls to dance with them. The food was tasteless, as usual, and Persin himself was far from pretty:

he had two middling sized horns, and his face was completely black, except for his lips which were paler; his eyes were enormous and frightening, entirely black with no whites, while his nose was hideous, big and hooked, with three points sticking out a long way at its end. Looking lower he saw that he had hairy legs, like a horse, as were his feet, except that they were divided in the middle, saying that nothing about him was more hideous than his nose.

45

The stuff of nightmares indeed, and the story seems to have left everyone perplexed. The case was referred to the duke himself, who kept delaying a decision, then died, so that it had to be reconsidered by his successor. The boy was only ten when he made his confession and had originally left home at the age of seven or eight to look for work after his father was killed in a quarrying accident. He spent nearly two years lodged with the local *prévôt*, who made a complaint about the danger to his own family. Finally the new duke sent him back to his mother, with orders to the local *curé* to teach him some sound religion.[54]

There are only two cases from Lorraine which include descriptions of a formal black mass, with a parodic elevation of the host using a turnip or a piece of wood. They come from the same group of trials from a remote valley in the extreme south of the duchy, so may represent a distinct local tradition. The trials began with a voluntary confession by Chretienne Parmentier, an illegitimate young woman of twenty-three, who was reported to have already been telling stories about her own witchcraft as a child. She poured out a long tale about an exciting night-life, during which she had ridden to the sabbat on a broom treated with special grease and enjoyed a good meal. On other occasions she helped make hail, but she also said sometimes she only went in her dreams and found herself in bed when she woke. Her ingenuous story that her devil Taupin wanted to marry her and raise children with her sounds like an attempt to compensate in fantasy for her difficult situation in reality; she had tried to win a young man who rejected her. Chretienne was evidently only too ready to confess and bring about her own death, which may be seen as an example of the tendency for the disadvantaged to put themselves in positions where they are liable to be destroyed. Her confession bridges the worlds of the child and the adult.[55] Chretienne's stories may well have influenced those told by the twelve-year-old Jean Colombain from the same village and group of trials. It is hardly surprising that after her apparently unprompted confession of a parodic Mass at the sabbat he should have been asked about this specifically six weeks later. Jean was another seriously disadvantaged child; his mouth was deformed after a babyhood accident, so that another boy had to interpret his speech. It is easy to understand why, according to the witnesses, the girls did not want to kiss him and why he resorted to threats, mixed with claims of supernatural experiences and powers. He told a story about going to an iron house that was the location for the feasting and dancing that seemed entirely on fire, yet gave off no heat. After telling of the diabolic mass with its parodic rituals, he produced a bizarre account of the use of the powder, usually envisaged as a deadly poison; he said the witches ate it and then showed it to wild boar that became unable to run away and were easily captured. His stories led to the trial and execution of his mother, although he himself was spared.[56]

The only rivals to these children for extended and imaginative descriptions of nocturnal activity are a group of witches from the German-speaking region to the east of the duchy. Although there is a considerable overlap, several elements in their stories make it clear that the linguistic divide between French and German speakers was also to be found in folklore. Here it becomes difficult to distinguish between the sabbat and acts of *maleficium*, for small groups of witches seemed to gather regularly with their master to conduct night-time raids on their enemies. They used a liquid poison to kill animals or sometimes humans, which required several pairs of hands to administer it successfully. This poison was fabricated by the witches themselves from the burned bodies of stillborn children, whose fingers were kept as candles which never consumed themselves. The myth of these 'thieves' candles', never mentioned in the French-speaking areas, was a widespread German folk belief also found in Bavarian trials.[57] Even the original seduction by the Devil seemed to be assimilated to this vision of a frenetic night-life, in which the sabbat was the occasion for feasting, dancing and marriages between young girls and demons, but some of its other elements were carried on separately. The witches met in small groups to make hail and carry out other crimes. It may be going too far to suggest that there is a curious Gothic quality to these confessions, but they are certainly different – and the general style is common to the dozen or so surviving cases from the region.[58] It is curious to note that a similar notion of how to harm enemies appears in the even more lurid accounts of the Basque *aquelarre*, where the Devil and other witches went to the victim's house by night in order to pour powder down his or her throat.[59]

Few of this group tried to escape from identifying accomplices with the usual claim they had been masked, nor could they very well deny their active participation, although it was in some sense under compulsion. Elsewhere, witches commonly went to some pains to present themselves as marginal and despised figures even at the sabbat. Few were more abject than Barbon Moictrier, who claimed the others called her 'la criarde' ('the blubber') because she would not join in. She alleged that the one accomplice she could identify, la Belle Agnes, 'was one of the most forward there, in status and in the dance, and even that once when she was crying the said Belle Agnes gave her a kick as she was dancing'.[60] It was always someone else who had taken the lead, unless one counts the rather ambiguous claim made by Marion le Masson, a woman of higher status whose husband had been mayor of St Dié, that among her accomplices,

> there were many who wanted to cause the loss of the grain crops, but she opposed this and said that it would cause great damage and be a great hardship for the poor, arguing that it would be much better to make a storm and wind to cause damage to the belltower at St Dié. This was agreed, and after beating the water of the spring in that place a great cloud and storm came up, which severely damaged the said tower, and when they had thus beaten the water they all found themselves back at home.[61]

Even here there is a claim to have attenuated the harm done to her neighbours in practical terms. In theory the sabbat might have provided the opportunity to plan a whole range of malicious acts. In Lorraine the Devil showed very little imagination in this direction, rarely taking the opportunity to address his servants. When he did, according to Claudon la Romaine, 'all his preaching amounted to nothing more than that they should do harm under threat of being well beaten'.[62] Often he seems to have imposed silence, perhaps because, as some witches claimed, his deformity prevented him from speaking clearly. Colas François did suggest an exceptional attempt to convince, when his master Navel called them together to tell them 'how it was much finer in his hell than in paradise, and that they would be very happy to be in hell with him'.[63] More typical was the mixture of apology and derision reported by Chesnon la Triffatte when, in the face of protests about putrid meat, Lucifer 'seeing some fastidious ones who did not want to eat such offal said that they ought to be very content, and that they were the best and most delicate meats he had been able to find'.[64] In just one case there is the hint of a serious discussion of practical politics. According to Marion Arnoulx, a leading witch named Jean Gelyat warned that the local mayor 'had undertaken, if he was allowed to proceed, to have all the witches of their group arrested'; there was some talk of taking measures against him, but this practical effort at self-defence came to no clear resolution, nor was it followed by action.[65] In other words, the confessing witch simply lost the thread of her own story, whose logic was not being examined too closely in any case.

Such details are really decorative and should not obscure the fact that like so much else in the concept of witchcraft, the sabbat was primarily concerned with power. Such visions were of course fundamentally deceptive. They could only be fulfilled in negative terms, through the destruction of the basic assets of rural society, the reverse of bringing any improvement to the lives of participants. A curious logic is evident, whereby the Devil needs the witches in order to produce corporeal effects and so uses a mixture of false promises, threats and compulsion to obtain their presence at his disgusting ceremonies. The betrayal which begins with the seduction and the pact is completed at the sabbat, where nothing is quite what it seems. The food, instead of being merely repellent might be entirely illusory, as for Hellenix Hottin, who reported that Persin 'had promised to give her a meal, but did no such thing, and those who had already eaten said that when they left they were dying of hunger'.[66] The basis for virtual enslavement to this deplorable master was never really explained, except as a result of the witches' own pathetic gullibility and the pact they made. As for the proceedings at the sabbat, these appear to prefigure Hell itself, in which respect at least we may fairly see the sabbat as the gateway to the land of the dead. For those who made the confessions death loomed in a very real sense, although many seem to have felt that by making a clean breast of their sinful relations with the lord of the underworld they ensured ending up in the other place. Fortunately the historian is not called upon to decide whether this amounted to more than the exchange of one fantasy for another.

What the Lorraine example also shows is how the stereotype was adapted to local conditions and to a particular pattern of persecution. In a rural society, where local judges and officials were very close to popular traditions, this seems to have been accomplished without great difficulty. It seems highly probable that many of those who made brief confessions could have elaborated them easily enough if pressed, and indeed there are instances of this in the trials. From the examples given it should be evident how a mixture of realistic and fantastic detail, rooted in local folklore, could be developed in this way. The evidence also suggests powerfully that this folkloric material was often mediated through personal fantasy and dreams to relate to the personal conflicts of individuals.

The mechanism of denunciations did contribute to some small local witch-hunts, although almost none claimed more than a handful of victims. Those who came to trial in this way always turned out to be men and women who already had a reputation for witchcraft among their neighbours; it is possible that where accusations were not followed up, as was often the case, it was because such evil fame did not attach to those concerned. Once a reputation had been established it might keep circulating. A curious case is that of Mathieu Blaise, an elderly and prosperous peasant from the large village of Ste Marguerite. He was brought to trial in 1592 after a denunciation but most of the witnesses testified for him rather than against him; as there was no serious evidence at all, he was released without even being interrogated. For the next decade local witches continually named him among their accomplices, often as one of the leaders at the sabbat, without any sign that further action was taken; he almost certainly died in his bed, like many other suspects.[67]

The people of Lorraine reduced the sabbat to a rather drab inverted reflection of their own hard but humdrum lives. Witches skulked away from their tiresome master and short-changed him on their obligations, as peasants commonly did with their real masters. Many of them told versions of a curious story, according to which they made an annual offering – usually a chicken thrown out into the garden – in order to be spared the tiresome and laborious duty of attendance at the sabbat. Like any feudal overlord the Devil evidently accepted the principle of commutation. Although the witches might emphasize how he had forced them to harm others, the Devil rarely appeared as very astute or terrifying. The occasional vivid splash of colour in an individual confession did nothing to launch panic or frenzied witch-hunting. The naming of accomplices followed rather than led the labelling processes whereby a category of suspects was created. It facilitated persecution to some extent, since perhaps a quarter of trials were actually initiated in this way, but it would be rash to assume that most of those concerned would not have ended up in the same predicament by other means. The belief itself certainly endured long after the trials were a distant memory; a century ago the folklorist Sauvé found the inhabitants of the Vosges still enthusiastically whiling away the long winter nights with stories about witchcraft and the sabbat, the latter reached by a magical flight after rubbing ointment on one's body. The Devil retained his conventional horns, claws and tail, and if he was better left unnamed this did not imply any great respect for his intelligence, since he seemed more often a buffoon than the cosmic embodiment of evil.[68]

The sabbat in Europe

If the sabbat myth appeared in some form virtually everywhere witches were detected, it was still very far from presenting a uniform pattern. The apparent coherence and normality of the Lorraine case must not mislead us here. This was an unusually stable and fully realized fusion of different traditions, which more often fluctuated violently over time and space. One version of this can be seen in the intense witch-hunts, among them that in the Basque country fortunately cut short by Salazar, where local beliefs seem to have displayed an astonishing capacity to ramify and develop. It was mostly in German cities that the juridical, political and social peculiarities of virtually independent urban communities interacted to generate terrifying outbreaks of persecution. The cities involved had populations of only a few thousand, and functioned as market, legal and clerical centres for the surrounding countryside. Surviving examples suggest a rather claustrophobic environment, with narrow houses packed tightly within the medieval walls to make an ideal setting for a satanic thriller. Small Catholic cities ruled by bishops also had abnormally large clerical populations, and would have been filled with the sounds and symbols of belief, yet also with petty rivalries and jealousies. While the dramatic episodes that took place against such a background only made up a relatively small proportion of known European trials, they have inevitably dominated most later thinking about witchcraft. The unrestrained use of torture to extract confessions and denunciations horrified many contemporary observers. In fact these persecutions turned out to be self-limiting, for they created such social instability and general fear that finally the ruling groups brought them to an end. It should be added that major cities and centres of government were never involved; the places concerned were always relative backwaters, where small groups of zealots could have disproportionate influence. The most spectacular cases of all were in some prince-bishoprics – Trier in the 1590s, Bamberg and Würzburg around 1628–31, Cologne in the 1630s – but Protestant towns were also affected. There are striking similarities with earlier persecutions of Jews on charges of the ritual murder of children and both types of outbreak brought efforts by the Emperor and his jurists to enforce higher judicial standards.

These intense persecutions were necessarily built around the sabbat, for it was only through the identification of numerous accomplices that the panic could spread as it did. It is also noticeable that as accusations spread to clerics and other members of the elites the confessions became more elaborate, with much emphasis on complex diabolical rituals at the sabbat. The poor might go on brooms or pitchforks, but the rich allegedly travelled in silver coaches or other luxury conveyances. A particularly unpleasant feature of these outbreaks was the way in which children became involved in large numbers as both accusers and victims. This had also been true in the Basque country and was to be a major factor in the Swedish witch-hunt of 1668–76. In this last instance the confessions made much of the legend of Blåkulla (the blue mountain), a Swedish equivalent of the German peak known as the Brocken, which shared the reputation of the latter as a meeting place for witches. The children elaborated this into stories of a great hall where devils and angels alternated amidst a series of bizarre and often playful inversions, intermixed with devil-worship and scenes of punishment. Here the meshing together of demonology and local tradition is particularly obvious, alongside the fertile qualities and danger of juvenile fantasy. The children were grouped together in special houses, supposedly for their protection from the witches, and this encouraged them further in their role as mouthpieces for local opinion. Although there was considerable elite scepticism from the start, the local clergy and community leaders took up the hunt with enthusiasm; the persecution was only stopped after it spread to Stockholm. Only at this point did the government itself come to appreciate the dangers properly. Under hostile questioning the whole great edifice of fantasy collapsed as the children admitted their stories were lies from beginning to end. Over the previous years they had brought terror and panic to large areas of northern Sweden. Yet because there were dissenting voices and there was no systematic use of torture, less than 15 per cent of those accused were put to death, with the total number of executions being around 200.[69]

In Sweden it was only during this late outbreak that ideas of the sabbat contributed much to witchcraft persecution. There were many other regions in Europe where the sabbat played a marginal role at best, appearing in small minorities of trials in other parts of Scandinavia or in Aragon and Hungary, for example. It is no surprise to find that it made only fleeting appearances in connection with Dutch witchcraft, while its absence from most English cases is often noted. In this context England seems much less exceptional than was once thought, and indeed the sabbat did creep gradually on to the English scene albeit in a rather tame and homely form. It surfaced hesitantly in the Lancashire trials of 1612 and 1634; these were unusually large group trials for England, and particularly good evidence has survived from the first, when nineteen persons were tried and most of them convicted and hanged. In 1634 an even larger group was tried, with seventeen known convictions, but intervention by king and council first stopped the executions, then finally exposed the main accuser, a boy named Edmund Robinson, as a fraud. There is an obvious natural association between these group trials and stories about secret meetings of the accused, and after this there are a few, more scattered references to witches' meetings in English trials. The sabbat as such hardly featured at all, however, in by far the biggest English witch-hunt, that conducted by Matthew Hopkins and John Stearne in East Anglia in 1645–7. Poor record survival complicates the task of reconstructing this famous affair, which probably claimed between 120 and 200 victims. Hopkins and Stearne are obscure figures; all we really know of the former is that he was the son of a local minister and that he died from consumption in 1647 (rather than being executed as a witch himself, as a tenacious legend would have it). Even less information is available about Stearne, while the Puritanism of the two men has often been exaggerated. The witch-finders used sleep deprivation and other forms of coercion to extract confessions, including much testimony about pacts with the Devil and the keeping of familiars. Hopkins himself alleged his local witches met in an attempt to compass his death, but evidence for such assemblies is absent from the testimonies. It is far from clear that this made much difference to the proceedings, for Hopkins and Stearne seem to have brought existing suspicions about *maleficium* to a head in a fashion very similar to the Swedish children. This was true in the case of John Lowes, vicar of Brandeston in Suffolk, who had a long history of disputes with his parishioners, including cases in the Star Chamber. He was evidently a violent and litigious man, given to imprudent verbal sallies against his neighbours. In 1615 he had attempted to protect a woman who was convicted and executed as a witch, hiding her in his own house and threatening the constable. He himself had been tried for witchcraft at Bury St Edmunds later that same year, but was acquitted. Hopkins and Stearne used their typical methods on him, according to the lord of the manor, who recorded:

> I have heard it from them that watched with him that they kept him awake several Nights together and ran him backwards and forwards about the Room, until he [was] out of Breath. Then they rested him a little, and then ran him again; and thus they did for several Days and Nights together, till he was weary of his life, and was scarce sensible of what he said or did. They swam him at Framlingham, but that was no true Rule to try him by; for they put in honest People at the same time, and they swam as well as he.[70]

It was hardly surprising that a man in his seventies broke down under such treatment; here as elsewhere one must assume that the absence of the sabbat from Lowes' rambling confessions indicated that Hopkins and Stearne were not interested in extracting material of this kind. They and their clients were still primarily concerned with *maleficium*, alongside the pact and the familiars which gave the witch the power to operate it, so that the alleged diabolism never became detached from the every-day reality of witchcraft belief, as it did in some of the German witch-hunts.

In north-western Europe the sabbat appears to have enjoyed greatest prominence in Denmark and Scotland, where there is a rather odd relationship. Danish witches often confessed to meetings with the Devil in their local churches and this has been plausibly linked with the wall-paintings in the churches, where scenes of temptation were com-monplace.[71] When King James VI of Scotland married Anne of Denmark in 1590 the storms which troubled the return voyage were ascribed to witchcraft in both countries. In Scotland around a hundred individuals, supposedly led by the Earl of Bothwell, were accused of high treason through meetings with the Devil in the kirk at North Berwick. This bizarre affair took the sabbat into Scottish witchcraft trials, where it subsequently cropped up in numerous confessions. Like those in Lorraine, however, Scottish witches were rather well behaved and in fact inversion played rather a limited role in most stories. In a society where almost all forms of spontaneous festivity were banned, the idea of disorderly gatherings was perhaps sufficient evidence of depravity on its own. In the coastal villages where many trials took place it was the sinking of ships, rather than the spoiling of crops, which exemplified the treason to the community.[72] There is another similarity to the Lorraine case in the way denunciations operated, for they seem to have concentrated on other local suspects with existing reputations.

Such links between different countries crop up in various contexts. The account of the Swedish trials in Glanvill's *Sadducismus Triumphatus* evidently influenced the New England clergyman Cotton Mather, and may have had some indirect bearing on events in Salem Village. The behaviour of the possessed girls during this famous episode has obvious parallels with that of the children in Sweden, although there is no sign of direct imitation. The sudden appearance of the sabbat in New England in 1692 remains mysterious; the children's stories have too much in common with European accounts not to have some literary or folkloric source whose exact nature is now impossible to recover. In comparison with their counterparts in the Old World, the authorities in the New came out remarkably well. Not only did they bring the trials to a close much more quickly and with a modest number of executions, they also sponsored public penitence for the wrongs committed, and ultimately rehabilitated both the accused and the dead. Whereas the Swedes executed four of the accusers, including a boy of thirteen, in Massachusetts the girls were left to wrestle with their own consciences. Another who engaged in painful self-examination was Cotton Mather, much troubled by his failure to intervene earlier and stop the persecution yet still fascinated by what he called 'the wonders of the invisible world'. For men like Mather, the Devil's anti-world remained a vital part of their cosmology, even when they saw how easily the great enemy could lead them astray.

In a very different context, the Inquisitors in the extreme north-east of Italy were confronted by a strange nocturnal world in the beliefs of the *benendanti* of Friuli, peasants with a peculiar folklore of their own. These belonged to at least one widespread belief system, for they were allegedly marked out by an accident of birth, having been covered by the caul (or amniotic membrane) at the moment of delivery. Various similar chances – birth at a particular time or at a particular place in the family – were supposed to confer special powers of insight or healing elsewhere in Europe. In Friuli the *benendanti* went out in dreams to fight the witches and ensure the fertility of the crops; some of them also claimed the power to identify witches and treat their victims. The Inquisitors tried with some success to assimilate these local traditions to orthodox demonology, turning the dream meetings of the anti-witch cult into versions of the sabbat. However by the time they had achieved this, around 1650, the sceptical attitudes of both the Roman authorities and the Venetian secular administration averted the danger of an ensuing persecution. While male *benendanti* allegedly fought witches, women seem to have been more concerned to make contact with the souls of those recently dead, bringing back reports of their condition and their needs. There are hints of similar beliefs elsewhere, but nothing remotely as complex or systematic as this strange corpus of folklore. If most scholars have seen the *benendanti* as an exceptional local case rather than the tip of a submerged iceberg, this must of necessity remain a matter of opinion. Where there is certainly no problem is in linking them to the role of the sabbat as an anti-fertility rite, for their stories exemplify this in a particularly vivid fashion.[73]

We must also suppose that a wide range of local folklore was caught up in the judicial machinery, through whose distorting lens it is preserved. The complex process of interaction suggested in this chapter provides a general model within which these beliefs can to some extent be reintegrated; it seems unlikely we shall ever be able to reconstruct them fully. What we do not need is any pseudo-empirical explanation, whether in the form of Murray's pagan covens or the early drug cults imagined by some others. It was often claimed in the course of trials that witches smeared themselves or the objects on which they flew with ointments, while there was quite widespread knowledge of various medical plants, including some hallucinogens. Dream experience is likely to have played a significant part in validating personal stories; it is even possible that some of it was drug-induced, perhaps by fungi with psychotropic qualities. When one looks in detail at the stories about ointments however, it becomes plain that the ingredients were usually magical in a quite different sense, for they only acquired their virtue by being placed in a symbolic system, through preparation at particular times and so forth. Powerful magical qualities were frequently accorded to human grease, simply because it carried such a charge of the forbidden. Wherever there is clear evidence about the alleged ointments they turn out to be harmless substances, identified or even deliberately manufactured to support confessions.[74] It is hardly credible in any case that drugs could have produced specific visions of goats sitting on thrones or of perverted rituals; at most they could be linked to general sensations like that of flying through the air. To give them more importance requires us to homogenize the confessions in disregard of the endless local variations.

This would be to repeat the error of demonologists like the Jesuit Martin Del Rio, whose enormous compendium on magic and witchcraft argued that the similarity of the confessions showed the sabbat was no illusion.[75] As a notorious library-bound pedant, he was predictably confusing scholarly syncretism with reality, for the confessions were anything but uniform when taken one by one.

While confessions were normally extracted under thumbscrews, rack, strappado or other refinements of the torturer's art, a certain proportion of the accused made 'free' confessions, which in some cases did not reflect even the implicit threat of torture. This led such a sceptical observer as Thomas Hobbes to remark that 'though he could not rationally believe there were witches, yet he could not be fully satisfied to believe there were none, by reason that they would themselves confess it, if strictly examined'.[76] Such confessions no longer seem as puzzling as they once did; some recent cases of alleged satanic abuse have provided yet more evidence of the way individuals placed under extreme stress will manufacture preposterous stories, apparently coming, at least for a while, to believe that they must be true. They mingle themes from their cultural milieu with elements derived from dream and fantasy, to generate self-incriminating narratives which have their own psychological significance (discussed more fully in a later chapter). Those witches who made a clean breast of such imaginary turpitudes were engaging in a form of self-purification, just as they should have done when they confessed to the priest, if they were Catholics. In the face of a terrifying situation, which saw them excluded and vilified by their own community, the confession represented an appeal for forgiveness and reintegration. The judges frequently emphasized the importance of a complete account, including all separate acts of witchcraft, as the condition for being received back into the church and rendered eligible for salvation. In practice they were very careless about enforcing this, but such exhortations produced statements such as that made by Claudatte Jean, who

> prayed for the honour of God that she should be put to death as soon as possible for the salvation of her soul, and wished that there might be no more witches in the world, but that she might be the last, so that the fruits of the earth might be more abundant than they had been, because so much and so long as there were witches it would be a great evil for the poor people. She then prayed she might have a good confessor to

secure the salvation of her soul, and begged all those she had offended to pardon her.[77]

As we have seen, however, others were better aware of the fictitious nature of their accounts, to the extent that they could explain how they had concocted them. We should also remember such terrible stories as that of mayor Junius of Bamberg, who wrote to his daughter explaining how the executioner – either very sly or unusually merciful – begged him to confess, rather than oblige him to inflict endless torment. These German witch-hunts were very different in some respects; since the accusations were spread by denunciations made under torture, the arbitrary nature of the process was far clearer to the accused and they were rarely suspected until the last moment. Those with long-standing village reputations were more likely to make a 'sincere' confession, as part of a psychological *folie à deux* with their interrogator, although one may wonder how long they continued to believe in it. A fair number of the Lorraine witches withdrew their confessions when interrogated again without torture; the inevitable penalty was to be tortured again. Only two are known to have resisted this second test.

The detailed accounts of the pact and the sabbat evidently reflect the everyday cultural and social concerns of their tellers, however fanciful the imaginary packaging may appear. They also reaffirm the creativity and significance of human fantasy, through which the juxtaposition of real and imaginary worlds took place. For their neighbours and the judges it was the witches who bridged the gap between the worlds, with the sabbats as the ultimate anti-world, hovering uneasily between diabolical illusion and some kind of perverted reality. Stories that the Devil incited those present to do wrong, then distributed the necessary powders or other poisons, sought to link the secret nocturnal meetings back to the *maleficium* the witches operated in the ordinary sphere of village life. The weakness or absence of this element in most accounts of the sabbat suggests how imperfectly this element was ever integrated into popular thinking. One must add examples, such as that of England, which demonstrate how persecution and witch beliefs could function perfectly well without the sabbat at all. It is not a case of there being a 'classic' type of European witchcraft built around the pact and the sabbat, with a few deviant types in peripheral regions; the picture is much more varied and the sabbat was only the central basis for persecution in a small number of extreme cases. What this complex superstructure does do is to give us enormously helpful insights into the minds of those concerned. Only so long as it is placed firmly in the mind, and allowed its full range of local variants, will its great symbolic richness help rather than hinder our understanding.

CHAPTER II

THE EXPERIENCE OF
BEWITCHMENT

The power to harm

WHEN THE DEVIL PROMISED witches prosperity and freedom from want he inevitably proved to have deceived them. It was very much otherwise with the power to harm others. His money might turn into leaves, but the powder or the familiars remained with his new servants and were all too efficacious. As far as other people were concerned, witchcraft was about power. To be bewitched was to suffer the effects of the witch's power; it was the defining experience of what this meant in the real world. In most cases a person or an animal fell ill; later they possibly died. There was general agreement that the affliction itself must be strange or unnatural, so known illnesses were almost never ascribed to witchcraft. Given the modest state of medical knowledge in early modern Europe, this still left a vast field open for argument. The potential opportunities for suspicion were so great that it is hard to see where it need have stopped. Once a witch was on trial witnesses from the local community often produced a great list of misfortunes as evidence, varying enormously in both their gravity and the strength of the causal links alleged. Since the main source for such beliefs is in the trials, with only a thin scattering of other evidence, there is no way of judging the ultimate extent to which sufferers and their relatives routinely invoked bewitchment as a possible cause. Plainly they did not go as far as the Azande of equatorial Africa during the 1930s, who attributed every death to witchcraft.[1] On the other hand, many suspicions probably remained latent, primarily for lack of a suitable person to whom they might be attached.

The most clear-cut cases were those of sick people who were convinced they had been bewitched and named the witch responsible. They might demonstrate alarming symptoms if the suspect approached, or even at the mention of their name. The violence of some of these episodes is quite startling. The possessed London girl Mary Glover, having seen her alleged persecutor Elizabeth Jackson in church, went home and fell into a grievous fit, which was through repetitions of the witch's view, increased both in strength and in strangeness daily. In so much as now, she was turned round as a hoop, with her head backward to her hips; and in that position rolled and tumbled, with such violence, and swiftness, as that their pains in keeping her from receiving hurt against the bedstead, and posts, caused two or three women to sweat; she being all over cold and stiff as a frozen thing.

We may well see this particular instance as a hysterical attack, with the additional motive of gaining power and revenge, for when later the old woman was brought before her during such fits, a strange voice apparently coming from the girl's nostrils repeatedly said 'Hang her'.[2] There is every reason to suppose that such conviction could be an illness itself and that in some circumstances it might kill, either on its own or in conjunction with another complaint. The phenomenon of 'Voodoo death' sees the level of anxiety rise to a traumatic state, so that normal body functions collapse, and death may follow.[3] In effect those who are cursed or believe themselves to be the target of witchcraft go into shock; in most cases the result is some kind of pain or neurosis, which may well redouble in the presence of the suspect. Such phenomena have long been remarked on by observers of primitive societies, while more recently doctors have come to recognize how the immune system is affected by emotional states. The current trend towards less mechanistic ways of understanding the causes of sickness is very apposite here. In certain circumstances, it would appear, people can effectively be scared to death; more commonly, their normal social functioning and sense of well-being can be seriously impaired. While Haiti may be an extreme case, where impressive rituals reinforce the process, there is a very striking example from rural France as recently as 1968. In this instance a nocturnal session of counter-magic was followed the next day by the hospitalization of a neighbour suspected of witchcraft, who would presumably have been well aware of what was going on, and that the magic was intended to send the evil back to its alleged source. The woman concerned baffled the doctors; she would only repeat endlessly 'I'm afraid', and was too terrified to eat properly, dying seven months later.[4]

In societies where people believe in witchcraft their own fears usually function in this way, so that curses, threats and other expressions of ill-will have genuine power against the suggestible. The crime itself may be imaginary, but the imagination can be an immensely strong force. It is not surprising that children and adolescents seem to have been particularly prone to such disorders. While it would appear that most cases did not involve the most intense forms of witchcraft paranoia, a much larger number included claims that one or more of the alleged victims had blamed the accused for their fatal sickness. This was usually explicit, but might be expressed in a more oblique fashion, particularly if it was in a face-to-face encounter with the suspect. Margueritte Liegey, known as la Geline ('the hen'), had allegedly been a much feared beggar in the villages around Mirecourt in southern Lorraine for twenty years. After Claude George refused her alms one day she fell ill with her mouth twisted; when Margueritte returned she told her she had been very ill since the refusal. The suspect had no difficulty understanding the subtext of this remark, retorting 'so she wanted to say that she had given her the illness'; Claude still thought herself bewitched when she died 3 months later. This was just one of numerous allegations in this case from 1624, which ended with the confession and execution of the sixty-year-old widow. Eighteen months before the trial, Humbert Journal's wife had died after a violent illness lasting six days, during which she named Margueritte as the cause. Humbert chased after the suspect to beat her but she took refuge in the house of Didier Mongenot; Mongenot's wife had at first tried to keep her out and now believed she was bewitched, because several rat-sized animals seemed to be running about inside her body. Margueritte's actual arrest was provoked by the suspicions of Didier Drouat and his wife Claudon. After the former had demanded sureties for debts owed him by Margueritte's son-in-law, Claudon became bedridden with great pains in her limbs. She 'could only believe herself bewitched', either by the suspect or by her daughter Lucye. Lucye's husband, Pierot Cugnin, then appeared to assure Didier that he wished him no ill and was not to blame for his wife's sickness, adding the astonishing statement that he had told his own wife and mother-in-law to harm no-one in their house, but had been unable to be master. When the time came for the witnesses to be confronted with Margueritte, Claudon Drouat claimed to have walked in from her village feeling quite well, but that pains had reappeared in her arm and throat as she approached the church where the confrontations were held. A young farm servant, who also believed himself bewitched by Margueritte, made a similar claim. Jean Vuillemin, who thought she caused the death of his cow after he refused her some wood, told how he followed the advice given him, which was to boil its heart, so that if it had been bewitched the person responsible would be the first to visit his house. Margueritte duly appeared to ask for the offal, which he seems to have given to her without revealing his suspicions. By their own account the witnesses in this case had reacted with a typical mixture of violence, threats, but ultimately caution; most had clearly chosen to placate the witch rather than pursue matters too far. Once the trial began, however, their accumulated resentments poured out, while it was plain that the son-in-law of the accused (who must have been her main source of support) had abandoned her. Where the judges noted her lack of emotion as she heard the charges, one can only suppose that the unfortunate old woman was numbed by the full revelation of what her neighbours thought about her. She offered little resistance to the torture, admitting that she had been a witch for some twenty years, having been seduced when in despair because her child had drowned.[5]

In a case from the German-speaking north-east of Lorraine, it was reported that around 1590 the _curé_ of Bisping had helped arrange a marriage and was roused early from his bed to join the party which fetched the bride. As they went on their way Senelle Petter, whose own son had been an unsuccessful suitor for the girl's hand, was seen looking over her door at them. The _curé_ started to feel unwell and on his return said 'O God what have I done, I failed to cross myself this morning, and I have an evil opinion of Senelle, because I helped Steffan to obtain that girl'. He took to his bed with fever and a swollen leg, to die maintaining that she had given him the illness. Four years later this was one of the stories told against Senelle when she went on trial, after a failed attempt on her own part to obtain reparation from Royne Marchal. The latter had put about the story that she had woken at night to see the accused kneeling on her husband Demenge Marchal, holding a candle with a strong blue flame in her hand; Royne had been unable to move or call out as she lay in bed beside her spouse. Other testimony from the twenty witnesses showed that Senelle had a long reputation, of which she was well aware, while she was in the habit of defending herself with threats and with claims that others were witches. A particularly damaging story, which she hardly attempted to deny, was that she had talked about a method of causing lameness and death to both people and animals. This involved sticking a needle previously used to sew up a shroud into the ground where the target had been walking. The court was so alarmed by this rather elementary piece of sympathetic magic that after her confession of guilt orders were given to omit this section from the customary reading out of the trial prior to her execution. Senelle was a

married woman of about forty, with some modest property, whose assertive methods of self-defence had caused numerous crises, but also carried
her through them. Eight years earlier she had cursed her half-brother
after an inheritance dispute ended up in court, for him to die within six
months, giving rise to local gossip. Another local man told of his wife's
miscarriage a decade before and of the suspicions she later voiced before
her death; there had been a quarrel over the herding of a cow, then the
sickness had begun when his wife ate some bread given to her by Senelle,
whom she later thought she saw by her deathbed. While the accused
was probably correct if she reckoned that this accumulation of rumours
was likely to end in a formal charge sooner or later and so had little
alternative but to persevere with an aggressive strategy, her own attempt
to face down the latest story was plainly the catalyst for the trial which
sent her to the stake.[6]

Witnesses undoubtedly liked stories about blame attributed by past
victims because they placed responsibility for the charges on persons who
were safely dead. When it came to their own suspicions they were often
more evasive, making use of various equivocations. Their testimony was
commonly structured as a narrative, in which the causal links were
by inference rather than direct statement. Isabel Bordon of Charmes,
testifying against Claudon la Romaine, told how when the latter was ill
she had asked the witness to visit her twice a day. She kept this up for
some time, but finally stopped. After her recovery, Claudon came to
Isabel's house to complain that the latter had begun her visits well, but
finished badly. She then told Isabel that she did not like the plate of
cabbage she was given, throwing it and the bread away. Isabel was angry,
telling her she should not throw away such gifts in the name of God,
when others might like them better than she did. This caused Claudon
to leave 'angry and grumbling', at which the witness felt a sharp pain
in her leg, which became so swollen she could only walk with a stick.
A week later the suspect returned asking to sit by the fire, only for Isabel
to tell her she could hardly make a fire for herself because of the bad leg
she had since her last visit, adding 'I don't know what devil has given
it to me, but if it is not taken away some people will have to be put to
death.' Claudon responded by advising her to rub it well with butter, a
treatment which succeeded.[7] Such statements arranged events in a
sequence which strongly implied that one thing caused another without
the need to state this explicitly. Some witnesses were prepared to affirm
their belief directly; most limited themselves to suspicion or even a rather

unconvincing pose of neutrality. Wherever possible the diagnosis of witchcraft was attributed to a third party. Jennon Napnuel might well have felt nervous when summoned as a witness against Georgeatte Herteman, since the latter, asked if she were not very vindictive, admitted she had a very quick temper. Jennon told of a quarrel at the mill and the subsequent death of a cow, whose flesh was rotting and coming away, so that the slaughterman 'gave it as his opinion that it was witchcraft'.[8] These devices can be seen as evidence for the reluctance with which villagers testified at all, and their desire to leave a way open for reconciliation in case of an acquittal. They may also reveal the genuine uncertainty most people felt about witchcraft as an explanation, an awareness that there was something fragile and unreliable about it.

There is some evidence that the kin of sufferers were inclined to discourage ideas of bewitchment, and might show reluctance at any proposal they should summon the suspect. When Catherine Ancel was tried in 1614, Bastienne Morel testified about an incident, around 1600, when her late husband suspected Catherine over the illness of a bullock and wanted Bastienne to fetch her. In the end she agreed, and Catherine gave it some salt to lick, after which it recovered; Bastienne and her husband continued to dispute over the matter, as he suggested the cure showed it had been witchcraft, while she insisted one should not think ill of anyone and they did not know she was the cause. Most witnesses in this case used formulae to the effect that they were not sure, one saying rather pointlessly that he did not suspect her unless she was a witch. Catherine herself responded to questioning with the sensible comment that 'other people became ill just as she did, without anyone making them so'. In this case it seems that the accused had not given many real grounds for complaint to her neighbours, and that the suspicions owed a good deal to her mother's previous execution as a witch; in the event she withstood the torture to win her release, nearly two months after her arrest.[9] Early modern European villages were not populated by a race of credulous half-wits who attributed any and every misfortune to witchcraft. Such people existed, but enjoyed little credit among neighbours who usually held more sophisticated views about causation and understood that sick people might be more desperate than wise. When Claudon Grand Demenge was on his deathbed he said a woman had caused his death; his brother thought he referred to his wife Jennon, but his sister-in-law thought it wrong to take any notice of what he said because he seemed to be out of his mind at the time. Since this was the most serious charge in a rather poorly supported accusation, these doubts may have been important in the subsequent decision to release Jennon without taking proceedings any further.[10]

Religion, medicine and misfortune

Misfortune has always been a difficult concept, both intellectually and emotionally. Very few people are content to accept that blind chance plays a large part in their lives; they seek reasons and logical connections even where these do not really exist. In early modern Europe there were two large-scale systems which claimed to offer general explanations for success and failure, health and sickness, life and death. To the modern observer both appear almost wholly false, with their genuine power to explain being as meagre as their claims were grandiose. The first was religious or providential: God was an active force in the world, rewarding the faithful and punishing the impious, showing his hand in the issue of battles or the infliction of famine and plague. Some clever sleights of hand were necessary in order to deal with the more obvious cases in which the divine verdict was patently unjust; the almighty perforce became a very crafty operator, lulling some into a false sense of security while others endured tribulations designed to test or consolidate their faith. Although the resulting system was a supreme example of circular reasoning, it underlay a vast network of spiritual and therapeutic agencies that provided real comfort for many. Just as witchcraft could kill those who believed in it, so faith in divine power might well cure or succour them. The Devil himself was part of this way of thinking, and a particularly intractable one. Theologians wrestled none too successfully with the problem of evil and the reasons why God either inflicted it himself or allowed the Devil to do so in his stead.

The other, parallel system was that of natural philosophy, largely borrowed from Greek antiquity and imperfectly merged with the Christian tradition. This was the world of the elements and the humours, fictitious categories which supposedly governed everything from meteorology to medicine. Balance and harmony were the keys to peace in the skies, the state and the body alike. A whole arsenal of powerful imagery, still present in modern language and magnificently expressed by such authors as Shakespeare and Racine, was deployed to support these commonplaces. These literary glories cannot disguise the fact that the theory was little more than sonorous nonsense, which a few bold spirits were beginning to undermine, and would finally start replacing, in the later seventeenth century. Such pseudo-sciences as astrology, natural magic and alchemy were part of this world-view, claiming to offer ways to understand and control the environment. The learned medicine of humanist physicians was firmly rooted in this seedbed of error. Its practitioners had no real understanding of reproduction, the digestive system, the function of the blood or the lungs, the nervous system or indeed anything much else. Most of their prescriptions were useless, disgusting or potentially lethal. To preserve the illusion that they were doing something useful they commonly subjected patients to a regime of emetics, purges and bleeding, the only forms of intervention readily available. It would have taken some ingenuity to devise better methods of undermining strong constitutions and finishing off weak ones; slavish obedience to orthodox medical theory was the quick way to the grave. Perfectly healthy members of the upper classes often 'took physic' (courses of purges or emetics) in the belief that it would protect them from future illness, a sad example of the triumph of doctrine over common sense. There is a certain irony in a situation where only the relatively rich could afford the fees charged by these pretentious frauds and hence were their chief victims.

In practice both these grand systems were alarmingly flexible and lacking in true logical coherence. Their purchase on objective reality was so weak that they were readily manipulated to deal with apparent inconsistencies. It was perfectly easy for them to incorporate beliefs about witchcraft, by opening spaces in which diabolical power could operate. Nevertheless they do seem overall to have acted as a brake on any generalized attempts to link witchcraft and misfortune too closely. The intellectual leaders among clerics and doctors may have been ensnared in defective systems of thought, but they were quite capable of sharp perception on specific questions. For various reasons (considered later), they were never won over to support for the stronger versions of witchcraft theory, some isolated individuals apart. More importantly in the present context, these world views were far from being unknown at the popular level. It was the business of the clergy to disseminate Christian teachings, while almanacs and local medical practitioners were among the agencies which put about a rather fragmented version of natural philosophy. For all their weaknesses, these schemes had a very powerful effect on the way people at all levels of society apprehended their world. Explanations in terms of divine purpose and natural forces were normal; they did not exclude witchcraft, but both had a tendency to push it to the margins.

Even today health care is far from being the exclusive preserve of doctors and in earlier centuries the very conception of a medical profession was in considerable doubt. Physicians did try to assert monopoly rights through closed corporations and licensing, without any perceptible effect on what actually went on. They were really only one among the many sources of medical expertise, which constantly tended to merge into one another. Surgeons and apothecaries, trained by practical apprenticeship rather than learning from books, were obvious rivals to physicians at the more professional end, as were astrologers. Clerics routinely offered medical advice, particularly in rural areas, alongside the wives of local gentry and other notables. Midwives and older local women had a vital role in attending childbirth, that most alarming of routine events. Large numbers of cunning folk – local healers who combined practical and magical techniques – provided more or less specialized services; there is no clear way of distinguishing them from those neighbours who might be consulted in an emergency. Ultimately every household was expected to provide much of its own care, a task which usually devolved on the housewife, so that popular medicine had a strongly feminine tinge. Nursing sick husbands or children was regarded as natural work for women, who pooled their experiences or discovered personal abilities as healers that might enable them to establish a local reputation. Local medicine was cheap, quite often provided free or as part of that general exchange of services so common at all levels of society. It was also very empirical, relying on a mixture of herbal lore, pilgrimages, magical formulae and so forth. In everyday practice the physicians were often just as empirical, abandoning their grand theories with suspicious ease. In the seventeenth century an enlightened few came to see the merits of letting nature take its course and confined themselves more often to sensible efforts to make their patients comfortable. The most useful and widespread of the official practitioners were probably the surgeons, who had considerable practical skills in dealing with fractures, wounds, abscesses and a range of other more or less 'external' complaints. In much of rural Europe, where physicians were rare, they provided the nearest thing to a general medical service.

This network of healers and carers naturally came into play whenever illness appeared. Who was consulted depended on wealth and status, alongside family opinions on the nature of the sickness; in sudden mortal illnesses there is often no record of any consultation, perhaps because the outcome was seen as inevitable. Prolonged illness, on the other hand, might lead to a whole range of potential healers being summoned, either simultaneously or in sequence. The diagnoses they offered were bound to be influenced by the input from the patient and his or her relatives, and this was one way the idea of bewitchment might make an entry. Although the evidence is too scrappy to allow any certainty, it seems probable that witchcraft was more commonly identified because of the patient's convictions than because the symptoms were thought strange and 'unnatural'. Even physicians who firmly believed in witchcraft were insistent that they could offer natural explanations for many apparently bizarre complaints. In those cases where people were convinced witchcraft was operating, they often ensured it was diagnosed by consulting an expert whose skill lay in identifying witches, one of those 'witch-doctors' whose role will be explored more fully in a later chapter. There are numerous instances, however, of physicians, surgeons and others making such claims without obvious prompting. In 1683 a Yorkshire dissenting minister, Oliver Heywood, was confronted by a worrying case:

> He lies in his bed, hath swelling in his throat, hand cannot stir, looks as one affrighted . . . One Dr Thornton . . . saith it is not a natural distemper that he is troubled with, but he hath had some hurt by an evil tongue. He saith he will not prescribe any medicine for him untill his water have been tried by fire, i.e. they must take his water, and make a cake or loaf of it, with wheat meal, and put some of his hair into it, and horse-shoe stumps, and then put it in the fire . . .

When Heywood paid a visit himself he 'perceived their imagination that, upon their using these means, the witch that had hurt him would come and discover all'; since he 'utterly disliked it' he persuaded the family to resort to fasting and prayer instead.[11] While a proportion of these diagnoses must have been made in response to suggestions not evident in the record, this was clearly not true of all.

It was a commonplace among critics of persecution to ridicule the way medical failure was explained away by alleging witchcraft. There is no need to suppose this was merely cynical, for baffled doctors might have perfectly reasonable grounds for deciding on a supernatural explanation. At other times, university trained physicians could behave like any local wizard, identifying witchcraft on the basis of a sample of urine without even seeing the patient. The 1597 case of Alice Gooderidge, from Stapenhill near Burton-upon-Trent, shows how a diagnosis could evolve progressively. An aunt to a sick boy, Thomas Darling, took his urine to a physician, who suggested worms, then suspected witchcraft when the illness worsened. The aunt rejected the idea, but the possibility was then discussed in the boy's presence, after which he came up with the story of his meeting with Alice Gooderidge and her anger against him. He had farted in front of her, after which she angrily said 'Gyp with a mischiefe, and fart with a bell: I will go to heaven, and thou shalt go to hell', then stooped ominously to the ground. At a later stage in this case a cunning man was called in who subjected the wretched old woman to a form of torture, putting her close to the fire with new shoes on her feet. This totally irregular (and indeed illegal) procedure was apparently carried out before an assembly of 'many worshipful person-ages'. Although she did not make a proper confession on this occasion, Alice finally agreed that she had been angry because the boy called her witch, then caused the Devil, in the form of a small dog, to afflict him; according to the pamphlet record she was convicted, only to die in prison.[12] Yet in the areas on which we have detailed information such episodes are relatively rare; it seems likely that a diagnosis of bewitchment was only made in a tiny fraction of all cases. This is particularly striking when one considers how much medical expertise was relatively amateur-ish and local. If practitioners had resorted to this technique to explain every failure, or those cases they did not understand, then accusations would have proliferated dramatically, far above the levels of which we know. In the absence of direct evidence one cannot know for sure why they were so restrained. They may have been so committed to their own approaches and methods that they preferred to seek explanations within the system rather than outside it; often they blamed the patient for not following the prescribed treatment.

Nothing in most of the illnesses seems to mark them off, apart from the reiterated claim that they were strange and unfamiliar, at best a highly subjective judgement. Sudden fatality and lingering decline might both be attributed to witchcraft, as might anything from eye trouble to a bad foot. People who felt sudden weights on their chest at night, so that they could not breathe, reported seeing other persons in the room, who might attack them physically. Jacotte Simon told a complicated story about how she had remained in bed after her husband rose before dawn to work, then she felt something press down on her. Although she could not move, she managed to make the sign of the cross with her tongue, calling out to her husband for help. Finally managing to raise her head a little she saw Penthecoste Miette at the foot of her bed, but there was no reply when she spoke to her. Her husband then rushed in, at which two cats, both 'marvellously big and ugly' left with a great noise. She suspected that Mengeatte Lienard had been the other cat.[13] On other occasions the cats spoke and might even hold a debate. Mesenne Vannier was ill in bed when three cats appeared and discussed whether to kill her, but decided that she was to be spared on account of her youth and recent marriage; their voices identified them as Jennon Zabey, the widow Rudepoil and Claudon Marchal's wife.[14] This sounds like a typical hallucination brought on by a high fever. Other incidents where the sufferer felt paralysed in bed probably resulted from the quite common phenomenon of regaining partial consciousness while in a deep sleep. In addition, the various panic attacks may well have had a strong psychosomatic component, making them particularly suited for witchcraft explanations.

In other instances the affliction is quite often readily identified in terms of modern medical science; strokes, tuberculosis, tetanus, cataracts and so forth. One obvious case is that of the pedlar John Law, who refused Alison Device some pins because she had no money then suddenly 'fell down lame in great extremitie', with all his left side paralysed, and unable to speak properly.[15] It would be hard to find a clearer description of a stroke than in this incident, which sparked off the whole series of trials at Lancaster in 1612. The accused had no access to such sharply defined medical categories, yet they often sought to defend themselves before the judges by challenging the idea that there was anything exceptional about the complaint. Sometimes they said it was a long-standing problem that predated the quarrel supposed to have been the motive for inflicting it. Accused of bewitching Jean Fleurat's wife, Demenge Milan objected that she had been ill for a year before the incident described.[16] They might also say that the afflicted person had behaved foolishly, in ways likely to encourage sickness or injury. On other occasions they would identify it as a common disease or point out that they had suffered in the same way themselves. Mengette Cachette said that if Jean Vannier's horses died, this was because he worked them too hard, while the wife and son of Dieudonné Demenge Alix had died from an illness which was going round the village.[17] Perfectly rational objections of this kind never seem to have had much effect, which rather emphasizes that the interest was in the circumstances rather than the illness. Once malevolence had been established, almost anything could be attributed to it; the link was essentially a causal one.

Usually it was also chronological, with much stress on the rapidity with which misfortune had followed a quarrel – sometimes the idea that it had begun exactly a week or a month later – or a combination of disasters. Jean Colas Lienard had talked in company about the rumour that Mengeatte Babé was pregnant by one of the soldiers lodged in the village; she heard of this and made threats against his animals. The next day two pigs were killed by a wolf, his best cow broke its leg 'in a strange fashion', and his finest horse went blind. Drawing the natural conclusion, he spoke angrily to her husband, after which she apologized for her threats while denying responsibility for his losses.[18] Although other witnesses felt no scruple about alleging bewitchment where there was no such tidy connection, the pattern was obviously a very well established one in many people's minds. There were times when the suspect had made open threats; although these usually amounted to no more than a statement that the other party would repent, they could be more specific. Gérard de Briatte removed some manure belonging to Aldegonde de Rue which was obstructing his entry, then refused requests for payment, at which her daughter said he had no right to take poor people's property in this way and he would have to pay for the manure; within days he had lost two horses.[19] When Mengin Badel reclaimed a field from Claudin Clerget, the latter threatened that 'the first time he went to it he would return having lost his health'. Mengin met Claudin when on his way to the field and had to crawl home, finally dying after two years of bad health.[20]

Angry exchanges and suspicions of bewitchment were much commoner than criminal prosecutions. A very powerful motive for accusing someone was the hope that they might offer a cure. This was likeliest if the charge were made indirectly, often in the form of an invitation to visit the sick person. There must have been a complex code in operation here, full of implicit understandings which are all too likely to escape the modern eye. In the negotiations which followed the witch was really being invited to accept responsibility, then secure pardon and immunity by removing the evil. Cures might be effected by touching, by bringing or preparing food, by more formal medical treatment with herbs or charms, or by pilgrimages and rituals. In the Labourd, according to de Lancre, it was customary to ask the suspect to wash their hands in a basin, then give the water to the sufferer to drink, a ritual with multiple resonances.[21] The display of good-will involved cancelled out the negative charge of the original ill-will; in many cases it must have made the sufferer feel much better. A good many of the witnesses in court cases were talking about episodes of this kind, which would have been regarded as closed until legal action started. The notion that illness might be related to the breakdown of inter-personal relations, also contained within this pattern of behaviour, was far from absurd. If the sickness resulted from a broken relationship with the witch, then the natural inference was that a formal display of reconciliation was a necessary part of a cure. When William Luckisone of Stirling was ill around 1653 he consulted Magdalen Blair, herself a suspect, who asked him 'if there was any enmitie or discord between Issobel Bennet and him'. When he replied that he sometimes threw stones at her chickens to drive them off his father's property, she advised him to 'go to Issobel Bennet and take a grip of her coat tail and drink a pint of ale with her. And crave his health from her thrie tymes for the Lords sake and he would be well'. William claimed he had not followed the advice, which is understandable, for such a confrontation required a degree of nerve.[22] Demands for signs of amity or neighbourliness further constituted a warning to the suspected witch, particularly in relation to the victim's family, with whom it would be wise to avoid further disputes. It was not unknown for the witch to make formal promises to cause them no further trouble. Claudon Renauldin was returning home with Didelon and Bietrix l'Huillier, whom he believed to have caused him extensive losses; when he thought of this he went to beat Didelon, who reacted with the highly unwise statement 'that he would never harm him, nor cause him further losses or damage'.[23]

Parents, children and witchcraft

Whereas illness was unpredictable, the dangers of childbirth were the opposite. Women had every reason to be nervous about the risks to themselves and their babies, against which they sought to mobilize help and protection. The presence of neighbours and relatives offered moral as well as practical support at a moment of great danger and stress. Failure to summon a neighbour with a reputation as a witch to either the birth or the christening was to keep them at a safe distance, while running the risk of giving offence that might provoke hostile action. This scenario appeared frequently in the trials as the explanation of a bad outcome for mother, child or both. Jacquotte Tixerand refused to attend the baptism of George Guyart's son, since she had not been asked to the childbed, but when she visited the house a week later she admired the child, telling the mother to keep it well; when it sickened the same day, to die a week later, the inference was obvious.[24] Similar problems were attached to godparenting, for it was all too easy to give offence over this important sign of mutual friendship and respect. Jehennon Foelix had suggested that Claudatte Mengin might act as godmother to her first child then had to withdraw the offer because another promise had already been made elsewhere. The subsequent loss of a cow was blamed on her witchcraft, but when a second child was born Jehennon and her husband tried to make amends by asking George Mengin, Claudatte's husband, to be godfather. This too turned out badly because the suspect wanted her son to take the role instead and was annoyed when the midwife said he was too young; when the baby died a few months later, this was inevitably blamed on Claudatte.[25] High infant mortality rates were general across Europe, with many babies languishing then dying for no obvious reason. These deaths inevitably formed one cause for suspicion; difficulties with breastfeeding, another very common problem, were often blamed on witchcraft too. Older women, who provided the normal source of advice in such cases, could easily find themselves in ambiguous positions. When Zabel Remy lost her milk, her relative Dion Remy (who was about seventy-five at the time) came to her aid; she made Zabel drink some wine, then damped some coarse cloth, warmed it by the fire and applied it to her breasts. Another witness remembered, however, that she had not been invited to the celebrations after the birth, was suspected by the parents, then invited to dinner in an attempt to secure relief.[26]

Professional help in delivery was normally provided by midwives and it has been widely supposed that any misfortune might be blamed on their witchcraft, allegedly linked to their position as 'popular' healers in traditional folklore. Midwives have thus become a paradigmatic case of female medical specialists under attack from men who wanted to control them and destroy their autonomy. Whatever truth there may be in these wider claims, the putative association with witchcraft is illusory. No statistical evidence of any significance has been produced to support it; where figures have been established they show that midwives were rather under-represented among the accused.[27] The theme is present in demon-ological literature mainly because the *Malleus Maleficarum* went on about witch-midwives at some length and was copied by later writers. There seems to be a connection with the idea that witches ate the flesh of unbaptized children or used their remains to make poisons; midwives were supposed to be the main providers of the bodies of stillborn babies. There are odd cases where this idea surfaced, as with the one Lorraine witch who actually fits the stereotype, Jennon Petit; she admitted digging up the bodies of the infants she had killed on behalf of her master Persin, who then made powder with them.[28] In general, however, it is easy to understand why midwives were rarely accused; they were selected pre-cisely because they were regarded as trustworthy persons by the com-munity, so that it must have taken a catastrophic drop in their standing for them to become suspects. A rare instance of association between child-care and witchcraft tends to bear this out, for in the German city of Augsburg a number of lying-in servants found themselves on trial. These were women who specialized in helping out in households around the time of childbirth, but they lacked the skills or status of midwives and were much more vulnerable in consequence.[29]

Another myth about early modern Europe is that parents were rela-tively indifferent to the fate of children because they expected them to die young and would not invest too much emotional capital when the risks were so high. The economic metaphor is patently unsuitable and inaccurate; the evidence suggests on the contrary that children were the objects of affection and concern to the vast majority of parents. A high proportion of witchcraft accusations were about their illnesses, frequently the reason for considerable expenditure of effort and money. There were practical as well as sentimental reasons for this concern, since preservation of the family line and property depended on bringing some children to adulthood. Women's status with their husbands and their peers was closely related to their role as mothers; the good housewife bore children and brought them up properly. In many respects this was a child-centred society and the demographic patterns ensured that at any given time a high proportion of the total population was made up of children and adolescents. The figures for England suggest that in the later sixteenth century, around 35 per cent of the population was under fifteen, with perhaps 54 per cent under twenty-five. Although these ratios had moved significantly downwards (albeit temporarily) in England a century later, it is doubtful whether this was true for Europe more generally.[30] There are numerous cases in which women who were accused of bewitching children turn out to have been childless themselves, either because their marriages had been infertile or because their children had all died. One suspects that their contemporaries drew the natural inference that it was envy of their more fortunate neighbours which motivated their choice of victims, although such subtleties do not really survive in the depositions. Such ideas may nevertheless help to explain why admiring and petting a neighbour's child could be interpreted as evidence of ill-will or an ostentatious display of hypocrisy. Catherine la Rondelatte was evidently deeply upset by the loss of all her own offspring, for one witness recorded her as saying 'I may well curse God', a blasphemy she then compounded by adding 'that he had done nothing for her when he took her children'. Later she explained her failure to cry – commonly taken as a sign of guilt – by the fact that 'she had cried so much for the deaths and loss of her husband and children that now her heart was so hardened she was finally incapable of crying'. Several of the charges against her involved the bewitchment of children, two of them after admiring babies in the cradle.[31]

Women who had difficulties bearing children, with frequent miscarriages or stillbirths, were liable to blame these on witchcraft, perhaps displacing their worries about their own failure to meet expectations. Mengeon Colin and his wife Agathe had objected strongly when the local mayor's wife proposed Fleuratte Chappouxat for election as midwife at le Vivier, drawing attention to the great misfortunes which might arise from having a witch in that position. She was naturally angry when they succeeded in getting someone else chosen, so now Agathe blamed her for three successive stillbirths.[32] Motherhood is, of course, a long-term affair and as children grew their own behaviour often appeared as the original point of tension. They might taunt supposed witches directly or perhaps insult them through their own children. Mothers were always defending their children against others who attacked them; this could be thought the reason for a witch's resentment, or if threats or violence to a child were followed by sickness, the moment at which the bewitchment had actually occurred. Didier Goeury's mother went to tell Jean Pelisson off after he had beaten her son for no reason, saying she could beat her own children if it were necessary and meanwhile he should attend to his own, who badly needed discipline. Soon after she fell fatally ill, while the surgeons and doctors declared her bewitched.[33] When the sons of Claude Henry and Barbelline Antoine fought, the former was hurt, which led to a quarrel between the parents and relatives; the following Sunday the boy's grandmother, Marion Henry, was met with silence when she greeted Barbelline in church, then promptly fell ill and died. She would have sent for the suspect if one of her sons had not prevented this.[34] When Marye Sotterel asked the eight-year-old son of Meline Hanry where he was going, he replied 'That's enough for you, great witch', after which she chased him and beat him; he fell ill next day and died a month later.[35]

Mental illness and marital problems

Children and adolescents were also prime victims for one form of illness which does seem to have been quite frequently attributed to witchcraft because of its nature. Dementia and other kinds of mental disturbance were readily interpreted in terms of demonic possession or obsession; it was often all too easy to incorporate the afflicted in psychodramas leading to direct accusations. In the long run the obvious danger of manipulation was to have some importance in discrediting the concept of bewitchment more generally. It was actually possible to falsify some charges arising from the alleged presence of the Devil in the body of the sufferer by detecting trickery or getting accusers to admit they had lied. Such cases could become very complex, giving rise to bitter disputes between clerical and medical experts of different schools. The use of exorcism as a therapy was largely rejected by mainline Protestants and raised increasing doubts at the upper levels of the Catholic hierarchy. In England the activities of Jesuit and Puritan exorcists in the 1590s led the official spokesmen for the Anglican church into taking openly sceptical positions to defend their ban on exorcism. Elsewhere in Europe the Catholic church usually continued to offer exorcism at the local level; it functioned not only as a therapy but as a mechanism for identifying suspects. There were occasions when groups of 'possessed' persons were used in a kind of litmus-paper test, with suspects coming before them voluntarily in the hope of clearing their names. Something of the kind was plainly going on at the chapel of St Anne near Goudency in the Franche-Comté when Jeanne Magnien went there in 1608, allegedly on a pilgrimage to seek a cure for her bad eyes. She was touched by a blind girl who was supposedly possessed by a demon called Joly and felt obliged to make a second visit (despite the opposition of her own *curé*) to get herself cleared of the resulting imputation of witchcraft.[36]

Such procedures, which caused great disquiet to many scrupulous clerics, were gradually brought under control during the seventeenth century. The popular view verged on treating possession as a simple result of bewitchment; the more extreme the symptoms, the greater the need to eliminate the witch responsible. Theologians, on the other hand, were inclined to define possession as a divine punishment for sinful individuals, whose status as mouthpieces of the Devil made them totally untrustworthy, so that their charges against others had no value whatsoever. If this was true, the diagnosis of possession came very close to a statement that the afflicted person was very wicked, and a rejection of their own view that someone else was responsible. Any cure was dependent on repentance and amendment of life as much as on exorcism, even where Protestant objections did not exclude the latter. The waters were muddied, however, by an alternative state of obsession that allowed the Devil power over the body alone; while this too was a punishment for sin, it was thought that a witch might be the effective agent who sent or invited the Devil in.[37] Until much later, most Catholic writers seem to have believed that possession could also be inflicted by a witch, increasing the chance that this notion could be exploited by those with an interest in linking disturbed behaviour to witchcraft. This did not mean, of course, that mental illness or disturbed behaviour was automatically explained in this fashion. For a start, the Devil was seen as perfectly well able to act on his own; many personified their own anti-social or unclean urges in this way, as direct temptations by the fiend. The Buckinghamshire cleric and physician Richard Napier saw hundreds of patients who believed themselves to have been bewitched, but they only represented a minority of his large case-load. Although Napier specialized to some extent in mental illness, his disturbed patients were not noticeably keener than the others to blame witches for their plight. The fact that Napier conjured spirits and used astrology in his diagnoses did not lead to quite the results that might have been expected. He only confirmed a handful of the suggestions that witchcraft was responsible, often in cases when the witch concerned had admitted guilt.[38] Other, less scrupulous, healers must have been readier to take the client's word, yet such patterns are not very prominent in known trials. Mental illness had plenty of alternative explanations, ranging from disappointed love through melancholia to fever, so that there was no need to resort to supernatural factors.

The supernatural might also be invoked to cover a rather different set of experiences. Strange happenings, sudden noises at night, whirlwinds and lightning strikes; these and similar events could easily be attributed to diabolic intervention. It seems most unlikely that such charges were ever more than decorative additions in an actual trial, rather than the occasion for starting proceedings, but they might contribute to the long process of building up a reputation. Similar comments seem appropriate to another common element in the trials, that of relationships with other people. These too appear as supporting evidence. Marital troubles could be blamed on bewitchment, with discord portrayed as an otherwise inexplicable affliction. This might be little more than an attempt to shift blame away from one's own folly or misbehaviour. Bastienne Simonatte suspected Chrestienne Barret over an estrangement from her husband Colas which had lasted three years; the accused retorted that she knew they hated one another, but this was already true before their marriage.[39] Hanry Jean Hanry failed to ask Jennon Bresson to his marriage feast, then she went and moved the beds around; he was very angry, but too frightened on account of her reputation to stop her. No sooner had he and his wife consummated their marriage than they fell into a state of divorce and hatred, which lasted several years, both thinking she had put something in the bed.[40] When Catherine Mathieu was on trial, she claimed that her first husband had run off after three months with a maid he had made pregnant and that this had been the result of a spell cast by Mansuy des Folz, which would have lasted seven years had he lived.[41] It was even possible for a husband who admitted ill-treating his wife to use witchcraft as an excuse; Dieudonné George le petit Colin explained a period of six weeks when he was constantly beating his wife as the work of Claudatte Henri, who had then secretly offered a soup which cured him.[42] It could also be given as a reason for adultery, as it was by the mayor of St Maurice, Jean de Fribourg. Pierrotte Roy had been his mistress for several years, while he neglected his wife and even threatened her with a knife; then, when he apparently wanted to return to his wife, he told her he thought he had been bewitched.[43]

Wives were supposed to be in a very favourable position to harm their husbands if they wished since they could readily add something to their food or drink. Several witnesses deposed that Demenge Pourlat suspected his wife Didie had made him ill by putting something in a dish of veal; when he went to another woman asking for some soup he explained that he did not trust his wife to make it, because 'she was a devil of a woman, who would bring him damnation rather than salvation'. The suspicions became stronger when she forbade him to take a purge as prescribed by the surgeon, saying there was no cure and he had already tried many. Demenge was safely dead, so it was easy for others to ascribe these ideas to him, but from further evidence it seems that this late remarriage for both parties had led to bitter quarrels about his drinking. In this case Didie admitted nothing about harming her husband even when confessing other acts of witchcraft, so one may question whether she ever had such thoughts.[44] On the other hand, while no early modern account of alleged poisoning can be trusted (since doctors were quite incompetent to test for it), we can hardly doubt that some wives did attempt such things, not necessarily with homicidal intent. They might obtain a potion from some local wizard which was supposed to restore a husband's love stolen by a mistress, or prevent excessive drinking in the tavern and the squandering of family resources. Jennon Villemin dite la Gargantine (one such practitioner) prescribed a drink made from wine, herbs, pepper and ginger that Barbon Saulnier was to give to her husband in the morning to stop his debauches.[45]

A particularly rich folklore surrounded the embarrassing subject of impotence, for which there were numerous alleged cures. The idea that a knot tied in a lace during the marriage ceremony would render the groom impotent was an obvious piece of sympathetic magic, found quite widely in Europe, although impotence might be attributed to witchcraft without this specific form being invoked. Equally, there was no compelling reason to think that tying the ligature made one a witch; given the jealousies and hatreds, among relatives and disappointed suitors, which formed the subtext of many marriages it is hard to believe that people did not try this rather nasty form of revenge. Since psychological elements must have been predominant in many cases, the various rituals and cures were probably quite effective. Most of them involved the obvious symbolism of pissing through a hole – the bride's wedding ring or the keyhole in the door of the church were favoured for this purpose. The doctors themselves often cited this as an instance of the powers of the imagination and might use some kind of pretence to persuade the sufferer that the spell had been lifted.[46] An earthier method still was suggested by de Lancre, never one to resist a spicy story; he reported a female specialist who sounds like a pioneering sex therapist. Her cures involved practical lessons by herself or her daughter during an overnight session with the husband in the nuptial bed.[47] Not only did her local community treat her with respect as an effective healer, but her services were often demanded by upper-class families, although according to de Lancre (who did not name her) she had admitted to him that all such cures contained a diabolical element. Apprentices and servants also fit into the family scenario; quarrels over who should serve whom might end up with allegations that the young person in question had been bewitched, if they happened to sicken.

Animals and bewitchment

If there was one area in which people thought of bewitchment more readily than in connection with their own illnesses, it was over the misfortunes of their animals. Domestic animals are extremely vulnerable to infectious diseases and small accidents; even with modern techniques their ailments can be difficult to diagnose and treat. Furthermore, a substantial amount of the capital of early modern society, especially in the rural world, was tied up in these fragile creatures. If the medical profession was rudimentary, the veterinary one hardly existed at an official level. Every peasant needed some practical skills in treating animals; in difficult cases they turned to neighbours reputed skilful in healing, including herdsmen, shepherds and smiths. The usual range of practical and pious remedies was on offer; quite large numbers of magical prayers survive. This was probably because suspected witches saw them as perfectly normal and accepted forms of treatment, so were ready to repeat them before the judges. There was more than a hint of dishonesty in the way these might suddenly call such prayers superstitious and blasphemous, as part of their general attack on the defendant. In other respects the bewitchment of animals followed the same pattern as that of humans. It usually followed quarrels and threats, was closely linked to these by its timing and frequently led to demands for the witch to effect a cure. On occasion there was a tighter logical link, when refusal to buy or sell animals was the alleged motive for harming them, but this looks like a convenient elaboration rather than a major theme. The sick animal often recovered after a simple visit from the suspect; on other occasions the latter might make more specific attempts to heal it, sometimes of a very practical kind. Jean Colas Claude Martin was called in to see Demenge Doienney's sick ox and cut away the hoof to release the pus, while someone else applied verdigris to complete the cure. It is not easy to see why this was regarded as evidence of witchcraft, although there was a claim that the animal had been lame for five months after a quarrel between the men.[48] Jean Claudon Thierion, finding his foal had stopped eating, drove it out into the village, saying the witch who was responsible should kill it outright. When it stopped outside Marguitte Laurent's house she asked his wife what was wrong, then put some flour down its throat, after which it promptly recovered.[49] Another common reaction, however, was to declare incompetence to help sick animals and refuse to come at all. Sometimes, as with human sufferers, some kind of deceit was employed to get the suspect into proximity with the supposed victim.

The possible impact of such losses, and the increasingly frantic reactions of those who incurred them, are wonderfully caught in an anonymous and undated document addressed to the Norfolk justices, which C. L. Ewen discovered among the Egerton MSS in the British Museum. The breathless recital has a rather comic effect which must have been very far from the mind of the writer:

[May it] please your Worships to understand what trouble sickness and losses your petitioner [hath] suffered and in what manner they happened and by plain tokens and likelihood by the means of this woman and others but chiefly by her as is gathered by all conjectures.

First of all a boar which I have was in such case that he could not cry or grunt as beforetime, neither could he go but creep until we used some means to recover him but all was to no purpose, until such time as we sent for Nicolas Wesgate, who when he saw him said he was mad or bewitched, and my wife using means to give him some milk he bit her by the hand, and I fearing he was mad sent after my wife towards Norwich, that she might get something of the Apothecaries to prevent the danger we feared, and that horse which my man did ride upon after my wife, was taken lame as he returned back again, and suddenly after was swollen like a bladder which is blown, and died within eight days.

Next a calf was taken lame, the leg turning upward, which was a strange sight to them who did behold the same, suddenly after that I had five calves more which would not have sold for 13s 4d, the calf being sound and well in the evening and the next day in the morning they were in such case as we could not endure to come nigh them by reason of a filthy noisome savour, their hair standing upright upon their backs and they shaking in such sort as I never saw, nor any other I suppose living; again within a short space I had another calf which was taken so strangely as if the back were broken, and much swollen and within the space of three or four days it died and within two or three days after another calf was taken in such sort that it turned round about and did go as if the back were broken, then was I wished to burn it, and I carried the calf to burn it, and after it was burned I was taken with pains and gripings and so continued in such sort, until she came to my house, whereupon I did earnestly chide her, and said I would beat her, and that day, I praise God, I was restored to my former health.[50]

Even this account makes it plain that in itself the loss of an animal was a routine experience, involving little of the trauma associated with the sicknesses of parents, spouses and children. A single cow, however, could be vital to the well-being of a poor family, while rich peasants were at risk if animals died in large numbers or over a long period. Repeated inability to keep them successfully might readily be attributed to a malevolent neighbour. Claudon Renauldin and his wife had numerous quarrels with Didelon and Bietrix l'Huillier, who blamed them for taking over a house they had previously occupied; their cows and horses repeatedly died as if they were rabid.[51] It was also possible for a whole village to blame local witches for what were obviously outbreaks of contagious disease. There were at least four cases of this type in the Cambrésis region between about 1609 and 1627, which saw groups of inhabitants, led by the local elite, send in formal requests for action. They also promised that the community would meet its share of the legal costs; one of these petitions carried the names of no less than forty-three householders.[52] With animals more even than with humans, one is conscious of how flexible the diagnosis of illness might be. Strangeness and suddenness were taken as signs of witchcraft – the cow which ate normally but wasted away, the horse which dropped dead in the stable. Slaughtermen and others who cut up dead animals would sometimes claim that they were rotten inside, something which must proceed from witchcraft. Mayette Gaste was suspected of causing the death of a horse whose flesh was found to be blackened as if burned, so that the butcher said it had been given a drink by some evil persons.[53] Commonest of all was the allegation, as in the case just cited, that an animal had died 'as if rabid', a curious example of having it both ways, with the natural explanation being simultaneously advanced and rejected. Perhaps the symptoms of animals which lashed out at their masters and foamed at the mouth were thought similar to those of demonic possession. The various infections which resulted in the feet and legs rotting away were also cited as proof of bewitchment, although they seem all too plainly natural to a modern reader. The accused were obviously bewildered by some of the charges, protesting that the sickness had been natural, that animals were always dying and that they had lost as many themselves. On other occasions they alleged ill-treatment or various faults in handling the animals. Claudatte Ferry argued that the goats and cows she was accused of bewitching had suffered from a sickness which had affected many animals that winter, while some of them might also have been weak because their owner was feeding them on a poor substitute for hay.[54] When Demenge Didier Ydatte threatened to kill Jean Cachette if he did not cure his sick cow, he replied 'when people had sick animals they were accustomed to blame witches, but most of the time the cause was bad handling'.[55] As with human illnesses, these arguments were never answered; if the witches confessed they usually ended up admitting just about every charge against them.

Milking cows were very susceptible to infections (such as brucellosis) and other disorders, which often coincided with minor disputes over requests for purchases or gifts of milk. A routine pattern saw these episodes interpreted as witchcraft. Demenge Saulnier claimed that Margueritte Liegey had asked his wife to sell her some wood and after several refusals went to the door of the stable, turned round and came back. This was repeated three times, then she asked to buy milk, responding to a further refusal with a threat that she would repent. Their only cow then sickened, only recovering within hours of a threat to beat her.[56] A more elaborate belief occasionally surfaced that witches had the capacity to take milk away from their neighbours, using a kind of snare or other device. The child Mongeotte Pivert, whose confessions led to the deaths of several members of her family, alleged that her father set snares for neighbours' cattle to pass over, then took the threads home and warmed them by the fire before rubbing the backs of his own cattle to obtain more milk.[57] This was one of the fairly rare occasions when modest prosperity rather than poverty was supposed to mark off the witch and appears to be commoner in modern witchcraft beliefs. Virtually all these beliefs seem to have been applied only to a minority of cases, so that yet again the identification of witchcraft must have depended as much on awareness of a suspect as it did on the nature of the misfortune.

This applied in the case of one specific nexus of beliefs, that in were-wolves. The notion that witches could be transformed into the likeness of other animals, such as cats and hares, was particularly threatening when extended to these dangerous and much feared predators. The number of known cases across Europe is very small, despite the fairly widespread belief, so it is very hard to understand why it occasionally surfaced in a prosecution. Attacks by wolves might be interpreted in this way on the grounds that a particular animal had been singled out, a notably unconvincing attempt to give the normal behaviour of predators diabolical purposiveness. More plausible stories picked up on claims that the wolves had an abnormal appearance; according to Boguet, when Perrenette Gandillon turned herself into a wolf and killed a child, the creature had no tail and human hands in place of its front paws.[58] In 1573 rumours were circulating that the villages near Dôle were 'infested with wolves the size of donkeys' that ate people and were impossible to capture; these were naturally supposed to be werewolves.[59] Alternatively they behaved unnaturally, like the wolf which strangled the foal of Claudon Jean Claudon, refusing to loosen its grip when burning sticks were put against its throat. Earlier the same day his son Curien (who was guarding the herd) had quarrelled with one of Claudon Marchal's sons, and this was not the only suspicion of the kind against him.[60] The extreme and sensational cases were those of wolves which devoured children, bringing together the werewolf theme with the cannibalism sometimes found at the sabbat. When the children of Grattain were running after the wolf which had taken Claudon Didier Vagnier's child, Claudette Dabo was seen in the vicinity and a strong rumour spread that she had eaten it.[61] The whole business of shapeshifting is a curious mixture of ancient folklore and practical everyday fears, which lurks around the fringes of witchcraft belief without ever becoming an integral part of it. Figures for later periods suggest that quite large numbers of children were attacked by wolves; apparently only a tiny minority of these events were openly attributed to werewolves.

Cows, pigs, goats and sheep were all potential targets for witches; these were the animals which were kept for meat, milk, hides and wool and can be assimilated to crops in general. They were also routinely kept in herds or flocks, overseen by individuals appointed and paid by the community. These positions were normally taken by poor peasants, who had to collect payments in money and kind from individual owners. This situation provided fertile ground for the kind of petty quarrels which could easily slide into accusations of witchcraft. There was friction over payment, whether the animals were taken out on time, when they went missing and so forth. Nicolas Chollat left the herd of Repas in the care of his wife at harvest-time, and she did not have them in the fields until four in the afternoon. When Nicolas Loys went to protest she retorted that 'he should not be so troublesome or he might repent', and next day a cow died.[62] Would-be herdsmen competed with one another, underbidding for the position, and this caused a fair number of feuds. Mengin Mathiotte lost the position of cattle herdsman at Mazerulles because he lost his temper after bidding successfully and refused to pay his share for the traditional drink to confirm the deal – he thought better of it overnight, but found it was too late. Both the richer peasants who ran the election and his replacement predictably suspected him of causing subsequent losses, while he had also managed an impressive number of petty disputes during his previous tenure.[63] It was easier for these squabbles to develop into witchcraft accusations because herdsmen were expected to have some primitive veterinary ability that placed them in the dangerous boundary zone of magical healers. Animals were also the source of quarrels because they were always straying, eating other people's grass or damaging their young corn. This frequently happened when they were under the care of children, whose own illnesses might also be explained in this way.

Horses and oxen were in a rather different category from the other animals, although there was a certain overlap. They provided the motive power for many agricultural activities, in which role they also marked out their possessors as a village elite. The substantial peasant whose draught animals started to die was threatened in his status as much as his pocket, and reactions may have been sharper in consequence. The elderly labourer Demenge Villemin and his wife testified that when they started losing many animals they had consulted a *devin*, who warned them that Mongeatte de Leuce and two others wanted to ruin him 'and that after all his means were lost, they would bring him so low that he would be on his back, which had happened through various misfortunes he had suffered, when his wealth was at risk, although he took all possible care'.[64] All animals posed problems when they sickened, for they became an unproductive drain on resources, calling for a decision whether it was better to sell them at a loss or keep them in the hope they might recover. Animals might suffer accidents in the herd, being gored or breaking legs in clashes with others. They could also become dangerous to their owners, as when illness made them frantic and uncontrollable. Falls from horses were a related misfortune; witnesses would insist that the road had been smooth or that the animal had thrown them repeatedly. The notary Nicolas de Lusse struck Didiere Failly after a quarrel, then set off towards

Domjevin. He fell off his horse twice, then it refused to obey at the river, so they were both covered in mud and he had to lead it to the stable. Things were even worse on the return trip, since the animal went wild when he approached it, then died, leaving him to walk to the next village.[65] Eight years later this story was evidence in the trial that led to her conviction and execution.

Accidents and poverty

At this point accidents to animals shade into a final large area of bewitchment, that of damage from a range of physical causes. People did not just fall off their horses; they also fell from carts, sometimes with fatal consequences. Falls from trees were another possible cause of death, while those who survived would insist that they had been standing on large strong branches which broke inexplicably. Collatte Lorette made matters still worse for herself. Marguerite Thibault told how Collatte had quarrelled with her uncle, who then fell to his death from a tree; in the frequent quarrels between the two women Collatte was in the habit of saying 'some had already had their necks broken, and there would be others yet'.[66] Work accidents – including injuries inflicted by sharp tools, falling objects and the like – made occasional appearances in the depositions. A variety of other accidents might be presented as life-threatening, as when millwheels disintegrated suddenly after a quarrel with the suspect. This happened to Colas Chretien at Moyenmoutier just as his wife was telling him of a quarrel with Mongeatte Johel and warning him to be careful how he tried to clear the frozen millwheel, which had only just been repaired.[67] Newly built structures were known to collapse after visits by local witches.

Livelihoods could be put at risk in similar ways. The frequent disputes over milk might be followed by an inability to make butter churn; there were various folkloric remedies, including putting a heated horseshoe or other metal object in the cream, a move some thought would cause severe pain to the witch responsible. Ovens or forges would mysteriously refuse to reach the correct temperature, however much fuel was added. François Pelletier had a dispute over the price of some work he did for Hellenix le Reytre, then found the hides he had in store had rotted, causing him serious losses. He wisely reduced his price, then she advised him to use his own cellar for storage in future, which proved successful.[68] No doubt these charges were often a cover-up for carelessness or ineptitude on the part of the victim. Envious neighbours might, in rare cases, attribute exceptional success in the production of some commodity to witchcraft. Synnelle Adam was called 'the butter-maker' at Insming, because she was said to be able to get more from one cow than others could from four. Two different stories were attributed to her in explanation; one involved collecting dew before dawn on May mornings, the other a magical thong for horses. She denied these, defending herself successfully by explaining that she was very careful with dairy products and mixed her butter in a specially prepared barrel, although she did admit to using magical prayers to heal animals and people.[69] The courts evidently found it hard to demonize such claims when they cut across the idea that the Devil's promises were always worthless, which may explain why they appear more frequently in recent non-diabolical witchcraft beliefs in both Africa and Europe.

Serious damage to crops was most readily linked to witchcraft through the stories of hail, rain or frost being made at the sabbat. Individual witches were much less likely to be blamed here, although very selective damage or marked immunity might start tongues wagging. Jeanne Lienard was playing with fire when she told several people at Laveline that they ought to be generous with their alms to her, since she had preserved their crops from hail three years earlier when she had let the neighbouring parishes be laid waste because their inhabitants were so ungenerous to her. It was hardly surprising that one of the witnesses said that everyone feared her, and for himself 'he would as soon see a wolf as her when she came to his house begging'. Under interrogation she freely admitted these remarks, giving the obvious explanation that she wanted to persuade the villagers to be generous, while admitting that she knew no way to protect them in fact. This was an odd case in many respects; the accused told a series of fanciful stories, sounding very confused or even deranged, confessed under torture, then withdrew the confession, resisted a second round of torture and was finally released.[70] Vines and fruit trees might suffer as well as grain crops, while gardens could prove strangely infertile. A run of bad luck was as threatening in these sectors of agricultural life as it was with animals. Behind local fluctuations there lurked the spectre of general economic failure, bringing personal ruin with it. For maritime communities, such as were found in Scotland, England, parts of Scandinavia or the Basque country, weather magic extended to the sinking of ships. Witchcraft was still readily suspected by seventeenth-century sailors, although the Navy Commissioners may have been surprised when an officer explained the adverse winds preventing his ship leaving Pevensey Bay in 1656 by the operations of an old woman who was prophesying it would be there for three months.[71] A still more spectacular misfortune was suffered by William Tompson of Dartmouth, who struck Alice Trevisard of Hardness when she laughed on seeing him fall. She then told him 'Thou shalt be better thou hadst never met with me!' and within a few weeks his ship caught fire and foundered, leaving him a prisoner in Spain for a year.[72] Fishing villages which lost significant numbers of menfolk were extremely vulnerable, for this was one activity in which women could not replace them. Violent suspicions of this kind might lead to direct action, as with an incident in 1573 involving some sailors from Enkhuizen, anchored off the Dutch island of Ameland. At the request of the inhabitants, who believed a woman living on the island to be responsible for wrecking ships, they threw her into the sea, then beat her to death with an oar.[73]

Like every other aspect of bewitchment, this one reminds us just how precarious life must have felt to most ordinary people. Neither prosperity nor good health were to be counted on for the morrow. Those who stayed fit themselves might still be dragged down by the burden of a sick or crippled spouse or child. The unlucky could end up as vagrants and beggars, despite the very real degree of charity and mutual help offered by the community. Often the loss of status was felt as keenly as the more direct privations. The fears and tensions just below the surface occasionally surfaced in witchcraft accusations, with specific threats attributed to the suspects. Marguerite Carlier of Oisy-le-Verger, tried in 1612, allegedly told Antoinette Pannequin 'that she would see her husband died in poverty, as had happened, and that she herself would have to beg, as well as telling the children of the late Wattencourt to their shame that they too would go begging'.[74] Jean Diez seems to have made a speciality of such threats, for Zabel Gillat alleged that he told her and her husband 'he would bring them down so far that they needed a beggar's wallet', and having been rich they lost so many animals that they indeed became poor. Her husband Demenge added that every time he quarrelled with Jean some misfortune followed, and that he told the witness 'as for him and le grand Colas, he would cause them to die shamefully, in public view, because of the charges they made against him'. The other man intended was evidently George Colas Bergier, to whom he remarked on the road from St Dié 'you see George, you are a rich man, comfortable and with much property, while I only have my bill-hook, but within three or four years at the most you will become so poor that you will have nothing left with which to beg your bread, while I will become prosperous'. George replied 'that this depended on the will of God, and it was for him to permit it or not', to be told 'that he knew for certain that it would turn out so, and that he knew many things'. According to his widow, although from that moment on they worked as hard as anyone else and were not extravagant, they were slowly reduced to desperate poverty.[75] This will not have been an isolated experience around this time. As will be seen later, the peak decades for persecution were ones in which communal and family bonds were being tested to the limit, for European society was passing through a phase of change accompanied by severe hardship for many.

Malice and envy

With a few exceptions of the kind indicated above, witches were among those who did badly amidst these stresses and had good reason to be resentful. Their power was essentially negative, to drag others down with them rather than to pull themselves up. Ill-will and personal hostility were the standard preconditions for bewitchment, as revealed in innumerable witness narratives. Since a fair measure of aggression was normal in personal relations, the materials needed to construct such stories were readily available. Witches were thought to deprive other people of their possessions or their health; in a sense they were thieves operating on a rather special plane. Most of the time the Devil appears as a very secondary figure, a shadowy presence behind angry neighbours whose normal inhibitions about showing their feelings might break down under extreme stress. Some of the exchanges reported are very suggestive. Jean Michault thought Jeanne Bigenel had bewitched him by making him sit in the place she had just left; when she later came to his house (according to another witness) his wife Mengeon burst out, 'Come here witch, don't you want to unwitch my husband – you were very quick to get off your seat to make him sit down and bewitch him, you have hated us long before today, and are envious of us, you have come just at the moment to do us harm'. On a later occasion, when Mengeon accused her of killing a pig, Jeanne retorted 'you wished me evil long before today, evil tongue'.[76] The records often convey a powerful sense of the malevolence and aggressiveness for which the suspects were known. An extreme case was that of Jeannon Poirot, who evidently startled her judges with her reply when they asked whether she had fought with Blaisette Breton:

> said that this was true, and she wished she had killed her, and had her tripes on her lap, and afterwards she would be content to be hanged and strangled. But she did not want to be burned, because it was said that someone who was not a witch did not burn easily, and if at the time of the dispute or afterwards she had been a witch, there was no doubt that she would have made her [Blaisette] die miserably, or witches had no power over anyone . . . [asked about her threats to Blaisette and her daughter Marguitte, she said she had intended to beat or kill them] . . . and if she had thought that she would now be arrested as a witch, they would not have had such trouble, for she would long before have been hanged and strangled, since she would have killed mother and daughter, and wished with all her heart she had done so, for she would never have repented it.[77]

More soberly, Jacotte Raon was said to be 'a bad neighbour, feared and hated by all her neighbours . . . a riotous woman'.[78] The power seemed inherent to persons, a direct emanation of their passions, possessed of great psychic force. It was expressed in threats like that made by Margrett Scherchen of Lohr to the miller Stoffel Ziegler in 1576; 'You're a proud miller, but I'll soon melt your paws, and you'll quickly be finished' – after which he promptly took ill and died.[79]

Pact or no pact, it was usually the witches rather than the Devil who called the tune in deciding whom to afflict and how. This was expressed in a particularly unpleasant way by Mengeatte Lienard, who said 'When they really hate someone, they make them suffer for a long time, and if they do not hate them excessively, they give them a quick death. If anyone is sick for forty days, it is too late to cure them'.[80] Threats and curses were the common sign of their malevolence, although they might sometimes be seen performing strange ceremonies. Mother Staunton of Wimbish was refused milk by Robert Cornell's wife,

> whereupon she sat down upon her heels before the door and made a circle in the ground with a knife.
> After that, she digged it full of holes within the compass, in the sight

of the said wife, her man and her maid, who, demanding why she did so, she made answer that she made a shitting house for herself after that sort, and so departed. The next day the wife coming out at the same door was taken sick, and began to swell from time to time as if she had been with child; by which swelling she came so great in body as she feared she should burst, and to this day is not restored to health.[81]

After such an obvious display of malice and some other bad-tempered exchanges, it is not surprising that Mother Staunton found herself on trial at Chelmsford in 1579; she was fortunate that none of her alleged human victims had died, so under the 1563 act she was not liable to the death penalty. Even if they made themselves more agreeable than this, those reputed to be witches could not even praise or caress children, still less animals, without risking further damage to their reputation. The terrifying possibilities of bewitchment are all too evident in the testimonies of those who thought it had fallen on them. Nevertheless, it is vital to maintain a sense of balance about the whole subject. Just as many misfortunes were not attributed to witchcraft, so those who supposed themselves bewitched often behaved in a remarkably cool manner. Confident that they knew the culprit, they found some comfort in the diagnosis. Those who had inflicted the harm could allegedly take it off again and found themselves under intense pressure to make signs of reconciliation. Endless little dramas of this kind were played out across Europe, few of which can ever have reached the courts; this was the enduring everyday reality of witchcraft beliefs. So enduring, indeed, that it can still be found in parts of rural France today.

CHAPTER III

SUPERNATURAL POWER AND MAGICAL REMEDIES

Elite and popular cosmologies

THE BELIEFS AND PRACTICES described in the last two chapters all formed part of a coherent, if rather fuzzy, world view. This held that the physical and social universes alike were designed to be ordered but were constantly menaced or disrupted by disorder. The prevailing religious myth expressed this through the story of original sin, the fall of man and exclusion from the Garden of Eden. The Devil, whose first revolt had led to all the subsequent trouble, was still hard at work preying on human weakness. This meshed neatly with the scientific myth, according to which the earth, and the sublunary region it occupied, was the sphere where the elements were mixed into a highly unstable cocktail. European intellectuals made sense of this world through an ingenious dialectical logic, working on principles of polarized binary classification. Ultimately everything was defined in relation to its opposite; good and evil, dry and wet, hot and cold, male and female and so forth. The diabolical anti-world, already invoked in relation to the witches' sabbat, was another example of this way of thinking. In its own terms this logic was capable of great virtuosity, which usually masked its artificiality and lack of true referential grip on the world. In the sixteenth and seventeenth centuries it was undergoing a kind of progressive internal disintegration that would ultimately destroy it as a general system. This collapse was very slow, however, and its implications for witchcraft long remained ambiguous. Debates over the meaning and reality of witchcraft were not just an offshoot of the creation of a new mechanical philosophy; changing ideas about witchcraft themselves contributed to these long-term shifts in thinking. It may well be that among the elites the process created strains and divisions which led some of their members to take witchcraft more seriously than in the past. In later seventeenth-century England, some Fellows of the new Royal Society such as Henry More, Joseph Glanvill and Robert Boyle, encouraged and publicized work on witchcraft and kindred phenomena; they saw this as a way to combat atheism and scepticism and to support traditional views about God's relationship to his creation. It was with rather similar intentions of supporting a highly religious world view that the New England divine Cotton Mather published his *Wonders of the Invisible World*. This was a commentary on the famous trials at Salem in 1692 that portrayed them as part of a much wider diabolical assault on New England. Other threatening agencies included sorcery, raids by the Indians, war with the French and several heresies, notably that of the Quakers. According to Mather's apocalyptic vision of the external forces inspired by the Devil

> The usual *Walls* of defence about mankind have such a Gap made in them, that the very *Devils* are broke in upon us, to seduce the *Souls*, torment the *Bodies*, sully the *Credits*, and consume the *Estates* of our Neighbours, with impressions both as *real* and as *furious*, as if the *Invisible World* were becoming *Incarnate*, on purpose for the vexing of us.[1]

As these examples suggest, the religious schism opened up by the Reformation did not have to imply any obvious division of opinion about witchcraft. Partisan scholars have spent much ink trying to demonstrate that either the Catholics or the Protestants were the real witch-hunters, with remarkably little success. The more we know about the local patterns of persecution, the harder it becomes to see confessional divisions as playing anything more than a marginal role. This is in some respects rather startling, since in theory the Reformation involved a full-scale attack on the previously accepted vision of relations between God and the world. With their assaults on images, the cult of the saints, the ritual calendar, the power of the sacraments and much else, the Protestants were striking at the heart of communal religion as it was practised in Catholic Europe. Salvation by faith alone left the believer wholly dependent on a single, hidden God, who no longer traded in terms of reciprocal services. While they could hardly turn ordinary believers into fully individuated ones overnight, the reformers did have the power, in some areas at least, to remove most of the rituals and props around which the old faith had been built. The vagaries of the campaign against idolatry and superstition were of course very great, and the picture is further complicated because a parallel movement existed within the Catholic church, albeit in a more limited form. In fact it seems unlikely that the Reformation shattered popular cosmology decisively; it changed the modes of relation between man and God, but left the world controlled by the hand of a strongly interventionist deity. In addition, a variety of surviving, hybrid, or alternative popular practices compensated for the demise of traditional Catholicism. The 'disenchantment of the world' was bound to be a slow, piecemeal process, even if its first phase looked like a revolution.

One slow and hesitant change in Christian moral teachings, which may ultimately have been of great importance, has been brilliantly expounded by John Bossy. Between the fourteenth and sixteenth centuries, the Seven Deadly Sins – pride, covetousness, lust, envy, gluttony, anger and sloth – were gradually replaced as the basic moral code by the Ten Commandments. Although this trend in the late medieval church was linked to the reforming movements which nurtured the Protestant Reformation, Tridentine Catholicism also took the Decalogue as a central text. The effect was to make sins against God – notably idolatry or the worship of false gods – the central offences, whereas the older system had given priority to sins against neighbours and the community. This shift provided a powerful motive for Protestant iconoclasm, with its corollaries that Catholic rites were diabolical and that the Pope was the Antichrist. The Devil, who had earlier been an anti-type of Christ, teaching universal hatred in place of love, now became an anti-type of God the Father, the centre of idolatry and false worship. Witchcraft had previously been the crime of harming neighbours by occult means; now clerical intellectuals tied it firmly to devil-worship. As Bossy shows, it was precisely those who pioneered the new moral code – Jean Gerson, John Nider and the Dominicans more generally – who also built up the new vision of witchcraft as the ultimate diabolical heresy. This included the condemnation of many kinds of popular magic and healing on the grounds that they involved either tacit or explicit pacts with the Devil. It is of course one thing to identify such changes, quite another to estimate their effects. Catechisms, confessional guides, sermons and a whole range of devotional and visual aids generalized this new vision of the Devil and must have had some influence at the popular level. As we have already seen, however, confessions about the pact and the sabbat often seem closer to the vision enshrined in the Seven Deadly Sins, with the Devil primarily interested in stimulating communal failings such as envy and ill-will. What seems to have happened, predictably, is that old and new ideas fused into an untidy composite, whose very instability was highly dangerous. Among the educated, the reclassification of witchcraft helped break down earlier scepticism, as witches became dangerous heretics rather than creatures of popular credulity, and thus opened the way to major persecution. While popular ideas generally remained much closer to the old vision, new elements were grafted on without any sense of strain, adding new dimensions of fantasy and anxiety. The traditional cosmology survived, but in a context where it risked becoming the target for violent hostility from zealous reformers of all denominations.

This popular cosmology allowed the sacred great influence within the profane world. It was a source of power that could be invoked in reaction to any disorders in nature and which expressed principles of cosmic order. There was considerable flexibility over the channels available to harness such power, so that Protestant fasting and prayer could take over some roles previously assigned to Catholic shrines and rituals. What such revised practices lacked was the outright materialism which led believers to attack the images of saints when they failed to guarantee suitable weather or other benefits. Formalized ritual was inevitably directed above all to securing the most basic needs of the community, those which ensured its continued existence. Social reproduction, exemplified by the repetitive processes that integrated the life-cycle of the individual into the family and the wider kin, was associated with the established rites of passage – primarily baptism, marriage and the last rites, but also such secondary observances as churching, confirmation and betrothal. Proper observance of a range of official and more dubious practices in association with these ceremonies would bring protection from the multiple dangers faced by every individual and family. Biological fertility, as it affected crops and animals, was similarly protected through the annual calendrical cycle, with its multiplicity of festivals, processions and ceremonies. Formal blessings were pronounced on various occasions, activities began or ended on specified days and holy water, bread, candles and other objects which had been blessed were distributed. These objects, known as sacramentals, provided a major agency of semi-authorized magical power. They were used in order to remove or prevent disorder in the natural world, of the kind which threatened household members and their basic resources. Illness, drought, plagues of insects and the like might be averted by such means. Protection and cures were also sought from conjurations, ranging from formal exorcisms carried out by the clergy to innumerable semi-pagan prayers. Whatever orthodox clerics might wish, there was tremendous scope for a do-it-yourself magical religion of this kind.[2]

Similar concepts underlay another very popular system, that of astrology. Skilled professional astrologers were relatively rare but with printing, the almanac had become the basic staple of the cheap book trade. The astrological calendar and lists of suitable days normally found in almanacs further buttressed the idea of external forces governing the world to which daily life must be attuned. Although orthodox Christianity had always opposed dualism and made the Devil subservient to God, there was a constant danger that harping on the idea that life on earth was dominated by the Devil would sustain a semi-Manichean popular cosmology. Sermons, wall-paintings, religious drama and ceremonies, chapbooks, miracle stories and much else contributed to this tendency towards polarization between good and evil. In symbolic terms, 'good' communities might be envisaged as constantly threatened by dangerous outside forces. Their protection was only assured if assiduous ritual practice and godly living maintained a carapace of positively charged supernatural power around them. Individuals and families needed to maintain their own security in similar fashion. When things went wrong, the cosmic balance might be restored through suitable rituals, such as processions, pilgrimages, or special offerings, which generated a flow of positive force. Serious Protestants had to resort to a more austere prescription of communal faith, godly living, fasting and prayer, whose psychological effects may have been just as powerful. The danger posed by witches in this context is obvious; they were the hidden traitors within, through whose apostasy and aid the Devil penetrated the protective carapace. Failure to keep the bargain with God was indicated by the presence of disorder, usually some version of the 'wickedness, cunning and tricks of the devil'. Sacramentals and conjurations played a double role, being both part of the routine protective rituals and a source of emergency power in crises. The church had traditionally sought to keep supernatural power under clerical control, but these practical expressions of it had largely escaped into the hands of the laity. Although this trend caused much theological anxiety, in early sixteenth-century Germany a popular preacher like Geiler von Kaiserberg was recommending the use of sacramentals as a form of counter-magic, even if at other times he seemed to doubt whether this was legitimate.[3] The church spoke with many voices, allowing ordinary believers to shape and select its message for their own purposes.

Such ways of thinking and acting make up a large part of culture, in the broad sense of the term. Yet this was much more a style of thought than a system, a set of metaphors rather than rules. Boundaries between sacred and profane were so ill-marked that they were easy not only to cross but to move. As usual, people found it much easier to multiply supposed causes than to test them. As a result the beliefs associated with both cosmic order and witchcraft were enabling rather than compelling, serving as a repertory or set of registers from which arguments or actions could be drawn as needed. This is a crucial reason why general theories about witchcraft very rarely led to systematic witch hunting. It also helps to explain why the laity often displayed no abhorrence for the demonic, treated witches as routine nuisances and cheerfully used professional magicians as sources of power. European folk-lore is full of stories in which the hero or heroine succeeds in exploiting the power of the Devil without coming to any harm, thanks to a little elementary trickery.

The Devil, the witches and the power to harm

It is no surprise to find that there was great confusion about the real power of witches. Were they merely the dupes of the Devil, who made them believe they had caused evil he brought about himself? This was essentially the position of such critics of persecution as Johann Weyer, who went on to argue that witches were melancholics in need of treatment rather than punishment (this seems to have been Montaigne's opinion too). Elite demonologists found this a difficult issue, which led into the even more awkward area of God's final responsibility for evil; as we shall see, Weyer's ideas were remarkably close to the orthodox Protestant position in most respects. Popular views, which juggled mutually incompatible ideas with some virtuosity, defy any attempt to reduce them to a system. They slipped easily between treating witches as independent actors, whose power was inherent to them personally, and suggesting that they were helpless tools of Satan. All one can do is to characterize certain typical positions found in the trials, without any claim that they represented a rigid predetermined view. For the specific areas of relations between witch and Devil, and the techniques of causing harm, such material mostly comes from the confessions of the accused, since witnesses were usually deliberately vague about how malice had turned into physical effects. Although all such statements tend to be concerned with fantasy more than fact, this probably renders them better indicators of the underlying concepts.

A very common implication was that witches had crossed a hidden boundary when they gave allegiance to the Devil. In consequence he could coerce them directly, beating them and even threatening to kill them. Witches might tell a variety of pathetic stories around this theme, portraying themselves as abused and unwilling agents of Satan. Laurence Tolbay claimed that 'she did many things with great regret, but she was forced into them by the cruelty of her master Persin, who tormented and beat them [the witches] when they did not wish to do as he wanted'. She had also been beaten every time she used white powder to cure, which made it rather hard to understand why Persin should have given her this at all. If this disobedience made it clear that she was not just his puppet, this was also true of some of her evil acts, for he knew when *she* was angry and would then appear with the powder needed to avenge herself.[4] Where the confessions go into any detail, they more often distinguish between the corporate acts against the crops at the sabbat, where the majority of the poor witches were coerced by the Devil and the rich, and the individual bewitchments, acts of revenge whose motivation came from the witch. Witnesses sometimes alleged the accused had shown physical signs of mysterious beatings or been heard crying out. They plainly implied that they had been maltreated by their master, so the idea that witches were to some degree the miserable dupes of the Devil was widespread. It was said that strange noises and talking were heard from Babillon Cherier's room at night, although she was alone. She gave a very mundane explanation – she was so exhausted after days spent labouring in the fields and had such pain from her limbs and her teeth that she could not endure it, and complained out loud.[5] Her accuser plainly wanted to suggest that she had been receiving regular visits from the Devil; the authorities cannot have been wholly convinced, since she was not tortured and was finally released.

When his servants had quarrelled with someone, therefore, it was all too likely that their infernal master would appear in person to suggest that they take revenge. They most frequently did this by physical means, employing the powders, poisoned sticks and similar weapons he had provided. On other occasions, however, he might propose to act personally on their behalf, provided they gave their consent. This was a confusing area, as appeared from Jean Martin's response when he was asked why the powder did not harm him when he touched it. He said that it 'could do no harm to the witches who touched it, and when they had thrown the powder on some person or animal it was the devil their master who subsequently made them die after the witches had given their consent'. In reply to a further question about whether he could use the powder on anyone he wished, he said 'neither he nor any other witch had power against anyone unless the devil approached them first, commanding them to do so, nevertheless he only did this when they actually wanted to harm someone, and that in the case of all the people and animals he had killed, the devil his master Persin had always driven and incited him to do this'.[6] Plaisance Toutblanc admitted that after the surgeon Maître Hanso had bled her husband, she was angry because they spent the next week drinking together; her master Jolybois suggested she kill him and offered to do this for her. During his subsequent illness she regretted her anger, because he was a very expert surgeon, but Jolybois refused to cure him and she found by experience that the spell, once given, could not be removed.[7] Sometimes the witches claimed to have bargained with their masters, finally agreeing on some lesser act of revenge. Georgette Malley would not agree to Persin killing Colas Charier, who had beaten her son, but finally agreed that he might make him ill.[8]

The implication of most of these stories was that the Devil only had power over other creatures through the agency of the witch, itself based on ill-will and envy. As George Gifford put it;

> It is the common opinion among the blind ignorant people, that the cause and the procuring of harm by witchcraft, proceedeth from the Witch, and that either the Devil could or would do nothing unless he were sent by her.[9]

This was why such traitors from God's camp were vital to him, since without them he could achieve nothing more than illusions. Even with their aid his power was not unlimited, for many witches stated that those who were strong in faith and performed the correct rituals – usually washing their hands and commending themselves to God – were guaranteed against witchcraft for the day. Too much consistency should not be expected from these beliefs; for example, witches might say they had left an enemy unharmed because they could not find a good opportunity to administer the powder, apparently forgetting that they could have asked their master to act on their behalf. The beliefs appear rather as expressions of psychic truth, of a sense that the evil was capable of taking both internal and external forms. The diabolical master seems to be a projection of the witches' own often frustrated malevolence, battling with his or her better feelings, even slyly suggesting that this was the day an enemy was ill-protected. Jeanne Martin explained that those who had crossed themselves and commended themselves to God were invulnerable for that day, but their animals were not. Asked how she could know when individuals were unprotected, she said the Devil told them and if they could not act themselves would do so for them, provided they gave their consent.[10] In psychological terms these ideas had great immediacy and conviction, beside which the efforts of some demonologists and theologians to claim that the Devil merely deluded witches when he performed the evil himself look rather feeble.

The weather magic allegedly performed at the sabbat also apparently required the consent of the witches, even a vote which parodied the proceedings of a village assembly. This allowed the accused to protest that they personally had resisted, but here the witches as a group were the agency for action. The standard defence against storms was to ring the church bells, a dangerous practice for the ringers in the absence of lightning conductors; witches regularly testified that their plans had been frustrated in this way. Conversations showing some kind of scepticism about the prophylactic effects of bell-ringing could be brought up in evidence against suspects. Jacquat Jean Adam had been ringing the bells when a storm threatened, only for Jean Marion to tell him he would wear them out with so much ringing, which reinforced his suspicions about him.[11] It was not a good idea to display too much confidence when a stormcloud blew up or to return afterwards from some remote spot. There were even cases when a suspect's house was struck by lightning, and this was interpreted as a diabolical visitation. A whole range of mysterious events might be alleged as evidence of connections with the Devil, from blue flames in a barn, through visits from unknown animals, to the sight of the witch flying overhead. Adrien Jacot testified that he had gone to thresh in Chrestien Pierre's barn before dawn, only for a dog to howl continuously, while a strange blue light flashed through both house and barn, both ceasing suddenly when the accused appeared some fifteen minutes later.[12] Denys Tourneur claimed to have seen a woman riding a distaff in the air, with arms and legs spread wide; he called on God, at which the distaff fell to the ground, then Synnel Stumpf appeared to claim it, saying her grandson had taken it there.[13]

Flying and shapeshifting

References of this type to actual flying were very rare outside the confessions, apart from the troubling accusations made by children or servants, who might tell how they themselves had been taken to the sabbat in this fashion. Witnesses were more often found making imputations of rapid or unseen motion. The witch would be seen as they left one place, only to turn up several miles away without passing them on the road. A linked belief was that witches knew far too much about other people's business, reporting secrets they could not have known or overhearing conversations from far off. Phelippe Phillepin told how he and Jean Girard had been threshing at Jennon Girard's house, where they hid a hatful of apples under some straw. Although no-one had seen them, Jennon knew about this immediately, so they suspected the Devil must have told her.[14] Claudon Bregeat knew when Jehenne Jennat had not used the herbs she gave her, but Jehenne thought only her evil spirit could have told her of this.[15] Such stories were told ingenuously, without any attempt to give a full explanation, but judges do not seem to have taken them very seriously, in comparison to the charges of *maleficium*. They attest to a general conviction that witches had access to a world of strange occult powers, akin to that of miracle stories and the marvels, monsters and prodigies which were the stock-in-trade of popular broadsheets. When a storm came up at harvest-time Petroniere Varnier seemed confused about which mountain she was looking at, so Demenge Biol remarked 'perhaps she was only a ghost, placed among them by the enemy, in place of her real body, which he might have transported elsewhere at that time'.[16] These episodes were as often bizarre or playful as they were threatening; sometimes it is obvious that they had circulated actively through the medium of village gossip, to be retold by numerous witnesses.

The widespread notion that witches anointed themselves with a magical grease in order to fly, already discussed in relation to the sabbat, was one instance where a semi-naturalistic explanation was attempted. Given the general belief in the power of words, the parallel claims that an incantation had the same effect are hardly surprising. Descriptions of shapeshifting, although much rarer, are also found in many areas of Europe. Here too one may suspect traces of ancient shamanistic ideas, readily assimilated into the folklore of witchcraft. Greases, special skins, incantations and the direct action of the Devil were all invoked to explain these transformations into animal form. Jean Callery explained that his master Houbelot had ordered him and an accomplice to take the form of wolves, using grease and skins complete with fearsome teeth.[17] Although these details are found in the confessions of the witches, they plainly reflected a stratum of folk belief which was much more widely spread and was implicitly present in numerous testimonies. These charges were often evaded or ignored by the accused, sometimes by alleging that their master had taken the form of the wolf, so that self-confessed werewolves are very rare among surviving cases. Pamphlets and serious demonological treatises spread these stories, with much disagreement about the balance of reality and illusion involved. There are occasional accounts of transformations into other animals such as hares, but the creatures which shared diabolical honours with the wolf were the cat and the dog, whose ambivalent status as predatory animals which worked for people (and whose behaviour might oscillate between the wild and the domesticated) may have encouraged such stories.

The appearance of strange cats, which found their way in and out of closed houses, attacked babies or tried to smother sleepers, was a fairly common theme, as we have already seen. These events were often nocturnal, as one might expect. Witches again reinforced the belief with confessions about how they had been changed into cats in order to reach their victims. Demenge Thiriat had told a story about how he awakened, felt there was someone else in the bedroom and touched a woman's clothes. He heard voices he thought were those of Marion Arnoulx and Barbeline Mareschal, but when his wife lit a candle the room was empty and the door locked. Both suspects later confessed that they had entered the room in the form of cats, after Persin had stripped them naked and rubbed them with grease. They squeezed painfully through the shutters to enter the room, then were transformed back into their normal shape in order to put a poisoned grain in Demenge's mouth; when he awoke, Persin hastily converted them back into feline form so that they could make good their escape. This elaborate scenario failed to explain how they came to be fully clothed in the room, but no-one thought to ask about this inconvenient detail.[18] In Lorraine there was a curious distinction between dogs and cats; witches took the latter form, while dogs were usually thought to represent the Devil himself. A typical story came from Jean Gerard, who thought he had seen Claudatte Jean in company with another unknown woman and a great black dog an hour before dawn, although the accused kept no dog; the group fled towards the mountain as he approached.[19] The demonologists circulated accounts – some of them drawn from classical literature – about injuries inflicted on witches in animal form that were then found on the person of the human suspect. The notion was wholly consonant with popular ideas, but such flights of fancy are exceptionally rare in actual trials. In symbolic terms, shapeshifting associated witches with predatory creatures, the night and the wilderness outside human society. At a more pragmatic level, wolves were a real threat in many areas, whose sudden appearances must have been a particular terror to the children who often guarded the animals; here one can sense a widely shared anxiety, even trauma, behind the stories.

The idea that witches could pass through locked doors might be advanced without any suggestion of transformation into a cat, simply as another sign of the supernatural. Richard Jean Collatte claimed that Catherine le Maire had been locked out by her drunken husband when they shared a house, only to be found back in bed in the morning.[20] Mongin André of Hymont thought that Jacquot Petit Jacquot had given him his fatal illness, telling his wife 'that an animal the length of a man had come into their bed and lain on him, being so heavy that he was unable to make the sign of the cross with his hand, but had to do it with the tip of his tongue, and that by the light of the moon he had seen him enter by the lock of the door'.[21] In general many of these elaborations seem to serve the basic purpose of emphasizing otherness, in order to stress the implicit meaning of the evidence as a whole. The witch was a carrier of malevolent power who operated outside the normal realm of physical causation; any behaviour or associations which could add to this impression were eagerly reported by hostile witnesses. A relatively common charge was that the accused was subject to trance-like states or fits. From the descriptions and explanations given, most of these were probably epileptic in nature, although such attacks could just as easily be regarded as a sign of bewitchment, and there is no reason for supposing that epileptics were normally classified as witches. The hostile interpretation of such states was that they showed the person's spirit to be elsewhere, presumably in contact with the master from whom the evil ultimately came. There was something in common here with the claims that witches could attend the sabbat while their body, or a simulacrum of it, remained in bed. The diabolical anti-world was ambiguously poised between reality and imagination, physical effects and fantasy, in a way which allowed it to absorb a mass of disparate material whose common theme was simply that the witch was somehow abnormal, a misfit whose oddities were deeply significant.

The techniques of bewitchment

When it came to the act of bewitchment itself, the range of possibilities was rather small. Witnesses were often content to suggest physical proximity or simple touching, obvious opportunities to administer the powder by which the accused themselves explained most *maleficium*. The powder was usually supplied by the Devil, often in a range of colours to indicate its different purposes. There were also stories of how witches themselves made it, at the sabbat or independently, using such constituents as the bodies of stillborn babies, toad venom and stolen hosts; these generally appear in the more fantastic and elaborated accounts of the sabbat. Sometimes there was a distinction between powders for humans and animals, more often between those to kill, to make sick and to cure. The colour-coding was very random and witches would contradict themselves in their confessions, claiming to have used the wrong powder according to their own classification. Claudatte Parmentier had received three kinds of powder, black to kill people, red to kill animals and white to heal. Having made Simon Hougney ill, she decided to cure him when he threatened to have her arrested and did so with the red powder.[22] There was also much uncertainty about the degree to which the powder worked automatically, although it was fairly clear it had no effect on the witch who handled it. In some instances it was suggested that it was dangerous to anyone else, in others that it only affected chosen targets, as if it needed to be charged up by specific ill-will. In a typical case, Margueritte François sprinkled powder near Bastien Mariatte's door to make his children ill, and they were the only ones affected when they walked over it.[23] Judges sometimes took a considerable interest in the powder, apparently hoping to find a more solid basis for their decisions; searches were conducted following the indications given by confessing witches, only to prove negative in almost every case. Margueritte Gallier told her interrogators where to find it on the windowsill in a barn, but they only found two small packets of cabbage seed, with a third empty packet from which she said the powder must have escaped.[24] The Basque witch Maria de Zozaya gave a list of powders and liquids, as well as 'dressed toads', hidden in various specific places in her house; when a search proved fruitless she said the Devil must have removed them himself.[25] Where suspicious substances were found they usually turned out to be quite harmless, although a few stories to the contrary got into the demonological literature. Witches usually claimed to have expended all their stock, or thrown the remainder away, when they feared arrest. During the great Basque country panic of 1609–11, some jars of witch grease were discovered, only for the accused to retract their confessions later and explain that they had manufactured these to satisfy the insistent demands of their accusers. They were made with such ingredients as pork fat, soot and kitchen waste.[26] As so often, the attempt to convert fantasy into fact proved self-defeating, bolstering scepticism rather than belief.

The idea that the Devil supplied a powder to heal was an important feature in the belief-system, although it did not appear consistently. It reflected the ambivalence of popular attitudes to diabolical power, seen as a possible source of advantage as well as harm, a viable alternative to that of God. At the same time, it was linked to the notion that diabolical illnesses were incurable by normal means, so that only the witch could truly alleviate them. By a roundabout route witchcraft therefore became a means to seek cures, with its practitioners having therapeutic powers they might be compelled to use by threats or force. These did not necessarily involve the use of powder, for the Devil himself might be asked to procure the cure; the accused, in an obvious attempt to excuse themselves from the full consequences of their ill-will, quite often claimed they had sought such aid, only to be refused by their master. The midwife Jennon Petit had been angered because she was not treated with sufficient respect, or given drink, in the bourgeois household of Bernard Huel, so gave his wife Anne her fatal illness. She claimed this was at the persuasion of her master Persin, but that when she repented – and declared she would have given the last drop of her own blood to secure a cure – he expressly forbade this and prevented her.[27] Others admitted they had inflicted illnesses in order to make money by healing them, employing a range of standard techniques behind which (when they were used as a mere pretence) the Devil often performed the real cure. The magical healer Claudette Clauchepied accepted a suggestion from her judges that her master had advised her to feign a religious life in order to operate more convincingly, telling people she had been born on Good Friday 'when she wanted to deceive everyone still better'. Although she had indeed been born on that day, 'it hardly made her worth anything more'.[28]

An alternative view of bewitchment was that it came directly from the witch, as an emanation of evil spirit. This might take the form of 'overlooking', a version of the evil eye beliefs, or of breathing over the victim. In these ways the witch became like someone suffering from an infectious disease. More directly hostile acts might also be the modes of transmission, when witches pinched or struck those with whom they quarrelled, their children or their animals. Jeannotte Toussaint accused a girl named Alison of stealing clothing from her washtub, only for it to be found later. She knew Alison was resentful and went up to her among the other girls saying 'these great lazy girls, you need to feel how big they are', gripping her round the thigh. The girl became all swollen and was sick for five months before her death, saying at the height of her illness 'the witch who has given me this sickness won't let me die.' As the other women were lamenting her state, Jeannotte said (with her 'habitual smile') that she would not die yet and she lingered several more days.[29] These methods could also work in reverse as a means of healing, often said to have been effected by simple touching or manipulation. Hellenix Hottin gave Jérémie Barbier's small son some gooseberries, asking him to bring her back some bread from his father. Since the father already suspected her, he told the child to be sure not to touch her – but his finger made contact with her as he handed over the bread, then he fell ill. Barbier then threatened to have her burned if she did not heal the boy, after which she prayed over him, traced the sign of the cross on his stomach and within an hour he was playing in the road with the other children.[30] The most overtly witch-like procedures were those which used the power of words, notably cursing or some form of threatening ceremony or ritual. Ursula Clarke of Dunstable wished in 1667 that William Metcalfe should 'waste like dew against the sun', adding that 'some people had wronged her, but they had as good have let her alone, for she . . . had seen the end of Platt, and she had seen the end of Haddon, and she hoped she should see the end of Metcalfe, and that she had never wished or cursed anything in her life but it came to pass'.[31]

At other times witches might force their victims, however reluctant, to consume food or drink they offered in an insistent fashion. Loudevic Thoussaint had been haymaking for Penthecoste Miette for five days but always refused offers of food in her house because he was afraid she would bewitch him. On the last night she pressed so hard that he accepted supper, only to fall ill as soon as he got home.[32] In 1649 it was alleged that a Yorkshire witch had followed a boy with 'an apple and a piece of bread and would not part with him till she caused him to bite both of the apple and the bread'; the child then started to spit blood and finally died.[33] The powders or other poisons were often invoked here, as obvious explanations for the subsequent illnesses. The accused might also reveal their uncanny knowledge when they reproached the recipients for failing to consume the dubious gift, or when domestic animals to whom it was given would die suddenly. Magdelaine Finance claimed that her husband brought home a pear Jeanne Martin had sent for her, only for it to turn black. When the stalk was pulled off it was seen to be full of grease, so he said she had surely intended to bewitch her. She threw it into a field where there was a sow, in order to test it, whereupon the sow and all her piglets died after she had eaten it.[34] Here too a similar exchange might bring a cure, for the response to an accusation was often a gift of food, later said to have been sprinkled with the healing powder. After her brother-in-law threatened to have her burned, Marguitte Lairain brought some porridge to his wife, whose illness had baffled the doctors, then she slowly recovered. Marguitte later confessed that her master Persin had given her yellow powder to remove the illness she had inflicted.[35] The system was almost infinitely flexible and could validate just about any claim about either harming or healing, whatever agents were supposed to be involved. In the English case the familiars or imps allowed action at a distance, just as the Devil did elsewhere. Ursula Kemp confessed to Brian Darcy 'that upon the falling out between Thurlow's wife and her, she sent Tiffin the spirit unto her child which lay in the cradle, and willed the same to rock the cradle over, so as the child might fall out thereof, and break the neck of it'.[36] Elsewhere familiars were mostly found in rather special roles, such as spirits who were supposed to bring luck at dice or cards; these were sometimes sold to the gullible by the cunning folk.

Fear, reprisals and healing

In theory the witches who had access to this store of supernatural power were the deadliest enemies imaginable; only those individuals who observed their religious duties in the most scrupulous fashion, thus ensuring divine protection at all times, could feel any confidence that they were invulnerable. Needless to say, this was not the way people actually thought and behaved in general, although there must always have been a few hag-ridden exceptions. Fear of witchcraft waxed and waned at both the communal and the personal levels according to circumstances. Devastating weather, plagues of insects, epidemics of animal disease and similar misfortunes might arouse villages or larger regions to peaks of anxiety. Despite a few well-attested incidents, there does not seem to have been anything automatic about this, at least in terms of waves of persecution. Events of this kind were commonplace in early modern Europe and were often interpreted in a relatively naturalistic fashion, with no suggestion of witchcraft. They might still be attributed to supernatural causes, in the sense that they were sent by God as a punishment for sin. The plague, for example, although recognized as an infectious disease, was commonly described in such terms, since God could work through natural causes. It was also possible, however, for stories to circulate of malevolent individuals using grease on doors or similar methods of spreading the infection; in Geneva two major panics, in 1545 and 1571, saw a total of sixty-five people executed on such grounds.[37] This rather localized belief seems to be connected with the role of Savoyard migrants as the specialists who normally took on the dangerous task of clearing away the bodies of the dead in such epidemics. Since they might be thought to profit from the infection, it was easy to think they would be tempted to cause it.[38] Where individuals are concerned the picture is still more shifting and ambiguous, for persons who were sceptical in one context often became fearful in another. Sickness might liberate people from the usual inhibitions, so that under the effects of pain or fever they expressed their hidden fears, even seeing hallucinations of their supposed persecutors. Jean Grand Didier had told Didier Grand Claudon that he should stay and confront the women who denounced him as a witch, attracting a very angry response. That night he felt a heavy weight on him, then saw five persons around him; Didier, the only one he recognized, was trying to strangle him. He commended himself to God and lit a light, but as soon as this was put out they reappeared, and this continued for several nights.[39] When such illness followed immediately on an angry interchange it required a stout heart indeed to doubt the connection between ill-will and mortal peril.

The normal response of the sufferers or their relatives was to summon the witch, by threats or blandishments, in an attempt to obtain a cure. It was commonplace to threaten the suspect with legal action and execution, even to beat them up. Catherine la Rondelatte went to Jean Grainel's house, complaining that he had not made a purchase from her on behalf of his master; she added 'I have kept some real pleasures for him, and I will keep more still', then clapped her hands saying 'I will do all that I can'. He then lost animals to the value of 500 francs and on meeting her outside the village told her, 'Witch, I have come to kill you since you have caused the deaths of my horses and cattle, now you too will die at my hands'. He beat her until she said 'I beg mercy, I will never cause you, or anything belonging to you, harm or trouble'. Still dissatisfied, he later beat her again, after which she complained to the local *prévôt*, who fined him sixteen francs and made him promise not to molest her any more. He did not pay her the fine, although she begged him to give her two pence so that some reparation had been made, and from this point his losses ceased.[40] Another woman who was regularly beaten was Mengeatte Jacques, of whom one witness said that anyone else would have been badly hurt, 'but she seemed to be hardened to blows, so that they had no more effect than if they had been struck on wood'.[41] A number of these cases ended with the death of the suspect; there are at least a dozen cases in Lorraine where the murderer obtained letters of remission from the Duke, while three men were hanged at York assizes in 1677 for the murder of a suspected witch from Wakefield. Another Yorkshire case shows that Elizabeth Lambe was beaten by several neighbours who believed she had caused losses of cattle, and were 'never after disquieted by her'.[42] The more timorous left the accusation implicit, hoping this would be enough to induce remedial action, or simply asked for suggestions about what to do. It is not always easy to tell from the evidence whether suspicions preceded or followed such encounters; indeed there may often have been doubt in the minds of those involved. Power to harm and to heal was so closely intertwined in the popular mind that they could never be clearly separated. All forms of healing formed part of a tangled web of cause and effect, into which the magical and the supernatural could easily be inserted.

As an alternative to confronting the witch, there was the possibility of obtaining such items as bread, salt, vegetables, or ashes from their household. This might often be done through a servant or other intermediary, after which the bewitched person would consume them and any improvement in their condition confirmed the original suspicions. In England and Scotland, thatch from the suspect's house was frequently burned as a remedy; the intention, as with other forms of remedy, was to compel the witch to appear, so that he or she might be put under intense pressure to offer help. The accused normally claimed total ignorance of such transactions, but these protestations do not always ring true. Very often the wisest course of action was to turn a blind eye to such covert accusations, for an attempt to challenge them carried its own dangers, seeming to confirm the existence of ill-will. Although witches sometimes refused to visit their alleged victims, they more generally yielded to pressure, putting on at least a show of neighbourly feeling. Aubertin Tripa believed that Sibille Vacquaire had made his wife ill because she refused to act as wet-nurse and told her he had fifty francs to make sure she was burned unless she cured her. The next day Sibille came to the house and asked if they had made a pilgrimage, suggesting the local shrine of le Bel Bernard; he had his wife taken there on a cart, after which she recovered.[43] Laurence Viney was haymaking for Jean le Clerc when a great cloud came up over the local mountain (the Kemberg or 'Cambas'), so the hay was hurriedly raked into stacks, but Laurence was leaning on her fork looking thoughtful. Le Clerc's wife Jennon called on her to hurry up and work, adding 'perhaps she was thinking she was on Cambas making hail'. The response to this provocative remark (by a relatively prosperous young woman of twenty-five to a poorer one who claimed to be eighty) was a warning that she would repent, after which she fell ill instantly and had to be helped back home. She thought she must die and asked for the last rites, but her husband sent their maid to ask Laurence to the house on the pretext of working flax. She said that she knew why they really wanted her and had expected them to come for her soon. Arriving at the house, she said 'she had been taken by an evil wind, that she knew the remedy to heal her, and they had done well to call her', then crossed her forehead five times with her thumb and said she would pray for her over nine days – her pains immediately ceased and she recovered.[44]

This kind of local crisis management carried long-term risks, particularly if it involved the formal asking of pardon (as seems to have been quite widespread in England), for it inevitably confirmed reputations, while very commonly defusing the immediate tensions. The balance of forces was restored with the renunciation of hostilities by the supposed offender, whose attack was thus repelled. Accused by the wife of Richard Wood of Heptonstall over the sickness of their cattle, Mary Midgely took sixpence from her, then advised her to put a handful of salt and an old sickle under each cow. When Wood later met Midgely in an alehouse he referred to the matter in equivocal terms, after which she gave him an apple 'and confessed she had done him hurt divers times but would never do more'.[45] It was through such exchanges, often deliberately kept ambiguous by all parties, that ideas of witchcraft could flourish without the law becoming involved at all. What they did involve was a confrontation which in several respects formed a mirror image of that other familiar scene, the witch cursing someone he or she felt had wronged them. As Jim Sharpe has remarked, such cases demonstrate that the interpersonal relationships between witch and accuser 'were vital not only in the formation of the accusation, but also to those subsequent stages during which the two parties negotiated their position, often in a public or semi-public forum, the accuser or victim at least frequently being assisted by the mediation and support of friends and neighbours'.[46]

The potency of the various rituals and observances to cure was often associated with the actual person of the healer, as some kind of emanation of their vital spirit. The simple physical presence of the witch was sometimes thought enough to effect a cure; more often this was extended to include touching the victim or the sick animals, or alternatively breathing over them. On other occasions it seemed that the only way for the afflicted to enjoy any rest was for the witch to make their bed. In England the touching might be reversed, through the general popular belief that scratching the witch and drawing blood was an effective way to negate the curse. At Windsor in 1579 a sick ostler consulted the wise man Father Rosimond

who told him that he was bewitched, and that there was many ill women in Windsor, and asked him whom he did mistrust, and the said ostler answered 'One Mother Stile', one of the witches aforesaid. 'Well', said the wiseman, 'if you can meet her, and all to-scratch her so that you can draw blood of her, you shall presently mend.' And the said ostler upon his oath declared that he watching her on a time did all to-scratch her by the face, that he made the blood come after, and presently his pain went away so that he hath been no more grieved since.[47]

Another very common reversal was that of the gift of food or drink; often thought to be the means whereby the original bewitchment had taken place, it was also a gesture of neighbourliness linked to cures. As already suggested, confessions regularly explained that this was how the healing powder had been applied, smeared on fruit or bread, or included in some soup – making soup for the sick was probably the most widespread of all these techniques. Hillevix Magister had been called to heal le Grand Martin Jacques, who suspected her of bewitching him, but he could not eat the soup she made and died. More than fifteen years later she offered a similar cure to the wife of Didier Maraise, only to have it thrown in her face by the sufferer, who cried out 'Witch, don't you want to heal me, must it be that by your wish I should die'.[48]

In a minority of cases more elaborate and overt methods of healing were employed. In Catholic Europe the illness might be identified as coming from a specific saint, whose favours must be sought through a pilgrimage, offerings and other observances. Jennon Villemin was a healer who specialized in this kind of diagnosis; she told Françoise Cochien that her bad leg was St Mimin's evil, advising a pilgrimage to his shrine. When Françoise proposed to send her daughter, she said it needed a woman who could speak German and 'Romand', then agreed to perform it herself for eight francs. She took a man's stocking containing horse-dung and five eggs with her, while giving the sufferer some ointments – but these made her leg swell up, so that she thought they would have killed her if she continued using them.[49] Jehanne Villaume had been angry because Jacquatte Contal was being given alms by a woman she feared would be less generous to her in consequence – then Jacquatte's small daughter fell ill. Jehanne was persuaded to visit the child, saying she was angry to be suspected and was not what they thought. Jacquatte said they had not accused her, but she should see the state of the child; she then asked if they had made a pilgrimage, adding that these were useless if made by the parents. Asked to do what was necessary, she performed a 'neuvaine' in the church with candles, later giving the child an apple and some bread, after which she recovered.[50] Eggs were used, either in specific numbers or when laid on particular days such as Good Friday. Herbal remedies also featured, sometimes as drinks, more often in the form of packets to be worn against the skin or herbal baths and fumigations. Various greases and ointments were provided. It is impossible to separate the elements of genuine folk medicine (if such a thing can be said to exist as a separate entity) from the magical beliefs in all this. Jennon Villemin faced a long series of testimonies from those she had failed to heal, but she was clearly genuine enough in her intentions, mixing herbal treatments with her pilgrimages and rituals; a group of doctors, apothecaries and surgeons was called in to test her drugs. In the end she was sentenced to whipping and banishment for superstitious practices, without any serious attempt to prove she was a witch.

Many remedies clearly relied on forms of sympathetic magic. Some of these saw the disease as something that could be transferred from one creature to another; at its most literal this might involve incorporating waste products from the sufferer in food given to the animal selected to receive the disease. When Jean Purel was ill and thought three local witches had gathered round his bed to strangle him, one of these, Claudon Demengeon, refused to come and see him because she thought he would reproach her. Instead she advised his wife 'that to relieve him she should make a cake of rye flour, mixed with her husband's urine, then put it alongside his bed, after which she should place it on the dungheap outside their house, after which a small black dog would carry it off and he would be well' – as duly happened.[51] On other occasions there was a much more general implication that one person had sickened on behalf of another. During his possession George Guerin had blamed Barbe Barbier for his affliction (he had earlier persuaded his mother, with whom she was living, to expel her because of her reputation as a witch), and she had agreed to come and make remedies for him. While she was in the house his small child laughed at her, to which she said 'Don't laugh, you will hardly laugh any more', and the infant was dead two days later. Her response was unexpected, for she commented 'praised be God, my prayers are answered, the child has repurchased the father, affirming that had she not come to the house the said Guerin would have been dead and buried, and she would swear this on all the gospels'. She later said the child had been sickly already and that these comments might have been made when neighbours came to see the body, since, according to her, it was a common saying.[52]

Disease was implicitly understood as a foreign element intruding into the sufferer's body; this idea received particularly vivid expression in stories of animals moving about in the stomach or elsewhere. After a dispute with Mengeotte Blaise over the rate of payment for hoeing, Annon Trippier suddenly felt a great pain in her throat; the next day she claimed to have an animal in her stomach which cried like a toad and gave her great pain, while she spat up stuff as black as ink. When she told Mengeotte that she believed the animals would kill her, she replied 'she had hardly suffered yet and was not ready to die', but Annon wished God would end her agonies.[53] The numerous magical prayers, whether passed on orally or taken from the various magical books and *grimoires* which healers kept, clearly express the related notion that religious language was itself a vehicle of power. There were also other, more mysterious practices, like using a dog's skull to rub ointment on the swollen legs of horses and cattle; this was supposed to be more efficacious if a priest had blessed the skull, according to some women at Leintrey.[54] The better trained clergy of the post-Tridentine Catholic church were unlikely to participate in such obvious superstitions, but there was a much wider range of fairly respectable prophylactic measures. Buildings could be blessed and sprinkled with holy water, prayers said, exorcisms performed. Although theologians worried about the use of the sacramentals mentioned earlier, it is unlikely that most ordinary clerics shared their doubts, at least until the late seventeenth century. Shrines and pilgrimages were cornerstones of popular Catholicism, sources of revenue and prestige for priests and churches, so that efforts by bishops and others to control them were often resisted. Their guardians and users were patently sincere in their faith in the therapeutic power of these sacred places. There were orders such as the Ambrosian friars that specialized in exorcizing the possessed, but it was only around the middle of the seventeenth century that major orders like the Jesuits and the Capuchins became seriously worried about the dangers of these activities, earlier seen as a source of spiritual prestige.

Superstition, magic and religion

The reformed churches might appear to have formally renounced the use of religious counter-magic, but it is far from clear what this meant in reality. There was a lengthy period in most parts of Protestant Europe during which many clerics persisted with old practices, while Catholic shrines and holy places seem to have retained much of their appeal. Even well-educated members of the Protestant elites were still liable to resort to folk remedies at the slightest provocation. A clerical healer like Richard Napier, using talismans and amulets alongside more conventional remedies, could still enjoy a thriving practice in early seventeenth-century England, with clients across the whole range, from the peerage to poor labourers.[55] Nevertheless, there must have been a serious reduction in the ritual equipment available for repelling the Devil and his minions. Burying a 'witch-bottle' under the threshold could not really replace the blessed candles or palms, still less the ubiquitous holy water – apart from anything else the comforting regularity of these observances was lost. While it is impossible to measure such things, the result may well have been a golden age for the cunning folk. Certainly Puritan clerics complained bitterly about their pervasive influence and popularity, describing their 'cures' as a combination of deceits and implicit compacts with the Devil. Gifford commented:

> The charmer often times knoweth no devil, but with his charm of words he can catch rats, and burst snakes, take away the pain of the tooth ache, with a pair of shears and a sieve, find out a thief. Many other pretty knacks he glorieth in, as if he had attained great wisdom. The art is devilish, when any thing is done the devil worketh it, he is the instructor of the enchanter.[56]

Attempts to pursue these people through the ecclesiastical courts seem to have proved largely futile, for the modest penalties imposed were no real deterrent and may have been outweighed by the useful publicity such appearances generated. Although it is tempting to envisage fear of witchcraft increasing as official remedies were withdrawn, comparisons with Catholic Europe do not really bear this out; it would be just as plausible to see the old observances as part of a symbiotic thought system which encouraged witchcraft explanations.

There was always a danger that cunning folk themselves would be accused as black rather than white witches, and a fair number did end up before the courts in this way. As a proportion of their total numbers, however, this was a minuscule fraction; this seems to be particularly true in Protestant areas, despite the strong line taken by the reformed clergy. Such cases arose naturally from the ambiguities attaching to the position and techniques of the healers. If taking off the sickness implied sending it elsewhere, or returning witchcraft on the original giver, then such reciprocal effects were hardly neutral. Behind this attitude one may perhaps detect the harsh realism of a society in which resources were scarce and one person's gain was commonly another's loss. In addition, the skilful operator surrounded himself or herself with a certain mystique, leaving the exact nature of the process obscure, and this too could easily be reinterpreted in terms of diabolical witchcraft. Muttered prayers, obscure gestures and an insistence on secrecy were all part of the act, but carried their own risks. Clients generally preferred to consult a magical specialist at a certain distance; displacement had its own special charge in such instances, analogous to that of pilgrimages. This could lead to the odd situation in which a positive external reputation was combined with a negative one in the healer's own community, where he or she was seen primarily as a black witch. Itinerant cunning folk represented another type who, since they lacked any natural defenders, were particularly liable to fall foul of the authorities. Ideas about superstition and diabolism showed their full elasticity when such persons were tried, for practices which were accepted without comment in witness testimony against other witches were liable to be reclassified as evidence of their dealings with the Devil. Contemporaries seem to have been simply unaware of the bad faith involved and happily manipulated their categories to suit the particular situation.

It has been suggested, principally with reference to the belated eighteenth-century peak in Hungarian witchcraft persecution, that the cunning folk were prone to accuse one another.[57] There must certainly have been a danger that the whole system of magic and counter-magic could overload in some such way, building up intense anxiety to the point where conflict might reach this deadly level. To date, however, there is little clear evidence that this was occurring in sixteenth- and seventeenth-century Europe, although the possibility cannot be wholly discounted. Such keen observers as Scot distinguished sharply between the witches and the cunning folk and failed to discern any marked tendency for them to merge. There appears to be no earlier analogue for one spectacular Hungarian trend, also found in some other areas of eastern Europe after 1700, which was for magical aggression to be attributed to vampires, recently deceased persons who emerged from their graves to suck the blood of the living. This conveniently displaced blame so that it fell on the dead, with action being taken against their corpses; this new form of counter-magic may in part be seen as a response to the growing hostility of the Habsburg state to witchcraft trials, but was itself quickly repressed by the authorities.[58] Another interesting local variation appears in the extensive records of the Venetian Inquisition. Here witchcraft was almost entirely associated with the cunning folk, who were mostly engaged in the sale of love magic and the pursuit of buried treasure.[59] These were traditional activities across Europe, as were the identification of thieves, the recovery of lost property and similar services. Elsewhere they do sometimes appear in the trials of magicians accused of witchcraft, in a rather incidental fashion, but not as a major element. Over much of Italy and the Iberian peninsula the Inquisition seems to have been more concerned with this traditional sorcery and magic than with witchcraft, albeit with considerable differences from region to region. Thus in both Portugal and Sicily there is a mass of information about local magical beliefs, coupled with a failure or reluctance to diabolize them fully, and remarkably lenient punishments (also found in Venice).[60] Despite its formidable reputation and highly sophisticated procedures, the Inquisition plainly did no more than ruffle the surface of popular culture and magical practice. Like every other repressive institution in Europe, its bark was infinitely worse than its bite; it lacked the finances, the personnel, the popular support and perhaps even the will to tackle so vast and amorphous a problem. In addition, most Inquisitors in Mediterranean Europe appear to have adopted a cool and cautious attitude towards witchcraft charges, tending to regard them as one more example of the superstition and ignorance they met on so many fronts. In this respect, as in many others, the popular reputation of the Inquisition risks being wildly misleading.

The use of protective magic could itself be interpreted as a sign of witchcraft. The Scottish witch Isobel Young was charged with attempting to cure her other sick animals by burying a live ox and cat in a pit with a quantity of salt, this being interpreted as a sacrifice to the Devil.[61] The idea of making one animal the recipient of disease transferred from the others was a widespread one that might normally have been regarded as counter-witchcraft; there is much evidence for this in England and elsewhere, while sometimes the ears of the sick animal were burned or buried. In this case the long list of other charges against Isobel explains the diabolical meaning the judges attached to her magical healing. In a similar fashion the treatment of animals with a dog's skull, mentioned earlier, became the starting point for the prosecution of a group of suspects in the Lorraine village of Leintrey, against whom there were many other accusations. In this thoroughly Catholic region the local *procureur fiscal* expressed sentiments that might have come from any reformed cleric, referring to the 'great abuses and superstitions' which might have caused some 'to have recourse to idolatry rather than remaining firm and constant in awaiting the help and confidence of God as we should do in all adversities'. An echo of this came from a witness who said she was ill and only able to walk with a stick, but did not know if the accused was the cause, 'or if it had pleased God to afflict her in this way'. In the course of the trials it emerged that the idea of using the skull came from the local slaughterman, who advised having it blessed to prevent its becoming infected by repeated use. No-one showed the slightest interest in prosecuting the slaughterman, presumably because he had no reputation for witchcraft; this reminds us yet again that ringing declarations of principle are usually a poor guide to actual practice.[62]

Protestant clerics and demonologists were particularly given to such declarations about the link between idolatry and witchcraft. Since they were inclined to see Catholicism itself as in some respects a form of witchcraft, there was a polemical aspect to this emphasis. In many respects, however, it was a natural extension of both their theological and their pastoral concerns. The providentialist view of the world they adopted found its central text in the book of Job; earthly misfortune was a test of faith and those who endured it patiently would be rewarded by God. Their deep hostility to any form of dualism made them insist that the Devil could *only* act with divine permission, despite the severe problems this created over responsibility for evil. As close readers of the Bible, they found it much easier to interpret the scriptural texts on witchcraft as referring to illicit magic, which is indeed their natural sense. Pastors were regularly appalled by the all-pervasive network of superstitious and idolatrous practices on which their flocks relied, whose influence showed no sign of diminishing over the post-Reformation decades. The moral absolutism favoured by the reforming clergy was simply incompatible with what the Essex minister George Gifford called 'Country Divinity', one of whose main tenets was naturally that the ends justified the means. As a result, Protestant writings about witchcraft placed their main emphasis on the spiritual dangers of the wider belief system, whose most obnoxious representatives were the cunning folk. This attitude brought two fundamentally incompatible views of the world into direct collision and left the reformers with the task of propagating a remarkably unattractive doctrine. They had to tell believers that it was sinful to look for relief against their troubles from the helpers on whom they had normally relied. The only concession was that purely natural means of healing might be used, after one had prayed for divine assistance, but this was to exclude most forms of popular therapy. It was actually better to die a pious death than to obtain healing by magic, a position more notable for its logic than its persuasiveness.

Ultimately this Protestant position led to a strange paradox, for the black witches became in one respect the agents of God, inflicting the trials he wished the faithful to undergo. Although this did not absolve them or render them exempt from punishment, the worst sin of the witches was to send their supposed victims to the cunning folk, so that the Cambridge Puritan William Perkins wrote:

> Here observe, that both have a stroke in this action: the bad Witch hurt him, the good healed him; but the truth is, the latter hath done him a thousand times more harm than the former. For the one did only hurt the body, but the Devil by means of the other, though he have left the body in good plight, yet he hath laid fast hold on the soul, and by curing the body, hath killed that.[63]

These commentators understood very well how, in their turn, the healers stimulated witchcraft accusations and therefore felt great concern about the way convictions were often procured through common repute and mistaken ideas about causality. For them witchcraft belief was an integral part of that popular culture they wished to eradicate, a noxious compound of pagan survivals and popish idolatry that constituted a massive barrier to the spread of the true faith. While one must doubt how many, even among the elites, were truly committed to this hopelessly ambitious programme, it clearly represented the official position of the Protestant churches. There is therefore a second paradox, for no important Protestant states actually undertook a major persecution of the cunning folk; indeed, they were probably at greater risk in Catholic Europe. It was still less likely that the judicial machinery would be used against the clients who sought help, despite the obvious corollary that they too were liable to punishment. In England the witchcraft acts, even that of 1604, continued to put the emphasis on black witchcraft, demonstrating that the parliamentary gentry found it easier to sympathize with their tenants than with their pastors. The idea that witches were totally powerless yet were justly punished for their intentions allowed zealous Protestants to support persecution; it was simply too counter-intuitive to command general assent at any level of society. It is highly doubtful whether a majority of the clergy themselves shared the austere official position, let alone contemplated trying to enforce it. Reginald Scot had heard some ministers claim that they had seventeen or eighteen witches in their parish, underlining the extent of this all too predictable failure; local clerics were clearly among those he had in mind when he wrote 'there would be none of those cozening kind of witches, did not witchmongers maintain them, follow them and believe in them and their oracles'.[64] It is easy to understand the attitude Gifford bestowed on a character in his *Dialogue concerning Witches*, who claimed that the local wise woman 'doeth more good in one year than all these scripture men will do so long as they live'.[65]

Catholic positions on such points as the powers of ritual and the operation of the sacraments made it impossible to adopt a similar position *en bloc*. It is all the more striking to find that virtually all the Protestant views are echoed in Catholic demonology, albeit with much less consistency or general agreement. The Lorraine judge Nicolas Remy, for instance, attacked the local peasant belief that eating something taken from the suspect's house would bring about a cure. The story he told of the Devil gloating over luring people into dealings with him made it clear the objection was not that the method did not work; it was – just as with Perkins – that 'we purchase a brief and uncertain bodily health at the price of sure and eternal damnation to our souls'. The only basis on which it was permissible to obtain healing (and even then he worried about possible sacrilege) was by threatening or actually beating the witch, because this did not involve any implicit pact.[66] The eradication of popular superstition was a central aim of the Catholic reform movements of the early modern period, which also stressed individual responsibility and the need for patience in adversity. The hostility between the parish clergy and the cunning folk may even have been intensified to the extent that they were rival claimants for ritual or magical power; priests did not need to make any radical change in their world view to justify action against these interlopers. In France and her borderlands (such as Lorraine and Franche-Comté) magical practitioners seem to have been unusually numerous among convicted witches, although there is no evidence of any deliberate policy behind this trend. Where some kind of statistical test is possible, such cases still account for less than 10 per cent of known prosecutions, so their significance must not be exaggerated. Again there is no reason to suppose that the occasional trial did anything to shake the hold the healers possessed over local society, or that elite attitudes were consistent. Judges were quite likely to ask how individuals should protect themselves against witchcraft – the usual answer was to live a good life, avoid swearing, wash one's hands, cross oneself every morning and commend oneself to God. They might also enquire whether an afflicted person could still be healed, to which the likely response was that once a witch had been arrested he or she became powerless. Jean Arnoulx said that Jean Gelyat le jeune would be ill for six years, until the poison finally left his stomach, but there could be no cure before then. Had Jean asked him for healing earlier he would have given him some black powder to eat, but he could do nothing now he was in the hands of justice.[67]

Much of the clerical writing on witchcraft is full of ambiguities, since the world is described in supernatural terms very like those used by the peasantry; the main difference is the use of the concept of diabolism to distinguish between lawful and illicit sources of power. This technique could at once bestow enormous power on the Devil and justify severe action against those who dealt with him, yet in taking this road the church embroiled itself in a mass of contradictions that made it more the servant than the enemy of popular beliefs. The dialectical confusions which could arise emerge vividly in a book by an early seventeenth-century French casuist, the Capuchin Jean-François de Reims. After identifying a wide range of practices as involving tacit pacts with the Devil, the author goes on to emphasize that men always lose from such contracts with their sworn enemy.

Furthermore he makes another gain when men employ his inventions, by causing them to lose that confidence which they ought to have in his divine providence; if he can he persuades them that he has far more power than God, which is one of the reasons why there are so many witches. But since he never brings any good either to men, or to all that which belongs to them, his cures, whether of beasts or of men, are normally imperfect; indeed he himself often causes their illnesses, when men use his inventions to heal them, something God permits to punish those who avail themselves of his remedies. As proof of my claims, experience makes it very plain that in those regions or villages where use is made of some prayer or other diabolical invention to cure some illness, either of men or animals, that illness will be much commoner in those places than else-where; I can bear personal witness to this. In this fashion the evil spirit gains twice over; for firstly he takes pleasure in tormenting all creatures and after tormenting them, he gives offence to God, by inciting them to make use of the remedies he has invented.

In addition when it is thought probable that some witch has cast a spell on a person or an animal, although it is safer not to make use of such persons, who as faithful followers of their master the Devil seek the ruin of men; nevertheless there is no sin in permitting him, even begging him, to remove the spell, so that the Devil's torments may cease, provided that one believes he will probably do so by lawful means; for if one believed that he would make use of a charm to remove it, then one would not be allowed to ask him. He should be believed to be using a charm if he gives some soup, drink, or anything else to drink or eat; if he uses strange words or gestures, or if he does or commands certain things, which are sufficient to make it clear that he is using a charm; but if he simply unties some ligature, or if he simply removes the spell he has put in a certain place, one can believe that he is not using a charm.[68]

This is very close in some respects to the Protestant position, yet there are vital differences. God and the Devil appear to be omnipresent active forces in the world of this casuist, with no real frontier between the natural and supernatural. The same attitudes are found in some early seventeenth century synodal statutes, like those of 1618 for the diocese of St Malo. These condemned popular festivities which led to drunkenness and immorality, and were particularly severe on the *veillées*, 'assemblies of the night invented by the prince of darkness whose sole aim is to cause the fall of man'. The statutes made much of witchcraft, claiming that those who were afflicted were usually lacking faith or in a state of mortal sin; if the just were affected, God allowed this as a test of their faith. Although here it was said that healing might not be sought, it was lawful to force a witch, even by a beating, to burn or break magical objects, which would prevent future evil.[69] The conflicts which emerge from such expressions of pastoral theology are surely over power and its legitimacy, so that there is little sense of a clash between mutually incompatible views of the world. The clergy did not deny the existence of a surrounding world of spirits, always ready to intervene in terrestrial affairs; they operated a split between good and bad, in order to denounce all rival powers as the works of the Devil, in opposition to God and the saints. The church remained the divine holding company on earth, controlling access not only to the afterlife, but also to protective and curative rituals in the everyday world. Sin, which polluted the order laid down by God, was fitted into this conception, since it might be expected to bring direct retribution against both individuals and communities; misfortune in this world, eternal torment in the next. Therefore the church proceeded against it in direct and indirect ways, attacking the occasions of sin and providing a mechanism for sinners to repent and purge themselves. Both necessarily involved an assertion of the power and authority of the clergy, its right to set norms and enforce them. In all this the problem for the historian is often to distinguish between rhetoric and reality, since the great assault on popular culture rarely lived up to its billing; the small groups of enthusiasts who wanted to enforce it repeatedly found themselves isolated.

Doctors and the supernatural

Alongside the zealous reformers there were always other clerics who employed the standard techniques to detect and attribute witchcraft, or who engaged in various forms of medical practice. They were bitterly criticized on both counts by another professional group regularly involved in witchcraft cases, the physicians. Here too one finds a wide spectrum of opinions, although on balance it does appear that doctors were inclined to prefer natural explanations and to limit the scope for supernatural causes. Their hostility to the cunning folk was naturally just as strong as that felt by the majority of the clergy. Both were clearly reciprocated, for the popular healers often told their clients they were wasting their money with expensive and futile official medicine or claimed that it would prevent the operation of their own cures. When Nicole d'Acraigne hurt her arm in a fall, Mengeatte des Woirelz treated her (successfully, as Nicole thought) with a mixture of vinegar, urine and beeswax, while insisting 'that she must not show it to the surgeons, or they would cripple her arm'.[70] In a similar fashion the administration of the last rites was widely supposed to negate any attempt at healing, putting the recipient into a liminal state where he or she was beyond help. Those rather dubious clerics who acted as witch-doctors themselves naturally shared this belief. When Nicolas Miclin's wife fell ill, he summoned a monk from Hauteseille who specialized in divination to be told that she had been bewitched by Claudatte Antoine, but because she had received the sacraments there was no hope of cure. Miclin remembered the lesson when he fell ill in his turn; instead of sending for the local priest he struggled to Claudatte's house and asked for some white cheese. When she gave him some, together with bread and salt, he found himself cured.[71] Medical and clerical expertise was particularly liable to clash over the vexed question of diabolical possession or obsession. As we have seen, an affliction of this kind did not necessarily imply witchcraft, for possession might be defined as the direct action of the Devil, operating on an individual whose own sins had exposed them to this terrible fate. This theoretical position was naturally a great incentive for the afflicted persons to identify a witch as the agency, not least as a form of self-exculpation; in the most scandalous cases this was a priest, whose apostasy was the ultimate success for satanic influence. The sequence of these major scandals in France reached a climax with the great affair of the Devils of Loudun, where the *curé* Urbain Grandier was burned in 1634. Here, however, the debate was over whether the possession was genuine; although the exorcists and doctors distinguished between the possessed and the obsessed nuns, Grandier was blamed for invading the bodies of them all.[72]

The lurid details and the theatricality of the spectacle put on by the nuns, together with the political machinations in the background, have given Loudun a permanent fascination; in our own time the book by Aldous Huxley has provided the basis for a play by John Whiting, a film by Ken Russell and an opera by Penderecki. Contemporaries too recognized that this was something out of the ordinary, so that the prioress Mère Jeanne des Anges achieved the celebrity she evidently craved in her own lifetime. Yet there was nothing exceptional about the methods attributed to the Devil in such cases. The difference lay in the imagined purposes and the reactions. Suborning priests and disrupting religious houses was seen as a direct attempt to frustrate God's work through his church. The more optimistic interpreted this as a sign that Satan was worried by the gathering pace of religious revival, which he hoped somehow to derail. Exorcisms which involved prominent persons or major political issues could attract an enormous amount of attention and spawn a considerable literature. They were sometimes seen as a peculiar opportunity to gain access to hidden information, a moment when the Devil could be interrogated under compulsion and forced to divulge his supposedly enormous range of knowledge. The results of such approaches were so pathetically small that they became a useful weapon for the sceptics. Everyone agreed the Devil was a trickster; most people also thought that possession might be faked. It was therefore conventional to apply various tests to the possessed, such as the introduction of fake relics and interrogation in other languages. Debate soon became bogged down in conflicting accounts of how such procedures had worked, believers alleging that supernatural power had been plainly in evidence, sceptics that there had been the most blatant fraud. Clerical and medical expertise was deployed on both sides without any clear winners emerging. In Catholic Europe the end result seems to have been much greater caution, with leading figures among the clerical elite anxious to restrain the enthusiasm of local exorcists. It has been suggested (with particular reference to Loudun and some lesser French instances) that these spectacular episodes discredited persecution more generally and there is plainly some truth in this view.[73] On the other hand, an emerging consensus on the matter is not visible until witchcraft trials at a more popular level were in sharp decline, so the causal links must work both ways.

The religious and political overtones of some of these cases gave some people powerful motives to look for evidence of fraud. When French Catholic zealots in the 1590s tried to use the demoniac Marthe Brossier to criticize the policies of King Henri IV, an impressive body of doctors was mobilized by the government to declare her an impostor.[74] This case was used by Anglican clerics engaged in the contemporary English debate over exorcism, who persuaded the now increasingly sceptical King James VI and I to take up their concerns once he arrived in England. The exposure of fraudulent possession through witchcraft, as in the 1605 case of Anne Gunter, was on occasion extended to witchcraft more generally; sharp questioning of accusers could reveal that the malice lay with them rather than the witch. In the celebrated Leicester case of 1616, the King himself established through his own questioning that nine women had been hung because of accusations by a boy of thirteen, whose simulated fits in the courtroom impressed the judges and onlookers.[75] In France the Loudun case evoked ambiguous responses, but in the 1640s blatant faking by 'possessed' nuns at Louviers in Normandy discredited them, contributing to the developing current of elite scepticism.[76] The struggle over the possession cases of the 1610s in the Spanish Netherlands, referred to earlier, had rather similar effects. Although the arguments over the boundaries of supernatural and natural power were impossible to resolve satisfactorily, the continuing debate itself tended to act as a check on excessive credulity. When magical beliefs were realized in such concrete and extreme forms, their internal contradictions emerged with unusual clarity, so that there was a marked tendency for them to autodestruct. Groups of possessed nuns would display ever greater wildness and indecency, while their exorcists took refuge behind increasingly flimsy and implausible claims. There were two obvious dangers which led external authority to clamp down on such outbreaks. A surge of imitative behaviour might threaten to run amok in other religious houses, and too much credulity by the exorcists must eventually make them ridiculous. Such awareness does not seem to have crossed national boundaries very readily, however, so that lessons about the dangers of taking certain kinds of evidence seriously had to be learned separately, or even relearned in the same place after an interval.

These arguments about the nature and limits of the supernatural were ultimately bound to end in various kinds of stalemate, for both the terms of the contest and the evidence were too slippery to permit satisfactory resolutions. There cannot be the slightest doubt, on the other hand, that the clergy were right in seeing a fundamental association between witchcraft and the cunning folk. They were indissoluble parts of the same belief system across most of Europe, feeding off one another and often giving the same individuals dangerously mixed reputations. In the millennia-old history of witchcraft beliefs this symbiosis must always have been absolutely crucial, energizing the whole structure and providing the mechanisms for local mediation. When clerical reformers identified this enemy and tried to attack it they overreached very seriously, for they had little to offer in its place. Nor could they ever persuade the ruling groups as a whole that this was a battle worth fighting; an attitude of amused disdain was more likely to emerge than a great moral crusade. As will become plain later, in reality the relatively brief persecution of witches drew heavily on just those beliefs, practices and people the reformers wanted to eliminate. If the system of thought they represented was weakened over the early modern period, this was far less through frontal attack than because it was undermined by a range of social and intellectual changes on a much wider front – but that is another story.

CHAPTER IV

THE PROJECTION
OF EVIL

Charity and vengeance

IN THEIR ACCOUNTS OF dealings with the Devil, witches placed decisive emphasis on the idea of vengeance. According to the Franche-Comtois judge Henri Boguet, the Devil told them at the sabbat, 'Avenge yourselves or you die'.[1] Elizabeth Stile of Windsor said of herself and her confederates that 'if any had angered them, they would go to their spirits and say, "Such-a-one hath angered me, go do them this mischief" and for their hire would give them a drop of their own blood; and presently the party was plagued by some lamentable casualty'.[2] Unmotivated malignancy was hardly ever suggested by witnesses and was almost as rare in the confessions. Witches were essentially reactive, responding to acts of aggression or hostility from others. Like snakes, they had to be provoked before they would strike. Although there was no absolute logical necessity for this general view, it must reveal the deep structural patterns of witchcraft belief. Whether from choice, compulsion or perhaps because he could not act without God's consent, the Devil only sent his agents into action where there was disharmony and enmity. It was these failures of charity and communal unity which caused people to apostasize and become witches in the first place, as the mythology of the pact showed. The elaborate rituals designed to preserve internal harmony were evidently fallible, despite their emphasis on identifying and reconciling disputes. The idea that witches could not take Easter communion, hiding the host rather than swallowing it, symbolized this gulf between ideals and reality. It also constituted another formal inversion, with the sabbat replacing reconciliation, the central meaning of communion, by vengeance. Behind this there seems to lie the fundamental idea that witchcraft only operated where protection failed and where punishment was due. If the more austere Protestant versions of demonology sometimes demurred, that was only another sign of how remote they were from popular attitudes. These writers agreed with everyone else, however, in portraying local society as riven by feuds and disputes, building up tensions that were the context for both the accusations, and the performance, of witchcraft.

Feuds, in the sense of entrenched family rivalries, do not appear to have been a major factor in the great majority of the original witchcraft accusations. Although the possibility of widespread and successful concealment must be envisaged, this is most unlikely for several reasons. The various legal systems were very sensitive to the dangers of false accusations, against which they provided certain safeguards. The jury was one, in an age when knowledge of the accused and the community was considered an advantage. The inquisitorial justice widely used in Europe included specific provision for the accused to challenge witnesses on the very point of previous enmity. Objections of this type, which were surprisingly rare, hardly ever included suggestions of anything resembling feuds between families, as opposed to personal enmities. Feuds were really antithetical to witchcraft in any case; they were public and predictable, between people who would avoid contact with one another. The families concerned would unite to protect their members, if necessary by launching a counter-accusation. When hostility was already known there were no expectations of good neighbourliness to be confounded, no reasons for anyone to feel guilt. Open enemies were fundamentally different from secret ones, so witchcraft was not readily suspected as a weapon in their quarrels, while it was unlikely most people would use it cynically as a means to discredit others. Apart from the dangers of retaliation, such actions were not compatible with a genuine and pervasive belief in witchcraft as an everyday reality. A high proportion of the clear instances of factional struggles being worked out through witchcraft accusations are associated with higher social groups and the special machinery of demonic possession, as at Loudun and Salem. There are some other interesting cases in which conspiracies were detected that will be discussed in a later chapter, but the implication of these is that such attempts frequently ended in failure.

When it comes to the quarrels and social situations involved, one can for once identify typical patterns across most of Europe. Witchcraft functioned in predictable, even stereotyped ways within a specific social context, that of the early modern village. Normally this constituted a grouping of a few hundred people who lived in conditions we cannot readily imagine. There were no shops, metalled roads, or public services, with the church serving as the only public building. This was a world of pedlars and local markets, of dirt tracks, wells, privies and fire or candlelight. Houses were damp, smelly and uncomfortable, sheltering animals alongside people. The members of neighbouring households, whose living standards were rarely above subsistence level, were virtually forced to interact daily, through small exchanges of goods and services; this was a largely unquantified system of exchange which was nevertheless supposed to balance out over the long term. In a generally poor society mutual aid was the norm, providing an elementary safety net for those in temporary difficulties. The community was responsible for all its members, at least in theory; this was the principle on which the authorities tried to make vagrants return to their original parishes to be supported. Regular beggars and recipients of alms were a recognizable group, albeit one with very elastic boundaries which responded to both seasonal and annual fluctuations. A much larger category was that of the semi-dependent poor, clinging on as best they could to their modest assets and relying on an economy of makeshifts. These people were a periodic burden on neighbours hardly better off than themselves who were not always in a position to help. It was entirely natural that the idea of charity as a central religious and social value should be very deeply imbedded in European society, for without it many families or individuals could not have survived. In the traditional religion it was the classic means of salvation for the rich, whose sins were otherwise thought so heavy. Protestantism may have scorned the whole system of redemption through good works but still placed great emphasis on social duties; in any case popular attitudes only changed very slowly, well behind formal doctrines.

The very intensity of the charitable impulse in early modern society helped to create serious tensions for all participants. There were no clear boundaries to what might be demanded or should be given, nor was it easy to see how there could be. Assumptions of reciprocity were inherently vague and only likely to be fulfilled in the long run, if at all. Ownership itself was a tenuous concept in a world of common fields and pasture, shared labour and innumerable residual feudal and seigneurial rights. Communal decisions regulated many aspects of life, yet the community was far from being egalitarian or democratic. Social relations were consequently full of ambiguities, reflecting latent conflicts which were very hard to resolve in societies of this type, where harmony was regarded as a normal state and there were few accepted ways of settling persistent clashes of interest. The charitable and communal aspects of life had to coexist with other highly competitive and disruptive elements; these societies, highly stable though they may appear overall to the modern eye, were in constant flux at street level. Peasants and artisans formed intricately differentiated groups, even if it was only in terms of relative deprivation; awareness of these gradations must have been heightened when ruin and famine stalked so close behind. Individuals and families contended all the time for status, power and resources. At the same time they accepted a degree of responsibility to the losers, who were entitled to some protection in hard times. There was a sense in which this communal attitude existed as a form of early insurance policy, for only the wealthiest were safe from the economic disaster which accident or prolonged sickness would bring. Everyone else had reason to think that today's charity to a neighbour might become tomorrow's charity to oneself. This has been characterized as the 'good faith' economy, one in which personal ties were constantly reaffirmed through everyday inter-action. Minor gifts and services were the small change of the system, whose larger denominations came in the form of shared rituals and formal ideology.

As will emerge in a later chapter, powerful forces were putting great pressure on local society in the early modern period. Economic and demographic change threatened the whole network of precarious balances and understandings on which it rested. These processes must have intensi-fied the tensions and disputes which gave rise to accusations of witchcraft, so that their interactions need to be examined with some care. For the moment, however, it is important to recognize that virtually all the characteristic types of friction might be found in any agrarian society, even a fairly prosperous and stable one. The occasional witness depositions surviving from the fifteenth and early sixteenth centuries appear little different, in essentials, from those of the peak decades of persecution a century or more later. The specific charges in these documents follow a simple dyadic pattern; there had been a quarrel followed by a misfortune, with the latter being interpreted as the hidden revenge of the witch. Within this general scheme a second pattern frequently appears that may be described as the refusal-guilt syndrome. The original dispute – often very muted – occurred when the suspect asked for a small gift or service from a neighbour, who refused it. The person who failed to give, however, was well aware of the breach of neighbourly duty and convention involved, even when there were good immediate reasons for the refusal. Turning others away was implicitly an aggressive act, placing one's own needs first and making the refuser feel guilty; this aggression was then projected into the other person, who was expected to be angry and resentful after being refused. In effect, the victims' own anger and wish to attack would seem intolerable to them, with the projection operating as an unconscious defence mechanism. If some misfortune followed, suspicion would naturally fall on the person with the assumed grudge – these intuitive suspicions were felt all the more strongly both because the grievance could so often be seen as justified and because the feelings imputed to the witch were internal to the accuser.

Many of the examples given in previous chapters have already revealed this process at work, so a single illustration will suffice here, albeit one which reflects the complexity of these relationships. Claudette Dabo was peculiarly unlucky to be tried at all, because a year earlier she had married for the third time, at the age of sixty, and thus managed to move a mile or two away from the village of Robache where her reputation was so bad. Among other stories, there was evidently a powerful rumour that she had turned herself into a wolf to kill and eat a child. Unfortunately for her, when her fellow-suspect Jehennon le Renard was convicted she implicated Claudette, whose previous neighbours were then called upon to testify. There is no sign that they would have bothered to pursue her on their own account, once she had disappeared from their immediate view. One of the witnesses, Marguitte Colas, described three separate episodes. Around St John's day some two years earlier the accused had come to offer her some hay, saying 'that she wanted to share it with those who made gifts to her such as milk or other alms', but Marguitte refused to take it or give her anything in exchange, to which Claudette replied 'that she was very haughty'. Her two cows then lost their milk and had to be sold, over which she suspected the accused in view of her reputation and this refusal. Around Christmas they had killed a fat pig, but when Claudette came to the house she did not offer her any meat, intending to give her some soup and 'boudins' the following Sunday. Marguitte believed the witch's resentment was the cause of a sudden illness which immediately afflicted her three-month-old child; this was so violent they did not believe she would live through the night. When Claudette returned to the house the witness told her how the child had become sick, to which she replied by asking if she suspected her of giving the illness. Marguitte responded 'she did not really do so, but many other people did not trust her over it', after which the child promptly recovered. When the plague arrived in her village of Robache, Marguitte went to lodge with the accused to avoid it, while her husband supplied her with food and wine. Claudette usually drank most of the wine, so her lodger removed to another house, but within a week became as if possessed; when the accused heard of this she said it would not have happened if she had stayed in her house, which made Marguitte believe she was the cause of her illness.[3] The two women obviously knew one another very well, so that their quarrels merely punctuated the regular exchange of goods and services. Theirs was a complex reciprocal relationship in which offence was repeatedly given, but reconciliation was sought with equal regularity.

The apparent simplicity of the general pattern risks being misleading, therefore. To start with, fuller narratives of the type just quoted emphasize how extensive social relations were, so that the testimony only selects a few significant events at most from the multiple contacts between the parties. The scope for petty conflicts of this type was so vast that there must have been huge numbers of such episodes which led nowhere, compared with a small proportion which ended up as part of local gossip, or even as testimony in court. Unfortunately there is virtually no evidence on which we can begin to assess whether the visible cases are merely the tip of a vast iceberg of latent accusations, or whether there was something exceptional about the encounters recorded in the trials. In other words, was the explanation of witchcraft a likely or an exceptional response, in cases where the rejection or dispute was not followed by angry and threatening gestures? A great deal surely depended on the reputation and behaviour of the would-be recipient, as it did on the subsequent course of events, but we lack any comparable group of non-witchcraft cases that might provide a control. All that can be said is that there were some witnesses who, by their own account, only made a hostile interpretation retrospectively, even when a prosecution had begun. Claude Dieudegnon, the mayor of Reillon, blamed Nicolas Raimbault for the deaths of two horses and a fine cow, but added 'at the time of the said disasters he did not think of the accused at all, and it was only since hearing of his evil fame that he had become of that opinion'.[4] Our inability to answer this crucial question about typicality is particularly frustrating, for it creates a curious paradox. Modern scholarship has identified these ongoing neighbourhood disputes as the pivot around which the whole social reality of witchcraft turned. This discovery (by Keith Thomas and Alan Macfarlane) brought the picture suddenly into focus, making blurred outlines and interconnections clear. In any case for which detailed evidence survives we can predict with some confidence that it will be organized around a series of little narratives of this kind. Yet this pattern does not constitute more than the beginning of a general explanation; it bears roughly the same relationship to the whole as knowing how to win a trick does to proficiency at the game of bridge. The trick is the basic unit which determines how the game works, but only yields its full meaning in the context of a range of broader skills and strategies.

At first it did seem as if a more general interpretation of witchcraft could be built around the refusal of charity, with specific reference to the apparently special case of England. Here the general sixteenth-century increase in poverty and vagrancy, whose broader European causes and consequences will be discussed in a later chapter, had a particular outcome. Political and social anxieties, combined with Protestant views about good works, led to the institution of a national poor law system in the 1590s. Here was clear evidence for the depth of concern about a growing social problem, coinciding with the peak in trials and bringing about a major shift from private to organized charity. In this argument, witchcraft persecution developed out of social relations under intense strain, with all the attendant confusion in people's sense of social duty, then declined as a new set of arrangements reduced the tension. While there are clearly some significant and valid relationships here, they do not constitute an adequate explanation. The poor law system long remained an alternative rather than a substitute for less formal relief and the changeover to new practices and attitudes came far too late to account for declining persecution. Moreover, the implicit contrast between English trials inspired from below and Continental ones driven by the obsessions of the ruling elites has proved false for the great majority of cases. European witches may have ended up confessing to a more elaborate diabolism, but their accusers were almost exclusively concerned with quarrels and misfortunes very like those alleged against their English counterparts. This is true of many Catholic regions where concepts of charity underwent no major change. Although very detailed analysis may yet reveal interesting regional patterns, with variations in the styles and subjects of disputes, it is the similarities which appear more striking than the differences. The chief qualification to this view is that the refusal-guilt syndrome may have been more prevalent in England than elsewhere, suggesting that charity was a particularly difficult issue for English villagers of the late sixteenth century and may have given rise to a high proportion of accusations. This would imply that there was a relative rather than absolute difference between the English and the Continental experience, with market values displacing communal ones unusually fast in England.

The origins of such accusations were already brilliantly described by the Kentish gentleman Reginald Scot as early as 1584; all he missed was the specific theme of guilt felt by the accusers. Writing specifically of old women, he claimed

> These miserable wretches are so odious unto all their neighbours, and so feared, as few dare offend them or deny them anything they ask . . . These go from house to house and from door to door for a pot full of milk, yeast, drink, pottage, or some such relief, without the which they could hardly live . . . It falleth out many times that neither their necessities nor their expectation is answered or served in those places where they beg or borrow, but rather their lewdness is by their neighbours reproved. And further, in tract of time the witch waxeth odious and tedious to her neighbours, and they again are despised and despited of her, so as sometimes she curseth one, and sometimes another, and that from the master of the house, his wife, children, cattle, etc. to the little pig that lieth in the stye. Thus in process of time they have all displeased her, and she hath wished evil luck unto them all, perhaps with curses and imprecations made in form. Doubtless at length some of her neighbours die or fall sick, or some of their children are visited with diseases that vex them strangely, as apoplexies, epilepsies, convulsions, hot fevers, worms, etc., which by ignorant parents are supposed to be the vengeance of witches . . . The witch on the other side expecting her neighbours' mischances, and seeing things sometimes come to pass according to her wishes, curses, and incantations (for Bodin himself confesseth that not above two in a hundred of their witchings or wishings take effect), being called before a Justice, by due examination of the circumstances is driven to see her imprecations and desires, and her neighbours' harms and losses to concur, and as it were, to take effect; and so confesseth that she, as a goddess, hath brought such things to pass.[5]

This picture was reinforced by several other English writers; in the 1650s Thomas Ady even hinted at the guilty conscience of the man who refused charity;

> for, saith he, such an old man or woman came lately to my door, and desired some relief, and I denied it, and God forgive me, my heart did

rise against her at that time, my mind gave me she looked like a Witch, and presently my Child, my Wife, my Self, my Horse . . . or somewhat was thus and thus handled.[6]

Although the Continental demonologists may have tended to get more excited about the exotic details of the pact and the sabbat, in France at least the themes of poverty and begging were still well to the fore. Pierre de Lancre found an ingenious way of linking the more general evil practised at the sabbat with the crimes of individual witches, as part of a diabolical recruitment drive. The general aim behind the destruction of animals and crops was to help the Devil attack mankind. 'For when people see themselves reduced to starvation, after the Devil has removed the fruits of the earth, they commit a thousand wickednesses to live, and Satan seeing them in this desperate need, forces them to beg his help, and from beggars turns them finally into witches.'[7] Bodin had earlier produced a complex position of his own. After stating 'the witches confess that the charitable person cannot be harmed by their spells, even if he is otherwise wicked', he went on to suggest that a failure to be charitable had the contrary effect

> This is why the witches who are compelled by Satan to do evil, to kill and poison men and animals on pain of perpetual torment, when they have no enemies on whom they can take vengeance, go begging and anyone who has anything to give and refuses them will be in danger, as long as he does not know they are witches. For the witch has no greater power than that over the person who gives alms knowing that he gives to a witch. And one must be very careful not even to give to those who are reputed so; but any who refuse them alms, not knowing them to be witches, will have great difficulty escaping unscathed, as has often been proved. And in truth when I was at Poitiers for the Grands Jours of 1567, as one of the *substituts* of the *procureur général*, I heard of two pitiful and poor witches, who asked for charity at a rich house. When they were refused they bewitched the house and all the inhabitants contracted rabies and died mad. It was not the cause for God to deliver them into the power of Satan and his agents the witches, but since they were wicked in other ways and had no pity for the poor, God had no mercy for them.[8]

In Lorraine Nicolas Remy wrote of the witches that 'they are for the most part beggars, who support life on the alms they receive'.[9] This was factually incorrect, for only a small proportion of the accused in the duchy were in this position, but most were poor enough to be potential or occasional recipients of charity. Even if the stereotype of the old beggar-woman as witch was not strictly correct, its prominence in such descriptions is suggestive.

Communal bonds and communal friction

The sheer range of disputes which emerges from the trial records in both Britain and Europe makes it plain that communal unity and values represented an ideal which was fairly remote from the reality. Perhaps such concepts had a peculiarly important function just because of this gap, acting as a counterweight to forces which constantly threatened to subvert community in all its aspects. If this was the case, then the public value system must have increased the tensions felt by individuals as they struggled to reconcile their personal needs with wider social obligations. On the whole it was the aggressors in conflicts who were also the subsequent accusers, often reporting reactions along the lines of 'you will regret this'. Claudon Colas Colin warned Jennon Etienne to keep her geese out of his meadow or he would have them killed by his servants. She passed before his horses and held out her arms, whereupon one of them fell down, dying a few hours later. Next day his servant was ordered to chase away any geese; when he met her she said 'you and your master will repent of what you are doing', after which another horse died suddenly. Claudon was sure this was her doing if her long reputation as a witch was correct.[10] The pattern is so strong that it must be functionally related to the social meaning of witchcraft, yet there was nothing which made it logically essential in individual cases; the question of whether there were strong psychological reasons to expect it must also be asked. The ill-will might also be generated by the witches themselves, whose anti-social nature was allegedly revealed by selfish and quarrelsome behaviour. The suspect who infringed communal norms, then reacted angrily when challenged, was thus capable of being seen as a servant of the Devil.

A case in point is that of Jean Gregoire Mathis of Bertrimoutier. He was denounced to the chapter for failing to take Easter communion or confess and being generally regarded as an atheist (in itself atheism would have been a capital offence, but it was virtually never prosecuted at this social level). When he was arrested, a series of witnesses testified to his aggressive and disruptive behaviour. Jean Didier Cunin claimed that as long as he had known him he had made 'crazy deals', then insulted those concerned and often gone to court. Cunin had heard from his brother-in-law Jean Charpentier that he had reproached him about failing to do Easter duty, but when he told him to go and apologize to the *Grand Prévôt* Mathis replied 'that the devil might carry him off if he went there', since when he had not been seen in church. Claudatte Gregoire claimed to have been told by several that Mathis had threatened to tire out her and her husband (his brother) by lawsuits until they were poor; this had happened and now their children had to go begging. He had deprived them of their inheritance by keeping various pieces of property, while her husband had had a near-fatal fall under a cart when in his service and suspected Mathis of causing this.[11] At the emotional level the quarrel and the feelings it left behind had their own significance, which can be partly separated from the often debatable question of who was to blame. Real aggression and projected aggression are not identical, but it would be hard to draw any clear line between the ways they are felt by participants. As far as the witnesses were concerned, they had provoked the witch just as effectively whatever the rights and wrongs of the original dispute. Although guilty feelings do make sense as a driving force contributing to most accusations, the predominance of such situations may just reflect the generally disadvantaged position of the witches. In other words, there was something of a vicious circle; weaker and poorer members of the community made more demands on their neighbours, risked being rejected or treated with less respect by them and could only attempt to defend themselves by displays of aggression. In the process they made themselves vulnerable to witchcraft charges, yet these only crystallized around a tiny minority of the potential victims.

Here we see another problem with this style of interpretation. The more functional and 'natural' witchcraft beliefs and persecution are made to seem, the more they become a mere expression of the social tensions identified behind them. There is a threat of slipping into a rather mechanistic approach, so that – for instance – fear of witchcraft becomes a useful check on selfish behaviour by the rich and powerful. The true situation was much less tidy or balanced, although such incidental effects may have been widespread and did indeed feed back into the complex networks of causation. In some respects this was fortunate, for if accusations had been freely generated by the kind of antagonisms we find in the trials, then persecution would have been far more intense. The links to misfortune, described in an earlier chapter, were so flexible that every quarrel posed a serious danger. As already pointed out, whenever possible witnesses picked out a temporal coincidence; the more rapid the onset of sickness or accident, the clearer the proof. There were alternative ways of making the same point; the same time of day a week later might also be cited as a significant link. In the last resort, however, lengthy delays before any effect was felt were no obstacle to accusations. Medical practitioners, slaughtermen and their like commonly aided and abetted the popular notion that any strange or sudden malady might be caused by occult power. The dangers become even clearer when one considers the fashion in which the testimonies illustrate virtually the whole of early modern existence. The range of disputes recorded is so wide that few common causes of ill-will can have been omitted.

This all-pervasive sense of friction in communal life needs to be balanced by an awareness that ill-will was as much a creation of fantasy as of external reality. There is no reason why one should automatically disbelieve the accused when they protested their lack of animosity against at least some of their accusers. Marion le Masson's heartfelt plea carries conviction; she said that the witnesses 'seemed to know more about her actions than she did herself, and that she would have had much greater reason to kill her husband during the said quarrel and so many others they had, even during the period of three years during which he was ill (if she had been a witch) than to cause the deaths of her good friends with whom she never quarrelled, yet of whose deaths she now heard herself suspected'.[12] If many charges represented the projection of inner feelings of guilt or hostility, they are unlikely to have required much corroborative evidence from the chosen targets. To take one common sequence of events, that when a young mother whose child was sickening blamed older women who had tried to help, we may reasonably suspect that repressed feelings of hostility towards her own mother played an important part, stimulated by an unconscious conviction that the mother should be there to help. Such situations were of course very likely to generate hostility, if the accusations became known and were thus to some extent self-validating. It was hardly suprising that witches quite often claimed to have acted against their victims out of anger because they had been defamed. Chrestienne Barret was one of those who explained her seduction by the Devil in this way; it happened when she was angry because some were calling her witch.[13] There were many other scenarios in which the need to explain a misfortune might link up with unconscious resentments to 'fix' suspicion on a particular individual. Although trial depositions are not very forthcoming on such matters, the bewitched may well have shown a propensity to create inner worlds peopled by powerful persecuting figures. How far the representation of God and the Devil by early modern preachers and religious writers actively encouraged such dangerous fantasies remains a fascinating, if ultimately unanswerable, question.

The emphasis on ill-will can also be related to the 'good faith' economy, with its varied strategies for building up moral and practical credit among neighbours. The point has been admirably made by Annabel Gregory:

> It may be suggested that an emphasis on the destructive power of evil will through witchcraft is the obverse of the belief that the goodwill of others is essential for the achievement of survival or success. If someone feels that they need to make a considerable investment in personal ties in order to protect their commercial interests, this may predispose them to see commercial failure as in some circumstances due to the ill will of others. If such a suspicion gets articulated as an accusation of witchcraft, it can then be seen as some kind of negative statement about traditional obligations – that they are being abandoned, abused or imposed too strongly.[14]

Another way to conceptualize the position is to contrast traditional or multi-stranded relationships with a somewhat idealized market economy. In the first, every transaction is a complex one, with the parties relating to one another on several different levels; people display a natural preference for dealing where the ties of mutual obligation are thickest. The ideal market, on the other hand, is built around exchanges between strangers, simply determined by price and convenience. In our own day using the supermarket rather than the corner shop may help drive the latter out of business, but even those who see the connection are unlikely to be haunted by guilt. Villagers who declined to enter into collaborative ploughing arrangements, rejected offers for their hay or refused to sell piglets to a neighbour were in a very different situation. However trivial in themselves, these actions were capable of being interpreted as denials of neighbourly feeling, implicitly rejecting any sense of mutual obligation. Although individuals were perfectly capable of justifying themselves with claims that they got better value or a better price elsewhere, thereby appealing to the values of the market rather than the neighbourhood, their unease was often palpable. George le Remendeur testified against Barbelline Chaperey, telling how some nine years before she had been getting milk from his wife for her child; at this point his father added three cows to the three he already had and he decided to seek a larger profit by using his milk otherwise. He told his wife to stop selling it, so next day she warned Barbelline of this – yet she came again next day and when refused asked if she had not paid before, at which his wife agreed she had. The same evening his best cow stopped giving milk and subsequently died. When the local executioner was called in to cut it up and see what it had died of, he found its organs all burned, while most of the flesh was black, so he told George it was 'true witchcraft'; he subsequently lost all the other cows and four oxen, over which he suspected her.[15] Unwillingness to accept commercial values is still less surprising when one recognizes that early modern markets were very erratic, dominated by shortages and gluts; it was impossible to see them as neutral or mechanical. Market movements themselves were commonly blamed on human agency, with middlemen stigmatized as monopolists who created artificial shortages. This idea also appeared in witchcraft trials, with the stories that the rich wanted to spoil the crops by making hail so that they would profit from high prices. The most important market of all, that for grain, was routinely controlled by both state and local authorities, using a clutch of regulations. The relationship between market and communal values was thus a highly contentious issue, at both the theoretical and the practical level.

There were many other respects in which interdependence and friction were closely related. The widespread practice of sending adolescents and young adults of both sexes into service in other households provides one example. Refusal to take a neighbour's child, or ill-treatment of servants or apprentices, could easily generate animosity and feelings of guilt. No fewer than fifty-seven neighbours testified against Claudon Bregeat, who emerges as something of a busybody, pushing herself forward as a healer while trying to get her six children established and complaining when they were not treated as she hoped. Among the witnesses was Jean des Vaulx, who told how seven years earlier her son Jean had been in his service while he was teaching him the trade of baker and pastry cook, but he was unsatisfactory – selling goods without keeping any record. He beat him for this, then his mother appeared and took him away. The wife of the witness, who was heavily pregnant, ran after them and objected that while he was in their service, he had no right to leave and they were entitled to punish him. The women quarrelled and pushed one another; the same day his wife had a stillborn child and was ill for more than three months before she died, always saying that Claudon had made her sick. Whatever Claudon's faults, she was a caring parent who was evidently distraught when her young daughter was induced to tell how they had visited the sabbat together. Her reaction was to abandon her own defence – quite determined up to that point – and admit that she was a witch, but devise a number of reasons why her daughter's account must be a childish fantasy, since she had never given her to the Devil.[16] Claudon's confession sealed her own fate; whether it saved her daughter we do not know.

In the St Osyth trials, one of Brian Darcy's deponents, Robert Sannever, told how 'about 15 years past, there dwelt with him the daughter of Elizabeth Eustace, and that for some lewd speeches and behaviour by her done . . . he used some threatening speeches unto her, being his servant'. After she had gone home and told her mother, the next day as he sat by the fire his face was suddenly twisted strangely. He was cured by a smart blow on the head by 'one of skill', on whose advice he immediately discharged the girl. Robert Sannever did not abandon 'threatening speeches' against Mother Eustace, however, for twelve years later his brother-in-law thought himself bewitched by her, and Robert said 'that if that be so, he then wished a spit red hot and in her buttocks'. When this was reported to the witch, she allegedly said 'His wife is with child, and lusty, but it will be otherwise with her than he looketh for', words which were remembered when she fell ill, to die after her delivery. After such a violent and specific expression of ill-will, one might well feel guilty and expect vengeance to be taken.[17] Other occasions led to bad feeling and open quarrels. As already shown, the appointment and support of herdsmen, or the discharge of their duties, appear in numerous depositions. Loans to neighbours might have been expected to cement friendship, but too often became the occasion for bitter resentment when repayment was demanded. Another charge against Claudette Dabo, made by Thomas Vagnier of Robache, was that around two years earlier he had been obliged by his need for money to seek the payment of eight écus which her then husband Jean George owed him. She did not want to pay, while there had also been a quarrel over some damage done by her husband's horses. Although he wrote off a small proportion of the debt, she told him he would repent. Shortly afterwards two pigs worth fifty francs became blind, then died, which he believed had been her witchcraft.[18]

Borrowers sometimes failed to return objects as well as money; more frequently it was the refusal to lend such things as tools which led to trouble. Mengeon Renouard's servant Catherine explained that some two months earlier Jean Jacques Gerardin had asked to borrow a sickle from Jean Lyenard, her fellow servant, but he had refused, saying he would not lend it to his own father for fear it would be spoiled. Jean only said 'in God's name', but about six weeks later Lyenard became violently ill and went home, asking her to tell the accused that he was a witch and had made him fatally ill – he died ten days later.[19] Tax and tithe assessment within the community could pose ticklish problems, generating claims of unfairness and fraud. Claudotte de Ranfaing claimed that when her husband had been collector of the *taille* Jacotte Raon had reproached him with taxing them too highly, 'then went back into her house, threatening and muttering between her teeth', shortly after which he had part of the fingers of one hand cut off.[20] The allocation of work, and its satisfactory performance, was another flashpoint, alongside refusals to perform tasks like ploughing and carting. Jennon Micquel recounted how around Christmas some five years earlier her late husband and Jean Perrin had been threshing together, when her husband told Jean that he had been asked to thresh for the mayor Demenge Parmentier of Mazières. Jean seemed envious and asked if he was sure he was able to go to do as he had promised. The same night her husband became suddenly ill and told her 'Jennon, I am very ill, I am bewitched, by Jean Perrin's doing', adding that Perrin was envious because he had much more work than him. He had felt ill since drinking with him the same evening and died in five days, maintaining the charge to the last.[21]

It is hardly surprising to find socio-economic relationships at the root of most of the disputes which underlay accusations; in a society where subsistence was so precarious this was surely inevitable. Apart from those already mentioned, such grievances could include the enforcement of regulations governing forests, animal husbandry, gleaning, selling salt and textile production. Trespass of various kinds saw fields and crops being damaged, wood and fruit stolen, straying animals injured or killed and so forth. Such conflicts reappeared endlessly in the depositions, in a thoroughly predictable fashion, so one example will serve. Catherine Colas told of an occasion when the servant guarding their animals was called off by a neighbour to help with his ploughing, after which the animals strayed, damaging crops belonging to Mengette Estienne. Next day the best milking cow, which usually gave a full pail of milk, would give none; after three days Catherine visited the suspect, accusing her of being the cause, then adding 'that she advised her to put it right, otherwise she would complain and have a judicial inspection of the cow, so that she might have her taken as a witch'. Mengeotte objected strongly to this accusation, but that evening the cow protested vigorously and gave milk as before.[22] Although local institutions provided for arbitration and restitution in such cases, attempts to use them might themselves prove contentious. In the case of Claude Mengeon Grivel, the assistant to the mayor of Clefcy, Adam Thiebault, explained that the previous year there had been a dispute at the local festival that he interposed to settle, but Claude was angry and spoke disrespectfully of his office, so he took him before the mayor. After this his daughter Dieudonnée sickened and died, which he thought was Thiebault's doing, and of which he had accused him directly.[23] Bidding for positions which involved election or competition was bound to leave unsuccessful rivals with a grievance. Herdsmen were prominent here, but any kind of local office might be involved, including such appointments as midwife and tithe-collector. Collate Andreu testified that some eleven years earlier Nicolas Claudon had been the forester for a particular wood, but was deprived of his post for not performing the duties properly, to be replaced by her husband. Six weeks later the latter suddenly became ill and died within a week, saying 'the cruel envy, if he had to die for that'. Later she heard that Colas had said her husband had wanted to be forester, but would not be it for long; in conjunction with his reputation this made her believe he might have caused the illness.[24]

Rivalries of various kinds naturally show up in the background to accusations. Craftsmen and traders were particularly resentful of inter-lopers who threatened their livelihood. Ulriot Colas Ulriot was accused of bewitching Claudon Girard, his ex-apprentice, who had set up as a rival shoemaker then became possessed; he later offered to cure him, by keeping him awake all night, but failed.[25] Such professionals as millers, bakers, butchers and their like quarrelled among themselves, but also had equivocal relationships with their customers. Annon Chauderat confessed that she killed the butcher Mongeon Failly, because he refused to sell her meat on credit.[26] Sales or mortgages of land were often tense affairs, particularly when they carried the implication that one party to the transaction was rising at the expense of the other. Behind this there lay that ultimate fear of losing position, status and security. Jennon Galdri-mey reported that ten years earlier her husband had sold a garden to Antoine Jean Marchal out of necessity, then decided the price was too low and reclaimed it. Antoine's wife Jeanotte had been furious, wanting to beat the witness, stamping her foot on the ground and saying 'that her affairs would go well, as straight as a sickle', and making her bring three pence she said were missing. They lost seven or eight cattle, all they had, in addition to a horse, which she believed was Jeanotte's witchcraft.[27] Among the less fortunate, beggars competed with one another, while being ready to avenge themselves on the officials who managed local charity. Ydatte Moine confessed that she had killed another widow and her small son who were begging with her five years earlier because the woman was 'more skilful in getting alms' than she was.[28] When they confessed, some witches did express regret at having supposedly harmed people who had actually been charitable to them, but this does not mean there had not been genuine friction in such cases. Claudon la Romaine confessed that she had used her powder to kill Thiebault Dorin, the governor of the hospital, because her weekly allowance had been reduced by two sols. She now realized that the responsibility for this lay with the administrators, while Dorin had always been good to her, so she had repented his death soon after 'causing' it.[29] It was possible for the normal patterns to be inverted, with those who normally gave charity finding themselves accused, which may represent accumulated resentment on the part of the dependant. When Marion Flandrey was confronted with one of her accusers, Mengeatte Jacquat, she said Mengeatte's children came begging at her door every day, which the other effectively admitted. Jean Demenge le Clerc believed he had been arrested because of an accusation by Valentin le Souche during his own trial; this might have been made after he refused him alms when he was begging, and he said 'he would remember this one day'.[30] Suspicions might prevent people being as charitable as they wished. Mongeatte de Leuce knew herself to be suspected by many, although she protested 'that she saw well that all those who were sick would say it was witchcraft, but God would never permit it to be so'. She had never harmed anyone, 'and it was no longer wise to be charitable, so that she had sometimes given meat to their pigs, fearing to give it to the poor, when evil suspicions might arise if any misfortune occurred'.[31]

Beggars and their discontents

Begging clearly imposed an unwelcome degree of subservience and self-control on individuals who had usually known better times and now found themselves in a humiliating position. It was predictable that some of them would not react gracefully, while others actually used a reputation for witchcraft as a way to extract gifts from reluctant but fearful neighbours. According to Edward Fairfax, one of the Yorkshire witches alleged to be tormenting his children 'had so powerful hand over the wealthiest neighbours that none of them refused to do anything she required; yea, they provided her with fire, and meat from their own tables, and did what else they thought to please her'.[32] A vivid example of the sort of exchange that might take place was described by Jehennon Gaultrin. One evening two or three years earlier, as the animals were coming home, Jehennon Colin

> came to beg alms at their stable door, but the witness, who was busy around her children and animals, replied that two of her daughters had been there just before and that since she was not among the richer people she did not have the means to give so many alms. When Jehennon heard these words she went away very quickly. The witness, seeing her depart in this way, remembered the evil rumours and reputation she had of being a witch and, fearing some misfortune, took a bowl of milk and a piece of bread, with which she went out immediately, calling her several times to give her these alms. But she turned a deaf ear, pretending not to hear, while the neighbouring women called out to the witness that she heard perfectly well but had no intention of responding, which was the reason she was in great fear that some evil might befall her.

The next day a calf died, while her small son, who was guarding animals with his father, became ill and died after languishing for some time. In view of Jehennon's reputation she believed that this had been her witchcraft. It took less courage than usual to make such claims, since the accused had wisely fled before she could be caught; whether her husband was sincere in his promise to turn her in should she reappear is perhaps better left unknown.[33]

As we have already seen in the case of Jeanne Lienard, beggars might try to encourage charity through rash claims of special powers. More generally, those who went away muttering threats were giving the impression that their ill-will was something to be avoided. The old beggar Gilette Page was alleged to have said 'that if people did not fear her they would give her nothing'.[34] Such people were literally dicing with death, yet their conduct was hardly entirely irrational. Those who already had a bad reputation, in particular, may have done better to exploit it in this way, since there was really no escape from the trap in which they found themselves. The evidence suggests that it was possible to survive for years despite fulfilling every stereotype of the beggar-witch. Neighbours may have been effectively frightened by various displays of aggression, which sometimes carried an implicit threat of vengeance against anyone who tried to organize some kind of action. When Bastien Lalemant thought that Thomasse Poirot had killed a mare and said to her 'that it was her doing, and she must be burned', she retorted 'that he should shut up, for fear of some greater inconvenience'.[35] Statements by both judges and accused reflect the view that individuals might prefer to risk death when life itself had so little left to offer them. When another woman made a casual remark to Mengeotte Durand, calling her Aunt Mengeotte, she replied that her name was Aunt Witch. Later, while lamenting that she was being called a witch through the town and blamed for the death of a child of Nicolas Guerard, she said they did her great wrong, that she was very unhappy and 'would be very happy if her soul flew away into the air'.[36] Confessions, notably those offered voluntarily, can imply a state of mind in which the accused gave way to self-hatred and despair, mingled with awareness of their own malevolence (however impotent) and were left with little capacity to resist their interrogators. An elderly widow, Claudon Wannier, went round saying she was a witch, then voluntarily submitted herself to the court at St Nicolas. Asked what a witch was, she pathetically replied, 'it is an evil person who wanders round the country and does harm to poor people like herself'. When she confessed to two killings, the judges remonstrated:

> it is difficult for us to believe in this, because there is no sign that the powder was real, rather that tired of life and seeing herself to have become old and crippled, poor and needy, without relatives or friends to sustain her, she was trying to achieve the aim of her own death, by means not only of declaring herself to be a witch who had been suborned by the Devil, but in addition a bewitcher and poisoner, and that if her confessions were

untrue, she would be the cause of her own death and therefore her own murderer, who was thus rendered unworthy of the kingdom of paradise.

Despite this unexpected response, Claudon continued to insist on her own guilt.[37]

Suspicion and harassment

Such tendencies to seek a quick end to their persecution were also found among witches more generally, not just the destitute; they must have been all the greater when trials were preceded by years of harassment and local hostility. Claudin Aulbry, although denying he was a witch (and ultimately resisting the torture) said 'that he was very glad to be a prisoner in our hands, so that people would have no more suspicions against him, and stop looking at him sideways'.[38] Arguments and threats about possible witchcraft constituted another double-edged game, for disputes arising from this process were often adduced as the origin of bewitchment. The very public nature of life provided the occasions for people to rub one another up the wrong way. The church was one point of friction, particularly over seats and position; pilgrimages and rituals also involved social gradations which might prove controversial. One of the occasions which led to the charges against Mengeotte Durand was reported by Claudette Guerard; some six years earlier she had a dispute with Mengeotte over a seat in the church, so that the latter became very hostile. Shortly afterwards Mengeotte touched her infant son Demenge, whom the witness was carrying, on her shoulder and arm and he fell very ill. The accused was persuaded to visit him, then said they should light a small candle at each corner of his cradle in order to find out if it was an illness associated with a saint, but he died after seven weeks, shortly after the accused had visited him and touched him again. As we have just seen, Mengeotte was well aware of her own reputation, which she almost seemed to encourage, so it was no surprise when she confessed rather than endure the torture. One witness had commented that when living with her son-in-law she seemed very devout, ostentatiously carrying a rosary, but was always quarrelling with him. Another told how Mengeotte had consoled her over the sickness of a child, saying that witches should all be cursed and burned, and she herself had a daughter who was currently bewitched.[39]

Neighbours met one another at market, oven, forge and mill. They were expected to attend, or be invited, to the ceremonies associated with the rites of passage – birth, marriage and death. There was an elaborate code governing such interaction, albeit one with its own ambiguities, which carried messages about reputation and status. Breaches of it were sure to be noticed, affected people's relationships and might be invoked as explanations for subsequent events. Bastienne Valot recalled how seven years earlier, her son's betrothal feast had taken place a few days before the marriage feast. Petroniere Varnier had been serving the guests, 'but she behaved herself very insolently after drinking too much'. The witness therefore decided not to employ her again and she was invited merely to sit with the other women at the marriage feast – but did not come. There were many accidents during the second feast; a fire broke out in the house, the bridegroom had a fall, a man was killed in the stable where the horses of the guests were kept and her husband Demenge Valot fell ill of the strange malady from which he died after languishing more than a year. Petroniere – a relative by marriage – was already suspected as a witch, so was held to blame for all these disasters. It was to be Bastienne's son Nicolas who brought about her trial and execution, when he attacked her with a sword, accusing her of being a witch, of killing his father and his children and making his mother ill. A formal complaint by her husband Jean Varnier rebounded, for the local *prévôt* noted that many inhabitants of the small town of Bruyères suspected Petroniere of witchcraft, and forty-two of them testified against her. Despite admitting she was a witch, she always denied harming anyone, insisting that her relatives the Valots had been her 'sole help and comfort'. It proved impossible to extract satisfactory confessions from her, despite three sessions of torture; at one stage she remarked that the judges 'could write what they liked, and if she was not saved through her sufferings, no-one was, but as she knew that some others were to be executed that day, she was content that they put her to death with them'. The ramshackle nature of Lorraine legal proceedings finally sealed her fate, for although the ducal authorities were so unsure that they opted for banishment, the local court (which had the final authority) went ahead with the execution anyway. It was all the *prévôt* could do to dissuade them from their original intention of burning her alive and to allow her to be strangled first.[40]

Good neighbourliness was a key element in the spinning bees or *veillées* that occupied long winter evenings across much of Europe. There was an obvious difficulty over those with reputations for witchcraft; no-one else would want them there, but exclusion carried other dangers. Two such disputes were reported in the case of Mongeotte Lausson. Seven years earlier two women tried to stop her and her daughters sharing their bench; one of them was Bastienne Hadiguey, and when Mengeotte Lausson met her husband at market he complained of how his family had been humiliated, asking if they stank. Within a few days Bastienne slipped on the ice, had a miscarriage and died, followed soon after by the other woman involved. Four years later Mengeon Claudon and his wife had to exclude the Laussons from their *veillée* because the other women would not accept their presence, only for one of his horses to die.[41] These meetings could also be the occasion for tricks which misfired or were supposed to have provoked bewitchment. Zabey Pierson told an elaborate story of how a group of women decided to play a trick on the members of another *veillée*, throwing hair and old cloth on the fire to make a bad smell and force them to leave. The witness was persuaded to have her hair cut for the purpose and Jennon Friot (with whom she had earlier quarrelled) insisted that she should cut it, 'which made her timid and fearful because she was frightened of her', but she did not want to go back on her word. After cutting her hair the accused put her hand on her head, saying 'that's good, off you go'; a day or two later she became ill and had to take to her bed. She lost the child she was carrying, which she had only conceived some five weeks earlier, then her arms became twisted below the elbow. Her husband finally spoke to Jehenne Jean, who told them a method to bring the witch responsible to their house. Within an hour Jennon came and asked how she was; she told her she only had cramp and manipulated her arms; she immediately felt the warmth returning and they were cured in three days.[42]

A whole repertory of insults and threats could come into play, creating another set of flashpoints. If there were witnesses the proper reaction was to bring an action for slander, either in a local court or through informal arbitration. Where records survive, such incidents are numerous, often involving suspects who never seem to have come to trial. Failure to seek reparation for being called a witch was one of the commonest charges made by witnesses. The accused produced various explanations, when they did not react with straight denials. The insult had not been heard by anyone else, so they could prove nothing, or it had been made in vague terms which did not specifically refer to them. Sometimes it had been true, as when someone whose mother had been executed was called 'daughter of a witch'. On other occasions the insults were allegedly reciprocal, with both parties calling one another witch, along with such amenities as 'whore' and 'priest's slut'. Very often the injured party would claim to have been too poor to risk going to court; there was normally a fine for those who could not sustain their case. Women frequently asserted that their husbands would not support them, thus barring them from taking any action. They also expressed their sense that they could do nothing but endure these verbal attacks, leaving the retribution to God. There were serious dangers in doing otherwise, for a slander action sometimes provoked the defendant into bringing a full-scale accusation of witchcraft forward. By taking the initiative in what could be seen as an aggressive fashion, the suspect allowed an opponent to assume an injured, defensive role which might well make it easier to rally local support for the prosecution. Other legal action could have the same effect. At Bouvignies in 1679, when Péronne Goguillon was insulted and ransomed by four soldiers, her husband took action against them, only to find a local man, with whom one of the soldiers was lodging, coming forward as a formal accuser.[43] The case of Petroniere Varnier, discussed above, is another instance of such intervention proving disastrous.

There were various ways for those who suspected witchcraft to make their feelings known without risking an action for slander. Apart from the obvious precaution of making sure there were no witnesses, they might refer to the need to burn witches in general rather than a specific witch. There was an extraordinary scene when Marguerite Jobarde had a row with Demenge Grand Colas, who had taken on a maid she had dismissed, as he worked at his bench. He answered angrily 'that she had spoken of his wife and called her a loose woman, which she was not, but that she should go to Dompierre to find out what was being said about her, while for his part he would never be easy until he had caused some witches to be burned'. At these words she angrily seized his measuring stick and made to strike him, but he grabbed his stool in both hands and said, 'God's death, witch, if you budge I will smash both your eyes with my stool', at which she prudently left – but he lost eleven cattle over the next eighteen months.[44] Another way of achieving such ends was to make vague threats. Toussaint Gomay was unlucky enough to live next to the house of the Pelisson family, much suspected of witchcraft in Moriviller. Over a nine-year period he lost valuable animals every year, some as if rabid, others with their muzzles rotting or as if they were burned. The only one to recover was a large pig with a twisted neck, after he said loudly outside their house that if it did not recover he would do things that would be talked of in a hundred years. This evidence was given ten years after the execution of Jennon Pelisson, at a time when her daughter Georgeatte was on trial, about to be followed by the father she herself accused, leaving the rest of the family destitute.[45] The suspect could also be summoned to visit the sick, then asked to suggest a cure; everyone knew what was implied, but there was no direct statement. A particularly effective means of pressure was through children, who were not liable to the same sanctions. Often they conveyed local opinion by taunting the children of those believed to be witches. This sometimes led to acts of violence, more commonly to charges that the child had been bewitched in revenge for such behaviour. Barbelline de la Gotte told how five years earlier her daughter had been guarding the animals with the son of Claudatte Jean, whom she called 'son of a witch' during a quarrel. A few days later she developed an abscess on her side that resisted expensive attempts at cure for two years, until Claudatte came to the house unasked to see the girl, telling her to be patient and that she would soon be cured. Within a fortnight she was healed, which made them suspect Claudatte had caused the problem in the first place.[46]

From suspicion to action

All these complex interactions were liable to accumulate over many years until, if the suspect lived long enough or some local crisis precipitated action, a prosecution began. The typical sequence was described with great force and precision by the Essex minister George Gifford.

Some woman doth fall out bitterly with her neighbour: there followeth some great hurt ... There is a suspicion conceived. Within few years after she is in some jar with another. He is also plagued. This is noted of all. Great fame is spread of the matter. Mother W is a witch. She hath bewitched goodman B. Two hogs died strangely: or else he is taken lame. Well, mother W doth begin to be very odious and terrible unto many. Her neighbours dare say nothing but yet in their hearts they wish she were hanged. Shortly after another falleth sick and doth pine, he can have no stomach unto his meat, nor he cannot sleep. The neighbours come to visit him. Well neighbour, sayeth one, do ye not suspect some naughty dealing: did ye never anger mother W? truly neighbour (sayeth he) I have not liked the woman a long time. I cannot tell how I should displease her, unless it were this other day my wife prayed her, and so did I, that she would keep her hens out of my garden. We spoke her as fair as we could for our lives. I think verily she hath bewitched me. Every body sayeth now that Mother W is a witch in deed and hath bewitched the good man E. He cannot eat his meat. It is out of all doubt: for there were [those] which saw a weasel run from her housward into his yard even a little before he fell sick. The sick man dieth, and taketh it upon his death that he is bewitched: then is mother W apprehended, and sent to prison, she is arraigned and condemned.[47]

This passage perfectly conveys the curious halting logic of the whole process, with the interaction between individual and communal suspicion. At the end it is the neighbours who invite the supposed victim of the witch to recall how *he* had offended *her,* while secret gossip becomes general, with new stories about familiars, until the particular solemnity of a deathbed accusation seals her fate.

Gifford's imaginary reportage achieves great economy and force, but anyone familiar with the trials will recognize the pattern immediately. Christina Larner deftly assimilated the Scottish evidence to the labelling theory developed by sociologists, which lays the emphasis on a dynamic process of social interaction, through which the deviant's identity and nature are defined, then reinforced. In effect, suspicions are turned into something like reality by a social mechanism that may even induce the suspects to live out their assigned roles. This happens at the three levels of collective rule making, interpersonal reactions and organizational processes. Collective rule making is represented by the exchanges between rulers, law-makers and popular opinion which made witchcraft a specific crime, albeit an unstable one subject to constant redefinition. Organizational processes involve the expanded criminal law system, alongside the various disciplinary efforts of the church, that provided the opportunity, even arguably some of the demand, for the punishment of witches. Larner seemed to attribute some causal priority to these two factors when she suggested that interpersonal hostilities were generated in the space between them. While this is obviously true, in the sense that the theory and practice of persecution made witchcraft a far more dangerous matter within small communities, the implied priority is unconvincing. The world of local suspicions, hostilities and counter-magic did not just predate the witch-hunts, it also made an indispensable contribution to the formal theories. Labelling theory works better, on the European level at least, if we think in terms of three mutually interdependent elements, all of which were equally vital for persecution. The labelling process had its own remorseless logic, once an individual had been identified as a possible witch; all subsequent disputes and tensions risked being associated with some misfortune, while the suspect must sooner or later become aware of the reputation that was building. Attempts to escape from it, or outface accusers, were all too likely to backfire and be interpreted as further confirmation. One natural response was to accept the label and claim special power, like Agnes Finnie, with her threat 'if I be a witch, you or yours shall have better cause to call me so'.[48] What the theory does not explain is why particular individuals were selected as suspects in the first place, and this is a very difficult problem. A number of overlapping groups seem to emerge from the records, but it would be very hazardous to offer even a guess at their relative contribution to the whole sample of those at risk. There were those who behaved like witches, usually too ready with their tongues and quick to follow quarrels with a threat. Children and relatives of convicted witches (or those so reputed who had died in their beds) formed another group, alongside those identified by the cunning folk. Then there were those identified by confessing witches; often these were other existing suspects, but spite or simple despair might see them lash out with charges in unexpected directions. However one entered the system, it contained a number of one-way valves which made escape very difficult.

Projection and fantasies

The sheer unpleasantness of this pattern of social proscription, in which the witch seems to acquire a magnetic attraction for all the negative charges in his or her immediate environment, reminds us yet again just how dangerous projection can be. When groups or individuals link their inner feelings to the human society around them in this manner, the results can be explosive. A purely social explanation is in fact quite inadequate to convey the power of the forces at work. The protean, multiform character of witchcraft beliefs, as they have emerged in this account, must be related to their extraordinary capacity to mobilize and express fantasy. This does not just mean storytelling; in its psychological context it stands, among other things, for the unconscious fears, hatreds and resentments which play such a dominating role in the human psyche. In their contacts with their neighbours, individuals relived their deeply ambiguous early relationships with parents and siblings, redirecting feelings they had never recognized or worked through. Particularly in situations where dependency played a strong part, it was all too possible for murderous hostility to develop and, as the material in this chapter has shown, much of the operation of early modern society can be described in relation to dependency. Normally one would expect most individual feelings of this kind to be contained by social restraints, but the corporate fantasy of witchcraft was capable of breaking down such controls and encouraging people to act out their beliefs. The importance of fantasy was explicitly recognized by that shrewd observer George Gifford, who made his mouthpiece Daniel urge, 'Let such men learn to know God, and to expel fantasies out of their minds that the Devil may not have such power over them; for he worketh in the fantasies of man's mind, and the more strongly where they fear him'.[49]

Historians who are aware of the extensive references to witchcraft in literary and judicial sources for the early modern period have concluded that people must have spent a good deal of their time worrying or talking about witches. This is corroborated by the remarkable findings of ethnographers working in parts of rural Europe over the past few decades. Here it emerges that there is a private world of belief and discussion, normally closed to outsiders, in which problems or misfortune are routinely ascribed to witchcraft. Although the Devil has apparently vanished from the picture, *maleficium* remains as a feature of everyday thought, part of a hidden (and perhaps imaginary) power struggle between individuals, families and nebulous broader groups. Such ideas are kept hidden by a mixture of natural caution, fear of provoking adversaries and awareness that they are regarded as a sign of backwardness. Once the cover is penetrated, however, it turns out that they are widely held and readily capable of being reawakened, even among the highly educated and travelled. Only among the clerical, medical and legal establishment are they normally rejected; this is not without some backsliding and has much to do with an assertion of rationality as a badge of superiority.[50] While one must be wary of extrapolating backward through time, it is hard to believe that such elements did not play an even greater role in the mental world of early modern Europeans. Their vigorous survival into a period where they are forced to exist underground, without the overt social supports found in the past, is yet another reason for giving due weight to their psychological force. It also gives some *prima facie* support to the idea that there may be at least some mental structures which have not changed greatly over the centuries.

There is of course no hope of making full-scale reconstructions of people's inner thoughts across time, still less of putting individuals on some kind of metaphorical analyst's couch. This is less serious that it might seem, however, since individual peculiarities are less important than shared patterns when one is trying to explain social phenomena. While the material from some witchcraft cases allows us to suggest very plausible explanations in terms of the personal experience of individuals, these are bound to remain conjectural when they cannot be tested by talking to those concerned. What is really significant, by contrast, is to find certain themes and processes repeatedly present in a large body of material and capable of fruitful exploration in psychological terms. In other words, it is not primarily a matter of explaining why certain people became involved in witchcraft conflicts on the basis of their personal histories. The objective is rather to understand how the typical relationships worked. This should in its turn help us to see how particular social, familial and other contexts could give rise to intense convictions that witchcraft was operating. Projection and associated ways of thinking are essentially concerned with the integration of the self into the external world, also with the defences human beings employ to protect themselves against too much uncomfortable contact with reality. They provide at least some relief for the greedy, omnipotent self everyone carries within them. We learn to repress socially undesirable feelings from a very early age, but they do not vanish in consequence. A particularly neat way of dealing with them is to split them off inwardly, deny possessing them at all and project them into someone else. The person who disowns his or her feelings in this way may even manipulatively induce another into expressing them. A whole range of fascinating phenomena cluster around this core, several of them with obvious relevance to witchcraft. Being on the receiving end of a powerful projective identification can be an intense and numbing experience. The behaviour of the accused might well be considered in this light, with the associated sense of being manipulated into playing a part. Fear of witches may be linked to the pattern whereby the more violent the fantasies projected towards an external object, the greater the simultaneous sense of terror induced by that object. Aggressive fantasies lead to an intense fear of retaliation, of precisely the kind that has emerged as characteristic of many exchanges between witches and their victims. Whole groups can develop concordant schemes of fantasy, maintaining inner solidarity at the expense of a common external enemy. This is closely related to the process of externalization, which allows those less directly involved to gain vicarious satisfaction by disclaiming unacceptable parts of themselves. In such cases unconscious fantasy penetrates and gives meaning to 'actual events' in the external world; that world itself bestows meaning in the form of shared unconscious fantasies.

Witchcraft narratives routinely placed great emphasis on envy as a motive force, leading into the more general affective states of anger and rage. Suspects were commonly described as acting from 'malice and envy'; anger had inspired them to take Satan as their master, while envy of the better-off frequently underlay particular acts. Envy can be traced back to the earliest phase of childhood, where it is part of the process which sees the infantile self detach itself from the mother. It is one reaction to the failure of the mother to be totally compliant with the narcissistic and omnipotent wishes of the infant. This leads in turn to rage, the withdrawal of love and feelings of hatred and hurt. Illness or other misfortunes in later life can reactivate such feelings, with being unwell assimilated to being unloved, unprotected, or even hated. In this scheme the mother represents the external will, an embodiment of menace and power which seems magically formidable; the gendering of witchcraft, to be explored in a later chapter, must reflect such patterns. Witchcraft trials suggest that our early modern ancestors were scarcely different from us in these terms, for resonances from such tensions are found in many places. There is certainly a central preoccupation with maternal function; parents feared that vulnerable infants would die, yet children themselves must have wished that younger siblings would suffer that fate. Fear and repressed guilt would then combine to direct suspicion at surrogate figures. This was achieved through the projection mechanism, which is most powerful when reinforced by external reality, in this case the aggressive behaviour of many suspects. We might even posit an unconscious psychic alliance between witch and victim, both acting out their part of the fantasy. Younger men, for example, typically feel a need to detach themselves from mothers, leading to hostile behaviour towards them and their surrogates. In everyday terms this might manifest itself as the refusal of normal courtesies or services to older women, followed by guilt and the expectation of punishment. At another level the relationship between the witch and her imps or familiars was a strangely distorted, parodic vision of human motherhood.

Seen in such terms, witches were intrusive, self-assertive figures, who posed multiple dangers. The anxieties they embodied led people to associate evil with human agents, modifying if not contradicting the various official theories which gave direct power to God and the Devil. This bundle of psychic threats left the victims feeling they had been invaded by forces they could not control, threatening their autonomy and integrity. This was well symbolized by the attacks on people in bed, or their children in the nearby cradle, which violated a particularly private space and implied that safety was impossible anywhere. In the encounters with witches, boundaries were pushed aside to give a sense that an outsider was seeking power over inner experience and well-being. Confronted with a supposed witch, it was easy to panic, becoming so flustered that one's normal functioning was impaired. People in this state had accidents or thought they saw strange occurrences, thus confirming their original belief. Catherine Granier was merely passing Jacotte Raon's house at a time when she was heavily pregnant, with another child round her neck. Jacotte, who was on the manure heap, looked at her, at which she was suddenly overcome with fear, fell and hurt herself badly.[51] The extreme case was that of individuals who effectively went into shock, overwhelmed by negative affect to the point where they might literally die. Isabel Famel had bought a chest from Catherine la Rondelatte but found it unsatisfactory, so she had not paid while waiting to return it or negotiate a reduced price. She was worried about what might happen as a result, and one evening saw a strange black pig rolling on the ice of the stream, at which she was so frightened she lost her wits and could not even receive the sacraments before her death, while repeatedly naming Catherine as its cause.[52] As Marion le Hire and her mother were going to Mass one Sunday in 1587 Jean Diez touched the latter on the arm, asking if she wanted to buy bread from him, to which she replied she did not.

Nevertheless her said mother felt herself struck with illness at that touch, and as she mounted the steps to the church, started to complain, saying she was chilled . . . as soon as Mass was over she wanted to return, and in fact went home, complaining she was terribly cold, and had lost feeling in the half of her body with Jean had touched. That same evening she took to her bed . . .

She duly died within a few days, maintaining that Diez had given her the illness. She had long been terrified of Jean and was always putting off going to see a farm they owned in his village of la Bolle for fear of meeting him.[53]

While there is no way in which we can be sure that any one such event can be attributed to psychological causes rather than some coincidental disease or crisis, some of those concerned were surely frightened to death. The physiological basis for such events is now well established, so that we must suppose that witchcraft fantasies could be lethal in more ways than one. The word 'victim' has a curious double sense here, for it often applied to bewitcher and bewitched alike; both might experience loss, suffering, fear and death, as projected evil reinforced belief and persecution simultaneously. The vulnerability of witches to counter-magic, violence and legal action was the other side of the alarming psychic power so many people felt as a deadly threat to their own well-being. A similar reciprocity can be found on another level, for the victims often appear as deeply uncomfortable about their own aggressive traits – just those impulses to intrude, dominate or attack they attributed to the witches. Projection of this type might endow their neighbour the witch with precisely those traits they most despised in themselves.

CHAPTER V

WITCH-FINDERS AND WITCH CURES

Cunning folk and their cures

THE CUNNING FOLK have already made numerous appearances in this book, surfacing as key figures in the whole nexus of belief and practice surrounding witchcraft. Witches and witch-doctors form one of the tightest of all symbiotic relationships; wherever one is found, there too will the other be. The two categories might be characterized as positive and negative poles, at least as they appeared in popular eyes. Yet we have also seen that it was dangerously easy for the charge to be reversed, with healers suddenly finding themselves accused of harmful witchcraft. Magical knowledge was dangerous and ambiguous by its very nature. Those who could heal could also harm, whether it was by counter-magic directed against witches or by displacing an illness onto another person or animal. Worst of all, they might actually be witches, pretending to cure the effects of their own malice and getting profit from it. Such accusations might result from failed attempts to cure, grasping behaviour or outright fraud. One Lorraine healer who attracted much unfavourable comment was Barbe la Grosse Gorge of Jarville, tried in 1591. Several witnesses alleged she had taken money for pilgrimages she did not actually perform, one remarking that when she had got what she could from her patients in money and food, she abandoned them. Faced by one discontented client asking for her money back, Barbe picked up a sickle and threatened to cut off her head. Before she was tortured and forced to confess she was really a witch, she was already prepared to admit she had defrauded some of those she treated.[1]

Behaviour of this kind, while certainly not unique, was relatively unusual. The cunning folk generally believed in their own powers, made relatively small charges for their services and looked after their reputations. Even Barbe la Grosse Gorge was evidently proud of some of the cures she claimed, however badly she behaved in other cases. It was typical of Reginald Scot that he took a more extreme view, linking the wizards and wise-women to the Catholic clergy as conscious frauds. He put his views with his usual trenchancy:

> It is also to be thought that all witches are cozeners, when Mother Bungy, a principal witch, so reputed, tried and condemned of all men, and continuing in that exercise and estimation many years (having cozened and abused the whole realm, insomuch as there came to her witchmongers from all the furthest parts of the land, she being in divers books set out with authority, registered and chronicled by the name of 'the great witch of Rochester', and reputed among all men for the chief ringleader of other witches) by good proof is found to be a mere cozener; confessing in her death-bed freely, without compulsion or enforcement, that her cunning consisted only in deluding and deceiving the people, saying that she had, towards the maintenance of her credit in that cozening trade, some sight [skill] in physic and surgery, and the assistance of a friend of hers called Heron, a professor thereof.[2]

Scot also told the story of Mother Baker of Stonestreet, near New Romney, who asked the relatives of a sick girl whether they suspected any malicious neighbours. When they named a woman, she immediately suggested she was 'the very party that wrought the maiden's destruction by making a heart of wax and pricking the same with pins and needles'. When a search of the suspect's house proved fruitless, Mother Baker claimed to be able to find the heart – only to be detected planting it herself.[3] This case seems to have ended with some kind of punishment imposed by the court of High Commission, but in general these Kentish cunning folk appear to have operated freely over many years. Scot thought it was time their claims were subjected to the same close scrutiny as Catholic 'church magic' had undergone:

> But some affirm that popish miracles are vanished and gone away, howbeit, witches' miracles remain in full force. So as St. Loy is out of credit for a horse-leech, Master T and Mother Bungy remain in estimation for prophets; nay, Hobgoblin and Robin Goodfellow are contemned among young children, and Mother Alice and Mother Bungy are feared among old fools.[4]

Scot's virulent scepticism was, as so often, well in advance of his contemporaries. It is also plain that he exaggerated the part played by conscious fraud, although his own examples may have been accurate enough. The responses of cunning folk who were on trial for malevolent witchcraft demonstrate very clearly that most of them believed in their own capacities. Over the whole of the early modern period only a tiny minority of people – mostly puritanical clerics and self-interested doctors – seriously challenged the notion that such individuals had genuine healing gifts. However much other members of the elites might scoff at popular credulity, once illness or misfortune struck they often sought help from these same quarters. After all, common observation suggested that many people recovered after consulting the local wizard or wise-woman. Since there was no obvious means of testing the causal links involved, it was reasonable enough to accord the benefit of the doubt. These ambivalent attitudes probably go far to explain why demands for action against magicians and healers had little effect in most of Europe. Even had local rulers shown more determination, however, they would have needed wider popular support to prosecute effectively in the ordinary courts. In England, the church courts, which had a simplified procedure and no juries, seem to have been quite active in pursuing the cunning folk at times, though the mild fines and admonitions they administered had little deterrent value. In Mediterranean Europe, particularly Spain and Italy, the Inquisition appeared a more formidable tribunal. Purveyors of love potions or spells, fortune tellers, treasure-seekers and the like passed routinely through its prisons. Yet the stories they told do not suggest that this repression was really any more effective, for many had been practising for years undisturbed. As has already been suggested, the Inquisition was careful, expensive and slow; it simply lacked the capacity to deal with more than a fraction of its potential clients.

Only a minority of the daring or destitute took the risky step of turning magical healing into a full-time profession. The majority of operators claimed limited or specialized powers, functioned intermittently as demand allowed and made their main living by more ordinary means. They were thus largely invisible to outside authority unless specific complaints were made against them. These might occur if a zealous local cleric was prepared to disregard local feeling, but enthusiasts of this stamp were rare. Most incumbents knew better than to offend their parishioners in this way, being well aware that the latter relied heavily on this informal local therapy. Although dissatisfied clients were a more serious danger, most only acted when there were serious reasons to suspect that the healer was really a witch and neighbours were willing to back such claims. Because the repression was so limited, it is hard to reconstruct this dense network with any great accuracy. On the whole these very local operators do not seem to have been major players in the witchcraft game. Often rather vulnerable and low-status individuals, they can hardly have been unaware of the possibility of counter-charges based on their own activities. Such consciousness probably led to a natural caution about accusing others; they were more likely to make a general suggestion that witchcraft might be at work than to name suspects directly. This might still be vital in building up local feeling against individuals, while in other respects these people had great indirect importance. Their sheer numbers and ubiquitous presence at once sustained the world view they represented and clogged any official attempt at repression. At the same time it was mainly from their ranks that a minority of more potent figures emerged, who can more properly be described as witch-doctors.

Witch-doctors in Lorraine

The extensive references to such practitioners in the Lorraine records permit an unusually complete reconstruction of their role. Here, as elsewhere, successful local healers might gradually extend their range, in both geographical and therapeutic terms. They became known over a range of perhaps twenty miles or more, to form part of a much more scattered network of well-known wizards and diviners. As they developed greater prestige, clients would come in larger numbers from further away. The commonest reason for these consultations was a mysterious illness that had resisted lesser practitioners, or was thought from the start to be supernatural. The diagnosis of witchcraft was therefore in a sense predetermined, although by the nature of the evidence we cannot be sure how often it was actually offered. In many instances the clients arrived with this expectation. They had chosen to consult one of the known specialists, often at or beyond the periphery of their normal social range, precisely because they suspected witchcraft, or had the idea suggested to them already. It was not easy to conceal a visit of this kind and there were occasions when the suspected witches protested. Chrestienne Barret of Domjevin went to court and obtained damages after Dom Jean de Xanrey was consulted about the illness of Gerardin Jean Thiriot in 1591; he had sent some herbs which the suspect was to be made to touch.[5] A bad conscience could even result in a shamefaced return without completing the mission. Jean Masson of Sachemont thought Epnon Charbonnatte might have caused the headaches which tormented him and told her and her husband that he was going to visit a man in Burgundy who might identify the person responsible. After setting out he 'felt remorse in his conscience and thought to himself that he did wrong to go to the *devin*', so turned back. He also thought that since he had revealed his suspicions to her she might do something to heal him, and did indeed recover on his return.[6] Though people were clearly aware that there was something questionable about such consultations, doubts of this kind were exceptional. In many cases it seems more likely that visiting the witch-doctor was at least in part a way of pressurizing the suspect to offer healing. In one instance the threat was explicit, when a man sought payment of a debt in the house of the supposed witch precisely in order to hire an expert with an original technique. The local *prévôt* had told him about a *devin* from Nancy who could detect the presence of a witch in a house simply by examining the smoke from the chimney. On hearing this statement the suspect, Jeanne Thihard of le Void de Belmont, made conciliatory remarks and sent the sick man some white roots; he recovered after eating these.[7]

Travelling specialists formed a special category, whose relationship to the long-established local practitioners is not easy to determine. Some may have taken to the road when their local position became too hot seriously compromised, while others were primarily healers who showed a dangerous propensity to identify witches as part of their standard repertoire. Since we naturally know far more about those individuals who were caught and punished, there are problems in assessing the strength and significance of this group, who flit through the records in a much more elusive fashion than their static rivals. Itinerants of this kind could arouse intense interest and excitement from those who saw them as possible agencies of relief, as happened in the case of Claudette Clauchepied. After she had visited another family at Bruyères, Jacquotte Vauldechamps complained to her associate that she thought he was one of her friends, but he had brought a woman to cure the daughter of the other family without telling her anything about it. Others in the region who heard of her were evidently anxious to persuade her to visit, even when she made difficulties. There were good reasons for her to be cautious, because like others of her type she was an obvious target for local law enforcement officers, hostile to vagrants of every kind and especially those who threatened communal harmony. If they were picked up where torture was in use, they were at the gravest risk of being coerced into confessing they were really servants of the Devil. Claudette was no exception, for sustained interrogation without torture was enough to produce a confession that she had been seduced by Satan when in desperate poverty after the death of her husband and other relatives. She implicitly accepted the suggestion by the judges that 'this art of divination comes from no-one but the evil spirit'. Extensive material in her own statements and the depositions of the witnesses shows that she employed three interlocking types of explanation and cure. These were herbal medicine, pilgrimages to the shrines of local saints and the identification of witchcraft by named persons; like many of her type, she had exploited the very belief system which eventually brought her to the stake.[8]

Some of the stories told by the vagrants give a picaresque view of life in this strange underworld of early modern society, where survival called for a mixture of deviousness and effrontery. Anthoine Grevillon was an ex-soldier in his seventies from the Franche-Comté who claimed to have been a pupil of a doctor in the German town of Spire. He traded in powder to treat worms, but also in familiar spirits, which took the form of flies in small boxes, using one of these himself to decide which remedies to give. Another appears to have been sold to a man who then committed suicide. In danger of arrest in his home village, he moved into the remote valley of Ramonchamp, near the source of the Moselle in the extreme south of Lorraine, where the local officials set out to hunt him down when they heard of his activities. No doubt it was in the hope of evading such attentions that he had established himself in the village of Urbès, just outside the eastern boundary of the duchy; it was on one of his visits to treat patients that he was caught. Under interrogation he described a range of techniques, including a method of establishing whether an illness was witchcraft by testing the patient's urine on a hot iron. If the sickness was natural the urine went red and boiled away, if it was witchcraft it went white and remained. He did not employ this in the one attempt at a cure described by a witness; on this occasion he told the sufferer that her illness had been given by someone who touched her on the shoulder within a few days of the last St Rémy and that if she wished he could cause the person concerned to appear, then make them sicken in the same way. Then he put his jacket on the table, saying no-one should touch it because there was a stone in the pocket that would make it jump at their nose, asked for three candles and took them into another room. After a strange noise he reappeared to say he had identified the witch, whom he could afflict with paralysis or catarrh if so requested. Altogether Grevillon had perhaps a dozen variegated cures and ways of detecting hidden facts, which he clearly manipulated with considerable virtuosity. Despite being tortured he did not admit anything which really amounted to witchcraft, so that it was with much brandishing of demonological texts that the local authorities decided he had made a tacit pact with the Devil and put him to death.[9]

Similar risks certainly awaited the other witch-doctors, yet here too it is striking how long they usually operated unchecked. When Remy wrote about his experiences in Lorraine, where as *procureur général* he was the chief ducal prosecutor, he expressed the wish that three notorious individuals, the monk of Niderhoff, the woman at the hot springs near Mirecourt and the discharged soldier of Nancy, should be brought to justice.[10] Despite his powerful official position he was apparently unable or unwilling to take steps to this end himself. When the soldier, Nicolas Noel le Bragard, was tried and executed a couple of years later it was at the instigation of a dissatisfied client; the monk, Dom Jean de Xanrey, appears to have escaped altogether. Noel's interrogation revealed a career stretching back many years, the attempted practice of several varieties of magic and the implied protection of some of his military superiors. His relatively humble origins had not prevented his acquisition of a smattering of Latin and a collection of treatises on the occult. A quick-witted autodidact of this type could evidently ply his trade under the noses of the authorities with remarkable impunity. There is no sign, however, that he was involved in identifying others as witches, his healing techniques being based on stroking and handling the sufferer to draw off the evil.[11] Dom Jean, by contrast, was primarily a straightforward witch-doctor. When his horses sickened, the mayor of a village some fifteen miles away visited him to be told that a woman from their village had caused it because of jealousy over a garden she wanted. He then said that this woman would often visit their house to comfort his wife during their absence, and Barbelline Goudot was duly identified. Although an informal accusation and a dispute followed, it was to be at least fourteen years before Barbelline went on trial.[12] This incident took place around 1589; twelve years earlier Pierre Bonnet, a weaver from Azelot near Nancy, had travelled forty miles to consult Dom Jean. Bonnet asked him who had stolen some cloth, but he said he could discover nothing about such a matter. Under pressure the monk then told him that the first woman who came into his house on his return would be the one who had caused the death of his children, and that she had long been envious of him. This is a curious story, since the charge had nothing to do with the ostensible motive for the consultation. It does fit with a well-established pattern, in which the client raises a relatively minor matter, only to introduce the real issue almost as an afterthought. One cannot be sure that this was true on this occasion, but it is hard to see an alternative explanation. Catherine Claude, an elderly widow who used a measuring technique with a scarf to identify the illnesses of children and prescribe pilgrimages, was first to come in after Bonnet's return. She too came to no immediate harm, for she was only arrested six years later, when no direct charge was made on this account – the visit was merely mentioned by another witness who had accompanied Bonnet, and it was other accusations that dominated the trial.[13]

Elsewhere in the south-east of the duchy, numerous trials around St Dié refer to several consultations with the *devineresse* of Thanville, a hamlet on the Alsatian side of the Vosges mountains. Unfortunately there is no surviving evidence of her own subsequent trial, which led to her execution as a witch, but she too had enjoyed a long immunity from prosecution. The kind of informal pressures which might be brought to bear emerged when Demenge Gros Demenge of Colroy visited her in 1594. After he made a general statement that he had lost animals, she established her capacities by telling him how many and of what kind. This is another familiar element in accounts from various places and times, no doubt reflecting either local knowledge or the use of accomplices. She was more coy in responding to his natural demand to know who was responsible, saying at first that her *seigneur* had forbidden her to give names, since when she had done so in the past there had been complaints and quarrels. After he had assured her he would say nothing she told him it was the woman whose meadow had been damaged by his horse; he then remembered that the horse had strayed in Marie Alexey's meadow and angered her. He told the story when Marie was on trial four years later, while she countered by claiming that he and others were worthless people, as was shown by their going to the *devin*. This particular *devineresse* told another client that his illness had been caused by a woman he had made very angry, then gave him an antidote made with herbs and roots, after taking which he immediately felt better.[14]

Near the Moselle to the south of Metz another woman was operating around the same time in the 1580s and is also reported to have been executed as a witch. La Queprotte of la Vanolbe was again an expert in the identification of illnesses, those who had caused them and the appropriate pilgrimages. She told one client a sufferer was bewitched by a woman who had placed a small object above her heart; if it had been below it she would have died within twenty-four hours. They were to follow a nine-day cycle of religious observances, within which the patient would either die or recover (in fact she died within the week).[15] Another client received similar advice about his wife's illness, accompanied by a refusal to name the suspect and the comment that it was one with whom his wife had quarrelled and she would know well who this was. The wife, who was so ill that she received the last rites, immediately suspected Jeannon Collignon, who then visited her and sent a drink like yellow milk which made her vomit up strange things, after which she recovered. This took place some eleven years before Jeannon's eventual trial.[16] A much longer gap occurred in the case of Nicolas Sermemont of Gripport, convicted in 1615. A witness told how twenty-six years earlier his father, who had already accused Nicolas of bewitching his animals and threatened to have him burned, visited a *devineresse* at Bainville-sur-Illon. She used the classic adjunct of a mirror to show him Sermemont and his wife and sister accompanied by a devil. It was a foreign beggar-woman, however, who advised him to get bread and salt from the suspected household as a cure; some of this was then blessed by a priest with relics of St Hubert to act as a permanent protection.[17] At the trial of Catherine Tarillon of Bassing in 1594, Claudin Haman told how his suspicions followed a quarrel and the loss of ten horses. He consulted Rose Tixerand, the *devineresse* at Bénestroff (only four miles away), who was herself called as a witness. She made no bones about agreeing the consultation had taken place and that Haman told her there must be a terrible group of witches in his village. After performing her ceremonies with a basin of holy water and a piece of silver, she confirmed the bewitchment of the horses, saying they had been given a drink and it seemed to her it was by Catherine.[18]

Counter-magic and manipulation

The themes of these various stories are clear enough. The cunning folk had no interest in promoting formal prosecutions, which endangered their own position, and were anxious to preserve confidentiality. They were cautious in naming suspects, exploiting the familiar techniques which persuaded the client to make his or her own suspicions explicit. Many of them offered cures based on herbal medicine or religious observances. It was common for them to provide a range of services, including love magic, the recovery of stolen goods, information about missing persons, the prediction of lottery numbers and searches for buried treasure. In several of these areas it is easy to see how the giving of advice could in itself be effectual, enabling the client to take decisions with greater confidence or frightening others into remedial action. Although techniques of divination could vary widely, two in particular seem to have predominated across Europe. One used versions of the 'scissors and sieve', in which objects moved in response to specific names or questions – similar in essentials to the poison oracle found in Africa. In 1680 Jan Mulder and his associates were fined at Vollenhove in Overijssel because 'they practised devilry, using a sieve with a pair of scissors and then, calling on the devil, they could see from the way the sieve turned whether the person they had mentioned whilst the sieve was still turning could indeed witch or not'.[19] The other was based on visual identification, employing mirrors, polished stones or water as a reflective surface. The effect could be enhanced by the use of incantations, or by placing an object – an apple or a stick, for example – in the water. It is hardly surprising that these practices routinely achieved the discovery of the suspect, as in the 1578 Essex case of the cunning man who made his client wait for nine days before visiting him. He 'brought with him a looking glass (about 7 or 8 inches square) and did hang the said glass up over the bench in his said hall, upon a nail, and had the said examinate look in it, and said as far as he could guess, he should see the face of him that had the said linen.'[20] Philibert Tabusset suspected a certain Billey of having killed several animals, so he went to a *devin* at Auxonne who confirmed this diagnosis, 'having shown him a mirror in which he recognized him very clearly, then asked him what harm he wanted done to the said Billey, that is to say whether he wanted him given a black eye, to have an arm cut off, or to be banished from the region'. Tabusset opted for banishment, then beat up the suspect, who was never seen in the locality again.[21]

Once the suspect was identified, remedial measures could follow, whether it was a matter of witchcraft or theft. Many practitioners avoided making an identification, instead using the alternative technique of advising methods which would force the guilty party to pay a visit.

There were numerous variants, usually involving acts we might think of as symbolic, but which contemporaries must often have believed to have direct physical effects, through the principles of sympathy which permeated their vision of the natural world. A variety of such techniques were employed in the vicinity of the German town of Esslingen. The urine of the sick person was mixed with wax and a piece of cloth placed in a glass, which ensured that the person who had given the sickness would appear within twelve hours. When she did so, bread, salt and a broom were placed over a door to stop her leaving; there are similar accounts in Lorraine trials, with the broom apparently creating an invisible barrier the witch could not pass. In another case a Stuttgart apothecary advised the afflicted family that they should fill a bucket with water in the name of Satan, then put it under the bed, again to compel the witch to appear. The same effect was allegedly produced by hanging the hide of a bewitched ox in the window, while those whose cows had lost their milk made them urinate on straw they then burned. More spectacular results were claimed for a remedy prescribed by an Esslingen 'doctor' (one can rarely be sure what kind of practitioner is meant); the excrement of the sick girl was hung in the smoke over the fire, then placed on the hot surface above the oven, at which the suspect became so disturbed that she jumped over hedges and had weals on her face.[22] In most such accounts the result was the arrival of the suspect, who was not merely identified but persuaded to offer relief. A German case which illustrates this is that of Barbara Rüfin, tried at Ellwangen in 1611, against whom Veit Miller testified; years before, his late father had gone to a white witch (also now dead) because so many of his animals were sick. She visited the house and declared 'that such misfortune originated with evil persons. But she would cause the witch responsible to reveal herself. As soon as she left their house, she said, a person would come asking for three things. If they gave her these things, their situation with the cattle would get worse than before'. Almost immediately Barbara appeared asking for four things, which were refused, after which all went well with the cattle.[23]

Some wizards occupied a curious intermediate zone, claiming rather dubious titles to bolster their social status, while employing a mixture of learned and popular magic. Simon Achard, 'sieur de Beaumont', was tried by the *présidial* court of Angoulême in 1596 and finally executed after the failure of his appeal to the Paris *parlement* the following year, despite alleged interventions in his favour by several powerful men.

Achard claimed in his defence that he had never harmed anyone; on the contrary he had healed many and discovered various witches. He used a mirror of polished steel to consult a spirit, but denied being in the power of the spirit because he only paid the fixed tariff established by those from whom the gift had been transferred (the last had been his uncle). The actual consultation was made through intermediaries – two young children specially blessed by a priest, who looked in the mirror after he had invoked God through prayers taken from his manuscript copy of a well-known magical text, the *Pentaculum et sigillum Solomonis*. He described a séance in which they saw the Demoiselle de la Barriere bewitched by a certain Chamoulard, who took powder from a leather purse and sprinkled it behind her back. Achard claimed that Chamoulard and his accomplice Dutreil had freely confessed their crime; perhaps he genuinely knew nothing (as he said) of the treatment to which they alleged they had been subjected, which had seen them plunged in water and having their feet burned. He also told a fanciful story about the power to use the mirror, conferred by a college based at Toledo with thirteen masters and seventy-three disciples. In his case he had simply inherited membership from his uncle, who had performed the elaborate ceremonies and fasting necessary. Pretensions of this kind no doubt went down well with gullible provincials, while Achard may well have been sincere in his claims; unfortunately for him, they were just the kind of thing best calculated to enrage the sceptical Parisian magistrates.[24]

The popular conception behind all these operations was one of competing forces; the supernatural strength of the *devin* was being pitted against that of the witch. The appearance of the latter was a sign of his or her defeat in this invisible combat, which could hardly fail to offer comfort and might well be followed by the lifting of the evil. In other cases the next step was counter-magic, perhaps by burning some object associated with the suspect, or by various rituals and prayers. The idea that some emanation from the witch was the physical cause of the trouble can be seen in the idea that plunging a red-hot poker into milk might cause actual pain. There was even a claim that one cunning man (a Dutch sexton) had stabbed the image in his bucket with a knife, after which the suspect was found to be blind in one eye.[25] There might also be the dangerous notion that sickness could be deflected somewhere else, as in a Holstein case which led to Detlef Wiese of Schönbeck being fined for superstitious practices. He explained that his wife had consulted a beggar-woman over a sick cow, asking how they could prevent the disease spreading; she was advised to cut off its head, smoke it and hang it up in their gable end towards their neighbour's house, while burying the body. After they had done this their animals had been free of sickness, but another villager claimed that since that time a large number of his animals had died.[26] Particularly common practices made use of urine and other bodily waste products or involved driving nails into a cow's heart, then burning it. The father of Elizabeth Chamberlain claimed that she had been killed by the witchcraft of Jane Kent; when his wife also fell ill he went 'to one Dr Ha – ks in Spittle-Fields, who advised him to take a quart of his wife's water, the paring of her nails, some of her hair and such like, and boil them, which he did, in a pipkin, at which time he swore he heard the prisoner's voice at the door, and that she screamed out as if she were murdered, and that the next day she appeared to be much swelled and bloated'.[27] The elaborate ritual details often laid down both added to the magical aura of the performance and provided ready-made excuses should it fail; it was easy to claim that some part of the complex ritual had not been properly executed. The injunctions to secrecy customary in these cases should not be taken too seriously, for part of the point was surely to frighten the suspect, while village gossip was hard to evade.

The kind of exchanges which might take place are illustrated in the case of Jeanne Mercier of Autrepierre, tried in 1613. Two years earlier Claude Jean Clerc and his wife had suspected her over the deaths of their horses, talking of sending to someone to find out who was responsible; Jeanne claimed they did wrong to impute blame in this manner. Around the same time Nicolas Zabey's son was ill and his family sent the niece of Jeanne's husband to consult the *devin*. She returned with some herbs for him to take and the message that he was bewitched to the extent that he would have died had they delayed another day (such claims that the consultation came just in time were common). Although it appears that no specific accusation was made, Jeanne was angry with the niece, allegedly telling her that she would have her or the Devil would. On her own admission she told the girl that she did ill to go to the cunning folk, and that it would be sufficient reason for the *curé* to chase her out of the village if he knew.[28] There was an implicit trial of moral and psychological strength going on here, perhaps also of weight in the community, conducted through minor confrontations, threats and coun-ter-threats. An extreme case of the cunning folk causing trouble within the household is provided by Catherine Charpentier of Remémont; at her trial in 1603 it emerged that almost twenty years earlier her husband had been to the *devin* at Épinal after losing many animals, only to be told 'he should seek the witches who were killing his animals no further than by his own hearth'. On hearing of this she rushed out of the house, saying her husband had been to the Devil and she would do the same. Although the family followed her to fetch her home again, the incident had been observed and remembered by their neighbours.[29] It is hard to think that such a charge was made without encouragement from the client, but that is the kind of information the documents hardly ever reveal.

Relatively few of the recorded consultations led directly to formal legal proceedings against those whom the cunning folk identified; in virtually all these examples the fact they had taken place only emerged as incidental material dating some time back. We know from much more modern times that witch-doctors and witchcraft can exist in what is effectively a closed system, with only occasional acts of violence to draw attention to its existence. The struggle is a covert one between opposed sources of supernatural power, with physical actions such as those using a cow's heart being supposed to produce effects at a distance. Persecution of witches in the lawcourts was not a necessary corollary to the operations of the cunning folk. Even such commentators as Perkins and Gifford, who were very severe on the 'white witches', were cautious in blaming them for the popular zeal to convict witches. Indeed Perkins managed to have it both ways, when he wrote,

> It hath been the ordinary custom of some men, when they have had any thing ill at ease, presently to go or send to some wise man, or wise woman, by whom they have been informed, that the thing is bewitched; and to win credit to their answer, some of them have offered to show the Witch's face in a glass: whereof the party having taken notice, returns home, and detecteth the man or woman of Witchcraft. This I grant may be a good presumption to cause their examination, but a sufficient proof of conviction it cannot be.

This was because the Devil might take the opportunity to mislead human justice, so that 'If this should be taken for a sufficient proof; the devil would not leave one good man alive in the world'.[30] The reason why Perkins could still think such evidence significant was because he believed the Devil's malice was so great that once witches were in his power his chief aim was to betray them. He was therefore able to combine warnings against possible injustice with a call for diligence in searching out witches. Gifford sounded more concerned about the situation, remarking of the Devil,

> He worketh by his other sort of Witches, whom the people call cunning men and wise women, to confirm all his matters, and by them teacheth many remedies, that so he may be sought unto and honoured as God. These things taking root in the hearts of the people, and so making them afraid of Witches, and raising up suspicions and rumours of sundry innocent persons, many guiltless are upon men's oaths condemned to death, and much innocent blood is shed.[31]

It would clearly be wrong to imagine that every witchcraft case involved the cunning folk, yet it is hard to think that either belief or persecution could have been so intense without the reinforcement they provided. Perhaps their apparent successes in obtaining healing, which were very unlikely to lead to an immediate formal accusation, were particularly important in confirming the whole way of thought they represented. Consultations of the *devins* are mentioned in almost a quarter of trials in Lorraine, but this is not a reliable guide to how often they occurred. Witnesses must have been reluctant to admit such behaviour, when they knew it was frowned on by the authorities, and often used vague remarks about having been advised by unidentified persons. In any case there is no easy dividing line between magical practitioners and helpful neighbours. It is impossible to give figures at all, however unreliable, for other parts of Europe. What can be said is that across the whole continent there is abundant evidence for the ubiquity of the cunning folk and for their propensity to identify witchcraft as the source of illness or misfortune. Nor is there any way of establishing how many of them were reclassified as malevolent witches and punished as such; this clearly varied greatly from one jurisdiction to another. The official clerical view that all such operations implied at least a tacit pact with the Devil did have a tenuous connection with popular ideas, through the notion that occult power was always ambiguous, capable of being turned to bad ends as well as good. No amount of preaching and catechizing, however, was going to persuade sufferers that it was inherently wrong and sinful to seek healing from both black and white witches. It was predictable that such efforts should be particularly intense in regions where the religious allegiance of the people was open to considerable doubt. In the Swiss

Pays de Vaud, nominally Protestant but with a largely Catholic population, the authorities in Berne put out a series of ordinances against superstitious practices, culminating in a particularly stiff one in 1597. This was the time when witchcraft trials peaked under their jurisdiction: it is interesting to find an almost parallel series of ordinances in 1600, 1609 and 1616, imposing restraints on local courts, especially in accepting denunciations by those who confessed. Attacks on abuses could go in more than one direction.[32]

These ambiguities were particularly evident in the United Provinces, the country we now know as Holland. At the beginning of witchcraft persecution at least one jurisdiction in Gelderland had been prepared to make use of the cunning folk during the trial itself. At Ratingen and Angermund in 1499, master Conrat administered a potion to the suspects, after taking which they were supposedly forced to confess if they really were witches.[33] Attitudes subsequently changed and for about a century the ministers and synods of the Dutch Reformed Church kept up a steady fire of denunciations against the cunning folk, trying to persuade the secular authorities to move against them. Although a fair number were convicted, the punishments of whipping and banishment from the area concerned seem to have proved ineffective; most of the offenders simply moved into the next jurisdiction and recommenced their career. In the end it looks as if the ministers and the judicial officials lost enthusiasm for this fruitless repressive campaign. The abundant evidence for the continuity of magical practices down to the end of the nineteenth century at least makes it plain that many Netherlanders continued to resort to cunning folk. Popular attitudes were neatly expressed in 1647 by a farmer's wife who replied, when asked why she did not pray to God rather than running to a witch-doctor, 'We can get that man, but we cannot get God'.[34] It is interesting that the northern Netherlands also had a low rate of formal persecution of witches, which came to an end almost everywhere in the region around the turn of the sixteenth and seventeenth centuries. Here the contrast between a flourishing underworld of witch-doctors and official scepticism about persecution emphasizes the substantial independence of the two elements. Comparable situations would appear to have existed in much of Europe; evidence for England, France, Italy and Iberia all points in the same direction, with witch-doctors flourishing in areas where trials and executions were uncommon.

One Dutch case which has been reconstructed in some detail is that of Jochum Bos, a young man of twenty-two who was banished from the Duchy of Gelderland for life in 1550. This sentence followed the collapse of a prosecution against five women whom Bos had accused of witchcraft; he was lucky not to suffer the death penalty they would have incurred if found guilty. The elaborate testimony in the case reveals that several clerics were engaged in forms of counter-magic, although none apparently went so far as to name witches. The popular conviction that the best cure for bewitchment was for the guilty party to pronounce a blessing must have provided an opening for others who were prepared to be more forthcoming. The analysis of the Bos affair by Hans de Waardt suggests that the neophyte witch-doctor was canalizing latent hostilities both within and between local families. He seems to have been a disreputable character who haunted taverns and seduced nuns; the more respectable among the accused found plenty of local defenders and the local magistrates were able to pick numerous holes in his story. This is one of those fascinating cases which reveal a great deal about the boundaries within which an effective witch-doctor needed to operate, precisely because Bos failed so abjectly. He had tried to create a position for himself far too quickly, without any background of successful cures or detection, clearly relying on a pretty brazen degree of cheek. In the process he exaggerated the strength of the evidence, only to find that the witnesses would not back him properly once it came to a legal showdown. It is likely this was partly because they were frightened to commit themselves too openly, in a context where family feuds were likely to polarize opinion rather than unite it. Bos was pretty evidently too much of a beginner and an opportunist to carry off his difficult role with success; he contrasts sharply with most of the other known cunning folk in the Netherlands, who conformed much more to the stereotypes already described, keeping themselves at one or two removes from any legal processes. Like others, however, he survived to resume his activities elsewhere, though with what degree of success we do not know.[35]

Witch-finders and witchcraft panics

Jochum Bos really belongs more with a rather distinct group of overt witch-finders, who shared some techniques with the cunning folk but operated in a much bolder and more dangerous fashion. The social and professional range of these witch-finders was also wider, ranging from itinerants and children through clerics and judges to local lords. Although it was quite common for ordinary witch-doctors to be marked out, by some element of education or minor social distinction, from the population among whom they lived, these differentials extended only as far as the ranks of the local clergy at the upper end. Another contrast was that the careers of most witch-finders were relatively very short, whereas the cunning folk could operate for decades. As usual the boundaries between groups are very untidy, with the crucial distinction centred on the positive manner in which some individuals set out to mobilize suspicions, rather than simply responding to clients who approached them. Witch-finding movements have been studied by anthropologists and others in the African context, where they have usually been linked with periods of crisis and disruption affecting particular peoples or tribes. While it is tempting to seek similar patterns behind European episodes, they only seem convincing in a minority of cases and vary considerably in character. Moreover, one must recognize the negative counterpart of such explanations; there were many other local crises indistinguishable from those to which we attribute a causal role, yet which produced no similar effects. When trying to account for witchcraft panics one still has to leave a large space for the merely contingent, for these were not the kind of social reactions which could ever have been predicted in a given case. Sometimes there is no evidence for anything other than a 'snowball' effect, with denunciations from one or two convicted witches implicating others in a circle which then widened inexorably.

In such instances we may well suspect that either the local court as a whole or an individual magistrate was unusually concerned to follow up such leads. Occasionally this is fairly obvious, as in the case of the St Osyth witches tried in Essex in 1582; the local Justice of the Peace, Brian Darcy, whose interrogation of the suspects suggested he knew the recent treatise by Jean Bodin, brought unusual determination to the search, although in the end only two of the dozen or so accused were hanged.[36] There was something of a ripple effect here, for in two of the villages concerned it was some of the more powerful men in the community who followed the lead given by the Justice and organized proceedings against local suspects. In formal terms, Darcy was of course only carrying out the duties of his office, like Roger Nowell who examined the main group of suspects from Pendle Forest before the Lancashire trials of 1612.[37] The attitudes of men in such positions naturally varied as between individuals and with the state of local feeling. In the 1650s and 1660s the Somerset JP Robert Hunt extracted a series of confessions of attending the sabbat that might easily have led to a wider witch-hunt. Fortunately we can note Joseph Glanvill's complaint that 'Had not his discoveries and endeavours met with great opposition and discouragements from those then in Authority, the whole Clan of those hellish Confederates in these parts had been justly exposed and punished'.[38] It is not difficult to produce a series of similar examples from continental sources. Jean Clerc, *bailli* of Luxeuil in Franche-Comté, hunted down witches with enthusiasm in 1628–31, but found the *parlement* of Dôle increasingly reluctant to confirm the harsh sentences passed by the local courts. Elsewhere in the same province between 1657 and 1660 it was a local Inquisitor, Father Symard, who encouraged a widespread campaign against witches, only to run into trouble with both the *parlement* and the authorities in Rome.[39] In the Spanish Netherlands Charles Van der Camere, lieutenant of the *châtellenie* of Bouchain, played a major role in bringing about the deaths of more than 150 witches in the decade 1610–20.[40] Among the numerous German examples is Dr Matern Eschbach, councillor of the Margrave of Baden-Baden, whose relentless pursuit of suspects between 1627 and 1631 produced at least 200 executions.[41]

Individuals of this type could do much to foster and multiply accusations, but it is hard to identify many cases where they initiated them without a large degree of local support; they were usually facilitators rather than instigators. Across Europe as a whole, local judges and officials plainly cannot have pursued a sustained campaign to encourage trials, for if they had the persecution would have been far more severe. There were various ways in which even an enthusiastic witch-hunter of this type was likely to be constrained. Some of his councillors lobbied the bigoted counter-Reformation Duke of Bavaria, Maximilian I, to enlist his support for more energetic measures against witches. They seem to have had some success with him, but far less in the duchy as a whole. This was as much a question of resistance to steps which would have increased the authority of the central government over local authorities and jurisdictions as it was of doubts over witchcraft trials.[42] The great panic in the Basque country in the years after 1608 produced complex reactions on both the French and Spanish side of the border. What seems to have begun with witch-finding by a petty nobleman who held a local military office for the king of France turned into a wave of accusations and denunciations, involving numerous clerics and lawyers. A whole range of witch-finding activities can be detected within this affair, spread out as it was in both time and space. There were Franciscans carrying out a preaching crusade in favour of more intense persecution, teenage witch-finders examining the eyes of suspects, local lynchings and violent disagreements among the various authorities. On the French side the rather credulous judge Pierre de Lancre made use of children and adolescents as informants; indeed they were prominent everywhere, making up the great majority of the 2,000 or so persons accused before the Spanish inquisitors. Perhaps the most remarkable feature is the relatively low number of people finally put to death, probably no more than a hundred or so, most of these by the French judges. Even on the French side of the border it seems likely that the prime concern of the authorities was to dampen down the crisis, allowing an initial burst of convictions to allay popular demands, then removing other suspects to be judged in Bordeaux.[43]

At the other end of the Pyrenees, in Catalonia, several individual witch-finders are known to have operated. The activities of the Valencian Juan Mallet in 1548 led to seven executions by the Barcelona Inquisition, then an investigation ordered by the *Suprema* which described the accusations as laughable and condemned numerous defects in the procedures. After this the Inquisition was solely concerned to try and prevent the abuses committed by the secular courts, with relative rather than total success. Two witch-finders brought before it in 1617 and 1619 used a technique of washing suspects with holy water in order to discover a crow's-foot mark. The second of these, Laurence Carmell, called in by various communities after crop failures in 1618, claimed to have identified 200 witches, of whom about twenty had been executed. During the ensuing investigation some magistrates were prosecuted and there were claims that a number of the accused had been found dead, supposedly killed by their own relatives to prevent infamy being attached to the family. Despite such alarming events and the difficulty of controlling local agencies in this fiercely independent region, none of the various spurts of persecution was very prolonged or severe; given the evident readiness of petty judges to break the rules this was a considerable achievement for the Inquisition.[44]

It would appear that no well-organized major state in Europe was prepared to tolerate genuine witch-hunting for very long. The legal and religious authorities in France, England and the Spanish dominions had their own disagreements about the reality of witchcraft and the ways to handle it, but they were determined to assert their own authority and maintain good order. Although partial exceptions may be seen in some of the more northerly territories of the Spanish Habsburgs – parts of the Netherlands, Luxembourg, Franche-Comté – these do not really challenge the general rule. These were 'difficult' political entities, where government was relatively weak and local rights were tenaciously defended, so that they rather resemble the German lands than the more centralized nation states. Middling-sized and rather 'underdeveloped' states like Scotland, Denmark, Lorraine and the Swiss cantons had a much more chequered record. In Scotland one of the most intense periods of persecution occurred in the early 1590s, when the young James VI was persuaded there had been a diabolical conspiracy against himself and his bride Anne of Denmark. The trials had less to do with the king's opinions, however, than with the zealots of the Presbyterian Kirk, who were temporarily allowed their head. A background of political and religious uncertainty, as in this case, could become mixed up with questions about the legitimacy of authority and the need to assert it by enforcing divine justice.[45] Something of the same kind may have been involved in the operations of the notorious 'witchfinder general' Matthew Hopkins and his associate John Stearne. As the English Civil War was drawing to its close the two men travelled around East Anglia offering their services to local authorities to search out witches; their crusade may have had as many as 200 victims, a high proportion of the total of those put to death in England.

Although Hopkins and Stearne have often been represented as motivated by financial greed or Puritan enthusiasm, neither claim is wholly convincing. The payment they took for their services was modest, no more than was necessary to meet their costs and provide a very marginal living, while Hopkins at least showed little sign of particular religious concern. A number of clerics did become involved as supporters of the campaign, however, just as others (including some strong Puritans) opposed it. The influence of Perkins may well be evident in the unusual concern with the diabolical contract found in these cases, which seems to derive more from English sources than from the Continental ones often suggested, but this does not have to imply anything about the religious views of those who followed his lead here, since his position can be found among Catholic as well as Protestant theologians. Hopkins and Stearne began as members of a group concerned about witchcraft around Manningtree, in the extreme north-east of Essex, from where their activity as persecutors probably extended naturally into neighbouring areas. Their own motivation is perhaps best explained as a mixture of genuine obsession with the threat of witchcraft and the satisfaction of playing a leading role around the country. The whole episode was only possible at a time when central authority had broken down, for the record of the royal government before 1640 leaves no doubt it would have halted the witch-finders from an early stage, more particularly when such methods as the swimming test, pricking for the mark and sleep deprivation were being used to extract confessions. Like almost all witch-finding movements, this one was dependent on local support; its effect was to mobilize existing suspicions rather than create new ones. The fragmentary records of the trials suggest that the accused were charged with very typical offences. They may have been rather younger than usual, with a relatively high proportion of servants among both the alleged witches and their victims and a large number of bewitchments affecting children. One striking feature is that a significant number of the witches seem to have presented themselves in order to be searched for the mark or subjected to the swimming test. The obvious explanation for this apparently suicidal conduct is that they were trying to clear themselves of pre-existing suspicions in the belief that the ordeal must confirm their innocence.[46]

It has already become plain that Continental analogues for the Hopkins crusade are numerous and as time went by these aroused increasing concern at the higher judicial and political levels. Two local lords in Peelland, then just within the Spanish Netherlands, launched a drive against witches within their jurisdictions in 1595, which resulted in at least fifteen executions. It seems likely that the lords, Erasmus van Grevenbroeck and Bernard van Merode, were influenced by their relative Jacob van Brecht, high sheriff of 's-Hertogenbosch, who already had a background in hunting heretics and witches. Here it is less clear that all the accused were plausible candidates for trial and the local Catholic clergy came out strongly against the prosecutions. Such reactions were sufficient to provoke the intervention of the Council of Brabant; although that body was careful to avoid any direct challenge to the authority of the lords and the local courts, the pressure from above was enough to avert further trials.[47] In France there were several outbreaks of local witch-hunting. In 1587 parts of Champagne saw local courts and officials using the water ordeal and other illegal tests against scores of suspects.

This episode was almost certainly related to the political-cum-religious tensions which had wracked French society for some twenty-five years, since the beginning of the Wars of Religion in 1562. Both Catholic and Protestant zealots were deeply affected by apocalyptic visions of a world nearing its end, while identifying their opponents with the Antichrist and the Devil.[48] Champagne was a stronghold of the Catholic League, which at this very moment was mounting a climactic challenge to the authority of the Valois monarchy, which Bodin believed to be soft on witches as well as heretics (he prudently put more of the blame on Charles IX, who was safely dead, than on the ruling monarch, his brother Henri III).[49] There was always a gap between the ideas of the aristocratic leaders and those of their followers, however, and ironically it was the Cardinal de Guise, one of the most prominent figures of the League and also archbishop of Reims, who joined forces with the *parlement* of Paris to put a stop to the witch-hunt.[50] Half a century later the same region was one of those involved in the most widespread outbreak of the kind ever to affect France. Another archbishop of Reims, Léonor d'Étampes de Valançay, wrote in July 1644:

> For several months great disorders have slipped into numerous parishes of my diocese near the frontier over certain individuals who are made out to be witches; they are maltreated, driven out, or physically attacked; they are burned, while it has become customary to take the suspects and throw them in the water, then if they float it is enough to make them witches. This is such a great abuse that up to thirty or forty are found in a single parish being falsely accused in this manner; I say falsely because some have come before me to be confessed and take communion who are completely innocent, and those who desire to avenge their passions or to seize the goods of their neighbours with impunity use this pretext ... these disorders multiply every day because the petty local judges condemn people to death on simple conjectures, with no other form of trial or attempt to consider the evidence.[51]

During 1643 and 1644 a wave of these local persecutions swept across large parts of France, from the south-west to the north-east. It is far from clear that there was much direct contact between the various areas affected, so this may have been a series of independent panics with very similar characteristics.[52] In the Bordelais, the Pyrenees and the Toulousain several witch-finders were active, going round and being paid by local authorities to test groups of suspects. The Toulouse *parlement* sent three of these to the gallows, declaring that 'to give some authority to their schemes, they pretend they have authority from the *parlement* to make these searches, by which means they demand large sums of money from the communities, extorting payment; and since they have no know-ledge of the art of surgery to distinguish natural and unnatural marks, they judge arbitrarily and accuse those they wish of witchcraft, and normally those who do not pay them'.[53] The sceptical attitude of the higher courts apparently saved virtually all those accused, while the communities were left with substantial debts for the costs of the oper-ation, which rapidly cooled their ardour. The other major region involved ran from Burgundy to Champagne; here, there is some evidence that exceptional late frosts and hailstorms in 1644, seen by many as classic signs of weather magic practised at the sabbats, were the catalyst. The comments of the archbishop of Reims, already quoted, can be set against those of the Capuchin Jacques d'Autun, who described how in 1644,

> most of the towns and villages of Burgundy were in a state of consternation because of the rumour which spread that the witches were the cause of the changes in the weather, that it was they who through their spells had destroyed the grains by hail and the grapes by frost . . . the least of the peasants set themselves up as judges, their fantasies and imaginings were treated as oracles, when they accused someone of *maleficium*, without thinking that they confused in the same persons the different qualities of witnesses and judges; they banished all the formalities of justice and only wanted to follow those of the swimming test . . . there was a young shepherd whom the villagers in their stupidity called the little prophet . . . his trick was to look into the eyes of those brought before him, to determine their fate; for it was enough that this miserable boy said he had observed the Devil's mark which only he could detect, for the suspect to be declared a witch and put in the hands of the lower courts, whose officials were at risk of their lives if they tried to examine these extrava-gances; the least evil with which they were threatened, was to suffer the reproach of being accomplices of the supposed witches, for having been reluctant to rush to judge them and send them to their death.[54]

The *parlement* of Dijon was kept busy commuting sentences and pursuing abuses, passing more than a dozen death sentences on those who had been involved in the latter.[55]

Although Jacques d'Autun displayed the common tendency of the educated elite to be scornful about peasant credulity and ignorance, he also had few illusions about the attitudes of the local officials, writing,

> I am astonished by the behaviour of some judges, who tremble at the simple name of witch, and believe that all those suspected of witchcraft are already convicted: the opinion which preoccupies their minds is a coloured glass, which transfers its hue to all the objects which come before their eyes . . . Their readiness to believe the witnesses who accuse an idiot (who does not know how to defend himself, nor sometimes even to respond to the questions put to him) deceives them to such an extent that the stupidity of the accused passes for a confession.[56]

These words date from around 1670, the time of the final burst of local persecutions in France. In Normandy, four or five boys aged between eleven and fourteen went around identifying witches, with the backing of a judge at Carentan. Teenage boys were also prominent as witch-finders in the south-west at the same time; one of them was eventually arrested and brought to Paris, where the royal minister Colbert rapidly concluded that he was an impostor. Although the *parlement* of Bordeaux had acted with some vigour to stop the pursuits, in Béarn that of Pau had a less glorious record. It had sent out three commissioners to investigate, who charged the communities fees much as the witch-finders did; moreover, one of them did nothing to follow up the exposure of one of the latter as a fraud, when he failed to identify a suspect presented to him a second time. It was the Norman *parlement* of Rouen, however, which displayed an obstinate determination to convict witches, only to be overruled by the direct authority of the crown.[57] Despite this somewhat aberrant case, there can be no doubt that the overall effect of popular witch-hunting in France was to discredit persecution more generally. Declarations by the monarchy and its agents laid great stress on the way popular credulity and the operations of itinerant witch-finders divided families and communities, thus threatening the fundamental pillars of hierarchy and social order. There was also a long-running concern on the part of the higher courts to control abuses by local judges and reduce their scope for independent action. These tensions brought together issues of authority, prestige and intellectual superiority in such a way that they all tended to work against continued persecution.

State-sponsored witch-hunts

In Germany the same process was much more tortuous and uncertain, although the time scale was not very different. The fragmentation of political authority within the Holy Roman Empire underlay enormous variations in local experience. As elsewhere in Europe, the majority of those executed as witches perished as a result of scattered local trials, each with only a few victims at most. It was in Germany, however, that the mass panics were most deadly and terrifying, always in smaller territories and cities which were yet important enough to control their own judicial systems. In the last decades of the sixteenth century the notion of the sabbat became more elaborate as trials multiplied, culminating in the large-scale persecutions in the prince-archbishopric of Trier in the 1580s and 1590s. Various calamities affecting the harvests were significant as a background to events here, but the crucial reason why several hundred trials took place lay in the attitude of the archbishop himself, his suffragan bishop Peter Binsfeld and other members of his circle. Their determination to stamp out witchcraft was so intense that judges and clerics who questioned the conduct of the persecution were themselves tortured into admissions of guilt and executed.[58] This pattern was to be repeated in the notorious trials instigated by other prince-bishops at Bamberg and Würzburg some three decades later, where there were at least 300 and 600 executions respectively. In Bamberg, the bishop's legal adviser Dr Ernst Vasolt was obsessed with the sabbat and took torture to extreme lengths; he was aided by special witch-finding committees. The Würzburg trials were notable for the fact that a minimum of forty-three clerics are known to have been executed.[59] In both cases the Jesuits appear to have played a major role in organizing the persecution, but it was one of their number at Würzburg and Cologne, Friedrich von Spee, who used his experiences to pen a devastating critique of the whole methodology of the trials. His *Cautio Criminalis* of 1631 was to prove one of the most powerful and influential of all attacks on witch-hunting, with its insistence on the way the remorseless use of torture and other abuses vitiated the procedures from the start. Spee and other critics homed in on the ways that accusations procured in this way were totally unreliable, the possibilities of manipulation by gaolers and executioners, the risks of malicious charges and the virtual impossibility of being acquitted.

The years between 1627 and 1631, which saw the climax of these gruesome persecutions directed by the prince-bishops, were also the peak period for similar outbreaks across south-western Germany. In most of these cases it is difficult to ascribe responsibility to particular individuals; city governments in particular often seem to have been carried away by the crazed logic of denunciations extracted by torture. In a curious example of misapplied bureaucratic sophistication, some towns kept elaborate lists of those denounced, which they might even communicate to neighbouring authorities. Legal expertise was supposedly provided by consultations of university law faculties, but this proved a most unreliable check on local excesses, because these academic lawyers rarely had sufficient practical experience. An exceptionally unpleasant trend, noted in an earlier chapter, was for children to become ever more important as both vectors and targets of the persecutions; their readiness to elaborate stories and denounce others made it all too easy for others to manipulate them, whether deliberately or otherwise. The general pattern was for the persecution in a particular town to build to a climax in which members of the ruling elites themselves were being convicted, then for some incident to focus accumulated doubts, followed by a sudden collapse of the whole process. In the longer term the effect was to instil a much more cautious attitude, which prevented any recrudescence of witch-hunting at this intense level. Although there were a couple of further episodes in the 1660s, they were not on the same scale and did not spread in the same fashion. It should be stressed that these German panics, which have so often been thought of as being typical of the so-called 'witch-craze', were really rather exceptional; they were only possible within a very special political and legal context. The motivation of those concerned remains largely elusive, since no witch-hunter left an autobiographical record of his actions. One can imagine a potent mixture of fear, sadism and civic and religious zeal behind their desire to purge the community of the agents of the Devil, but it is impossible to be more precise. Some allowance must clearly be made for the general atmosphere of political and religious tension, at a decisive moment in German history. The 1627–32 peak coincides with the moment when the Counter-Reformation reached its political zenith in Germany with the victories of the Imperial armies in the first phase of the Thirty Years' War. The witchcraft persecutions, however, took place in areas hardly touched by the conflict. While in a general sense they must have incorporated a drive towards godliness, there is no good evidence (despite the activities of some Jesuits) that this was more than an ancillary factor in causing them or explaining their intensity. There has been a long battle between Protestant and Catholic historians, each trying to represent the other denomination as primarily responsible for the horrors of persecution. In south-west Germany the statistics are inconclusive; the Catholic areas appear rather harsher towards witches, but not to an overwhelming degree. Nor did the collapse of the trials have anything to do with the advance of the Protestant champion Gustavus Adolphus of Sweden, as has repeatedly been asserted, for they had virtually ceased before his first great victory at Breitenfeld in the autumn of 1631.[60] On the other hand, as Wolfgang Behringer has pointed out, the ten most violent persecutors of witches in Germany were all Catholic prince-bishops; apart from those already mentioned, these included three Electors of Mainz and – worst of all, with perhaps 2,000 victims – Elector Ferdinand von Wittelsbach of Cologne.[61]

Protestant states were certainly not immune from their own outbreaks of witch-hunting. Apart from the English and Scottish cases, the countries around the Baltic were particularly affected. In Denmark, King Christian IV and some of his councillors were responsible for a package of moral reforming legislation, including new rules on witchcraft, introduced in 1617. Over the next seven or eight years persecution ran at a far higher level than at any other time in Danish history; one historian has suggested that the subsequent drop in the number of trials came about because virtually all the prime suspects had been convicted.[62] This was of course far more like the Hopkins episode than the German panics, since high-level intervention was facilitating the proscription of typical village witches on *maleficium* charges, not spawning an uncontrollable wave of denunciations. The belated Swedish witch-hunt, occurring between 1668 and 1676, presents a strange mixture of characteristics. The central mechanism behind most of the accusations was the use of groups of children to identify witches, whom they had supposedly seen at the diabolical festivities in Blåkulla. Popular concern seems to have centred on the idea that large numbers of children were being corrupted and persuaded into serving the Devil although, as might have been predicted, many of the accused had previous reputations. In several cases the practice of keeping the child witnesses together provided an ideal environment for them to synchronize their fantasies and charges, while in others poor children went round as witch-finders, operating a mixture of begging and blackmail. The course of events was shaped by the discrepant attitudes of the royal government and the nobility, who seem to have been sceptical from the start, and the local officials and clerics who often joined in enthusiastically. The result was a curious compromise, with a modest number of executions over the first few years; in effect the government was allowing these to operate as a kind of safety-valve for popular feeling. The traditional practices of not allowing torture and only convicting those who confessed also kept the numbers under control at first, but over time these rules were eroded. The fact that around half the 200 or so executions took place in 1675 suggests that the 'middle way' attempted by the government was stoking up persecution rather than controlling it. When the trials moved to Stockholm itself in 1676, decisive action was finally taken to stop them and, as described in chapter one, the fraudulent basis of the whole process was exposed.[63]

The clergy and witchcraft persecution

Many of the brief accounts of witch-hunts given above have revealed the clergy, whether Catholic or Protestant, as leading participants. There is a risk that this may give a rather skewed picture, for selecting these moments of intense excitement and terror is to privilege the exceptional, and usually to present the most unfavourable examples. The difficulties of generalizing are immediately obvious, nevertheless. Whom should we regard as typical, the acutely sceptical Salazar or his two credulous and bitchy colleagues in the Logroño Inquisition? Are writers like Perkins and Gifford to be regarded as clear-sighted critics of the popular methods of identifying witches or as sponsors of a would-be persecution of the cunning folk? Reformers of all denominations certainly emphasized the Devil and his works, and this all-pervasive rhetoric must have had some effect on the recipients. Confessional friction and the struggle to cleanse religion of contamination by popular superstition both found natural expression through identifying what was to be rejected as evil and diabolical. Witchcraft had a natural place at the top of any hierarchy of sin and it must be the duty of every Christian to oppose it. Everyday pastoral work gave endless opportunities to propagate such views; it is evident that had the clergy across Europe been committed enthusiasts for persecution, they could have mobilized local feeling to devastating effect. The very modest levels of persecution and formal accusations in most areas are therefore *prima facie* evidence that the clergy (like the local judges) were very much less strident against witches than a rapid selection of texts would suggest. This conclusion is reinforced by the study of a large number of trial records, for only a very small minority show signs of more than the most marginal clerical involvement. Where attitudes can be discerned they are often ambivalent; were the beliefs part of the superstition which must be eradicated, or was it the witches who must be attacked?

Explaining why things do *not* happen is inherently difficult and this case is no exception. Several possibilities may be considered, albeit on a hypothetical basis. In much of Catholic Europe, the effort to raise the educational and moral standards of the parish clergy took a long time to have much impact and only seriously affected the generation of priests in place around the time persecution went into sharp decline; by the time the change was fully effective trials had either ceased or become a rarity. These men tended to be more socially distinct from their parishioners than their predecessors, while both their background and training probably increased their sensitivity to the dangers of popular superstition. Previous generations would have been closer to their flocks, more disposed to share a 'popular' view of the world as permeated by miraculous and supernatural forces. If they did not participate more in the processes whereby witchcraft was identified and managed, this is most plausibly explained on social grounds. For a variety of reasons – including nominal celibacy, outside origin, tithes and fees, dislike of confession – a certain wary distance characterized the priest's relationship to his parishioners. He was particularly excluded from the world of feminine sociability and gossip, through which much of the labelling of suspects took place. There may also have been a preference for consulting specialists outside the parish, as was the case with the cunning folk, while resort to the latter, the perpetual rivals of the clergy, would also have generated mutual mistrust. On the other hand, as we shall see, clerics who took on the role of witch-finders performed it very effectively; it was fortunate that for whatever reason they were not more numerous.

The Protestant churches also had their fair share of pastors who were not distinguished for either education or holy living, although in the crucial decades their average standard was probably rather higher. There were of course very significant theological differences, notably over what the reformers saw as idolatrous or magical practices; they were adamantly hostile to most of the traditional modes for giving protection against or relief from witchcraft. There was less agreement about the exact scope for the Devil and witches to inflict real harm. There were those like the Lutheran Johann Brenz, writing well before Weyer, who insisted that misfortunes such as hailstorms were sent by God, while the witches were merely deluded by Satan into thinking they had caused them.[64] Those who took this view often went on to argue that popular enthusiasm to convict witches was dangerous and often misguided. On the other hand there were plenty of divines who insisted that the pact with the Devil was enough on its own to justify the severest punishment, even if the witches were relatively impotent. The kind of enthusiasm for persecution found in Scotland probably rested most firmly on a determination to root out all the 'relics of popery', seen themselves as essentially diabolical, coupled with a fierce insistence on godly discipline within the community. Protestants may have been particularly liable to see themselves as isolated within populations which remained stubbornly attached to older ways, and resorted to extreme forms of black-and-white splitting as a reaction. If ministers were much less likely than their Catholic counterparts to engage in witch-finding and counter-magic, they may have compensated with a greater willingness to support formal charges through the legal system. The virtual absence of Catholic priests as witnesses does suggest some kind of informal taboo, perhaps connected to their privileged but delicate position as hearers of confession.

These reservations about the *general* behaviour of the clergy are particularly important as a counter-balance to the numerous individual cases which give a very different picture. Spectacular instances of clerical zeal for persecution can be found in some of the German episodes just described and among the exorcists dealing with diabolical possession. The latter often encountered resistance or scepticism from other clerics, including their own superiors, however; those not exposed to the violent immediacy of contact with the supposed devils naturally tended to take a calmer view. Among Catholics the situation was greatly complicated by the multiplicity of different orders, which made it impossible to enforce a coherent view or to discipline offenders effectively. There were orders such as the Ambrosians which made something of a speciality of possession and bewitchment. In the case of Chrétienne Simon of Domjevin, tried in 1607, testimony was given about how a sick girl had been taken to their convent at St Nicolas-du-Port, where she was diagnosed by one of the fathers. He told her to return at a specific time, when he made her kneel before him in the choir, where he used various 'conjurations' on her, then asked if she felt something moving in her body. She replied she felt something moving from her stomach to her throat, at which he continued his operations and asked if she still felt it. When she told him it had now descended to her stomach he declared that she was bewitched by someone who wished them great harm and would ruin them if they did not take action. Asked who it was, he replied that she did not live far from their house. This naturally directed suspicion at Chrétienne, who was the nearest neighbour and already possessed a reputation for witchcraft. No *devin* could easily have improved on this accomplished performance, with its play on the unfortunate girl's sensibility and its nicely judged vagueness.[65]

It was the religious orders, rather than ordinary local clergy, who tended to assume star roles as exorcists. This was the kind of special duty both they and the general public saw as particularly fitting for these spiritual athletes of the early modern world. Their theological and philosophical learning was one quality which surrounded them with an aura of special power, supposedly giving them a peculiar ability to discriminate between true diabolism and mere simulation. At the same time, a reputation for personal austerity was naturally linked in the popular mind to special powers of intercession; holiness was a potent weapon in the struggle against the demonic. It is therefore no surprise to find orders like the Jesuits and Capuchins, which really did maintain very high intellectual and moral standards, to the fore in several famous episodes. Students of early modern Catholicism have often noted how the period between the Council of Trent (which ended in 1563) and the middle of the seventeenth century had its own special tone and characteristics. This was an age of new beginnings, of combativeness and mystical and spiritual enthusiasm. For a few decades a heady mixture of old and new elements flourished, to create an atmosphere which was as fertile as it was incoherent. Despite a series of bitter disputes, which foreshadowed later difficulties, a remarkably wide range of views could still coexist, from the miraculous to the disciplinarian. Neither spiritual nor secular authorities could easily control the situation; only from the 1640s onward did a much tighter and more internally consistent style of belief and behaviour tend to become dominant. One of the striking features of this shift lay precisely in a deepening suspicion towards the kind of enthusiasm and therapeutic practices previously associated with sainthood, but now increasingly identified as superstitious. Relics, pious traditions and local saints with their shrines came under critical scrutiny they were ill-equipped to resist. This was a relative shift over a long time scale, so its effects should not be exaggerated. Traditional ideas and practices proved to have immense powers of endurance, which have carried many of them through to the present day, albeit often in rather modified forms. The trend, however, has been for them to become marginalized, with the authorities displaying a growing anxiety to avoid both contamination of the pure faith and possible ridicule. By the later seventeenth century, clerical enthusiasts for exorcism and the pursuit of witches found themselves in a new and less favourable climate almost everywhere in Europe. Leading figures in the great counter-Reformation orders such as the Jesuits and Capuchins clamped down on what were now seen as deviant and dangerous views; in the case of the Jesuits there was a virtual purge against mystics during the middle decades of the century, particularly in France. Although these changes did nothing to reduce popular demand for help against witchcraft and possession, in the long run they made the clergy more cautious in their responses.

One of the signs of this caution was the reluctance of superiors to allow involvement in highly publicized exorcisms. As the scandalous affair of the devils of Loudun pursued its course in the 1630s, with the enthusiastic help of no less than six Jesuit exorcists, the General in Rome wanted them withdrawn as soon as possible, complaining of their imprudence and hoping they could be brought under control by another father who would be less 'credulous and *naif*'.[66] Cardinal Bérulle, who had defended the false demoniac Marthe Brossier in 1599, seems to have learned from the experience, for he later advised his new order of Oratorians to have nothing to do with possession cases, in which there were 'many things which are fraudulent and difficult to detect . . . in general one should very rarely interrogate the devil and believe him still less'.[67] In 1688 another leading Catholic reformer, Louis Tronson, advised a colleague, 'Concerning witchcraft, it is impossible to be too sceptical about those who confess to it, and our experience has convinced us that without the greatest precautions it leads us into terrible labyrinths and embarrassments which consume all the time of the missionaries, with very little fruit'.[68] By this time undue credulity was readily mocked by educated Europeans, so that even those who wanted to defend the reality of diabolical phenomena were usually anxious to distance themselves from past abuses. This was an untidy and uncertain change of opinion, spread over many decades and only reaching down to local level in a very irregular way. Giovanni Levi's excellent study of the Piedmontese priest

Giovan Battista Chiesa shows how his mass exorcisms attracted enormous audiences as late as the 1690s, before he was disciplined by the officials of the Archbishop of Turin. Chiesa had treated over 500 people and in more than half the cases where the complaint was identified it had to do with possession or witchcraft.[69]

Clerical caution was evident very early in the Netherlands, as it was in England, where the exploits of Catholic and Puritan exorcists at the end of the sixteenth century led the Anglican church to adopt a highly sceptical position that was then reinforced by the new king, James I, with his enthusiasm to search out fraud. Here both Catholic missionaries, led by Father Weston, and Puritan specialists, such as John Darrell, were claiming that their ability to drive out devils showed they represented the true church; such supernatural powers were the sign that God was with them. The popularity of their séances, with the attendant publicity, worried the authorities greatly and exposed a dangerous chink in Anglican armour, for the official position that the age of miracles was past had little popular appeal. Bishop Bancroft of London took the lead in organizing a counter-offensive, as part of which his chaplain Samuel Harsnet struck out against the enemies on both wings in works entitled *A Discovery of the Fraudulent Practises of John Darrell* and *A Declaration of Egregious Popish Impostures*. Darrell himself was suspended from the ministry and briefly imprisoned by the court of High Commission, after his star patient William Somers had been induced to confess that his fits were fraudulent.[70] Official disapproval did not prevent a series of radical ministers and writers claiming through most of the seventeenth century that the 'cures' effected by Darrell and others had been genuine. By the time nonconformity became a serious alternative church, however, the leading ministers, such as Richard Baxter and Oliver Heywood, took a more cautious approach. This became evident in the rather laboured controversy which broke out in the 1690s over the Lancashire affair of the 'Surrey demoniac' Richard Dugdale. The dissenting divines who had treated him by fasting and prayer were obviously uncomfortable about some of the stronger claims made by one of their number and shared the distrust of their Anglican opponents towards popular beliefs.[71] By this date, it would appear, there was a virtual consensus among the educated elite in favour of naturalistic explanations; possession was still admitted as an exceptional event, but attempts to link it to witchcraft found very little support.

England produced an exceptionally rich witchcraft literature, covering the religious, legal, medical and sociological facets of the topic with remarkable thoroughness. It is hard not to conclude that this extensive public debate fostered greater sophistication among the national and local elites whose opinions were so crucial, making them ever more cautious. There were other Protestant countries like Sweden and Scotland, where ministers were still capable of taking an active part in local persecutions towards the end of the seventeenth century, and which possessed nothing remotely comparable. Ever since Sir Walter Scott and Lecky, historians have laid much of the blame for Scottish witch-hunting on the ministers of the Presbyterian Kirk. In the most general sense there is clearly something in this; the General Assemblies routinely called for the punishment of witches, ministers hectored and questioned suspects, then gathered the evidence against them, and there was a good deal of ineffective clerical grumbling when the repeal of the English Witchcraft Act in 1736 carried away the Scottish legislation with it. In the Highlands, where the Kirk's writ did not run, persecution never got going at all. One can scarcely imagine a more chilling or truly evil misuse of religious rhetoric than that by the elderly minister James Hutchinson, whose sermon to the Commissioners of Justiciary at Paisley in 1697 insisted on their duty to convict the accused, including young children, and put them to death. He blamed the outbreak of witchcraft in the area on the 'prevelancy of unmortified lust and corruption' adding that it was the means whereby 'others of the poorer sort could get their malice and envy satisfied'.[72] Without the intellectual underpinning the Kirk provided there might well have been no witch-hunt of any significance in Scotland, for the lairds and lawyers were deeply influenced by its teachings. Yet it was these holders of secular power who ran the trials that mobilized popular suspicions in the fashion familiar across Europe, while ministers rarely seem to have played more than an accessory role in the process. After about 1680 the secular authorities had effectively ceased to prosecute virtually everywhere, although the clergy continued to restate their formal position. As this case demonstrates, doctrine was very powerful and represented an independent causal factor, but it was not enough on its own, unless it interacted with other social and political forces.

An interesting feature of the persecution in Scotland is that it was heavily concentrated in a series of short bursts. The years particularly concerned were 1591–1597, 1628–1630, 1643, 1649 and 1661–2, although these dates are necessarily somewhat approximate. Rather unusually, it is possible to discern some meaningful patterns behind these episodes, thanks to the superb analysis of the subject by the late Christina Larner. The first began with the supposed conspiracy to shipwreck James VI and his Danish bride and the issue by the Privy Council of a general commission for examining witches that allowed local courts a virtually free hand. The peak of trials in 1597 was associated with Margaret Atkin, known as 'the great witch of Balweary', who declared after her conviction 'that they had a secret mark all of that sort, in their eyes, whereby she could surely tell, how soon she looked upon any, whether they were witches or not'. It was said

> that she was carried from town to town to make discoveries in that kind. Many were brought in question by her dilations, especially at Glasgow where divers innocent women, through the credulity of the minister, Mr John Cowper, were condemned and put to death. In the end she was found to be a mere deceiver (for the same persons that the one day she had declared guilty, the next day being presented in another habit she cleansed) and sent back to Fife where first she was apprehended. At her trial she affirmed all to be false that she had confessed, either of herself or others, and persisted in this to her death.[73]

It is all too easy to see how Margaret Atkin, already condemned herself, found both a compensating sense of power and a stay of execution in this fashion. Her case seems to have been instrumental in persuading the Council that delegated powers to try witches were being abused, while more generally it was asserted that individuals had been exploiting these to pursue personal grudges. From now on witchcraft was only to be prosecuted under specific commissions issued by the central government.

Over the next century this centralization created a rather peculiar situation in Scotland, also conditioned by the perpetual struggle between secular and religious authorities. The General Assembly of the Kirk regularly complained that the Council was slack on moral offences; when the latter wanted to show its godliness it allowed prosecution of offences which interested the church. The wave of trials after 1628 formed part of a general law-and-order campaign; those of the 1640s were related to the intense political atmosphere of the Civil War period. In 1649 the Parliament refused requests for special measures against witchcraft, while issuing large numbers of individual commissions for trials; it thus kept the clergy in their place, while satisfying the demand for godly severity against the servants of Satan. The Cromwellian régime took a very different line; the imported English judges were horrified at the flimsy evidence brought forward and the use of torture. Trials dried up almost completely, although numbers started to increase in the last year or two of the Protectorate. The Restoration saw the new Privy Council issue commissions in the old style, with the result that between the spring of 1661 and the autumn of 1662 there were perhaps 600 trials and 300 executions. This finally provoked an official reaction, with prohibitions on arbitrary imprisonment, pricking for the mark and the use of torture. Revealingly, the Council also denounced several witch-prickers who had been active in the persecution. One of these, John Kincaid, who had also been involved in the 1649 hunt, admitted using fraud. There seems little doubt that such men, apart from using fake bodkins with retractable blades, were well aware of the ways bodily sensations can be confused or lost.[74] After 1662 there were no more major hunts in Scotland, now that procedures had been tightened and scepticism was growing among the lawyers. In the short run it may also have been true that most obvious suspects had been eliminated in the great persecutions of the past three decades.

Some spectacular examples have already been given of Catholic clerics involved in major witch-hunts. These include priests in the Basque country, some of them acting as local inquisitorial commissioners, and the German prince-bishops with their entourages of Jesuits and others. At a much more local level there were *curés* who operated as *devins*, like the one at Raimbeaucourt near Cambrai. Françoise Brulois consulted him when two of her children died in 1665, to be told that the bewitchment came from someone who posed as a friend. This led her to suspect her neighbour Jeanne Bachy, who was always visiting the house. When the troubles continued, with a rumour that the spell was intended to kill Brulois's children, the Capuchins from nearby Orchies were called in to exorcize the house. They provided something to be buried under the threshold, saying that after this the witch would never enter; Jeanne duly ceased to visit, even when urged to do so by the local priest, and this was then reported at her trial in 1679.[75] At Douai in 1610, the mother of a sick child accused Isabeau Blary, threatening 'that she would go to the Capuchin, who would make the woman who had made him sick pass across a mirror'.[76] In the 1620s there were at least three *curés* near Épinal in Lorraine who were conducting exorcisms on the supposed victims of witchcraft, which included getting them to name the witches responsible. These cases also include descriptions of exorcisms in the same style carried out by monks at the local houses of Moyenmoustier and Autrey. The *curés* further suggested the investigation of bedding, in which strange substances were duly found. When Annon Bourguignotte of Bettoncourt was charged, she said all she knew was that the *curé* had found spells around the village and blamed her for them.[77] This was Dominique Gordet, *curé* of Vomécourt, whose activities were mentioned in several cases and eventually got him into serious trouble. In 1631 he himself was arrested and tortured by the ecclesiastical court; he admitted sexual relations with a woman already executed as a witch (claiming he had been drunk) and that he might have abused the use of exorcisms, although he insisted he was not a witch and that his intentions had been good.[78] Pierre de Lancre cited the trial of Pierre Renoux, a priest-schoolmaster apprehended by the *sénéchal* of Montmorillon in 1599, 'who unwitched and cured the sick, by illicit prayers. He made waxen candles to kill witches, saying that if they were placed in their room at night they died as soon as they had seen their light and flame. He alleged that a priest-witch named le Pic had died in this way, with various other superstitions I shall not report'.[79] Cases such as this do suggest that priests had good reason to be cautious about anything which implied they had magical powers. A fair number ended up in the courts, undergoing the familiar process of being converted from white into black witches; their high profile in local society probably left them more exposed than the ordinary cunning folk, while the range of authorities to which they were subject may have made denunciations easier and more effective.

Medical expertise

Doctors were not generally accused in this way, although there was an exceptional case of demonic possession in Lorraine which led to a physician being executed as a witch.[80] They were quite often blamed, however, for resorting to witchcraft as a cover for their own inadequacy. Scot had complained of 'unskilful physicians' in the course of alleging that the ills ascribed to witchcraft were no more than natural maladies.[81] As Thomas Ady, almost certainly a doctor himself, put it:

seldom goeth any man or woman to a Physician for cure of any Disease, but one question they ask the Physician is, Sir, do you not think this Party is in ill handling, or under an ill tongue? or more plainly, Sir, do you not think this party is bewitched? and to that many an ignorant Physician will answer, Yea verily; the reason is, *Ignorantiae pallium maleficium et incantatio,* a cloak for the Physicians ignorance, when he cannot finde the nature of the Disease, he saith, the Party is bewitched.[82]

Some instances seem to support these claims. In the celebrated case of the possession of the Throckmorton children of Warboys, a Cambridge physician named Barrow was consulted in 1589; after two unsuccessful prescriptions, he diagnosed bewitchment on the basis of a further sample of urine.[83] During the trial of Rose Cullender and Amy Duny of Lowestoft in 1665 it was revealed that some years earlier Dr Jacob of Yarmouth, who had a reputation for helping bewitched children, had offered an interesting prescription. One of the sick child's blankets was hung up and anything found in it thrown into the fire. A toad obligingly appeared and exploded when put in the fire, after which the suspect was discovered much scorched. At the trial itself Sir Thomas Browne offered the subtle but damning opinion that various children's fits were natural, 'and nothing else but that they call the mother, but only heightened to a great excess by the subtlety of the Devil, co-operating with the malice of these which we term witches, at whose instance he doth these villainies'.[84] The idea that the Devil could worsen natural ailments, which was perfectly consonant with the views of several demonologists, gave virtually unlimited scope for accusations. The failure to use it more extensively reminds us yet again that theory was regularly subordinated to common practice and belief. There is no reason to suppose that Browne was concerned to advance a general proposition for its own sake; he was called on to testify in a trial, and offered a medical opinion which allowed the accused to be convicted.

At the level of routine trials for witchcraft, doctors were not in fact very often involved in this way. The English instances just cited are among ten or so cases of medical diagnoses of witchcraft to be found in the extensive materials collected by Ewen, to which Keith Thomas has added a few more. The generally patchy nature of English records might justify the supposition that a number of other medical interventions have left no trace, but it would be hard to justify a claim that they were at all common in relation to the number of trials. The much fuller sources for Lorraine contain only a handful of cases, perhaps around 5 per cent, where men with any sort of medical expertise took any part in diagnosing or treating bewitchment. The status of the practitioners involved is decidedly obscure and their methods sometimes as dubious as those used by Dr Jacob; some appear to belong more to the world of the popular healers than to that of qualified physicians. The natural inference would be that such diagnoses were relatively rare and that the position of most doctors was probably well represented by the Northampton physician John Cotta. He insisted on the need to consult learned physicians and to apply the same standards of proof as for other crimes, while attacking superstitious and miraculous techniques for combating witchcraft. Cotta remarked:

> Nor do I deny or defend devilish practices of men and women, but desire only to moderate the generall madness of this age, which ascribeth unto witchcraft whatsoever falleth out unknown or strange unto a vulgar sense.

He emphasized that a combination of diseases might produce results which would puzzle the most expert observer yet remain perfectly natural:

> Many diseases single, alone and apart by themselves, seem strange and wondered which therefore in their strange forms united, and in their mixture one with another, must needs arise much more monstrous and Hydra-like.[85]

A more radical critic of witchcraft beliefs in the next generation, Thomas Ady, has been plausibly though not certainly identified as a local Essex doctor; his attacks on 'witch-mongers' contain strong echoes of Scot. Ady stressed the danger of blaming witches for misfortunes which really came from the hand of God, while denouncing both ignorant physicians and the cunning folk. He ended his summary list of fifteen 'Causes of upholding the damnable Doctrine of Witches power' with:

> Another abominable cause is the suffering of Impostors to live, such as silly people call Cunning men, who will undertake to tell them who hath bewitched them, who, and which of their Neighbours it was, by the delusions of such Impostors, many poor innocent people are branded with a report of being Witches, by reason of which report coming from a Witch, they are in process of time suspected, accused; arraigned, and hanged.[86]

In about 1580 Thomas Death took a sample of his apparently paralysed daughter Mary's urine to a physician named Bert in Ipswich, asking if she were not bewitched.

> But he said that he would not deal so far to tell him, whereupon he not satisfied to his mind met with an acquaintance of his, and asked him where he might go to a cunning man, telling him in what case his daughter lay in; who then sent him to a man whom he knew not, nor his name he now remembereth not, with whom after he had conferred and showed his daughter's said water . . . he told him if he had not comen with some great haste to seek help, he had come too late . . . he told him that within two nights after the parties that had hurt his daughter should appear unto her and remedy her . . .

The girl was duly given the remedies, and claimed that around midnight she saw the two suspects standing before her, telling her not to be afraid, after which she promptly recovered. Here we may note the reticence of the doctor, the warning that help was only just in time and the father's studied vagueness about the identity of the cunning man.[87]

The professional hostilities between official and unauthorized practitioners were surely one reason why doctors often tried to distance themselves from witchcraft charges. Despite the desperate inadequacy of their techniques, the physicians were inching towards a better understanding of both illness and their own limitations; given the absence of any satisfactory general theory, this could only take place on a piecemeal basis. The whole witchcraft debate needs to be seen in the context of the doctors' struggle to enhance their professional standing and establish both their authority over rivals and their intellectual respectability. This inevitably drove many of them into various degrees of scepticism, for here was a welcome opportunity to assert their superior rationality. Their own inadequacies could be largely forgotten when they dealt with the frauds and superstitions which were relatively easily identified in supposed witchcraft and possession. Here Weyer's notion of melancholic delusions was particularly useful, because it allowed them to turn round one of the strongest points in the demonologists' case and make the confessions of witches into an argument for the illusory nature of the whole notion. Witchcraft raised questions about knowledge, authority and power which were at once political, ecclesiastical, legal and medical. Although specialists in each field disagreed with one another almost as much as they did with those who professed a different expertise, the situations were not identical. Clerics and lawyers had to work with a body of authoritative texts which seriously circumscribed their freedom to argue against the witchcraft explanation, even in specific cases. Doctors also appealed to a corpus of texts, but one which was largely independent of the Christian tradition and minimized the opportunities for supernatural intervention. Furthermore, it was only the doctors who could readily deliver a knockout blow in any particular case, for unchallenged medical evidence that a disorder was wholly natural almost always carried the day. This is not a straightforward point, for there were many who argued that the Devil operated more through natural than supernatural means. In practice, however, there does seem to have been a widespread belief that diabolical afflictions ought to be different in kind from natural ones, which was too strong to be shaken by the various theoretical attempts to get round the problem. It is also likely that most defenders of the reality of witchcraft and possession preferred the 'strong' position, in which the abnormality of the affliction reinforced their other arguments, and only resorted to the argument that diabolical effects were natural when forced to do so.

Many of these issues surfaced in the case of Mary Glover, whose alleged possession through the agency of the witch Elizabeth Jackson became a *cause celèbre* in London in 1602. Rather like Weyer, the physician Edward Jorden, who took a leading part in the case, has become something of a proto-rationalist hero of scientific medicine. His *A Briefe Discourse of a Disease called the Suffocation of the Mother* has been described as a major turning point in the history of both hysteria and medical attitudes to witchcraft. The recent study of this episode by Michael MacDonald is particularly attractive because it shows that Jorden really was important, for reasons which are much more complex than those hitherto alleged. His pamphlet itself seems to have been relatively ineffective, for it was never reprinted, nor is there any good evidence that it influenced later writers. It is very much a *pièce d'occasion*, whose innovations were primarily an attempt to wriggle out of severe difficulties. These arose partly from the need to adapt the conventional opinions on hysteria to the case of a fourteen-year-old girl who had not started to menstruate when her symptoms began; this probably explains why Jorden relocated the source of her troubles in the brain and the imagination rather than just the womb. His medical arguments are respectable rather than truly convincing, while he studiously avoided any direct reference to the case itself. This was prudent, for his own appearance for the defence had been a fiasco, during which Chief Justice Anderson trapped him in an untenable position and the trial ended with the conviction of Elizabeth Jackson. Opinion in the Royal College of Physicians was divided, with Fellows appearing on both sides in the court, although it does appear that the larger number and the more influential group were to be found on Jorden's side, at least in doubting the diagnosis of possession. This is no necessary proof of enlightenment, since the doctors, who were no innocents abroad, would have been well aware of the wider context within which the trial took place, with the Anglican establishment determined to assert its control over Puritan enthusiasts for religious healing. It was a session of fasting and prayer which finally brought Mary Glover's possession to an end in December 1602; no doubt it is irreverent as well as anachronistic to see exposure to a whole day of sermons and prayers as an early case of aversion therapy.[88]

For Jorden, the real importance of the case was that it established him as a close ally of Bancroft, with whom he helped to win the battle for the ear of King James in the crucial first stage of the new reign. Credulity about the operations of the Devil in the world was now strongly associated with the wrong politico-religious groups, while possession cases allowed for direct disproof in a manner ordinary witchcraft did not. In 1605 the king sent Jorden to investigate the case of Anne Gunter, a young Berkshire woman who was allegedly possessed; this time the diagnosis of hysteria mixed with fraud was triumphantly successful, when she was interrogated by James in person and confessed to her deceits, leaving a number of eminent physicians and divines looking rather foolish. This was one of the numerous cases during the reign in which similar frauds were exposed, encouraging that attitude of practical scepticism about witchcraft which seems to have become widespread among the English elites.[89] Medical expertise was not necessarily involved, nor can one assume that all doctors would exhibit the same rationality as William Harvey, under whose directions a group of midwives and surgeons found that the supposed marks and teats identified on the bodies of some of the accused in the 1634 Lancashire trials were perfectly natural. The best-known story about Harvey is that he dissected the supposed toad familiar of an old woman living near Newmarket in order to show that there was nothing abnormal about it; unfortunately the source for this tale is very dubious and it is not clear what such an experiment could have been held to prove.[90]

Leading French doctors also appear to have been very sceptical about witchcraft and possession cases. Writing about his experiences in the 1580s the royal surgeon Pierre Pigray described how he and three doctors examined fourteen witches on trial before the *parlement*, to judge them in need of purging rather than punishment, 'and it is better, it seems to me, in matters where proof is difficult, and belief dangerous, to lean more towards doubt than certainty'. He argued that the tying of a lace could not cause male impotence, attaching all the blame to the power of the imagination; elsewhere he described how he had exposed a possessed girl as a fraud.[91] In the celebrated case of Marthe Brossier in 1599 the supposed demoniac was visited by no less than fifteen Paris physicians, led by the king's principal doctor, who found there was nothing unnatural in her behaviour. The group of Catholic zealots who were trying to exploit her possession for political ends mobilized a much less impressive group of doctors to declare in their favour, but their arguments were easily ridiculed by Michel Marescot in his highly sceptical account of the affair. Marescot summarized his position pithily:

> In brief, there are an infinity of things which are accomplished by the secret virtue of nature: and if on account of this secrecy it was necessary to attribute them to the devil, to explain physical and medical matters, from the beginning to the end of these two sciences, one would always be obliged to have recourse to demons.[92]

The Brossier case provides a striking link with contemporary events in England, for there was a similar line-up of forces, with the Crown anxious to dampen down a potentially disruptive scandal.[93] Marescot's work was immediately translated into English, with a dedication to Bancroft by Abraham Hartwell, who had read out the evidence against Darrell at his trial.[94]

There are numerous further examples of doctors who denied the reality of possession in various seventeenth-century French cases, notably the famous scandal of the devils of Loudun, which reached its peak in 1634 and its pale imitation at Louviers in the 1640s. In the first case the prioress and nuns of a recently-founded Ursuline convent put on flamboyant and theatrical performances directed against a prominent *curé* in the town, Urbain Grandier, whom they effectively charged with having bewitched them. A series of exorcists tried their strength with the Devils, getting rather the worst of it. This could be argued away as a further sign of the power of Satan, but the exorcists were severely embarrassed by the interventions of the most prominent local physician, the Protestant Marc Duncan. When the prioress Jeanne des Anges was wounded, he pointed out how easily she could have concealed a weapon and that the wound had been made from the outside. Then he accepted the challenge of the exorcists, easily holding her down and preventing her moving during her convulsions; the exorcist feebly claimed that the Devil was only as strong as the body he was occupying.[95] At the time Grandier's defenders pointed out that no doctors from the major towns of the region were called in to validate the possession, suggesting that 'they did not want to have any who were too clairvoyant'.[96] The subsequent debate on paper was more evenly contested and demonstrated once again that medical theory could never decide such difficult cases. At the intellectual level Loudun could be plausibly seen as a drawn battle, yet its moral effect does seem to have been very different. The obvious manipulation of the whole procedure by the royal agents and the exorcists generated wide unease, which was compounded by Grandier's courageous refusal to confess any guilt, even under the atrocious tortures to which he was subjected before his execution. The reactions of the intellectual elite were probably well captured by another local doctor, Claude Quillet, whose opinion was trenchantly expressed in a letter from Gabriel Naudé to Guy Patin:

> It would be preferable to call it hysteromania or even erotomania. These poor little devils of nuns, seeing themselves shut up within four walls, become madly in love, fall into a melancholic delirium, worked upon by the desires of the flesh, and in truth, what they need to be perfectly cured is a remedy of the flesh.[97]

Doctors were particularly infuriated by the ways in which some clerics tried to stage-manage the possession cases, often passing information secretly to the possessed and refusing to consider any evidence which did not fit their purposes. It seems certain that such faking was quite common, the motivation and self-justification being akin to those found in connection with forged charters, fake relics and fraudulent miracles. In his withering account of the feeble frauds offered by the nuns of Louviers, the royal doctor Yvelin was indignant about the behaviour of various clerics who, in contravention of their own rules, would allow no leeway for medical opinions and who endangered both the dignity of religion and the pursuit of truth by their credulity.[98] There were always local medical practitioners willing to support the possessions, but commonly they were men of far less professional standing than the critics, who laid heavy emphasis on their own qualifications from the prestigious faculties of Paris or Montpellier.

Executioners and gaolers

Elite figures of this kind would have been very remote from the experience of most of the accused. Executioners and gaolers, on the other hand, were thoroughly proletarian, the kind of underlings who were given the dirty jobs to do and who communicated readily with the typical suspect. Some sophisticated jurisdictions, like that of the Paris *parlement*, had surgeons present for torture sessions; more commonly it was the executioner who decided how far it was possible to go in order to extract a confession without killing or maiming the subject. Such positions opened up possibilities of bribery and corruption and there are some sinister accounts of executioners growing rich as the number of victims increased. The executioner of Luxembourg was put to death for such misconduct in 1603, while a decade later his counterpart in Nancy was threatened with the loss of his position.[99] One of the most dangerous areas in which justice might be perverted was over the naming of accomplices, with names being suggested and last-minute reiterations or withdrawals at the stake asserted. In the nature of things it is impossible to know how far such abuses went and it would probably be unwise to exaggerate their scale; torture sessions and executions were quite well controlled, with numerous people watching the proceedings closely. The individuals with the best opportunity to pressurize the accused were the gaolers, who determined the conditions of their existence in prison and had the chance to work on them over a period of time. It was of course well understood by everyone that prisoners were treated according to what they were willing or able to pay. There are quite numerous instances where misleading promises of release seem to have been made in order to extract confessions, others where ill-treatment or threats of the unpleasantness to come had the same effect, although again these can only be plausibly suspected in a small minority of cases. Anyone who has seen surviving examples of the dank, airless dungeons in which prisoners were normally held must be surprised at the physical and moral resistance they put up, since most of them only confessed under the most severe pressure and after actual torture. A fair number died in prison, their decease laconically attributed to cold and humidity if they had not succeeded in doing away with themselves in some way.

Hangmen were a peculiar group, excluded from normal social relations and forced to marry among their kin; they commonly pursued parallel trades as undertakers, coffin-makers and slaughtermen. As relatively scarce specialists, they often had to be summoned to smaller places as and when their services were required. The costs and delays involved may well have been among the factors which tended to limit formal persecution. Their close familiarity with the accused often included shaving off their hair, which might supposedly conceal charms to make the torture painless or prevent confession of the truth. This notion empha-sized the idea of the wily devil, anxious to keep control over adherents who were being exhorted to save their souls by returning to God. Confessing witches quite often claimed that the Devil had been in their body, preventing them from speaking, until he said that the (implicitly divine) power of justice was too strong for him and suddenly departed. Given the variety of superstitions associated with executioners and their recognized expertise in dealing with witches, it is no surprise to find that they could function as witch-finders in their own right. A spectacular example was that of Jean Minard, hangman of Rocroi in north-eastern France. Hundreds of suspects, almost entirely from the neighbouring Spanish Netherlands, made their way to be pricked for the mark by Minard. Some were apparently forced into this by their neighbours, others merely preferred a verdict one way or the other to remaining perpetual objects of distrust. When the Paris *parlement* caught up with Minard in 1603 he was sent to the galleys for life.[100] The need to seek out signs of witchcraft, whether in the form of the swimming test, the insensible mark found by pricking, spots detected in the eyes or, in England, by identifying the teats sucked by familiars, is highly suggestive. Many people evidently believed that there must be such infallible signs of belonging to the secret army of the Devil that could be uncovered with sufficient aptitude; perhaps this betrayed a certain unease with the whole business of extorting confessions under torture. In England and her American colonies these tests were usually carried out by special feminine juries of matrons and midwives, who form one of the most unexpected groups of witch-finders. Indeed the names of Hopkins and Stearne should be linked with that of Goodwife Mary Phillips, also of Manningtree, who was the third of these 'unspotted lambs of the Lord' and accompanied them on their expeditions, organizing such juries to search women.[101]

As has repeatedly been shown, the relationship between traditional witch-finders and formal persecution was complex; the unwary risked becoming victims themselves and attracted much hostility from the ruling elites. Their activities could set off serious panics, but more often they formed part of a routine of suspicions and cures which permeated normal village life. It was predictable that the attempts to diabolize them and persecute them directly should have such limited effects, when their services were so widely valued by the vast majority of the population. Like the beliefs they epitomized and helped maintain, they would endure long past the age of persecution, just as they had preceded it. Other types of witch-finder, such as the adolescents who went round selling their services or clerics who thought they could use exorcisms to unmask the Devil and his servants, were much more closely linked to the specific conditions of the time. Changes in intellectual fashion and judicial practice therefore brought about their rapid disappearance from the end of the seventeenth century. Before we feel too smug about this, it would be wise to note how quickly our own age has seen the emergence of semi-professional experts on ritual satanism, whose standards of proof would not have passed muster with sceptics four centuries ago.

CHAPTER VI

LOVE AND HATRED: SPOUSES AND KIN

Marriage and parenthood

THE FAMILY HAS PROVIDED the basic structure of all developed human societies. Affective, economic, political and social life have all revolved around it throughout known history. There have been important senses in which the individual could only exist through the family, and this was certainly more true in the early modern period than it is today. With rare exceptions, Europeans lived and died within the milieu of their birth; mobility was strictly limited both geographically and socially. The elites were defined by inherited wealth and position, even at the level of village oligarchies. Some of the consequences will be studied in more detail in a later chapter; it is the affective and social aspects of the family which will detain us first, together with their multiple reflections where reality and fantasy meet in witchcraft. The term is itself ambiguous, of course; it applies both to the wider kinship networks and to the household unit. Through most of Europe in the early modern period the latter was typically 'nuclear', in the sense that it comprised a married couple and their children, with perhaps a single servant. Large households including grandparents, adult children and grandchildren were relatively uncommon. This was at least partly because the late age of marriage and relatively low life expectancy precluded them in most cases. The most important variation was that found in large parts of Mediterranean Europe, where men typically married much younger girls; in consequence middle-aged widows frequently presided over households of unmarried children. The rich had their own distinctive household patterns, but these only impinged very occasionally on the plebeian world where witchcraft beliefs flourished most vigorously.

Marriage was the crucial social transaction in many respects. It was the mechanism whereby families constantly renewed themselves and formed links with others, like cells splitting and recombining. As an exchange in which property was involved as well as persons, with the establishment of a new household, one would be hard pressed to exaggerate its structural significance at every level. No wonder that marriage was surrounded by an elaborate ritual marking it out as a 'rite of passage', whose repercussions extended far beyond the couple themselves. So many interests came into play that the celebrations carried a necessary subtext of tension and dissatisfaction. Uncomfortable presences at the feast-table might include resentful parents and siblings, rejected suitors with their kin and groups of mutually suspicious new in-laws; other neighbours might be muttering because they had not been invited at all. Eating, drinking and dancing could all too easily become the setting for insults or acts of violence that left a shadow across the future. Jean Grand Didier must have wished he had avoided the marriage feast of Colas Ferry at la Vacherie in about 1586, where he seems to have been in a singularly quarrelsome mood. He got into a knife fight with another guest, who died of his wounds some days later, so that Jean had to flee, then secure a pardon from the duke at a cost of 700 francs. He also quarrelled with the brothers Mengeon and Colas Moullot, nearly provoking another fight; at the end of the evening Jean insisted that Colas have a drink with him as a sign of reconciliation. After several refusals Colas agreed, but instantly felt a great pain in his body when he drank, crying out that he had been given his death-blow. He died after an illness lasting just three days, saying that Jean had given him his death and they should open him after he was dead to find the poison. Fourteen years later his brother testified that they had not done this because they lacked the means, but had always imputed his death to Jean's witchcraft.[1]

The commoner form of animosity dating from the wedding festivities was resentment at not being invited at all, which might appear later as the alleged motive for bewitchment (a theme which passed into folklore in the familiar form of the excluded witch taking her revenge). Marguerite Menginat testified that just three months after her marriage six years earlier, Barbelline Chaperey had come to her house and said to her 'that she might well eat and drink, making use of hens and other good food . . . but that her husband's first wife had hardly known any good health while she lived with him, and she would be in the same case, nor would she have children by him or others'. Although they had not quarrelled, Marguerite's mother had told her Barbelline was angry because she was not invited to the wedding feast. Since that time the witness had been in poor health in both body and mind, so she suspected the accused of being the cause.[2] Other complications arose in the frequent instances of remarriages, inevitable when so many unions were terminated by a premature death. The complex emotional and financial tangles often associated with such second or third marriages have also left their mark in the trial records.

There have been some historians who have depicted early modern marriage in depressing terms, as a functional arrangement devoid of affection and feeling, based on crude economic calculations and patriarchal violence. By the same token, a 'black legend' of early modern childhood has been built up, according to which beating and emotional deprivation were the common experience. At its most extreme, this vision has brought the bizarre claim that sexual intercourse was nasty, brutish and short until the eighteenth century. This at least can be satisfyingly refuted from the confessions of the witches, in a rather unexpected fashion. Intercourse with the Devil was routinely described as painful and degrading; to make the point more clearly, the accused quite often contrasted it with the pleasure obtained from normal relations with their husbands. The broader questions about marriage and childhood are harder to resolve, and indeed it is difficult to see how they ever could be, given the limitations of the evidence. What was clearly absent was the modern notion of romantic love as the only proper basis for a lasting relationship, which is hardly surprising given the recent and culturally bounded nature of this ideology. On the other hand, there is abundant evidence for expectations of mutual attraction between prospective partners. It remains arguable that in basing choice on a mixture of sexual compatibility, matched social position and the capacity to run a household, our ancestors held to a more realistic view than ourselves. Perhaps the harsh specificities of their lives gave them little alternative. My own subjective view is that expectations were rather lower than today, while satisfaction was probably somewhat higher, with most marriages proving reasonably durable and effective. There was the usual spectrum from deeply satisfying to miserable and violent, which makes generalization doubly hazardous.

The witchcraft material provides a good deal of fascinating evidence on these matters, although here too interpretation is fraught with difficulties. Marital discord was sometimes blamed on witchcraft, in terms which clearly envisage it as something exceptional and unnatural, just the effect the Devil and his agents would like to produce. On occasion some type of counter-action had been followed by a startling improvement; perhaps the need for such measures had made the parties realize how serious the situation was, causing them to modify their behaviour. Claudon Durant and his fiancée saw Claudatte Antoine pass them one evening, at which he wondered aloud 'what was the old witch looking for there so late', although he did not know if she heard this. For the first eighteen months of their marriage he and his wife could not bear the sight of one another and were always fighting. Finally Claudon visited a wise-woman, and after he explained his problem she told him repeatedly 'that he had a fantasy and suspicion that an evil woman was responsible, so he must name her'. When he would not agree, she herself named Claudatte, and after taking something from her garden to eat with his wife, the two of them lived 'in peace, friendship, and mutual affection'.[3] Spouses often went to great lengths to care for sick partners, spending more than they could readily afford on medical care, or lashing out at suspected witches, while showing obvious signs of distress and grief. Only a small minority emerge as callous and uncaring. Even in these cases it was known for them to describe their own behaviour in bewildered and critical terms, as strangely impelled from outside, possibly yet again only explicable as the work of the Devil. The negative images of witch-craft belief suggest a much more positive ideal which was being sub-verted. As for children, their illnesses or sudden deaths plainly caused real anguish to their mothers in particular. A fiercely protective attitude was often evident, as were signs of tenderness and affection. A curious version of this appears in the confessions of Mongeatte Tendon, who offered two different stories of her seduction by master Persin. In the first she said she had been in despair two years earlier, because one of her sons, who was accused of being a sodomite and making a cousin pregnant, had been arrested and taken to St Dié. She was weeping in her garden when a hideous figure in black, complete with claws, appeared with an offer to get her son out of prison if she would believe in him. At her next interrogation she replaced this with an account of how some thirty years earlier her daughter Marguitte, then aged seven or eight, was lost one night when looking for animals. She was still looking for her after noon the next day when her husband returned from St Dié and said that he heard a girl had been eaten by animals, who had only left her head. She thought this might be her daughter and was in despair when Persin appeared, promising to find her daughter if she would give herself to him. After she consented he found the girl sleeping under a bush, so she had to keep her part of the bargain.[4]

Although an excessive number of children might be felt as a burden, childlessness was the state most people seemed to fear or regret, for both practical and emotional reasons. In the case of Margaret Moore, from Sutton on the Isle of Ely and a victim of the Hopkins and Stearne crusade in 1647, the confession again suggests a great deal about the vulnerability of the accused to threats against her children. Moore had lost three children, then claimed to have heard their voices telling her she must give up her soul to the Devil, as the only means of preserving her fourth and only surviving child. Strange dreams or hallucinations of this kind are well-known consequences of bereavement, which appear in some other witchcraft cases, and imply real anguish about such events.[5] There is little in these documents to suggest a world deficient in affection, or one in which suffering and hardship had dulled the sensibilities. While long-term destitution plainly can have such effects, the experience of the mass of the population was rather different in this period, hard though it was. The problems were with short-term crises bringing famine, plague or war, rather than with permanent states of deprivation; this followed inevitably from large fluctuations in production, which ensured that dearths and gluts would alternate unpredictably. Personal relations must have come under periodic strain in such circumstances, but are unlikely to have been permanently damaged.

Family loyalties under pressure

Witchcraft accusations, on the other hand, were very dangerous when they interacted with families. This was a process on multiple levels. Suspicions and charges originating from outside could generate enormous tension and even dissolve the normal bonds between family members. Differences and disputes which began within families not only left their members far more exposed, but often lay at the root of personal reputations. In other cases quarrels between families were expressed through allegations of witchcraft. Many of the elements of fantasy incorporated in witchcraft beliefs had their origin in the crucial early stages of development, so that patterns of infant- and child-care fed through into some of the more outlandish features of confessions. These are among the most obvious of the ways in which one cannot understand how the nexus of beliefs and practices worked without relating them to the familial context. One commonplace observation too often forgotten is that the closest bonds and the most bitter hostilities are linked, as opposite but insepar-able polarities; if the ties of blood bind people together, it is often with a special intensity of mutual hatred. Among the most disconcerting features of close relationships is the way they frequently alternate between opposite poles, and encourage patterns of quarrels and reconciliations. Often they also seem to liberate individuals' ability to express violent feelings they would conceal or sublimate in more external situations. The endless dramas played out on this semi-public stage fed into witch-craft, both directly and through the inner psychic worlds they shaped.

Official doctrines of patriarchy made the husband and father the unquestioned head of the family. Although reality was never so simple, at the legal level wives and children had little chance of acting except with his consent, and under his name. This was particularly important when wives were suspected of witchcraft, rumours began to circulate and neighbours insulted them by calling them witch. Failure to respond to such provocations was routinely cited in court as evidence for the suspect's guilt when the trial finally began. In fact it was far from easy for those concerned to know how to react. The best outcome was a formal sentence from a local court awarding damages, but such proceedings could go badly wrong if the other party decided to fight; in such circumstances they could turn into a trial for witchcraft. Action of this kind was likely to be safest if undertaken early on, before suspicions had accumulated to the point where wide support could be mustered for such a counter-attack. While there are plenty of judgments awarding small fines, it seems likely that more of these cases were settled by informal arbitration, carried out by local office-holders, clerics, or leading members of the community. That was a prudent low-level response, but many people simply ignored the insults or responded in kind. When answering their judges they resorted to three main strategies to explain their conduct. The first was to claim there had been no witnesses, the second to allege they were too poor to risk losing a case and having to pay themselves, the third to blame their husbands. The latter were said to be too soft or cowardly to help, with the implication that they had chosen to distance themselves from the whole affair. This was understandable, for these men were caught in the problem faced by families more widely; one set of rules enjoined support between kin, another the avoidance of suspected witches.

Neutral attitudes of this kind were evidently common, although they are bound to be over-represented in surviving records, since where husbands took an active part in defending their wives' reputations this is likely to have been quite effective, reducing the chance that these cases would come to court. Given the adhesive quality of suspicions, it was hardly possible to dispel them completely, so damage limitation was a more plausible hope. Husbands could confront potential accusers and ask them to declare their opinions; this might well shame or cow them into silence. Claudon Thonnere believed Mongeatte Johel was responsible for his illness, a suspicion his wife told her and her husband about when they met at the mill. The husband then came to see him, 'asking if he wished to declare that his wife was a witch; to which he replied that he did not, but if she was such as many suspected he blamed her for his illness'. Mutual threats of legal action followed, but Claudon's recovery allowed the matter to be dropped.[6] At other times more direct threats or violence might be employed, or alternatively excuses and pleading, even promises there would be no repetition. Ten years before Catherine Ancel was finally arrested, Demenge Alix had lost many animals, so he and several others from Benifosse resolved to seek out the *prévôt* to ask for her arrest. When her husband heard of this he went to see him, begging him not to proceed, while promising to talk to her and ensure that she gave no more cause of discontent. He touched his hands as he said this, and finally Demenge agreed to withdraw.[7] We may note that in this case, as in a good many others, action was only taken when the husband was dead – and that some of the suspicions came from the wife of Catherine's stepson.

There were occasional allegations that kin had attempted bribery towards gaolers or hangmen, but few substantiated cases. An inherent danger in any kind of intercession was that of being tarred with the same brush as the suspect; there are some cases where married couples or larger groups of relatives were tried. This normally seems to have resulted from widespread pre-existing suspicions rather than the immediate circumstances of the trials, but on occasion confessing witches were put under pressure to incriminate their spouses or children, particularly on the theory that they might have inducted them to the Devil's service and taken them to the sabbat. If the bemused or broken victim complied, horrible and heartrending scenes might follow when they were confronted with those they had virtually condemned to death. Ysabel Seguin declared that her seventeen-year-old daughter Gauthine had been to the sabbat with her, to which the girl replied 'that she must be out of her mind and understanding to bring about her death in this way'; the ludicrous response from the mother was that she was in her right mind, but one must tell the truth. It must have taken enormous courage for Gauthine to resist four sessions of torture and win her release.[8] Another line of questioning concerned the deception necessary to attend the sabbat without detection by one's partner. The answers revolved around illusions procured by the Devil, whether the inert body of the witch remained behind (what might, irreverently, be called the doctrine of the witch's two bodies), or some object such as a hayfork took on his or her shape. Some of the witches from Spanish Navarre offered a kind of double insurance policy; the Devil ensured that all other members of the household fell into a deep sleep, but also provided a demon in their likeness to occupy their place in bed.[9] There were households which had a generalized reputation for witchcraft, such that both spouses, or even larger groups, were accused simultaneously. There might be stories of how they had been overheard trading insults, or making other compromising statements. A curious example was that of Ulriot Colas Ulriot, who was (rather implausibly) alleged to have said to his wife eighteen years earlier, 'Marie, I have no idea whether you are a witch, nevertheless you have been arrested as such, and brought great dishonour on your family. As for me, I am a witch, yet have not been arrested or dishonoured my family, despite being the master of the witches'.[10] Sometimes witnesses put their charges in the form that one or other of a married couple must have caused a bewitchment, perhaps after a provocation offered to the household as a whole. Several witnesses hedged their bets in this way by declaring suspicions against Jean Cachette, his wife Mengette and their daughter Jehenne.[11]

A small minority of husbands revealed themselves as actively hostile to their wives; Bastien Bourguignon actually appeared as a witness against his wife Françoise, to tell how he had become suspicious of her after discovering that she had been accused by a man and a woman on trial at Neufchâteau – he had checked this with a judge at Nancy who had possession of the papers in the case. He had therefore watched her carefully, but could only add that she had sometimes mysteriously got back into the house overnight after he locked her out.[12] Second marriages (like this last example) look as if they were more vulnerable to such breakdowns, with women who remarried in middle life either proving less tractable than their juniors, or bringing dangerous reputations with them. Their husbands may also have been particularly vulnerable to the kind of taunts sometimes recorded from the tavern and similar settings.

Sometimes these men appear positively determined to get rid of a detested spouse, on other occasions merely keen to avoid any hint of guilt by association. More ambiguous cases had angry husbands calling their wives witches, with these insults being noted by attentive neighbours and later cited as evidence. Straightforward maltreatment of wives, who were beaten or locked out of the house, could be interpreted in similar ways. Unfortunates subjected to this kind of abuse had to hope for support from neighbours or their own kin, and it was hard to keep such goings-on quiet. In one or two exceptional cases the abuse was so extreme that the husband rather than the wife attracted obloquy and came under suspicion. The sensational case of Jean Aulbry, who confessed to an impressive list of sexual offences, thefts and blasphemies, came to court after he was so violent to his wife that she fled to take shelter with neighbours, then herself asked the abbot of Étival to take action.[13] The confessions also provide indirect evidence, when women admitted they had been driven to despair by maltreatment, and then succumbed to the blandishments of the Devil. A quarrel with one's spouse competed with poverty as the commonest explanation witches offered for their peculiar vulnerability to the tempter; this is double-edged as evidence for marital relations in general, since the despair might be the result of exceptional rather than typical treatment. Those of either sex who remarried several times were also liable to come under suspicion of having disposed of previous partners, since some of the deaths were likely to have been sudden or unexplained. Jean de Socourt was questioned closely about the deaths of his four wives; at first he offered very sensible natural explanations, but in his final confessions included two of them among his victims, killed because they were disobedient to him.[14]

Women who confessed did sometimes claim, often without evident prompting, that they had killed their husbands. Their responsibilities for providing food and drink made it all too easy to explain how they had slipped in a poisonous diabolical powder. Marguitte Laurent said she had put powder in her husband's soup after he beat her with the fire-irons, giving her a painful blow on the head. After adding that she had killed her nephew she went on to demand her own punishment, saying 'it was high time they put her to death, considering how many crimes she had committed over twenty or thirty years'.[15] Even more pathetically, Marguitte Digard confessed to following her master's instructions to put black powder in her bedridden husband's soup, because she saw she could not feed him or her children.[16] Admissions of this type were horribly risky, since the judges were liable to treat them as parricide or petty treason, and add gruesome penalties, such as the application of hot irons or burning alive, to the sentence. One can only presume that once the witches started to list the grudges for which they had supposedly avenged themselves, deep-seated feelings of guilt or hostility towards their late husbands surfaced in this pathetic form. A slightly different case was that of the Swiss witch Clauda Brunyé, tried at Neuchâtel in 1568, who had been asked to kill Don Claude Jacquet by his wife Franceysa. Together they prepared poisons, first by using items from a chicken carcase which had gone green, then part of a donkey's hoof; yet again soup was the chosen mode of administration, and the unfortunate Don Claude 'dried up immediately and died in six days'.[17] Stepchildren might also bring accusations of this type, as Nicolas le Jalley did against his stepmother Barbelline. He claimed to have left home himself because he was so frightened she might bewitch him, then suggested that his father had fallen ill on drinking some soup which tasted bitter, after which he lost the power to feel or speak. Nicolas asked Barbelline what had been in the soup, adding 'that if he did not recover quickly he would go to consult a *devin*, and if he learned she had bewitched him he would have her taken and burned' – as soon as he had said this his father became a little better, although still far from well.[18]

Household responsibilities and conditions are often evident in the sub-stratum of depositions and confessions. Friction naturally arose over money, with women complaining that they were not given enough to feed themselves and their families. Drinking was far the commonest culprit, with gambling and business incompetence occasionally mentioned. Boon companions, blamed for encouraging such conduct, were usually the targets for malice and bewitchment in these cases. Demenge Jean Gerardin told how fifteen years earlier Françatte Camont had spoken to his wife, asking how they could separate their husbands, who got together to drink. Some weeks later he was at her husband's forge with some miners, and they sent for a pot of wine. She drank some from a glass, then handed the rest to the witness, who drank it but was soon afflicted by a chill through his whole body, lost the use of his limbs, then after three months had to take to his bed. A consultation of the *devin* identified Françatte as the cause, leading to his eventual recovery after two separate exchanges with her. When she confessed, she said she had been angry with him because he made her husband go drinking, while there was not enough money for their food.[19] Men obviously spent a good deal of time in the tavern, and indeed the uncomfortable physical conditions of most dwellings meant that life was carried on in public spaces as much as weather and convenience allowed. If the tavern was a masculine space, the street and the houses which sheltered the *veillées* were mixed, even predominantly feminine. All this militated against privacy, as did the tendency to share the same roof, especially among the poor. People knew what their neighbours were up to and how they lived; they overheard conversations and spied on one another. Although this nosiness had its virtues – for example it may have protected children against the extremes of neglect and cruelty found in our own society – it was also oppressive and liable to magnify both discords and suspicions once they arose.

Servants and witchcraft

Servants occupied a marginal position in the household and were found surprisingly far down the social scale, with only the really poor not employing them at all. The combination of late marriage ages for both sexes (at least in northern Europe) with the general practice of sending adolescent children into service made them a very numerous group. For both young men and young women, service represented a very prolonged liminal or marginal state prior to full adult independence, one from which it was important to emerge with a good reputation and some modest savings. The arrangements for hiring and keeping them represented another of those points of tension around which grudges and accusations could cluster. People were naturally wary of accepting the children of suspected witches as servants, but such refusals were perceived as dangerous and provocative and could lead to bitter quarrels. Bad treatment of those in service was similarly adduced as a motive for revenge in some cases. Apprentices were in many ways a sub-set of the same group; here too the practical and financial details might be disputed, especially if employers punished or dismissed those they found unsatisfactory. It was unusual, although by no means unknown, for servants to be accused of witchcraft themselves, in line with the general tendency not to see young people in this light. Older servants, like the lying-in maids of Augsburg (mature women who looked after infants for their first few months), were much more likely to fall under suspicion. As in this special case, it was probably in connection with child care that disasters most readily occurred, and were attributed to malice on the part of the servant or their family. Mengeotte le Compaing was a single woman in her thirties, who had been in service for a number of years, then gone to look after her widowed brother's children. Numerous depositions revealed that her fellow servants had suspicions of her, disliked having her bring them food and blamed her for various illnesses. Her mistress Catherine Petit Didier accused her over the death of a three-year-old daughter, and afterwards called her witch when displeased with her – yet it is plain from this account that she was not immediately dismissed from service, merely not re-engaged for the next year, which suggests that the suspicions must have been rather tentative. Mengeotte defended herself with the comment 'that she would have had a wicked heart in her breast to cause the death of such a pleasant child', and was clearly distressed by the accusations.[20]

The other roles in which servants routinely appeared were as victims and witnesses. They were quite likely to bear the brunt of a witch's anger as the agents who refused some small charity or help; at other times it seemed to be assumed that ill-will towards the household as a whole might fall on them just as easily as on its more permanent members. When Denyse Pottier went to fetch fire from the house of Claude le Noir she exchanged angry words with the chambermaid, whom she struck on the arm, saying 'wicked slut, may God preserve your arms and legs to serve your master and mistress'. The girl promptly lost the use of the arm on which she had been struck, but was healed after Denyse was called in with the promise of some reward.[21] Another servant girl, Pierratte Colas, faced complaints from Laurence Viney because she did not bring her enough to eat when she was reaping. Pierratte replied that she should complain to her master and mistress, since she was only a servant, to which she said 'that she would have her in one way or another'; the girl fainted in the field and was ill for a year.[22] Deaths and illnesses of servants were quite frequently explained by witchcraft on such grounds, by both employers and relatives. Those who served in households where witchcraft was supposed to originate were in a different position. Sometimes they came forward voluntarily as witnesses against ex-employers, yet many others seem to have appeared rather unwillingly and often failed to support the allegations. While there is the odd hint of malice or revenge in these depositions, it is far from being a powerful theme overall; the general tone is one of caution, even prevarication.

When Didier Jean Charpentier was on trial in 1601 the judges questioned Marguitte Jeandey closely about an illness more than twenty-five years earlier, when she was in Didier's service. She explained that it was only after she had married several years later that she heard he 'had been to the *devin* or magician, to discover who had stolen his grain, when the magician made all the inhabitants of Remémont appear before him, telling him that she was the one who was the thief'. When she heard this she did wonder whether he might have caused her illness, possibly with the aid of the *devin*, but this was no more than a speculation. Asked whether she had been suborned or bribed to tell less than she knew, she denied this, adding 'that God sends illnesses to people according to his will'.[23]

Children and tales of the sabbat

The most extreme visions of the family as a centre of witchcraft naturally used the sabbat as their organizing principle. The idea that whole families might be seen there found peculiarly vivid expression in the Basque country, where the theme of child witches taken to the *aquelarre* appeared with monotonous regularity in the confessions. There and elsewhere the Devil was reported as keen to attract these young recruits, pressurizing parents to have them initiated. An exceptionally high proportion of those accused in the 1609–11 panic were children and young people, so the stories were in a sense circular, fantasies adapted to the situation of their tellers. Some at least were also collaborative, since the children were often kept in groups awaiting interrogation; the emphasis on large-scale collective activities may also reflect this special circumstance, for there are striking parallels with the Swedish episode in the 1670s. There are indications that children came to play an increasing role in witchcraft from the late sixteenth century onwards, at the informal level as well as in the trials. Their appearance as witch-finders has already been noted. They were also prominent among the supposed victims of diabolical possession, usually believed to have been inflicted through the agency of a witch, whose identity the Devils within them might then be 'forced' to reveal; others simply claimed to have witnessed the meetings and evil-doing of witches. In some instances these children, like Darrell's accomplice William Somers or the Lancashire boy Edmund Robinson in

1634, appear to have been directly manipulated by older men or parents, while hidden pressures must have been very common. A rather pathetic Essex case in 1622 saw Elizabeth Saunders of West Ham confess that she had taught Katherine Malpas to simulate bewitchment and possession, so that people would be drawn to the house and give money. This had included accusing two local women of being the witches behind the counterfeit possession.[24] On the other hand, the sick children who were often at the centre of those formal accusations which initiated a trial were quite capable of acting independently. Living as they did in a world where stories of witches and their powers were common currency, it was natural for them to generate such suspicions themselves, however much the later stages of the process were controlled by their parents or other adults.

Children's appearance as accusers, witnesses and suspects was particularly dangerous, yet also double-edged. As repeated experience in our own time should have taught us, it is all too easy to extract false statements from young people in such circumstances. It would have been hard to devise a more insidious method for procuring convictions. There were terrible scenes when children were induced to denounce their own parents; sometimes the latter raged against these unnatural offspring, often they crumpled in despair and confessed their own guilt. After Didier Pierrat had stoutly denied all the charges against him he was confronted with his daughter Marguitte, aged eight or nine, who insisted that he had taken her to the sabbat, carrying her on his back with a broom under his arm while they flew out of the chimney on the way to a mountain. Then she gave a description of the sabbat, where they ate poor meat and her father danced with the others, led by a black man. Didier responded that if this was true they should burn him alive, and that his daughter had been suborned; she was in the hands of the scribes and Pharisees. When she repeated her story, however, he said he saw he was damned and would have to admit things he had never done.[25] In a peculiarly nasty case, a girl of eight or nine, Mongeotte Pivert, was apparently manipulated by her uncle and cousins into accusing her whole family of attending the sabbat, sending five of them to the stake. The uncle had been vowing to take his revenge since he had been fined for assaulting one of his relatives by marriage; these childish stories gave him his chance. As the danger became apparent one of Mongeotte's aunts and another woman she had accused were looking for her with the intention of drowning her, in which they failed because the other accusers intervened to protect her. Among those she claimed to have seen at the sabbat was her eleven-year-old cousin Georgel; although the judges noted that his admissions were dubious, because the fear of whipping would make him say anything, they continued to extract them none the less. It does not say much for their humanity that they finally let him off with yet another whipping after forcing him to watch the execution of his parents.[26] It was fortunate that, like so much else to do with witchcraft, these practices for mobilizing child witnesses remained episodic and localized rather than becoming truly general.

In England a productive technique was the interrogation of very young children about the animal familiars or imps supposedly used by their mothers, which not surprisingly elicited some garbled but incriminating stories. Brian Darcy found his St Osyth witches particularly vulnerable in this way. Typical of several depositions was that by Ursula Kemp's eight-year-old son Thomas, who said that she had four spirits,

> the one called Tiffin, the other Titty, the third Piggin, and the fourth Jack, and being asked of what colours they were, saith that Titty is like a little grey cat, Tiffin is like a white lamb, Piggin is black, like a toad, and Jack is black, like a cat. And he saith, he hath seen his mother at times to give them beer to drink, and of a white loaf or cake to eat; and saith that in the night-time the said spirits will come to his mother and suck blood of her upon her arms and other places of her body.[27]

Although no writer of the period seems to have appreciated the full extent of children's suggestibility, there are some signs that excessive use of their testimony could lead to public concern and encourage wider scepticism over questions of proof. Perhaps it was the St Osyth cases, very close to his own parish, which led Gifford to remark,

> Yea sundry times the evidence of children is taken accusing their own mothers, that they did see them give milk unto little things which they kept in wool. The children coming to years of discretion confess they were enticed to accuse. What vile and monstrous impieties are here committed.[28]

This may be one of the several ways in which persecution tended to overstep unseen boundaries and discredit itself. When younger children confessed to being witches themselves, and to committing acts of *maleficium*, they set the authorities a difficult problem. There was natural reluctance to carry out capital sentences, yet on occasion children as young as ten were put to death. An even more horrible solution was adopted at Bouchain in the Spanish Netherlands, where three child witches were held in prison until they were thought old enough to be executed; it looks as if before the Council in Brussels intervened some of the total of eighteen children condemned to death may have been executed before they were ten.[29] Elsewhere more merciful councils normally prevailed, and quite a common solution was to send children off to receive proper religious instruction, so that they could be reclaimed from the Devil.

Many of the stories told by children, far from being the result of interrogation, were directed at their own peer group. Once beyond infancy the children of the neighbourhood formed into bands, playing and often working together, as well as having a distinct place in many religious and secular rituals. Claims of access to occult power or hidden riches evidently provided a possible way to enhance one's own status, even to frighten and overawe rivals for dominance. Occasionally a string of children or adolescents would be produced in court to testify about what had been said; it is hard to know whether these stories developed from existing reputations or actually created new ones. Jean Colombain told a particularly rich series of stories, reported by numerous children; Claudon Demenge, aged eleven, had quarrelled with him as they were guarding the animals a month earlier, receiving threats to kill him and make his teeth fall out. Jean added that he had made him ill already – Claudon remarked that it was true that a year earlier he had been very ill for two days, without knowing the cause. A year earlier Jean had told him and other boys 'that he went to the sabbat with his mother, and that his father went to collect money among the rocks in a meadow called Menaprey, mounted on a small black horse with big ears but no hair, and which was hard to ride, saying that his mother told him to say nothing about this to others'. They were again with the animals when Jean became angry with them, saying 'my father will soon have your beasts', at which a big wolf appeared and carried off a goat.[30] Another boy of the same age, Colas Henry, told his mother of a dispute in which Curien Marechal was arguing with another boy about which of them had been further. Anthoine Claude said he had been to Ramberviller, whereupon Curien said he had been to the Devil with his mother, where he had eaten little birds and a man dressed as a gentleman in black had danced with his mother.[31] It may well be that the growing importance of children in the whole structure of beliefs and accusations can be related to the absorption of material from the trials, as well as from village gossip, into this area of childish talk and boasting, where it could be developed and exploited in various ways. Another rather elusive theme is resentment against parents, latent or overt, which might easily find expression in this exceptionally dangerous form. While such motivations are hard to detect, trials certainly empowered family members to act against one another with no regard for the normal hierarchies. Parents must have been acutely conscious of their vulnerability; there are instances where they are reported making promises of special rewards to children if they would keep quiet when interrogated. Another child witness claimed that Jean Colombain's father had promised him a coat and a pair of breeches like those of the forester's son if he would hold his tongue before the judges.[32]

Vulnerability and reputations

If complete breakdowns of family bonds leading to accusations between close kin are rarely apparent, there were other situations which manifested themselves repeatedly. Families were often disrupted by the deaths of adults, and relations between step-parents and stepchildren could never be without problems. Since widows with dependent children did not find it easy to obtain new partners, stepmothers were much commoner than stepfathers; the folkloric commonplace of the wicked stepmother was an exaggeration based on a well-known phenomenon. Women routinely accused one another of failing to feed or care for their step-children properly, while as we have seen the adult children by a previous marriage often displayed marked hostility to the replacement wife. Such tensions were exacerbated by latent or open quarrels about inheritance, which could also influence the relationships between half-siblings, with unfairness almost bound to be felt by some if not all parties, whatever efforts were made to avoid it.

These tensions could spill over into the kind of charges made by Didier Hanna against his sister-in-law Thomasse Poirot, whom he believed to have caused the death of two of his daughters, aged eleven and thirteen. Didier had tried to dissuade his brother from marrying her, while there had been various other disputes subsequently, and 'a wise-woman had told his wife that another woman who sought to get their property had caused the death of those children.'[33] Worst off of all were those children who lost both parents and became orphans; unless they had some property they had to rely on charitable relatives, supposing these could be found, or eke out a precarious existence by minding animals and other similar tasks. Marginal individuals of this kind, who typically wandered from one community to another and lacked any support from kin, sometimes acquired an aura of malevolence which turned into a dangerous reputation. In one spectacular late episode, the Zaubererjackl trials in the archbishopric of Salzburg, such people were to become the specific target of persecution. The rarity of such cases, however, suggests that such an evolution was unusual; orphans were numerous, yet few show up in the records of trials. Most of them probably learned to be subservient towards the more fortunate, and simply could not afford the self-assertion commonly associated with witchcraft. Guardians or tutors would be forthcoming where there was property involved, but these arrangements were often unsatisfactory, giving rise to claims of dishonesty or embezzlement. Conflicts of these types might seethe just beneath the surface of witchcraft accusations, only partially visible to the historian's eye; often they are easier to intuit than to demonstrate.

Parental attachment to children, and valuation of them, is also a widespread theme with complex ramifications. The most persistent note sounded by many of the accused, in respect of their own situation, was not anxiety about their personal fate, but concern for their children. This was true of men as well as women, giving rise to some heart-rending appeals to the authorities. After Jean Pelisson confessed he was a witch he begged the local chapter to have pity on his poor wife, who had no property of her own, and their four small children under seven, otherwise they would have to go begging; he would die more easily if he knew something would be done for them.[34] Across most of Europe, as in this case, the situation was made worse because the property of a convicted witch was confiscated by the authorities, leaving the survivors impoverished. Although evidence for this aspect is limited, it appears to have been common for the family to repurchase land and other goods at less than their official value, perhaps with the connivance of either the officials or the community. Such arrangements could only mitigate the disaster, of course, and had no effect on the other consequence of a conviction, the creation or confirmation of a family reputation which might haunt the descendants through several generations. This was a dangerous reinforcement of the labelling process, with the trials helping to build up family, as opposed to individual, reputations. In most areas persecution did not last for long enough for the full implications to become evident, but there are some signs that a growing proportion of the accused may have been identified on this basis. In other cases there are later reports that the children of convicted witches had later left the neighbourhood, perhaps a sensible move, but one which may well have reduced them to the level of the vagrant poor. Nor was there any guarantee that moving would wipe the slate clean, since incomers were closely scrutinized and reports travelled quite readily over considerable distances.

There are signs that women with dependent children put up a stiffer fight than most; those who made remarks such as 'who will feed my children?' sometimes resisted intensive torture to assert their innocence. Those who had no children surviving, or had lost contact with them, on the other hand, plainly felt themselves to be isolated and disadvantaged; one or two felt so unwanted that by their own admission they hoped to secure their own deaths. Nicole Nigal, whose two surviving children had absented themselves long since, tried to drown herself in a well, saying she would rather be drowned than burned, and when on trial continued to say she wished she were dead, since there was no-one to defend her.[35] Claudon Wannier also insisted there was no-one to take her part, crying as she told of the death of her daughter and saying, 'a terrible death for me'.[36] As a matter of self-interest, all other considerations apart, adult children had good reason to defend their parents as far as they could; the simple awareness that they would bear a grudge against accusers must have been a restraining factor in many cases. In addition to lacking this protection, the childless often seem to have been feared, suspected of envy and malice towards more fortunate neighbours, an impression they were liable to intensify by taking a pathetic interest in other people's children. Admiring a baby or giving a child some titbits could be as risky as muttering a curse if illness followed. Chesnon la Triffatte, a childless widow in her seventies, was alleged to have approached a baby's cot during wedding festivities, remarking, 'Jesus, what a beautiful child'; the wet-nurse became alarmed when the child failed to wake, and found its face to be black and swollen. Another servant said in the street that some witches must be burned, at which la Triffatte rose from the bench on which she was sitting, and the infant recovered. It is perhaps significant that during her subsequent confessions the old woman told how her master had instructed her to kill some children in the fields, but when she approached two who were collecting pears she spared them, because they were friendly, one even sharing his bread and cheese with her – a poignant memory of one small act of kindness. Later she added that the Devil feared children, so when she wanted to avoid him she often kept company with them, for which he would beat her.[37]

Children also played a considerable part in creating or worsening disputes between neighbours. Heavy-handed intervention to break up fights and punish another child could easily cause bad feeling, or again activate witchcraft suspicions when illness or injury could be linked to it. Allison Claude testified against her near neighbour Mathieu Margeron, whom she blamed for the death of her son aged seven a decade earlier. The boy had gone out and she had not paid attention to where he was going, as one would not normally bother with children of his age. He had the better of a fight with Mathieu's son, was told off by the accused, then developed a pain under his arm and died in two or three days; the accused was reported to have said he would not recover, while his wife, who saw the quarrel, told the boy 'she would have his sauce made for him by the said Margeron'.[38] These clashes often involved the familiar projection mechanism, when the aggressor feared punishment and might display symptoms as a form of self-protection. This is evident in the famous case of Mary Glover and Elizabeth Jackson, when the girl had behaved badly to Jackson's daughter and was faced with the prospect of parental discipline. Mary Glover's subsequent 'possession' has all the marks, in its early stages, of a hysterical reaction to a persecuting figure readily assimilated with her own parents (as it developed her behaviour was shaped to meet the expectations of those around her).[39] Contemporary physicians seem to have realized that there was something odd about these episodes, rightly feeling that they went beyond simple fraud, without being able to penetrate the powerful psychic mechanisms at work. In other cases mysterious symptoms disappeared abruptly when the suspected witch offered some kind of conciliatory gesture and the threat of punishment was lifted. Jean Mulot testified that a few years earlier his son Jean, aged six, was playing with other children when he called Jacquot Petit Jacquot's daughter 'black beast'. When Jacquot heard of this he said the boy would repent, then next day he fell ill in an extraordinary fashion, with his stomach very swollen. Jean was considering going to the *devin* to see who had given the illness, but a woman suggested 'that she had heard a rumour that he might be cured'. Therefore he decided to call some friends to supper, and ask Jacquot and his wife; as they left they visited the sick boy, who had had a blessed candle in his hand all day, and was expected to die. During the night he called out for some bread, ate it readily and next day was recovered, running around the street with the others.[40] We should note the way in which children could transmit or enhance reputations through the familiar practice of name-calling, for one of the favourite insults was to call another child the son or daughter of a witch. This bred quarrels between parents, who may all have been embarrassed by behaviour they could not really control, when as so often children subverted the restraints set by adult society. The process may also have typecast the children of suspects, encouraging them to construct the compromising stories which simultaneously won them a certain respect, if only through fear, and threatened disaster to their whole family.

Mothers and their fears

Childrearing and childcare are such fundamental elements in shaping any society that it is deeply frustrating to know so little about them in the past. This is particularly true in relation to witchcraft, when the classic image of the witch is that of the bad mother. She was supposed to kill children, even sometimes eat them, rather than protect and nourish them. One of her favourite forms of revenge was to become the bad mother at one remove, damaging another woman's capacity to give suck; troubles with breastfeeding were frequently blamed on witchcraft. The expectation that older women would be able to give advice made it unusually easy to call in the suspect, then attribute any improvement to her having lifted the spell. These were exclusively female crimes, never to my knowledge found in the accusations against male witches. They can of course be linked to the broader, non-gendered offence of depriving the whole community of sustenance by damaging the crops, but this was rarely a specific charge, being rather a transposition of the theme into the mythology of the sabbat. The associated notions of witches killing and eating babies represent oral aggression in a particularly violent form, at the same time inverting the normal pattern whereby the infant uses its teeth on the mother. Perhaps the intense sensory experiences of motherhood were being transmuted into these fantasies of ultimate evil, while at another level accusers and judges projected their own aggression against mothers into the persons of the accused. Whatever the mechanisms – and they surely varied from case to case – a powerful and dangerous layer of sado-masochistic feelings might be brought into play through the medium of witchcraft beliefs, with the witch becoming the container for ugly and violent impulses her persecutors could not avow in themselves. Among the many imponderables in the background is the effect of the widespread practice of swaddling infants, which saw them held immobile within a cocoon of drapery. Although this was probably comforting to the new-born, it may have meant intense discomfort and frustration for slightly older infants, with implications for mother-child relations. One practical reason for swaddling was that women needed to return to work as soon as possible, and trussing infants up in this way was thought to ensure their safety as well as helping them to grow straight; periodic abandonment by the mother appears to have been part of the normal infantile experience in early modern Europe.

Young children were also regularly exposed to the traumas associated with siblings. Although prolonged breastfeeding and other factors did tend to lengthen the intervals between births, a majority of children would have experienced the arrival of a younger brother or sister before they were three. Among these siblings many would have sickened, and a high proportion of them died very quickly. Such events were bound to leave the survivors with intense feelings of guilt, since they would have experienced the normal impulses of murderous rage towards infants who supplanted them at the mother's breast, yet never had the opportunity to work these through to a more balanced relationship. Instead they would have learned that anger was so dangerous it must be suppressed, been unable to come to terms with this aspect of reality and perhaps become subject to later murderous impulses. The imagined responsibility for infant deaths was a peculiarly intense version of that conjunction between ill-will and disaster which lay at the heart of witchcraft beliefs. This pattern did of course operate far more widely, since similar feelings of being to blame would have been aroused by the death of a parent or a spouse as well. Where some historians have seen the widespread experience of sudden deaths within the family as a cause of emotional atrophy, it is more plausible to think of them as reinforcing a syndrome which linked covert hatred to physical effects. Emotions of this kind may actually have been more corrosive among full biological kin, who could not readily avow them, than they were between step-parents and their adoptive children or between half-siblings, who evidently found it easier to express hostility directly. Conflicts arising from broken homes and remarriages are certainly important, however, as part of the difficult world through which individuals had to make their way to maturity. When death and disaster were such constant presences, by the time they reached maturity many people could look back on a history of profoundly disturbed or broken human relationships. How far this was particularly true of either suspects or accusers it is impossible to judge, but some individual cases do reveal such patterns. More generally, the assumption must be that early modern Europeans (not unlike ourselves) were always liable to mobilize latent fantasies shaped in their formative period, which they projected into women who in one way or another stood for the mother.

Childbirth itself was naturally surrounded by a complex accretion of beliefs and practices that emphasized both its importance and its dangers. While it could be seen as the ultimate emotional and social fulfilment of a woman's life, it also made her exceptionally vulnerable. For some women it took the agonizing form of repeated miscarriages, which cast doubt on their capacity to bear children successfully at all; this quite common situation was readily blamed on witchcraft, and it is easy to see how it fitted the image of the malevolent enemies of all natural processes of fertility. In the case of Margueritte Martin there was a background of family disputes over inheritance; her sister was one of those who testified about the misfortunes of Françoise Jacquemin, who was married to Margueritte's nephew. She had suffered three miscarriages, and herself suspected Margueritte of wanting to ensure that all the property reverted to her, especially since she was said to have caused the illness of her brother-in-law. She had been heard saying they were the two richest young men in the village, a comment readily interpreted as a sign of envy. When the witness was pregnant the first time she sent her a roast, which her husband advised her not to eat, but she was tempted and did so, after which she felt no sign of life from the child. There was a similar event the second time, but they burned the gift. Then at the third childbirth she arrived early, although not summoned, and interfered with the midwife; when she suddenly felt cold Margueritte insisted on putting her feet in hot water. She visited her three days later and, when she was lamenting what had happened, told her it would not occur again – which she could not possibly know, so this encouraged her suspicions.[41]

Even those who carried their babies satisfactorily through to delivery were then unusually dependent on the goodwill and assistance of family, friends and neighbours. The expertise of older women was at a premium, whether they were official midwives or not; sometimes individuals tried to take charge of the whole event in an intrusive fashion which would be recalled later. This was actually the case with Margueritte Martin, for the midwife testified that the baby was well positioned, so that an easy birth seemed certain, when she arrived and insisted on directing affairs despite protests from the witness. A small group of perhaps half a dozen other married women and widows would surround the woman in labour, often sealing all doors and windows to keep out both witchcraft and draughts. This was one of those occasions when a very local community was supposed to unite, and by implication protect mother and new-born through a public display of goodwill. There was something shocking and threatening when some women were absent, whether they chose not to come or were pointedly not asked. It was one of those occasions when widely feared local witches had resentment thrust upon them, and were liable to be blamed for any misfortune whatever they did. Similar concerns gathered around the subsequent ceremony of baptism, with the associated celebrations for a successful delivery, while the choice of god-parents might prove a vexatious matter. Insistent demands for this sign of reciprocal trust might force latent suspicions into the open, whatever perfectly reasonable excuses were made for failure to nominate a particular neighbour. It was even worse if the refusal had more sinister implications. Jennon Valtin asked to be godmother to Noel Prevost's child, but on account of her reputation they asked someone else. She was very angry and said 'that they had not wanted to accept her as godmother, but they would have hardly any benefit from their child'. Predictably the infant sickened, to die nine weeks later, which was attributed to her witchcraft.[42] The whole situation of childbirth was so fraught with emotional tension, set within an elaborate social setting which gave ample opportunities for friction, that its prominence in depositions and charges is no surprise. A wide range of magical, para-liturgical practices underlined the anxiety felt by the women, their families and their friends; many of these were specifically directed against witchcraft.

Death, inheritance and ill-will

The rites of passage surrounding death could cause trouble just as readily as those associated with birth; failure to attend or invite, unsuitable behaviour and so forth. For the family this was another moment of extreme stress, particularly when the death was that of a parent and implied a major restructuring of several lives. The situations were of course varied; the death of a mother could mean that the eldest daughter effectively took her place, that a stepmother would soon arrive, that the widower must now be cared for by one of the adult children, or that the final redistribution of family property must take place. The father's death might also have very different consequences according to the stage in the life-cycle when it occurred, but was certain to raise issues about inheritance. When one considers the emotional trauma involved and the immense importance of the division of property for the heirs, the legendary propensity for families to split and quarrel at this point is not hard to understand. The danger was such that a range of legal provisions had been set up to restrict the freedom of testators; these varied locally all the way from strict primogeniture (eldest son takes all) to equal shares all round. None of these systems appears to have been fully watertight, and in any case all could be subverted by private agreement among family members, provided none of these reneged and went to law. In practice, therefore, they probably did little to prevent discord. If a small minority lived at a level of absolute poverty which made disputes pointless, most peasants in western Europe owned enough – parcels of land, animals and houses – to be worth squabbling over. In addition, most of this property was difficult to value or subdivide precisely, opening up further prospects of dispute and resentment. Rich people could fight it out in the courts, at the risk of mutual impoverishment; the majority of the relatively poor simply could not afford this option.

Inheritance was absolutely vital for one's status and prospects. Those who did not own enough property to be self-sufficient – probably approaching 90 per cent of the population – had no chance of altering this situation, because all paid work was essentially at subsistence rates. Entry to more highly rewarded professions was controlled so that only the sons of the better-off were eligible. The oligarchies of wealthy peasants, of which the English yeomanry were one example, formed the lowest stratum of the privileged orders, alongside the small urban bourgeoisie to whose members they were often related. There is not much sign that inheritance disputes at this level enmeshed with witchcraft accusations; it could be a different story lower down, however. A peasant with an acre or two of land in his own name, or even just a decent house and garden, still enjoyed an enormous advantage over the truly landless. Rural society below the level of yeomen and their like was far from being composed of an enormous mass of equally deprived, half-starving labourers; on the contrary, it was finely graded along a spectrum of valuations which were readily understood at the time. Some of these had to do with the ability to stand one's ground and not be put down, an issue which could be as important in inheritance disputes as the actual value of the property concerned. Those who betrayed weakness and gave up without a fight were liable to be considered fair game by other potential aggressors, from tax-collectors to trespassers. So there was a double incentive to press one's claims as hard as possible, which added to the inherent tensions of the situation. Certain specific problems seem to crop up in the witchcraft cases. Although it was very rare for siblings or in-laws to initiate charges, they did sometimes appear as hostile witnesses, exposing the latent tensions within the wider kin group. Angry words over inheritance might lay the foundations for suspicion, often with the same implication of guilt being projected as in disputes over charity. Lucie Rozieres had made no secret of her anger when her half-sister's husband Claude Borrellier sold her half of a house they shared; she said in public that although her sister might have agreed to the sale, 'she would never enjoy the money it produced in good health'. The sister soon became ill, so bent that she could not walk and had to be carried like a child. When her husband asked her about the opinions he heard that Lucie had given her the sickness, she persuaded him not to believe this, only for him to change his mind when she died after eating an apple sent by her sister.[43]

Elderly parents who had not provided for all their children, or were failing to pay dowries in full, could create animosities leading to great bitterness among the younger generations. Demenge Demongeot was reproached by other villagers for his failure to give his married daughter Nicole the dowry he had promised, at which he flew into a violent temper, making threats against Nicole while insisting that she and another daughter had taken so many household goods from him after their mother's death that he owed them nothing. Nicole subsequently fell ill, then recovered after there was a great public reconciliation with Demenge, who plied her with food and drink, so that she said 'she had left her sickness at the mill with her father.' Unfortunately when someone then stole some corn from him, he was told it was Nicole's husband, at which he repeated his threats, her sickness returned and proved fatal. There was a savage confrontation between the miller and his son-in-law, whom he called a thief, only to attract the charge 'that he was a witch, that he had already brought about the death of his other three daughters, that he was now killing the last who was his wife, after which he would have none at all'.[44] The treatment of foster or step children was liable to arouse concern among neighbours, who detected ulterior motives behind neglect or incompetence, whether in caring for such marginal dependants or in managing their affairs. When witches confessed they rather confirmed that hostilities of these types were widespread, since they quite often explained particular acts of malignity as inspired by jealousies over inheritance. Jean Cachette actually confessed to killing his own father by throwing powder on the cart where he was loading dung, so that he fell into the road – he did this because his father had said he was angry with him, would not live with him any more and was leaving his property to his sister Claude and her husband.[45]

Reputations resembled property in some respects, for they were inherited in the first instance and were much easier to lose than they were to recover or improve. European witchcraft was not conceptualized like that of the Azande, as a physical substance one might inherit quite unawares; the idea that the witch deliberately chose to serve the wrong master was an established part of popular belief. As was explained earlier, even where the idea of the diabolical pact was not found, as in Elizabethan England, relations with the familiars had similar connotations. Nevertheless, the idea of a taint in the blood was just as firmly rooted, so that the children and siblings of convicted witches were always in danger of being drawn in after them. Testimony in the courts often shows how retentive the popular memory was for any lapse within the wider kinship system, later cited as if it were evidence. No doubt this was aided by the insults which seem to have flown about so freely, acting as a reminder of past disgraces or failures. A common claim on the other side was that one's race or lineage had been clean from any charge of witchcraft. The legal systems themselves, with their provisions for the accused to challenge witnesses on the basis of reputation, enshrined such ideas. They were also found in respect of healers, who often took over from their parents;

here too it could be a moot point whether the magical powers were learned or inherited. There was plainly a serious danger that an unwise marriage into a family tainted by witchcraft would have repercussions for the wider kin, and this concern emerged when family members investigated the reputations of prospective brides. Sometimes the result was to break off the negotiations, leaving a legacy of resentment; on other occasions the marriage went ahead, only for the husband to reveal the reservations felt by his relatives or friends. When Mengette Estienne was tried, two members of the Connis family testified that their mother had tried to dissuade her first husband from marrying her, on the grounds that she was reputed to be a witch. Mengette later said that since she had used such words 'she would hate her for that all her life, with all her family'. One of the sons had so many sicknesses among his family and animals when he was her neighbour that he finally moved house.[46] Even if there was no direct evidence the advice was known about, the fear that the husband might have spoken would have been quite enough to set off the familiar mechanism of projected guilt on the part of those who had tried to dissuade him, with potentially disastrous effects if they experienced misfortune of the kinds normally attributed to witchcraft.

Courtship and sexuality

Courtship was fraught with related difficulties, since reputation and connections were so central to the whole process. One pathetic case was that of Georgeatte Pelisson, a young woman of twenty-four whose mother had been executed a decade earlier, while her father was strongly suspected and would follow her to the stake (partly because she accused him). Georgeatte was evidently thought to be similarly tainted; she admitted she had become angry when repeatedly asked to visit the sick, and blamed for their state. Two witnesses told stories which demonstrated how her position drew her into understandable – if foolish – displays of resentment towards the more eligible. Marguitte Vicaire said she was dancing with other girls on a Sunday when a young male servant came and danced with her. Georgeatte glared at her in a way which made it plain she was angry, so that she wished she had never seen him, and was frightened of the vengeance Georgeatte might take. At the moment Marguitte thought this, she felt something prick her behind the ear, then the pain spread to her throat and she had to take to her bed, unable to speak properly. She remained in this state for a week, while everyone thought she was dying, and she vomited up nut-sized lumps of something like flax with a terrible smell. The other girls begged Georgeatte to come and see her; eventually she did so, and lay down beside her without touching her or saying a word. She started to feel better immediately, and was out working in the vines next day. Thiebault Vicaire told how his young sister Catherine had fallen ill with a strange malady, crying night and day to God and the saints to help her. This lasted two years, and finally he asked her how she had come to be ill; she said that she was sure Georgeatte had bewitched her, in envy of the fact that a young servant was making love to her, when she had tried everything to attract him herself. When he asked her to visit his sister, she said she wished all those who came to ask her to visit the sick might burst – then he called her witch, threatening to beat her, kill her or have her burned if she did not cure his sister, but the latter died a week later, insisting to the last that Georgeatte had bewitched her.[47] In the cases of Jean Grand Didier and his wife Georgeatte, tried one after the other, both were accused over the death of a young couple three years earlier. The man had courted one of their daughters, but then became betrothed to another girl. He fell ill when about to buy the food for the marriage feast, followed by his fiancée who had been nursing him; both attributed their sickness to the accused, and Georgeatte had brought the girl some milk saying it would cure her – only for her to die as soon as she drank it.[48]

Men married to suspects were liable to taunts with a strongly sexual content, along the lines of 'go off and mount your witch of a wife'. How far this implied some broader association between witchcraft and sexuality it is hard to say; modern ideas about the appeal of the forbidden may not have much relevance for ordinary people in this period. It would be difficult to portray the world of peasants and artisans as one in which basic instincts were repressed by internal psychic mechanisms. Constraints on behaviour were external – social, economic and cultural – rather than being internalized. It was precisely a new style of self-control which the religious reformers, both Protestant and Catholic, sought to generalize among the laity; for them the repression of sin, in the form of libidinal impulses, was the principal objective. Such doctrines proved extremely hard to inculcate on a general basis, even among the educated classes, and their attractive power at popular level was minimal. The associated ideology, however, could be developed into much cruder justifications for direct external action to control disreputable behaviour. Indeed, those members of the ruling elites who participated in such campaigns were likely to project their own repressed libido into the deviants they were attacking. Pierre de Lancre and his like were behaving in just this way when they attached fantasies of unbridled sexuality to the sabbat. Children and adolescents, in particular, readily told suitably libidinous stories under interrogation, for the witch-hunters to reproduce with gleeful prurience, accompanied by unconvincing cries of outrage. Sexual fantasy was a perfectly familiar genre for them, as one would expect; what they lacked (as reforming clerics often bewailed) was any sense that it was sinful. In consequence there was no compelling reason for ordinary people to include this element in their construction of the witch as a bundle of deviant characteristics.

This may be one reason why sex with the Devil was generally described in a very banal fashion by confessing female witches, as a kind of rape which symbolized their subjection, an infernal *droit de seigneur*. Only a few admitted it had been a common occurrence, and they usually represented the Devil as the sole instigator of these unwelcome couplings. While the Devil could technically have been considered as an adulterous lover (and in German Lorraine was often referred to as a lover in the confessions), this theme never seems to have acquired any prominence. Men occasionally confessed to having been tempted by a succubus (a supernatural being in the form of a woman), but more often the sexual element was entirely missing from their stories. Homosexual relations with the Devil, which would have represented a splendid display of deviance, seem to have been outside their imaginative repertoire. The only clear-cut case I have encountered, in a German trial, has been convincingly explained as an expression of guilt from a boy of seventeen who had been seduced by a fellow servant.[49] This was at Esslingen, where the local witch-hunter Daniel Hauff showed an obsessive interest in such themes. When aberrant sexuality does appear in the trial records, it is mainly in those forms which threatened the norms of local society. Individuals who led a dissolute life crop up fairly regularly, and there is a suspicion that women with illegitimate children were more at risk than others. It would be hard to demonstrate this statistically, however, while these individuals might also have been picked out as among the poorest and least protected members of the community. Promiscuity was the basic material for insults among women, notably where relations with priests or soldiers were involved, and the numerous folkloric sanctions using varieties of shaming emphasize the point. It is easy enough to see how a male-dominated society would have sought to enforce such values on its womenfolk, yet the putative link to witchcraft accusations remains rather weak; the theme emerges in too patchy and incidental a fashion from the records to be given great significance.

A reputation for predatory sexuality was less damaging for a man, but was likely to create dangerous animosities. In one German case this was probably the reason why Grethen Michel of Lisdorf testified against Augstgen Mattheis, a suspect who had been having an affair with his wife.[50] Jean Gerardin blamed the frigidity of a wife he had never really wanted to marry for his remorseless pursuit of other village women, conceding that he deserved death for his immorality while insisting to the end that he was no witch.[51] In another case, a man subjected his wife to violence and humiliation, demanding that she use contraception and accept a *ménage à trois* with a concubine. He later admitted that his desires and rages were mysterious to himself, suggesting that some other witch might have caused his aberrant behaviour – 'when he was in his furies he felt that he should do anything he thought or which came into his head, so that he even sometimes wanted to kill his wife, yet when he returned to his senses he repented for doing and saying what he had'. The charge of witchcraft in this case revolved partly around the notion of forbidden knowledge, in the form of his ideas about contraception; there is also the possibility that the wife's family and friends were ganging up against the brutal and debauched husband.[52] At a more elevated social level, the notorious seducer-priest Urbain Grandier did become the victim of his own reputation, for when he refused to become the father-confessor of the young nuns in the Ursuline convent of Loudun, this fascinatingly ambivalent figure in their minds became the love object who spurned them. It is hard to disagree with the sceptical local doctor, already cited, who detected a strongly erotic impulse behind their behaviour. For all his courageous refusal to confess, and intelligent self-defence, Grandier paid for his earlier womanizing by being subjected to atrocious tortures, then burned at the stake. An even more highly spiced brew of love magic, black masses, poisonings and child murder was offered in the *affaire des poisons*, which scandalized the court of Louis XIV in the later 1670s. The king's mistress and other leading figures were involved, and although the stories were wildly exaggerated, there was plainly some small element of rather grubby reality behind them. These sophisticated imaginings have no real equivalent in the village world, where the more extreme sexual deviations take the depressing forms of bestiality and incest, aberrations which usually seem rather incidental to the cases in which they occur, and probably had only a marginal role (if any) in provoking accusations.

The ambiguous family: support and betrayal

However much the family might be threatened by internal tensions or the misbehaviour of individual members, its members normally rallied to defend one another in a crisis. Mutual protection was a basic expectation which everyone understood. Weakness and division, if revealed to the outside world, exposed all members to the dangers of isolation, when few could feel much confidence that some grave crisis might not strike at any moment. Help given to one's kin was the most basic form of insurance policy, building up a credit to draw on in one's own turn. Witchcraft accusations strained these loyalties to the limit, however, and could on occasion break them irreparably. The rumour that a family member was to be arrested might provoke anxious meetings, at which bitter arguments were liable to break out. When Didie Pourlatte was accused of causing the sickness of a young man who was vomiting strange substances, her brother and her son by an earlier marriage came to visit her, but several witnesses claimed that they had disagreed violently; when she foolishly claimed to be as good as the Virgin Mary, her brother said 'that if she was a good woman she should defend herself, but if she was otherwise he wished he was already far away'. This was hardly the kind of help she needed at this critical moment.[53] In general, the male line predominated in structuring allegiance, placing women at something of a disadvantage; there must always have been a temptation to try for self-preservation by effectively rejecting the outsider brought in by marriage. After all, witchcraft could be construed as a treason against the immediate family as well as against the wider community. Aulbry Colin claimed that when Jeanne Mercier was accused, her husband (who was also Colin's cousin) had told him he had been to see a relative about her arrest, who said 'that he should not spend any money defending her, since it would be a complete loss, because they knew well that she would not return'.[54] The grievances over ill-treatment and beatings, by which so many women explained their initial apostasy, also implied deep resentments against the husband and, by implication, his kin. There is no way of telling just how far these factors operated in most cases, since messages about family solidarity or its absence would have been conveyed in many subtle ways which leave no trace behind. There would have been a serious difference between displaying hostility to known enemies and accusers and merely observing a prudent silence. Ultimately protection may have depended on the implicit threat that the matter would not be forgotten, and retribution would be sought sooner or later. Many potential accusers must have been deterred by the knowledge that there were suspects among their own relatives who might easily fall victim to a counter-charge, although there was no shortage of other ways in which enmities could make themselves felt.

In those exceptional cases where families could not contain their internal disputes, and these took the form of witchcraft accusations, the effects could be devastating. The way such hostilities could fester, while becoming entangled with other suspicions, emerges from the trial of a Saarland witch, Lauers Barbell of Merchingen, who was executed in 1593 at the age of fifty-three. She was a married woman with just one daughter, although she had earlier given birth to an illegitimate child. Her repu-tation may have begun because she was friendly with another woman who had to leave the village in 1583 on suspicion of witchcraft. That same year Barbell, who had quarrelled with her own sister and brother-in-law, was accused of killing a horse belonging to them. She threatened her niece, whose whole body became swollen, so that the local pastor (in whose service the girl was) said it was witchcraft. Two years later her brother-in-law died, accusing her of being responsible – but it looks as if her husband and friends prevented any action being taken. Her sister continued to put about stories over the next seven years, while Barbell evidently tried to win over public opinion by behaving generously, as by providing additional drink for her husband's workers. One of the events leading to the dénouement was the sickness and death of one of these workers, who accused her of being the cause, while she was named as an accomplice by some convicted witches at Siersburg. The nephew of the dead man finally organized a prosecution; Barbell's accusers included her sister Sunna and her seventeen-year-old nephew Lorenz. After being imprisoned for seven weeks she was tortured and rapidly confessed to having been seduced six years earlier during the dearth, when she had nothing to eat. Although she escaped that night, she was soon recaptured begging in a nearby town and duly executed. She had her revenge at the last, however, for her sister and nephew were among a total of twenty (including other accusers) whom she named as fellow-witches; within a month they too had been tried and executed.[55]

Another trial which illustrates the uncertain quality of family loyalties comes from Schleswig, in the extreme north of Germany, in 1551. The central figure was Caterina Eggerdes, the wife of Hans Toffelmaker and sister of the *Stadtvogt* Peter Eggerdes, a powerful local official. Caterina had a long reputation for magical knowledge and the giving of advice, and may have been a wise-woman of high-status. For a long time it appears that her brother protected her, but in 1546 he quarrelled with his brother-in-law in a beer-cellar at Schleswig. He called Hans a philanderer and adulterer, adding that his sister was a witch and would have to be burned. This altercation, with its implication that he would no longer defend his sister, was too public not to become widely known, although action did not follow immediately. In 1551 Caterina was suspected over the long illness of Hans Bunthmaker; she was heard to say that nothing would cure him, and made threatening remarks about the doctor and healer Christoffer Smyth, who may well have encouraged the patient in blaming her. This dispute, which includes elements of the traditional hostility between competing healers, led to a complaint by Smyth, on which Caterina was arrested. She denied the charges, but then suddenly died, amidst extensive rumours that her brother had given her a poisoned drink. The case spilled over into accusations against a woman who had been Caterina's maid, with about fifty individuals being accused, and seven women executed.[56]

Relatives make more sympathetic appearances in the documents taking on various supportive roles. They might offer advice on how to respond to the court, or come to the prison window and call out encouragement. Barbelline le Jalley went to consult her relatives but could not find them; she was on her way back when she saw a man coming after her fast, and hastened on because she was afraid it was an officer coming to arrest her. When he did catch up he proved to be a friend, whom her nephew's wife had sent to accompany her. On the way he advised her how to reply when charged, 'even about the way they would put her to the torture' (he had previously been an officer in the court). He told her about how she would be racked, and 'would endure much torment, but if she could endure them she would do well and would escape' – unfortunately she was 'so terrified that she could remember nothing of what he said'.[57] At a more active and potentially dangerous level, they were found threatening hostile witnesses, helping prisoners escape and concealing fugitives. They must have been worried about the possibility of having their own reputations tarnished, so that often they merely advised suspects to flee. When Huguette Menestrey tried to take refuge with her brother Jehan at Semmadon around 1610 he summoned some friends, including the local *curé*, to his house, where they agreed to send her to safety across the border into France. This prudent decision was highly unwelcome to Huguette, who started to curse them all as she was taken on her way, threatening to render them and the inhabitants of the villages concerned the poorest of the whole country; the man escorting her was so enraged that he killed her.[58] There is little sign that attempts to help relatives were punished by the authorities, however, presumably because assistance of this kind was regarded as normal, even natural. On the other side, we must suppose that familial links often underlay the decision to make a formal accusation; it was to one's own kin that one would naturally look for support at such times. Only very rarely do the records give us a glimpse into such patterns, because the complex ties of kinship and faction are so difficult to reconstitute. There is a sub-text here which is probably lost forever, except at an imaginative or hypothetical level.

It is much easier to see the special problem faced by older women in particular, who had neither children nor close kin to fall back on. Around 10 per cent of marriages proved barren (presumably for medical reasons), while a rather higher proportion had no surviving offspring, and there were always some individuals who remained unmarried. Between a quarter and a third of the old women in a community would have had no direct descendants alive; most of these would have been at least partially dependent on formal or informal charity for even basic subsistence. While there are indications that they tended to band together in small groups, they were also implicitly in competition for scarce resources, so quarrels between them were frequent. Claudon la Romaine was accused by another widow of Charmes, who alleged she had made her ill when angry because she had received alms when Claudon had not. Claudon herself claimed to have been accused by the convicted witch la Mallebarbe out of hatred, after she had reproached the latter several times for hindering the other poor from gaining access to houses; she would demand alms for her husband as well as herself, refusing to leave until she had them.[59] The persistence of this grim aspect of the life-cycle across the varied societies of the continent reminds us that family was not everything for everyone. It was a precarious and often transient form of social organization, with many casualties and breakdowns in every generation. As a source of security, whether in terms of prosperity or emotion and affect, the family was as deeply ambivalent as through all its long and complex history. Although its problems do not explain witchcraft, they do provide an indispensable context without which the phenomenon could never be understood.

CHAPTER VII

MEN AGAINST WOMEN: THE GENDERING OF WITCHCRAFT

Theories and realities

FAMILIAL PROBLEMS LEAD inevitably into the fascinating, difficult and highly controversial question of gender. The one thing everyone 'knows' about witches is that they were women. Although every serious historical account recognizes that large numbers of men were accused and executed on similar charges, this fact has never really penetrated to become part of the general knowledge on the subject. The *Malleus Maleficarum* is routinely quoted to establish that witch-hunters were woman-haters, and one can hardly deny that its principal author, the Dominican Henry Institoris (Heinrich Krämer), blamed witchcraft largely on unbridled feminine sexuality. It is not often recognized, however, just how far this was a peculiarly misogynistic text, many of whose assertions are very misleading as a guide to what happened in typical trials. Later writers were often content to repeat such material uncritically, while their statements about gender are usually both sketchy and inadequate. Pierre de Lancre stated that the Devil 'wins over more women than men, because they are naturally more imbecile. And we see that among those brought before the *parlements* on charges of witchcraft, there are ten times more women than men'.[1] Jean Bodin went further still: 'When we read the books of those who have written about witches, it is to find fifty female witches, or even demoniacs, for every man.' He did concede that women often endured torture with more resolution than men, only to continue with the assertion 'that it is the power of bestial desire which has reduced women to extremities to indulge these appetites, or to avenge themselves . . . For the internal organs are seen to be larger in women than in men, whose desires are not so violent: by contrast, the heads of men are much larger, and in consequence they have more brains and prudence than women.'[2] The identification of witches with women was already standard form, it would appear, in the decades when trials were at their height. The demonologists would have been shocked to find their confident assertions turned against them by modern writers who use the persecution as prime evidence for men's inhumanity to women, often seeming to assume that the sex ratio was not de Lancre's 90 per cent, or even Bodin's 98 per cent, but a stark 100 per cent. When this misconception has been coupled with vast exaggerations of the numbers executed it has proved all too tempting to create the image of an earlier holocaust, in which millions of women perished.

The best-informed recent estimates place the total number of executions for witchcraft in Europe somewhere between 40,000 and 50,000, figures which allow for a reasonable level of lost documentation. Men actually made up around 25 per cent of this total, although there were large variations from one area to another and between different types of trials. Bodin and de Lancre were simply wrong about the facts, before they proceeded to offer explanations which merely repeated the conventional wisdom of the day, and now appear remarkably feeble. Their inability to observe the reality around them is significant. It suggests that received opinions were blinding them to the obvious; in this they were actually typical of most traditional thinking, much more concerned with concept affirmation than with referential accuracy. What made their error so egregious was that their own country, France, was in fact a fascinating exception to the wider pattern, for over much of the country witchcraft seems to have had no obvious link with gender at all. Of nearly 1,300 witches whose cases went to the *parlement* of Paris on appeal, just over half were men. The appeal system may have been invoked more often by men in the years before it became automatic, yet there are many reasons to doubt that this has more than a modest effect on the figures. In around 500 known cases which did not reach the *parlement*, although there is a small majority of women, men still make up 42 per cent of the accused.[3] Some local studies also show a predominance of men, as do the court decisions which de Lancre himself collected and printed in one of his works. There are variations within the *parlement*'s jurisdiction (covering nearly half the country), for towards the east the proportion of women rises towards 70 per cent, which fits very well with the picture just across the border, and suggests that the figures are trustworthy, while the central and western regions had a clear majority of male witches. The great majority of the men accused were poor peasants and artisans, a fairly representative sample of the ordinary population.

Relatively high proportions of male witches are common elsewhere, as the overall statistics would lead us to expect. In south-west Germany, the figures were typically rising towards 25 per cent by the 1620s, while in another sample of well over a thousand cases from the Jura and the Alps the proportion of men was 22.5 per cent.[4] For the modern French department of the Nord, then mostly in the Spanish Netherlands, men comprised 18 per cent of a much smaller group of 294.[5] The Saarland and Lorraine correspond closely with eastern France, around 28 per cent of those tried being men; for a sample of 547 in the neighbouring duchy of Luxembourg it was 31 per cent.[6] There are some extreme cases in peripheral regions of Europe, with men accounting for 90 per cent of the accused in Iceland, 60 per cent in Estonia and nearly 50 per cent in Finland. On the other hand, there are regions where 90 per cent or more of known witches were women; these include Hungary, Denmark and England.[7] The fact that many recent writers on the subject have relied on English and north American evidence has probably encouraged an error of perspective here, with the overwhelming predominance of female suspects in these areas (also characterized by low rates of persecution) being assumed to be typical. Nor is it the case that the courts treated male suspects more favourably; the conviction rates are usually much the same for both sexes. These data create as many problems as they solve, not least because of the 'dark figure' familiar to criminologists. Formally accused witches were predominantly women, but was this also true of those suspected and never charged? Might men typically have found themselves better placed to stave off their accusers? How do we account for accusations being gender-biased, yet far from gender-specific? Is there any rational explanation for the massive variations between different regions? This last question is perhaps the most baffling of all, particularly in a case like the French one, where large differences are found within a single jurisdiction and there are no obvious cultural or social differences to invoke. Recent work on contemporary witchcraft beliefs in western France strongly suggests that the pattern has endured to the present day, without providing many clues to its rationale.[8] It is possible that there may have been a particular tendency in these areas to see the cunning folk in very ambivalent terms, so that a high proportion of the men accused were 'good' witches reclassified as bad, but this only pushes the problem of explanation back another stage.

It remains true that most accused witches were women. Careful reading of the trial documents suggests that this was an accurate reflection of local opinion, in the sense that those tried were fairly typical of the wider group of suspects. Confessions include lists of those allegedly present at the sabbat, which obviously reflect local rumours about witchcraft, and some general statements about the attendance. Both of these usually (though not always) specify a majority of women, in line with the proportions found in the trials. Witchcraft was not a specifically feminine crime in the sense that infanticide and prostitution were, almost by definition; these offences, and domestic theft (the other crime often linked to women), were of course different in that there was something much more real to get a hold on. Infanticide and prostitution actually exemplify the double standard far better than witchcraft, since almost all those punished can fairly be depicted as the victims of male oppression, although this hardly exonerates them totally. Their seducers or clients, often from higher up the social scale, almost invariably escaped unscathed. A new punitive attitude towards these 'social' crimes, whose only direct victims were the new-born babies, was a striking feature of the sixteenth century; more women were probably executed for infanticide than for witchcraft. With very few exceptions they were denounced by other women, without whose participation the legislation would have remained a dead letter. The whole process is best seen not as the deliberate criminalization of women, but as part of a much broader drive to exercise greater moral and social control by labelling and punishing many kinds of deviant behaviour. This process was often deeply unfair and hypocritical, but patriarchy in this sense meant first and foremost the tyranny of the rich and powerful over the poor and weak. Social and gender hierarchies were naturally interlinked, so it comes as no surprise that harsher repressive policies had unfortunate consequences for women, as they did for vagrants, beggars and many others.

Historians who emphasize the social and psychological aspects of witchcraft beliefs are nevertheless bound to reject the idea that witchcraft persecution can be satisfactorily explained as the product of a great conglomerate of patriarchalism, absolutism and moral rigour. The point is not to deny all relevance to such factors, but rather to insist that witchcraft is much more than an elaborate delusion manufactured by outsiders, then misapplied to popular beliefs. It does rather seem that many interpretations imply, indeed require, such an underlying structure. At its crudest this can be seen in suggestions that clerics and judges diabolized feminine medical practice, or that women were the scapegoats for a variety of natural disasters. At a more respectable intellectual level, we have had attempts to show how a range of intellectual and symbolic devices (ranging from the equation of virtue with masculinity, through claims that women were biologically just incomplete men, to images of women as temptresses) were united by a persistent denigration of women. In its own terms there is much to be said for this view, provided we recognize the peculiar character and limited application of this kind of misogynistic language. What it cannot do is to provide a convincing explanation for persecutions which were largely initiated at village level, and whose motivation was quite clearly fear of witchcraft in the most direct sense. It is also very important not to confuse the rhetoric of justifications with the real motives for action. Another result of the tendency to see persecution as inspired from above is to give vastly exaggerated significance to the theories of the demonologists, attributing to them a causal role they simply did not possess. These approaches end up with the idea that witch-hunting was thinly disguised women-hunting, the diabolization of the feminine. In other words, here is the war between the sexes in a peculiarly violent form. Even if this were true, we would still have to account for change over time, since variables cannot be explained in terms of constants. The problem with these crude views goes deeper, for such generalized notions are too remote from the real world our ancestors inhabited. Gender did play a crucial role in witchcraft, but we will only understand this properly as part of the whole system, within which many other forces operated. What we need to explain is why women were particularly vulnerable to witchcraft accusations, not why witchcraft was used as an excuse to attack women. To achieve this, we must be constantly aware of gender as one of the crucial polarities within the vital frontier zone where beliefs and accusations interacted. Then we must tease out the ways in which it helped to structure the various operations which turned theory into action. In the process the information from the trials can tell us a great deal about gender, establishing a rewarding dialogue.

Counting heads is a useful way of shaking our ready assumptions, and of bringing a degree of rigour into the discussion. The figures can be broken down into numerous categories, to show distribution by age as well as gender, social and economic status, marital situation, childlessness and so forth. There has been no systematic work of this kind across Europe, and one would expect to find considerable variations by region. My own findings for Lorraine cannot therefore be regarded as a safer guide to general patterns, yet they do seem to conform to general impressions from several other regions. In this area of steady but very local persecution accused witches were on average much older and slightly poorer than their neighbours. Around half the women accused were widows, of whom a fair number appear to have had no surviving children. Some men seem to have been tainted by association with a suspected wife, but they were a minority; overall the masculine group formed a diverse cross-section of the peasant community. Although this evidence might seem to offer limited support to the stereotype of elderly women as witches, a more careful look at the material tells a different story. Age at the time of the trial is an artefact of the whole process by which reputations were built up. Since it took fifteen or twenty years for the typical witch to get to court, most were first suspected when still in the prime of life. There are signs that for women this transfer into the pool of suspects had a modest tendency to coincide with the menopause or the end of childbearing; while it would be rash to build too much on this flimsy basis, there may prove to be an important relationship here. This was an important watershed for everyone, physically, emotionally and socially, and, if the change of roles were not successfully accomplished, might prove an alienating experience. Those who missed out in some sense were likely to resent this, something their neighbours were all too likely to perceive. John Demos has suggested that midlife – roughly between the ages of forty and sixty – was the time when the exercise of power usually became central to personal experience. Wealth, prestige and responsibility all typically reached their highest point in these decades; while this was most obviously true for men, it was bound to affect women as well.[9] Many themes could be related to this one; if illegitimate and misused power was a key meaning of witchcraft, then it is not surprising to find this age group notably suspect.

Counting witnesses by gender is also an interesting exercise. In Lorraine the majority were men, particularly when other men were on trial, yet women did testify in large numbers against other women, making up 43 per cent of witnesses in these cases on average, and predominating in 30 per cent of them. There are some signs of interesting differences in the contributions made by male and female witnesses to the trials. Women were more likely to make allegations about human sicknesses and deaths, in respect of themselves, their children and even their husbands. Men might echo these charges, but often placed greater emphasis on the loss of animals, so crucial to peasant wealth and status. There was also a marked tendency for women's testimony to stretch much further back into the past. These patterns – which of course are only relative – can be fairly easily related to the gendered nature of specific activities or responsibilities and to the manner in which men often entered the scene towards the climax represented by a formal trial. A more sophisticated count for the English Home Circuit, by Clive Holmes, shows that the proportion of women witnesses rose from around 38 per cent in the last years of Queen Elizabeth to 53 per cent after the Restoration. This is convincingly explained on the grounds that the courts, applying a progressively more restrictive interpretation of the 1604 Witchcraft Act, were unlikely to convict without evidence of human fatalities attributed to the witch.[10] It appears that women were active in building up reputations by gossip, deploying counter-magic and accusing suspects; crystallization into a formal prosecution, however, needed the intervention of men, preferably of fairly high status in the community.

Feminine society and women's quarrels

As we have already seen, the witnesses gave an extraordinarily detailed picture of life in the local community, for witchcraft could allegedly disrupt normal functioning just about everywhere. It was also associated with all kinds of quarrels and tensions between neighbours. The link between ill-will and misfortune was the pivot on which everything turned. It cannot be emphasized too strongly that the typical trial was about witchcraft, in the sense of actual and palpable harm experienced by several other households. This is part of the answer to Stuart Clark's question; why should accusations against women concern witchcraft, rather than any other crime?[11] Witchcraft was peculiarly malleable, available to fit any kind of discord, because the link between ill-will and physical effects did not need to be demonstrated. Although this gap would eventually play a vital role in encouraging elite scepticism on legal grounds, at the psychological level it allowed fantasy to run riot. The fact that the causal system employed was wholly false according to our criteria has nothing to do with its subjective force for those who believed in it. To read the testimony is to be plunged into a dark world of fear and hatred, in which hardship, pain and death were the issues. Witchcraft was a lived reality for these people, not some kind of cover for gender conflict. Marguitte le Cueffre believed that Marion le Masson had bewitched her with some soup which had grains as black as coal in it. After drinking this she felt great pain throughout her body and ran up and down like a mad or rabid person, then became all swollen as if pregnant. She had been unwell ever since, with her stomach full of animals which gave her no rest, except when she drank cold milk, while she was forced to eat and drink at all hours of day and night. She spat up black and infected matter every morning, and the animals could be seen running about in her body when she was in bed. Marguitte was sure Marion had given her the illness by means of the soup, and had always said so in public. Whatever the true nature of this illness, which had lasted five years, the sufferer had evidently fixed the blame on a female neighbour with a widespread reputation, although unusually no actual quarrel was reported. As so often, relations were close – Marion claimed that if she had given Marguitte food and drink once, she had done so a hundred times. As we shall see in a later chapter, she tried to exploit her own superior status by getting her associates to pressurize Marguitte into withdrawing her persistent accusations.[12]

Such individuals, who were terrified by what was happening to them or their families, invoked witchcraft as both an explanation and a hope of relief. In most cases they were speaking of events in the past, when identifying the witch had usually led to a cure. Judith Huguenin knew that Fleuratte Maurice was hostile to her because Judith had been the first to suggest she was a witch. When two oxen fell ill she spoke to Fleuratte's daughter, threatening that harm would come to her unless she cured them; the suspect duly visited them and they recovered. A year before the trial she thought that Fleuratte had made her maid ill, then cured her, while an even more serious allegation was that she had given her sick daughter honey which had led to her death. This was part of a series of alleged bewitchments against the Huguenin family stretching back twelve years, yet no formal accusation had ever been made. When Fleuratte was accused of making a young girl from another family ill, she advised offering a live chicken at the shrine of le Bel Bernard. The girl then recovered (while the chicken died), and she told the mother to throw it into the river. Sitting outside a house with other women, she later 'gave the child great caresses, saying that people had no patience, and she had always said she would recover'. Later she believed the household concerned was still speaking of her as a witch, so gave a warning 'that it would need the wealth of three villages like Docelles to have her taken'.[13] Such evidence reinforces the general picture of recourse to the courts as an extreme step, which required either desperation or the mobilization of a body of local opinion. Normally witchcraft was a closed system that remained within the community; it only escaped into the public eye in a minority of instances. Of course those suspects who lived longest had the maximum chance of ending up at the stake. This emphasizes the importance of the process whereby reputations grew over time, to the point where individual suspicions crystallized into an image the witch could never escape. For many the best solution was to accept the situation, for there were actually some advantages to being feared by neighbours who might be more generous or respectful in consequence. Those who routinely employed curses or veiled threats and used various magical techniques for healing, may easily have come to believe in their own powers, and have had little difficulty producing a plausible confession when arrested.

Some historians have suggested that women testified against other women under pressure from a patriarchal system, presumably in the hope of making their own obedience to the rules clear and reducing any risk they might be suspected themselves. It is hard to see how this claim can ever be tested properly, but it certainly does not seem to account adequately for much of the surviving evidence. Other women appear to have feared reputed witches, talked about them among themselves and expressed their suspicions to them directly. This is hardly surprising when women lived much of their lives in one another's company, and were far from being confined to their homes. Although larger towns were probably rather different in this respect, the vast majority of the population lived in small towns or villages that were the setting for typical witchcraft cases. In the small Lorraine town of Blamont, Jennon Merviller told Jennon Ramaixe several times not to bring her dough to the communal oven, explaining that the other women were frightened she might touch theirs, and asking her not to bear ill-will. She replied that she bore her no resentment and had heard their talk herself, which would not trouble her but for the shame it brought on her children.[14] Many daytime activities were group or communal ones. These included work in the fields, baking, washing, journeys to market and religious rituals. Women occupied a distinct social space of their own, which also extended to leisure activities, notably spinning bees or *veillées*, the standard way of passing winter evenings. Groups of women gathered for all these purposes, as they did at the mill or around the village well. At all these nodal points they exchanged gossip and advice, while engaging in more or less subtle contests for status and esteem. Men might be present on some of these occasions; others were exclusively feminine. There was a spectrum here, from times when only one sex would be present through a middle area which was predominantly rather than exclusively gendered. As in most societies, there were relatively few instances where an equal balance between the sexes was to be found, even in terms of numbers. Some religious ceremonies would qualify – although men were usually more likely to miss out. So would weddings and funerals, village dances and festivals. Otherwise all but pre-adolescent children spent most of their time in company with their own sex. They may have preferred this, and social convention gave them no choice in any case. It is striking that those few occasions when both sexes were present in numbers often included arrangements to separate them; it was the widespread, although not universal, custom for men and women to sit apart in church. Festivals and celebrations also tended to have conventions which emphasized the gender divide.

Within the peasant family there was a further gender division in terms of production and commerce. This can be roughly represented as outside/male and inside/female. Men took responsibility for field crops and livestock, women for house, dairy, poultry and garden, including the marketing of surplus produce from these areas. The need to handle both production and marketing in these areas had considerable implications for wives, not least because their market activities were more extensive than those of men. They were required to behave aggressively in this respect, whereas general conventions indicated that they should be submissive.[15] A number of consequences might be thought to follow. Aggression and competitiveness by women were primarily expressed in relation to other women; direct quarrels between men and women were rather less common, outside the family itself. If the position of women deteriorated in a general sense in early modern Europe, this had less to do with public doctrines than with the decline of the household economy. As the peasantry was increasingly pauperized, so many families found themselves without land or animals, dependent almost entirely on day labouring. Women may well have done more of this than men, since they were cheaper to employ, but it brought no status or independence with it. In this area women were in competition with one another for the finite amount of paid work available; differential rates of pay and conventional divisions of tasks meant that they did not compete directly with men. While the expansion of the rural textile industry also made heavy use of female labour, this was commonly under the direct control of husbands. Declining living standards also had a disproportionate effect on women, who were expected to manage the household budget and care for children, since husbands continued to spend money on themselves in traditional style. Drinking in the tavern was a constant source of friction within families, much criticized by clerical moralists and others. It also seems to have provided Dutch courage for the making of insults; quite often men said they had called women witches when in drink, while the accused would give this as the reason why they had taken no action. The tavern was the male social space *par excellence* and features more often in cases where other men were on trial. The role of the calculated insult and the well-aimed riposte in peasant culture is one worth investigation in this context; here too there is a striking gender divide, for women were much more frequently accused of sexual misconduct than were men. Witchcraft depositions at least suggest that other women were very often the makers of such charges.

In both rural and urban environments women evidently passed much of their lives in the company of other women, often competing for apparently minuscule satisfactions in terms of social esteem and personal standing. Older women quite often appear as regular if unwelcome visitors to the houses of their younger neighbours, like Jennon Mengin of Fouchifol, against whom Jean Bertremin testified that his first wife Marion had 'always told the witness that she feared the accused, who was already suspected of being a witch, marvellously, yet in the absence of the witness she made herself very familiar in their house, going there to make herself friendly to the said Marion, his late wife. She always satisfied the said accused with good words, for fear she might do her harm'. Nevertheless, none of their four children survived, and his wife herself had died suddenly. All these deaths 'he imputed to the witchcraft of the accused, on account of her excessive familiarity in their house, or in anger because perhaps she was not given what she asked'. Despite this last speculation that Jennon was resentful because she had been refused something, the story suggests that she was more interested in a close relationship – which her neighbour found oppressive – than in any economic gain.[16] When witches confessed their crimes they often explained their hostility to the victims by the excessive pride the latter had displayed, probably another reflection of the hostility intrusive older women risked arousing. It is easy to see, in contrast, how Catherine Mathieu put herself at risk, for the witnesses said 'she is a woman who wants to know everything, and meddles in other people's business', while 'it is her habit to utter curses and ill wishes, against her husband as much as others, and she likes to show her pleasure, when she sees her neighbour in need, from famine or other causes'.[17] This sounds like a fairly comprehensive definition of anti-social conduct in village terms. Self-assertion in these face-to-face societies was at once a necessity and a dangerous game that could lead on the one side to ill-will and bewitchment, on the other to identification as a witch.

The pattern of quarrels and succeeding misfortunes, the basic stuff of witchcraft accusations, was inevitably related to this general social context. Childbirth and childcare provide one obvious example. A married woman's status rested partly on her ability to bear children and bring them up successfully, and this was bound to be a nerve-wracking business at every stage. An inability to conceive or to carry a foetus to term was quite likely to be blamed on witchcraft, perhaps in part because it was such a standard reason for seeking help from shrines and other forms of counter-magic. This extended over to the linked problem of masculine impotence, widely blamed on deliberate sorcery (whose perpetrator need not be a witch) through the use of the ligature or *aiguillette*, based on the simple symbolism of tying a knot in a lace. Jealousy is such a powerful emotion that one must believe this obvious form of revenge, available to any rejected suitor, was quite frequently attempted in reality. Childbirth itself was a traumatic event, which took place in a predominantly feminine circle of relatives and neighbours. As we have already observed, those who were not invited to the birth or the christening were readily thought to have caused the illnesses and deaths of infants, as could be those who tried to force their way into control of the proceedings. Such suspects were virtually bound to be women, and while fathers were quite capable of leading the outcry, it is hardly surprising that mothers appear more often in this role. The tenacious myth that midwives were regularly accused as witches, which appears to be completely unfounded, has actually obscured these genuine relationships. What can be said is that women were expected to offer basic medical care to their own families and routinely consulted experienced neighbours or known feminine healers, another regular source of suspicions. As children grew they remained vulnerable; now their illnesses often followed incidents in which they quarrelled with other children, or annoyed adults by letting animals stray. Once again these conflicts normally opposed one woman to another, with men being liable to become involved only at a later stage as ancillaries to the original dispute.

Women's economic role was particularly strong in pastoral economies, where they participated in looking after animals and had the management of dairy produce. As David Underdown has pointed out, the use of the cheesemaker's ladle in the skimmington ritual – an English practice involving the public humiliation of wives who ruled their husbands through a noisy demonstration – was intended to symbolize unhealthy feminine dominance.[18] Milking cows were at the centre of many disputes with overtones of witchcraft. They were always liable to die, or lose their milk or their calves inexplicably, while the everyday arrangements for supplying milk generated a lot of friction, with resentments easily aroused among both producers and consumers. Market criteria, such as the search for better or cheaper milk, were simply incompatible with neighbourly bonds, which dictated loyalties and obligations of a much more complex kind. It is by no means clear that upland areas really produced more witchcraft trials than lowland ones, but the arable-pastoral balance might be one of the keys to such local variations. This was only one of the areas in which gendered economic activity must have influenced the trend of quarrels and accusations. Women and children were usually in charge of animals not in the village herds or flocks, and when these strayed it was commonly into gardens, themselves the province of women. It was generally women who quarrelled with one another about who went first at the mill or the communal oven, although such disputes might involve men, particularly the miller or baker concerned. Tensions bred readily among the groups of women who worked together in the fields; domineering individuals frightened others, who might then blame them for subsequent misfortune. Mengeotte Michel was frightened when she saw Marye Sotterel already in the fields, because she knew she was proud and overbearing; sure enough Marye taunted her, then threatened she would have to stay by her fire for seven years. Later Mengeotte had an accident loading hay, so that she was crippled and had to walk with a stick.[19] In a different vein, those who were shunned as suspects were expected to resent this, which made them natural scapegoats too. Once the researcher plunges into the trials themselves it is this universe of local feeling and feuding which dominates the scene. It is indeed gendered, as was the society it reflected, but not in ways which made it easy for men to take charge of the whole process and use witchcraft persecution (formal or informal) as a simple agency of male power.

Demonic possession and women

In possession cases the great majority of the afflicted were women, although it was often male exorcists who manipulated them. There was no necessity for witches to be involved in demonic possession at all, since the Devil was plainly capable of carrying out the operation unaided; indeed, according to some austere theologians genuine possession could only be caused in this way. The popular view, which enjoyed widespread support even among the educated, was the opposite one, with witches normally blamed for initiating the possession. This was, for example, true in all the cases handled by the Puritan exorcist John Darrell, and may have contributed both to his success and to the disquiet of the authorities.[20] The psychological appeal of these performances to children and adolescents, in particular, is obvious enough. They provided a licensed opportunity to break the normal taboos, giving free expression to feelings and fantasies, in particular those which voiced resentment at various forms of discipline. A fair proportion of the afflicted in Protestant countries were being brought up in strongly religious households; in Catholic Europe convents were notably vulnerable. Some were also neglected by their parents, so can be seen as making a desperate bid for attention and affection to remedy their emotional deprivation, often with some success. Brian Gunter 'cared less for his daughter Anne when she was well than for any of the rest of his children', but after her supposed possession 'he made exceeding much of her'.[21] The possessed showed considerable ingenuity in pursuing these unconscious desires; their extreme suggestibility also rendered them very open to manipulation by the 'experts' who surrounded them, so that many aspects of their performances were learned through a complex process of interaction. In England at least, as Clive Holmes has perceptively suggested, the clerics who busied themselves in such cases had their own agenda. They were normally holders of extreme and probably atypical opinions about witchcraft, and saw the possessed as offering powerful evidence in support of their own highly-coloured view of ubiquitous diabolical activity in the world. Possession was much more impressive, and manifestly diabolic, than the small change of village quarrels and sick animals mocked by some sceptics.[22] It would also turn out to be a double-edged sword, however, because exorcists often allowed their own convictions to lead them into rash, even fraudulent behaviour, while too many of the possessed themselves were caught out in obvious deceits. In our own day disturbed adolescent girls are often characterized as masochistic, fantasy-laden and manipulative, terms which seem very appropriate to many of the possessed and help to explain some of the oddities of their repetitive behaviour.

The crucial gap: from rumours to trials

Possession amounted to a demand for attention and publicity. Ordinary witchcraft cases, on the other hand, often seemed to skulk in the shadows for years, the classic material for angry whisperings just out of earshot. As we have seen, one of the fundamental puzzles about European witchcraft is why suspects were not taken to court more readily. This was a highly pervasive and powerful system of belief, shared by the vast majority of the population. People really believed that pain, death and crippling economic losses resulted from the malevolence of their neighbours; they had the strongest motives for acting against them, yet displayed marked reluctance to do so. Gender differences may actually help us to understand this enigma better. The division of social, work and leisure activities virtually segregated the worlds of masculine and feminine gossip, so that reputations were largely formed within rather than across gender boundaries. If it is correct to suggest that most informal accusations were made by women against other women, then they would only have leaked slowly across to the men who controlled the political structures of local society. This made it relatively difficult for suspicions to coalesce, and for the accusers to feel sure they would have enough support. The primary way the gap was bridged was through the family, with husbands and wives joining their knowledge. This is one reason why the afflicted household is so often found at the centre of accusations, with husband and wife activating their separate groups of allies in the community. There are also reasons to suppose that women were less able to mobilize groups of kin than were men; they were more likely to marry away from their own village and family, while patriarchal family structures tended to separate them much more firmly from their blood relations. This affected their ability to bring charges as well as to resist them. The crucial point which emerges from many cases is that women did most of the work in creating reputations for their female neighbours, but were much less likely to organize support for a prosecution. This was the point at which men took over, whether it was husbands who shared their wives' suspicions, or the local magistrates and clerics who might also initiate proceedings.

Women's position in the household had its own ambiguities and dangers. Wives were always to some extent outsiders in the families they joined, much more so if they became stepmothers in existing households. This surely rendered them more vulnerable to witchcraft accusations in various ways. Tensions over inheritance were among the most intense and widespread in a society where property was so crucial; sibling rivalry was probably the norm rather then the exception, exacerbated by the imprecise nature of most inheritance systems. At the same time it was regarded as unnatural and improper, so that there was a great temptation to displace it and blame wives – who had no wider loyalty to the patrimonial kin – for hostilities which may not have been their doing. Such feelings were almost certain when stepchildren came into the picture, at least in those families where there was something to squabble over. Among the very small and probably atypical sample of women accused in the English colonies in America, there is some evidence for hostility to women who were significant property-owners in their own right, whose status was to some degree anomalous in consequence. Carol Karlsen has suggested that 'as women without brothers or women without sons, they stood in the way of the orderly transmission of property from one generation of males to another'.[23] Even here this appears to be only one of the numerous factors behind local suspicions, and it is very hard to detect at all in European cases. The chief reason why many suspects simply cannot fit this pattern is that they were too poor; inheritance disputes are only evident in a small minority of cases, although they may have provided hidden motivation in rather more. There is a small but sinister group of cases in which husbands were clearly eager to dispose of an unwanted wife, a larger number in which they were unwilling or unable to defend a suspected one. These must be balanced against many other instances where spouses defended one another vigorously; it would be quite wrong to suggest that witchcraft cases give a generally negative picture of marital relations. Although there are a fair number of drunken, brutal or sexually abusive husbands, these do not appear more characteristic of early modern society than of any other. The small but significant number of cases in which we find wives being accused as a weapon in local power struggles among the peasant elite rather points to the assumption that they were greatly valued by their husbands, who were being attacked through them. There were of course practical reasons why spouses should defend one another; the property of a convicted witch was usually forfeit to the ruler. More importantly still, the reputation of witchcraft usually passed from parents to children, so the whole lineage risked being tainted. The latter factor did not operate for childless couples, while there was a good chance that women without surviving children would either be genuinely resentful of others, or simply thought to be so.

At this crucial point, when a prosecution was to be launched, there is no doubt that men had to take the lead, yet of course one can often detect their womenfolk close behind. Sometimes they were the more insistent, as when Jannon Estienne wanted to blame Fleuratte Maurice for the loss of an ox and other animals, but 'her husband persuaded her otherwise, arguing that since misfortunes often affected people, there was no reason for astonishment if they also befell animals'.[24] There was often much hesitation and manoeuvring up to the last moment, which might include demands that the husband exercise his authority. In the case of Laurence Tolbay of Sainte-Marguerite the local mayor tackled her first, after the miller Jean Musnier, who suspected her of causing his bad leg, had consulted the *devin* at Avould, to be told that it was her witchcraft. The mayor told her to put matters right and find a remedy, since otherwise he had instructions to collect evidence against her; she sent food and wine to the miller, who duly recovered. The next year, however, he told her husband 'that people had great ideas and suspicions about his wife, on account of various bewitchments she was alleged to have committed, and that he would do well to put this in order, otherwise they would be obliged to arrest her and put her on trial, which words only moved her husband to say that he wished she was already burned if she were such, without ever demanding reparation'. While this brutal indifference may have contributed to the relative ease with which Laurence confessed, it should be said that her son-in-law emerges as far more supportive, making gifts of food and helping her against her enemies.[25] In contrast, one apparently well-intentioned husband, Demenge Romary Petit Colin, brought about the trial and conviction of his wife Jacotte by demanding reparation for the accusations against her. Arnould Jacquel testified that just before Christmas his wife had been in danger of death until Demenge visited her; he knelt by her bareheaded, and asked pardon in his wife's name. Jannon replied that she pardoned her if she cured her, to which he said 'that if his wife knew something appropriate she would cure her', since when she had been well. Quite why Demenge chose to pursue a quarrel which appeared to have been successfully terminated it is hard to understand.[26] Another husband who intervened (more successfully) to protect his wife was Joseph Parsons of North-ampton, Massachusetts, who brought a successful action for slander on her behalf in 1656. Here it is interesting to note that the plaintiffs were significantly richer and more powerful than the defendants; between the first depositions and the final ones several crucial witnesses withdrew their hostile testimony against Mary Parsons, and it is plain that both sides had been putting pressure on witnesses, with the stronger family winning out.[27]

Another group of women who were particularly at risk were the dependent poor, those in receipt of regular alms. Remarriage was the normal response for both sexes on loss of a spouse, but was less readily available to women. Those with a family of young children, or those past fifty, might find themselves unable to attract a new partner. This exposed them in two ways. Firstly, the kinship network was liable to be drastically reduced, so that there were few who would defend them, and would-be persecutors felt free to express their suspicions. Their routine explanation for why they failed to take those who insulted them to court was that they could not afford to do so. Secondly, their dependence on begging exposed them to the classic refusal-guilt syndrome, in which those who refused charity (thus breaking with the normal expectations of neighbour-liness) felt at once angry and guilty, then projected their own feelings into the other person. If the rejection was followed by a misfortune, the supposed ill-will became witchcraft. Worsening economic circumstances both increased the numbers of beggars and made others more resentful of the burden they represented. Those who were obviously destitute may have been more readily accepted than neighbours in a marginal position; these could appear to be claiming aid within a reciprocal system, then failing to honour the implicit obligation to repay. While the dynamics of such systems were both complex and flexible, it was usually women who appeared at a neighbour's door asking for small loans of milk, grain, butter and so forth. As usual any dispute which followed was likely to be between women, although it sometimes occurred because the husband had forbidden his wife to continue humouring a demanding neighbour. Catherine Demenge had supported herself by begging at St Dié until she was chased out on suspicions of witchcraft; when she came to trial two years later a local notary and minor lawyer, Christophe de Forges, testified that on a late summer Sunday evening about five years earlier he and his wife were sitting outside their house when they saw some beggar-women approaching, Catherine among them. He told his wife not to give to her, since she had been begging at the house recently, and took their child indoors himself before she arrived. When she asked if there was any soup, his wife rudely replied that there was not, and she should go away. Soon afterwards his wife's face began to hurt, as if she had toothache, while that evening a large cat appeared in the house and proved difficult to chase away. When the doctors and surgeons could do nothing to ease his wife's pain he reckoned it was witchcraft, thought of the refusal of alms and her reputation, and told his wife to seek her out and see if she could help. Catherine suggested that she should go to bed and make herself sweat, but this did no good. The witness became more angry, and one day called Catherine into the house, took a stick, then told her she was a witch, threatening to beat her and have her burned. She told him not to do so, saying his wife would recover. After this she did improve, but was still not wholly cured, so when he saw Catherine passing he looked out of a window and threatened her again with his stick. After this his wife recovered, although she still felt some pain when the weather changed.[28]

Cunning folk, midwives and healers

One way in which older women might try to secure greater toleration and prestige was as holders of skills or knowledge. There was a natural extension from women's responsibility for the health of their own house-hold to wider medical activity. This relates to witchcraft in two ways. Firstly, it has often been suggested that there was a campaign against female healers, who were supposed to be replaced by approved male specialists. Secondly, it was precisely these healers who were likely to diagnose witchcraft; they functioned much as witch doctors do in tribal society. There is some truth in the first claim, for as the number of more or less qualified practitioners rose, so they became more anxious to exclude rivals. It is far less clear that this was primarily a gender question, except in so far as the would-be persecutors were inevitably male. In many parts of Europe the attack was on male and female cunning folk alike, with the former sometimes appearing to come in for harsher treatment. Some old women, evidently conscious of the danger witchcraft persecution represented for them, expressed some reluctance to give advice in future. In 1584 Jeanne Housel asked Mengeatte des Woirelz of Saint-Nicolas to help her daughter, saying that 'old people like her customarily had knowledge of various things'. After touching the girl Mengeatte said, 'when you want to teach people something, they form a bad opinion of you'. During her subsequent interrogation she claimed 'that they did her very great wrong, and that because she was ugly, old, and decrepit people seemed to fear her, and impose such an insulting and injurious accusation on her'.[29] Thirty years later in the same town Abraham Thomassin asked Barbe Barbier to suggest remedies, which she did with reluctance, for 'she feared to do it because as soon as old people teach some treatment for the sick they are said to be witches'.[30] As these cases suggest, in the prevailing familial systems of north-western Europe such old women seem often to have found themselves dangerously isolated; once past the stage of bearing and caring for children, their main claim to consideration lay in experience. Knowledge of remedies was a widespread form of this that did not have to imply any pretensions to special gifts as a healer, so that the request to advise a neighbour was commonplace. It must have been hard to know when it concealed suspicions of witchcraft, although the reactions of these particular suspects may imply that they sensed the danger all too well.

Information about the activities of such informal healers is inevitably scrappy; we have a fairly good idea of how they operated, much less of their numbers or gender distribution. In the only case I know of one testifying, with no sign that anyone thought this incongruous, it was a woman, Rose Tixerand, who gave evidence against Catherine Tarillon in 1594.[31] Whereas it was commonly women who made pilgrimages on behalf of sick people, consultation of the cunning folk seems to have been more a masculine preserve. After numerous quarrels with the suspect and her husband, Jean Colin said he had suffered various losses, although he could not now remember all the details; one of his children died, and many animals. To find out the truth he consulted a *devineresse*, who said 'it was done by the woman he suspected, and to confirm what she said took a glass, in which she put something like a round apple, and having done something showed him the effigy of a woman resembling the said Françatte, asking if it was the person he suspected. He looked at it carefully several times, then replied that he was sure it was her'. He was only one of several villagers who admitted similar consultations in the case of Françatte Camont.[32] Like the pilgrimages, these usually involved a journey outside everyday range. The art of the practitioner was to get the client to articulate his own suspicions, so if men were the interlocutors this would have given them a certain power, but hardly establishes that they were the original source of the accusation. In any case the point of the whole operation was to seek a remedy, partly by means of an implicit threat to the supposed witch. In the case just mentioned, Françatte Camont complained that a neighbour was sending to the Devil, but she also went to visit some of those who consulted the cunning folk, presumably responding to the suspicions they had made plain in this way. One may reasonably infer that such practices were more widespread than the rather cautious hints in the trial records would show. They were part of the elaborate history behind so many of the cases which finally made their way into the courts. The illnesses of animals were treated by a motley group, including herdsmen and smiths, but more broadly anyone who was supposed to have the necessary touch. Men may have predominated here, whereas it seems likely that informal healing for human beings was more often the province of women – they were prepared to spend long periods in another house as men were much less likely to do. All these activities were ambiguous, for while they gave the opportunity to denounce others as witches, they also risked implicating the healers themselves. Overall, gender divisions are hard to establish with any clarity in this large sphere, which was so important in the social construction of witchcraft.

As has already been mentioned, the idea that midwives were commonly accused of witchcraft has proved quite untenable; although the denunciations in the *Malleus Maleficarum* may reflect real events in the late fifteenth-century Alps, surviving European records show very few such cases. All later demonologists seem to have referred back to the *Malleus* and to a brief reference by Nider; these early authors were appropriating a standard charge against the Jews, then turning it into a typical inversion motif, with the midwife killing the babies instead of protecting them. This would have been a terrifying fear had it been as widespread as has often been thought, but a painstaking check of all known British cases reveals precisely two rather dubious instances in England, and fourteen out of some 3,000 accused in Scotland. In both countries midwives, far from being prime targets, are under-represented among the suspects.[33]

It is a similar story in Lorraine, where Jennon Thomas, one of only three midwives known to have been tried, despite confessing numerous acts of witchcraft, pathetically yet rather touchingly insisted that she had always done her duty as a midwife.[34] In response to a relatively small group of accusations concerning dead infants she asserted that it was the habitual carelessness of mothers which should be blamed, rather than witchcraft. One other accused did exemplify the alleged stereotype in sensational detail; Jennon Petit, who was tried in 1609, had been a midwife in the town of Raon for twenty years. There were many charges relating to disasters in childbirth, notably the death of Anne Huel after the surgeons had been called in and Jennon made no secret of her hostility. Under interrogation she blamed them for Anne's death, commenting that it was not their business to attend women in labour. When Jennon was tortured she admitted that her master Persin had instructed her to kill all the babies she could, then take the bodies (which she dug up) to the sabbat for him to turn them into powder. In total she avowed causing the deaths of twenty-five infants and children, eight women, and one man.[35] This exceptional case shows how a 'bad' midwife, supposedly corrupted by the Devil, could indeed become a nightmarish image of murderous power, but isolated instances of this kind are no basis for the sweeping claims made on the subject.

In England and her colonies midwives did become increasingly prominent in trials, but in a quite different context. The notion of the animal familiars was developed and exploited in an opportunistic way, as a supposedly objective test that might provide the satisfactory proof it was so difficult to find. In a fairly obvious adaptation of the diabolical mark theory, the witches were expected to have teats, usually around their genitals, from which their imps took suck. Feminine juries of midwives and matrons were assembled to inspect the suspects, with somewhat mixed results.[36] The process rather resembled the various ordeals, in that the evidence was open to more than one interpretation; what was normal and abnormal in these matters? Such tests are often interpreted as a method of allowing popular feeling to make itself felt, since the inherent ambiguities left wide scope for manipulation. The activities of Mary Phillips and Priscilla Briggs, who accompanied Hopkins and Stearne on their witch-hunting crusade, were probably very questionable on these grounds, although not necessarily amounting to deliberate fraud. On the other hand, midwives in particular proved rather hard to convince on numerous occasions, or disagreed among themselves. As we have already seen, a group of London midwives, summoned with the famous royal physician William Harvey to inspect some of the Lancashire witches of 1634 on their arrival in the capital, flatly contradicted the claims of their provincial counterparts by declaring that they displayed no abnormalities of any note.[37] The supposedly impartial test tended to become yet another bone of contention, which ultimately lost credit and helped further to undermine the credibility of the whole operation. There was a striking resemblance to the frauds associated with pricking for the witches' mark, whose contribution to judicial scepticism operated in much the same way. It is hard to know what to make of the fascinating case reported by Christina Larner, when in 1662 the prickers 'Mr Paterson' and 'John Dickson', who had been detected in such malpractices, also turned out to be women in disguise.[38] Whatever the effects of their activity, the use of these feminine juries is a fascinating example of power being vested in women, admittedly in a very limited sphere, and wholly contradicts the idea that female midwives were under serious attack.

A much more plausible correlation emerges from the recent study of Augsburg trials by Lyndal Roper. Here it was the specialized group of lying-in maids who were regular targets of what she describes as 'murderous antagonisms between women'. As she also says, these women seem almost overdetermined as the culprits; temporary intruders in the household, past childbearing themselves, readily construed as gripped by envy.[39] What becomes mysterious is why so few were accused, when neonatal mortality rates were so high and the displacement of blame had such attractions. It remains to be seen whether such cases will now be identified in some numbers in other cities, or whether there will turn out to be something peculiar about Augsburg arrangements for lying-in. These were of course practices associated with an urban bourgeoisie, by definition only likely to be found in larger towns, and essentially foreign to the peasant world where witchcraft beliefs were most pervasive and tenacious. Nevertheless, this instance reminds us yet again how the cases which came to court represent just the visible tip of a great hidden iceberg of fear and tension. It does seem at least possible that it only needed one or two individual trials in a city, with the attendant publicity through public executions and pamphlets, to create a local syndrome which led to a modest trickle of cases over several decades.

Psychology, misogyny and witchcraft persecution

These cases also provide a particularly rich context for investigating witchcraft from a psychological standpoint. As Lyndal Roper states, 'witchcraft confessions and accusations are not products of realism, and they cannot be analysed with the methods of historical realism'. She draws out how individuals borrowed the language and stereotypical images of witchcraft to express their own psychic conflicts, which centred on the earliest stages of the mother-child relationship. Although this approach is particularly effective for the Augsburg material, with its exceptional focus on the care of infants in a strictly feminine space, it can be extended more widely. After all, we need to question why, as witchcraft has receded almost entirely into the sphere of fantasy in the modern world, it has come to be completely sex-specific. The witch is the bad mother, a being who subverts the basic duties of her sex by direct hostility to fertility and nurture. She also embodies the envy which originates in early mother-child relations. Again and again the details of cases can be assimilated to these underlying patterns; they are not 'caused' by them so much as structured through them. Every individual carries around a permanent legacy from the formative period of life that includes negative elements capable of being activated under stress. Such reactions are very likely to employ the processes known to psychoanalysts as splitting and projective identification, both of which first take shape in relation to the mother. Every individual's fundamental experience of love and hate is with a woman, in the mother-child relationship, or whatever surrogate takes its place. How far this creates a predisposition, perhaps independent of gender, to make women the target for murderous hostility, it is impossible to say with certainty. Nevertheless, the historical record suggests that both men and women found it easiest to fix these fantasies, and turn them into horrible reality, when they were attached to women. It is really crucial to understand that misogyny in this sense was not reserved to men alone, but could be just as intense among women. Behind it lay the position of mothers as primary objects who were felt to possess magically formidable qualities, and whose very intentionality (independent will) was perceived as dangerous.

Such analyses have severe limitations, above all because they are too general to offer useful explanations for change and local variations. We cannot suppose that child-rearing practices changed dramatically in ways which would even begin to account for the rise and fall of persecutions; no independent evidence suggests this, while only exceptional shifts would be likely to affect relations between mothers and babies significantly. Wet-nursing might seem to be a candidate here, but it simply does not correlate in any plausible way; it was characteristic of those urban and elite groups which seem to have been least involved in persecution. It is more helpful to think of numerous distinct factors meeting around a central void filled only by fantasy, a structure which related to the essential nature of witchcraft as a crime which never happened. Some people tried to practise it, although they were a minimal fraction among the accused; many more probably died of it, but in both cases the effects were only because of what people believed. The most enduring structures still persist in modern peasant societies, including some regions of Europe. They are to be found in parts of France, for example, as earlier variants of them doubtless were in Merovingian or pre-Roman Gaul. These include both social and psychological determinants, the elements which make all witchcraft beliefs fundamentally similar across great expanses of time and space. More ephemeral factors include the religious, legal and economic shifts which help to explain why persecution occurred when and where it did. It appears that certain combinations of the latter have been sufficiently powerful to deflect a normal tendency for witchcraft to be heavily – but not exclusively – attributed to women. We are unlikely to get much further on this last point until there has been a meticulous study of a region where men comprised the majority of the accused. A great deal might also be gained from a comparison between northern and southern Europe, with their strongly contrasted marriage systems. Mediterranean culture appears to have combined powerful witchcraft beliefs with very low rates of persecution, perhaps because older women were protected by their families, and enjoyed more power and esteem. This derived from a marriage pattern in which brides were much younger than their husbands, then commonly took over as effective heads of the household when they were widowed. Such women had to expect less power during their childbearing years, frequently dominated by mothers-in-law as well as husbands; it was only in mid-life that they acquired a new authority and status that was widely regarded as legitimate. By contrast, the theoretically more equal marriages of north-western Europe actually left older women at a grave disadvantage, unless they had the good fortune to find a caring, long-lived and forceful husband. Although it would be absurd to claim that one marriage system is more 'natural' than another, one of the most obvious biological differences between the sexes lies in the ages at which they cease to be fertile. The pattern of very late marriages for women, which was an essential condition for the closely-matched ages of spouses in the north-west, has long been regarded as an exception by historical demographers, and a puzzling one at that. It is at least possible that it may have made its own contribution to 'fixing' witchcraft accusations.

There are still reasons for linking witchcraft persecution to the assertion of patriarchal values, which can be seen as one aspect of a search for order in a period when many established patterns underwent severe disruption. Temporal coincidence does not establish causal relationships, however, and it is only by adopting a quite implausible picture of persecution imposed from above that patriarchalism can be made to carry direct blame. It is much more a case of underlying causes producing parallel effects, which were only mildly self-reinforcing. In a period when all tensions were being magnified by extremely harsh and painful social and economic pressures, those between the sexes were bound to be among them. The idea of the female sex as scapegoat misdescribes a situation of this kind, in which anxieties might be displaced into the area of gender. It is also dangerous to put too much weight on the kind of discourse employed by the demonologists. Their referential system was self-confirming, with the positive and negative polarities used for rhetorical purposes. As Stuart Clark has pointed out, they took the link between women and witchcraft as a given, rather than spending much time debating it.[40] Even the overt misogyny of the *Malleus Maleficarum* really falls into this category. Within the confines of an agrarian society and early modern intellectual styles, it was virtually impossible for anyone to rethink gender relations, because everything was referred to ideal types. Polarized binary classification was the dominant style of early modern thought, so that demonologists had no choice but to associate women with evil and inferiority. For them gender took the form of polarity, rather than a range of overlapping possibilities, because this was how it was always conceptualized. This was such a powerful 'mindset' that it could override empirical observation, as it often did in the medical theory of the time. At the popular level such views were expressed in the form of proverbial wisdom, later reinforced by chapbooks and almanacs. The result was an unfortunate mixture of fear and aggression towards women, whose passions were seen as a grave threat to husbands and society alike. Deficiency in capacity to reason supposedly left women unable to control the baser part of their nature, while their mysterious cycles were evidence for the way they were dominated by the womb. Eve had been responsible for original sin, and women's attraction for men led to corruption and death; women's inconstancy and self-love made them natural allies of the Devil, an eternal danger of betrayal for the men they lured on. The commonplace idea that women were more sexually voracious than men was just one expression of these attitudes, part of an association between women, original sin and sexual pollution.

Despite the pervasiveness of these grotesque misogynistic doctrines, it is not easy to find evidence that they functioned as a direct cause of action. They may indeed be evidence of a mixture of fear and ignorance which dominated gender relations, and whose roots are better sought in general psychological structures. Early modern Europe was a society in which women got a raw deal in many respects, but this did not often take the form of direct persecution; rather it operated through indirect pressures that frequently led to women accusing one another. It was of course inevitable that the courts which heard these charges would be male, but among the judges it was often those elite jurists most strongly linked to formal patriarchal theories who treated witches leniently. Ultimately witchcraft was a theory of power; it attributed secret and unnatural power to those who were formally powerless. In this way it allowed men to project their own aggression into women, notably those with whom they or their wives quarrelled. This tendency must have been strengthened because women typically responded with threats and curses, which then became part of the evidence for their malevolence. The evidence of the trials, however, suggests that quarrels between women followed much the same course as those between men and women, and often underlay subsequent direct accusations made by men as well as women. In this sense women too could use accusations as a vehicle to assert themselves and claim power against their enemies; seen in this light witchcraft did nothing to reinforce gender solidarities. The highly stressful circumstances experienced by early modern communities produced at least as much friction between those who were closest to one another as they did between those at opposite ends of the grids of wealth and gender. We do find peasant oligarchs accusing poor women, but only in a small minority of cases, compared to the significantly larger groups in which poor peasant households directed their suspicions against tiresome neighbours or persistent beggars.

It is all too easy to fall into anachronism when writing about witchcraft and gender. This is one reason why explanations should always be firmly bedded in the surrounding social realities. It should also warn us against the kind of knee-jerk reactions and facile assumptions which have too often resulted from failure to recognize the otherness of the past. We need to ask whether explanations that invoke gender as a motive could possibly apply in this period. It seems highly unlikely that any contemporary could have seen matters in this light. One must beware of false analogies between the past and the present. Gender is now an issue everyone has to confront, whereas at the time of witchcraft persecution it was a bundle of shared assumptions. Although there was a Renaissance debate about the status of women, it took place within strict limits, and hardly touched on the central questions as we might see them. In other words, modern views tend to be held consciously, whereas earlier ones were almost wholly unconscious. This did not necessarily make them less powerful, but it did mean that they were unlikely to motivate action directly. Gender differences are bound to remain a permanent and overt issue in our world, since the clock of consciousness cannot be put back. This also applies in reverse, however, and we must not project modern ideas and feelings back on to our ancestors, nor make them fight our battles. In the specific case of witchcraft we have a phenomenon which was permeated by gender, yet in much more subtle ways than any simple argument can convey. Hostility to women did play a crucial part at several levels; no general interpretation of the subject can or should obfuscate this basic truth. At the same time, this can only ever be part of a much more complex set of causes and connections. As so often, witchcraft tells us as much about the context from which it sprang – in this case gender relations – as that context helps us to understand witchcraft.

CHAPTER VIII

THE AGE OF IRON

Hard times and witchcraft persecution

CYCLICAL THEORIES HAD great appeal for early modern Europeans, whether it was a case of Fortune's wheel, the rise and fall of empires or the predetermined shape of human history. This was commonly identified with the age of iron, as a period of hardship and decline, implicitly or explicitly contrasted with a golden age in the past. The Elizabethan preacher Henry ('silver-tongued') Smith remarked, 'In these days, and in this iron age, it is as hard a thing to persuade men to part with money, as to pull out their eyes, and cast them away, or to cut off their legs, and throw them away'.[1] His comments on the failure of charity were all too apposite in relation to witchcraft. To some extent the idea of decline could be combined with the Christian eschatological view of the world proceeding towards a period of chaos and shaking, which would usher in the Last Judgement and the end of time. How far people took such notions literally, or acted on them, varied enormously according to circumstances and is not particularly relevant here. When they perceived an age of iron, however, they were not just engaging in self-deprecating rhetoric. For the bulk of the population the sixteenth century brought a sharp worsening of their living standards, with virtually all the indices reaching record low points in the 1590s, improving only very slowly thereafter. Wages declined in real terms, work became harder to find, pauperization spread inexorably, while beggars and vagrants multiplied. Social tensions, riots and crime were associated with these trends, as the gap between rich and poor widened. Other non-economic evidence could also be used to deepen the gloom, notably the Reformation and the collapse of Christian unity, with the related religious wars and massacres. There was also the Turkish threat, and that very different menace from the east, the bubonic plague. Astrologers and prophets of doom were not likely to run out of bad news quickly, even if in a pre-statistical age the long-term movements were felt rather than understood.

Broad-brush treatments of such themes inevitably conceal significant variations in both the temporal and the spatial dimensions, some of which will emerge later. Nevertheless, it can be said that the later sixteenth century was a peculiarly bad time for most people across the whole continent. At the most basic level, European economic and social organization was proving unequal to the task of employing, feeding and clothing a rapidly expanding population. This is emphatically not the same as saying that population increase was the sole or fundamental cause of the problem. Although the exceptionally high rates of growth in this period were bound to create some disruption and local crises, the failure to raise production to anything like the levels that were possible even with existing technology must derive from major rigidities within the system. Europe had actually been here before, in the sense that population levels in the early fourteenth century were probably comparable with those at the end of the sixteenth; that earlier period had also given signs of major strains threatening social order. When the Black Death burst upon Europe around 1347–9, followed by repeated waves of plague, that situation changed dramatically. For reasons which remain partly obscure, but must be linked to the persistent virulence of the epidemics, it was only around the end of the fifteenth century that population growth resumed significantly in most areas. During the interval the western European peasantry – or at least those of them who survived the repeated visitations of the plague – came to enjoy something of a golden age. Land was relatively plentiful, wages high and both personal freedom and nutritional standards increased. This was not achieved without a struggle, for the lords reacted by trying to enforce feudal rights and intensify compulsory labour services. A wave of peasant revolts, including the French Jacquerie and the great English revolt of 1381, bore witness to the intensity of these conflicts. Whereas the peasants finally had the better of things in the west, east of the Elbe it was a very different story, with the lords succeeding in imposing serfdom on their estates.

Relating these long-term trends to witchcraft is a difficult and potentially controversial task. Social anthropologists working on Africa have been able to make quite effective use of a 'strain-gauge' theory, according to which outbursts of witchcraft accusations, witch-finding movements and the like are very largely a response to acute social tensions. The theory is a 'weak' one, in the sense that local societies undergoing such crises do not necessarily turn on witches; a range of other conditions must be satisfied for this to happen. To apply it successfully calls for a fine-grained interpretation of events, explaining how the processes actually worked, not merely a set of chronological coincidences. This chapter will show that it does explain quite a lot about European witchcraft, at more than just the crude level of the rate of persecution, without providing anything like a complete explanation. We will see how the very broad shifts across long time spans made themselves felt in much more immediate and local terms, rather in the way the movement of tectonic plates produces earthquakes and volcanic eruptions. Interpretation at the microscopic level does empower some rather cautious conclusions of a macroscopic kind, which tend to correspond with certain patterns that make good intuitive sense. It should always be remembered that levels of persecution cannot be assumed to relate at all closely to the prevalence of witchcraft fears at the local level. It seems much more likely that the latter built up slowly across much of the continent in response to growing socio-economic tensions, particularly from the middle decades of the sixteenth century. In comparison, the persecution took a long time to get going in earnest and was always erratic, sporadic and localized. Where it became intense, of course, there was a serious danger that it would reinforce popular fears and thus raise anxiety levels further.

Where these arguments provide very little assistance is in accounting for the early phases of persecution. There is nothing to suggest that the social crises of the early fourteenth century exacerbated fears of witchcraft, still less precipitated any kind of legally sanctioned witch-hunt. Lack of evidence may be concealing more than we suspect, of course, but it looks rather as if some necessary conditions were simply lacking. It is at least arguable that late medieval economies coped with the strain considerably better than their sixteenth-century successors. If anyone was being blamed for hard times or shared misfortune (and general scapegoating theories are particularly dubious in any case) it seems to have been more clearly identifiable groups such as lepers and Jews. The first significant persecutions of typical local witches came half a century after the Black Death, in a period of relative prosperity, and our information about them is inevitably too sparse to permit fully detailed analysis. Nevertheless, it may be significant that the first group, which took place between the late fourteenth and mid-fifteenth century, were located in some of the Alpine valleys. These were far from being the backward zones envisaged by some historians; on the contrary, they had highly developed economic, social and religious institutions. Their complex, largely pastoral economies were associated with the precocious development of market relations and the inevitable disruption of older social structures these brought. There were also considerable political tensions, as neighbouring rulers and cities started to enforce their authority over these outlying regions. The very first known persecutor in the area, Peter von Greyerz, was an outsider acting as *landvogt* for the Bernese overlords of the Ober-simmenthal region between 1392 and 1406; he was also the chief inform-ant of the pioneer demonologist John Nider.[2] These trials may therefore have a special local dynamic of their own. It could also be argued that their failure to spark off wider epidemics of witch-hunting, and the low level of persecution in the early sixteenth century, did reflect a generally positive economic climate in most other regions. Although several other preconditions for persecution, including some specific legislation, were fulfilled in this earlier period, it was only as serious, sustained hardship and disruption developed in the final decades of the century that trials multiplied dramatically across western Europe. One special feature of these years was the highly divisive impact such trends had on the local communities; at this level, where suspicions and charges originated, peasants and artisans were often more conscious of conflicts with one another than with the ruling classes. Virtually everywhere it was the half-century between 1580 and 1630 which included the great majority of all trials; however dubious one may be about mere chronological links, it is hard to avoid the *prima facie* inference that a simultaneous sharp decline in living standards and individual security played a large part in this.

Most of the obvious counter-examples, where persecution peaked con-siderably later, are found in precisely those areas of eastern Europe which followed a very different socio-economic evolution. While some of these areas are still too little studied to permit much in the way of generaliz-ation, detailed work on Hungary supports the idea that here and in Poland rather similar social tensions occurred around a century later, tying in with a surge of witchcraft trials in the early eighteenth century.[3] There are also some cases, notably in northern Europe, where trials continued at a high level longer than elsewhere.[4] This is most convinc-ingly explained by the relative slowness of the ruling elites in these peripheral areas either to adopt or to enforce the sceptical attitudes which quickly developed elsewhere. Legal persecution and popular belief need to be distinguished carefully here, for there is much evidence indicating high levels of popular anxiety enduring for decades after trials had become rare. In the 1640s, for example, there were epidemics of popular witch-hunting in England (the Hopkins crusade) and eastern France. In both instances we can detect a background of warfare, high taxation and disruption, analogous to conditions behind some modern African outbreaks. The French case, as already noted, followed devastating late frosts, an agricultural disaster specifically associated with witchcraft in the mythology of the sabbat as a conspiracy against natural fertility. The German pandemic of 1627–31, which pushes the balance in this area unusually far to the end of the peak period, also involves a range of local explanations, which will be discussed later.

Modern ecological studies suggest that human beings resemble all other known species in having an excess reproductive capacity, so that over time numbers will increase towards the limits set by resources. Single births and a long, vulnerable maturation period put us somewhere towards the bottom of this particular league, which may be just as well. Nevertheless it is only in the present century, with the availability of effective birth control, that parts of the developed world have seen birth rates fall below the levels needed for simple replacement, in a situation where early mortality is statistically insignificant. Previously it was only high mortality, especially among infants and children, which prevented populations growing at very fast rates indeed. There were areas with persistent demographic deficits, including insanitary, unhealthy cities and those regions where malarial mosquitoes proliferated. Healthier zones exported surplus population to these centres of economic opportunity and high risk. This regular self-limiting mechanism was seconded by the unpredictable incidence of epidemic disease, whether this was the plague, influenza, smallpox or the numerous other killer strains which emerged from time to time. Even when there was no specific outbreak of this kind, a routine mortality peak in late summer seems to represent gastric troubles, probably caused largely by poor hygiene and diet. Again in line with other species, humans also have ways of responding to a shortage of resources by cutting fertility. Malnutrition affects ovulation and the capacity to carry a foetus to term, although such effects are rather marginal outside real famines. Prolonged breast-feeding, which lengthens the intervals between births, ensured that the 'baby every year' pattern was never the general experience in Europe. Clearest of all reactions to hardship, in north-western Europe, was late marriage for women, which might come close to halving their effective fertility by enforcing celibacy until their mid to late twenties. While women in this region married relatively late even in good times, presumably in response to a complex set of cultural and social constraints, age at marriage moved up quite sharply as living standards fell.

Mortality, mobility and crime

Adjustments of this kind had their hidden social costs as well as demographic ones, as will become evident later. High rates of infant and juvenile mortality may look routine at aggregate levels. Their subjective effect was a very different matter, because their distribution was so irregular. Famines and epidemics tended to strike unequally across age groups, leaving depleted generations which would inevitably produce less children themselves. This would also have left unusually large numbers of households without any surviving children, a fact which could well relate to some categories of witchcraft belief and action. Major population losses, especially when on a patchy local basis, implied high mobility, but this could also arise from overpopulation and from seasonal labour patterns. Although this last form of mobility was of course temporary, it might still add to some of the social difficulties associated with migration more generally. Historians sometimes distinguish between 'betterment' and 'subsistence' migration, the latter – undertaken as a direct response to hunger and deprivation – naturally being regarded as a sign of greater dislocation than the former. While this is certainly true, one must again recognize that every kind of migration carried risks, both for those who attempted it and the communities through which they passed. Early modern commentators and law-enforcers probably tended to exaggerate such effects, since they generally subscribed to a rather static view of an ideal society, and rarely seemed to understand the important socio-economic functions performed by the migrants as a whole. These reactions bore witness to the unease and fear generated by the whole phenomenon, which seems to have helped create a pervasive sense of insecurity at all social levels. Not least among the poor, who must have seen the enforced departure of neighbours as a dire warning of the fate which could await them too. Their resentment of avaricious landlords and lenders could only be sharpened by the awareness of such ultimate consequences, just as their own charitable impulses were kept alive by the knowledge that their own turn might easily come.

Wealthier people evidently tended to see the wandering poor as a serious threat to law and order. Swarms of beggars gave rise to a rhetoric, accompanied by a picaresque literature, of 'sturdy beggars' and a criminal underworld in the big cities. The legends of a subversive counter-culture included stories of hidden organizations run by beggar-kings, who sound like prototypes of Fagin in *Oliver Twist*. These imaginary secret societies, with their private languages and parodic rituals, have some curious resemblance to the myths about the witches' sabbat, while many other aspects are uncannily reminiscent of contemporary attitudes to social security 'scroungers'. From the 1530s, European cities began to establish security and poor relief systems which were largely designed to keep unwelcome intruders out, while averting dangerous discontent among their long-term residents. This meant drawing up lists, making rules, levying local taxes and appointing administrators and policemen to enforce the policy. Everywhere the idea that communities of origin should be responsible for their own poor seemed to gain ground, with legislation to send migrants back home as an obvious consequence. In England the organized relief system pioneered by towns on an independent basis was gradually extended to the whole country, with parliamentary legislation in the 1590s, empowering local justices to levy poor rates, organize workhouses and distribute relief on a regular basis. Although it took many decades for the 'old poor law' to become a truly effective national system, its conception was a sign that traditional informal methods of relief were breaking down for both practical and ideological reasons. This process must have had some bearing on the special prominence of disputes over begging and charitable obligations in English witchcraft cases. While such themes do appear across Europe, as one would expect, there still appears to be a significant correlation between their relative frequency and the extent to which the old rural economy was undermined in sixteenth-century England.

The propertied classes, who generally did well out of the economic and demographic pressures which disadvantaged the poor, were uneasily aware of the resulting social dangers. Major revolts, such as the German Peasants' War of 1525, the English uprisings of 1549 and the widespread French peasant disturbances of the 1590s, reminded them that the social order which enshrined their domination was fragile. More generally, there was a widespread perception of a crime wave, readily associated with vagrants and 'masterless men', whose most obnoxious varieties were highway robbery and other kinds of brigandage. Coupled with internal developments in the legal profession and legal thought, the growing power of the 'new monarchies' and the effects of printing, the fear of popular disorder can be detected behind the great expansion of the instruments of repression in the sixteenth century. Law codes were drawn up or expanded, with new courts and police officials created to enforce them. Governments also came under pressure from reforming clerics of all persuasions to reinforce social discipline in the cause of the godly commonwealth. The result was a marked tendency to treat even minor crimes as offences against society as much as the individual, imposing harsh exemplary punishments rather than helping victims secure compensation. Although proper figures are lacking, it does seem likely that the period saw an exceptionally high rate of capital sentences, alongside the extension of inquisitorial procedure and judicial torture. The relevance of these trends to witchcraft persecution is very obvious. Provisions against witchcraft and sorcery were included in the law codes, or developed as a matter of local practice, then the crime was incorporated into the wider repressive drive against criminals and the socially undesirable.

Inflation and social problems

Crime is not just a product of poverty or social resentment. The high levels of personal violence in early modern Europe related most obviously to local rivalries and to drinking; violence by the destitute merely aped the behaviour of their betters. The most successful thieves were the officials and local agents who siphoned money out of taxes, tithes, feudal dues and rents. Nevertheless, it is evident that much minor pilfering was the work of desperate individuals, who were starving or hopelessly indebted. Sixteenth-century society was being tossed around by powerful forces men could neither understand nor control, above all by inflation. Over the century prices typically rose to stand at four or five times what they had been in 1500. As an annual rate of inflation this is remarkably low compared with the kind of figures often found in the modern world, but it had devastating effects on societies which almost wholly lacked mechanisms for adjusting to it. At the time it was hard even to realize that it was occurring, because prices of foodstuffs in particular fluctuated so much with harvest variations that general trends were almost completely obscured. The most intelligent contemporary theory was first advanced by some Spanish theorists, but most famously some years later by none other than Jean Bodin, author of the *Démonomanie des sorciers*. Bodin argued that the influx of gold and silver from the New World had increased the monetary stock, with much the same effect as printing additional banknotes in a modern system, so that too much money was chasing too few goods. Others had already recognized that debasement of the coinage by greedy rulers had a similar effect. National experience naturally varied in this respect; in England the spiral of debasements initiated by Henry VIII ceased with the Elizabethan recoinage of 1563, whereas the kings of France and Spain continued to manipulate their coinage well into the seventeenth century.

Monetary chaos certainly created difficulties for ordinary people who were, predictably, the ones who usually lost out, short changed by unscrupulous traders or finding their small coins had been devalued. Villagers would have been surprised, however, to hear that there was too much coinage in circulation. Their own experience was rather that it was rare and unreliable, so that they often preferred to carry out transactions in kind. In the case of the tithes at least this was obligatory, at the point of payment; every tenth sheaf could mean just that. This did not prevent attempts at fraud or false accusations. When Demenge Mathis was tried, several witnesses recounted the ways he had tried to practise such tricks, or persuade others to be his accomplices. Jean Colin Dieudonné recalled how when they were collecting tithes together, Demenge had wanted to put an extra sheaf in the stack of Jean Blaise Laynel, so that there would be eleven and he would be found to be cheating. When the witness objected 'that he did not want to live by such bread', Demenge replied 'that if he feared the ill will of his neighbours he would never be rich' – a striking if impolitic view of early modern village life.[5] Tithes gave particularly attractive openings for middlemen, usually drawn from among the richer peasants, who leased them on monetary terms and reckoned to take advantage of market conditions, if necessary by hoarding grain until prices rose. Although much criticized by others, this practice actually had serious merits for the community as a whole; storage facilities and reserve supplies were vital if famine was to be avoided after bad harvests. Rather similar observations might be offered about the collection of feudal dues and rents, which tended to be operated by the same rural oligarchy. Payments in kind also operated to the advantage of millers, always suspected of cheating on either quantity or quality.

Demands for payment in cash, however, could be equally oppressive; they were a particularly obnoxious feature of the tax system for many people. The various levies, in kind and money, did enforce a market economy up to a point, although in much of Europe one has the impression that local autarky asserted itself as far as possible. Transfers of both foodstuffs and money usually took place only at short range, with the local town serving as the centre for such exchanges. Only where there was a large city to create a commercialized hinterland for itself, or good water transport, did more active market conditions develop.

Local economies functioned extensively on credit, so that *postmortem* inventories commonly show the deceased holding long lists of small credits and debits, stretching back for years. It is none too easy to determine how this network of submerged mutual indebtedness functioned in reality, but it is striking how attempts to get payment often figured in the quarrels reported in witchcraft trials. Owing a debt and actually paying it were evidently rather different things in the popular mind. While modern historians accept that Bodin and others were right to blame bullion imports and debasement for some of the problems, these are now seen as only partial explanations for the great inflation as a whole. Not only was the process already under way before these factors could have become important, differential price rises for separate commodities suggest another and equally powerful force was at work. This was also a demand-led inflation, fuelled by the tension between expanding population and relatively static production; this was why the price of agricultural goods rose at almost twice the rate industrial prices did. Largely unfettered markets behaved in a thoroughly perverse manner, as might have been predicted. An abundance of labour held wage rates down, in a situation where underemployment became general; demand for all but essential commodities was thereby depressed, as real incomes fell dramatically and nutritional standards dropped. Ultimately the effect was to jam on the brakes across most sectors of the European economy, so that the expansionist tendencies of the early sixteenth century gave way to stagnation, or sometimes actual decline. Meanwhile anxious rulers, at both national and local level, tried to dampen down popular discontent by controlling the grain market through various devices, including price fixing, export prohibitions and compulsory sales. It is a moot point whether these measures did more harm than good in the long run.

The agrarian economy did possess some scope to expand cereal production, in the forms of wasteland which could be brought under cultivation and pasture convertible to arable. Initially good yields soon declined, however, as nitrogen reserves on this generally poor land were consumed. Switching to cereals was bound to limit numbers of animals, when these were vital sources of both fertilizer and motive power; although it is impossible to calculate these effects precisely, productive capacity must have suffered to some extent. Overcrowding animals on the remaining pasture carried further dangers. They were unlikely to thrive, while fodder shortages made it hard to keep large numbers through the winter and epidemic diseases became more likely, as did the inability to work properly. Friction over the various mutual help arrangements involved in ploughing and carting, for example, was bound to increase in consequence. Communal herds and flocks were traditionally kept on common land, which now became an increasingly valuable and scarce resource, steadily eroded by legal or illegal means. Communities resorted increasingly to stinting, the arrangement under which animal numbers on the commons were controlled, usually to the advantage of the richer peasants. Many of the poor could only keep animals at all by leasing them from wealthier individuals (most probably town-dwellers), often on share-cropping terms. This was just one of many ways in which a tentacular system of debt and exploitation expanded through the rural economy, frequently to the benefit of outsiders.

The limits of resources and self-sufficiency

The effect of high food prices and lagging wages was so powerful because the vast majority of peasants were not self-sufficient on their own land. Their small plots could only produce a fraction of their subsistence needs, so wage labour was the mainstay of their lives (although of course many payments were in kind rather than cash). When household budgets were dominated by the need to buy food, a fall in living standards might have widespread and unpleasant effects. It could mean children crying with hunger or suffering from diseases of malnutrition such as rickets, while a monotonous cereal-based diet had more general effects on health and work capacity. These patterns were inevitably far from uniform, for there were many regions where climate, soil type, or relief dictated a more varied agriculture. Generalizations about the European peasantry are bound to be inaccurate in detail, yet it is startling how the same themes do reappear in local studies across a very wide area. One important common factor was the way in which hardship was actually experienced from month to month and year to year. Plenty and dearth alternated, cyclically yet unpredictably, within a system whose annual productivity was dangerously unreliable. This was partly because crop yields were so low, with perhaps four or five times the amount of grain sown being harvested. When such a large proportion of the crop had to be held back as seedcorn, a fall of a quarter in average yields became one of a third in the marketable quantity. Bad years could be much worse than this, and since a poor harvest meant less work there was an internal multiplier, which made the effects on the poor even more severe. As the system approached something like its natural limits, in terms of the balance between population and resources, the margins of safety were reduced, so that such crises became both more frequent and more savage in their impact. At the limit large numbers of the poor literally starved to death in terrible famines which also tended to produce epidemics of disease. Anyone who lived to late middle age was likely to have survived at least one of these appalling experiences, which cast a shadow of fear and insecurity across the whole society. In a more routine fashion they knew the fears which pushed grain prices up whenever bad weather seemed to threaten the next harvest, and the hard times of many a spring and early summer, when the remainder of the last year's crop had to be eked out until new produce was available.

Most subsistence crises were relatively local, but they did not have to be very extensive to overwhelm any possibility of effective relief. In much of Europe markets were too local, and communications too bad, for supplies to move any great distance in quantity. The Dutch, and to a lesser extent the British, were fortunate in having extensive water-borne transport systems, for these were the only way of shifting bulk commodities efficiently. They encouraged the development of a more specialized and market-oriented agriculture; even if this did not raise yields much, the infrastructure for moving grain around served as a vital protection against outright famine. Towns generally escaped the worst of the problems because they had more extensive storage facilities, and the authorities were always anxious to forestall popular discontent, if necessary by using reserve stocks to depress prices or by organizing direct relief. Governments would have liked to achieve similar results on a national scale, which is why the grain trade was so tightly policed in most countries. Problems were routinely blamed on traders who operated monopolies and tried to drive prices up; there was just enough truth behind this to make it plausible, although it completely ignored the vital function of a market based on anticipation, which was to use prices as a mechanism for eking out supplies as long as possible. This governmental rhetoric found a ready echo at popular level, where crowds would seize grain or bread supplies and force their sale at 'fair' prices, thus imposing the moral rather than the market economy. More fundamentally, everyone knew that high prices favoured the rich, those with surpluses they could hoard to sell when prices peaked. We have already seen how this theme surfaced repeatedly in the myth of the witches' sabbat; it is also found as a routine grievance of poor peasants against their rich neighbours.

A second basic need of all populations, given the European climate, was fuel for both heating and cooking. In most places this meant wood, since only small areas used peat or coal for these purposes. Wood was also vital for building, furniture, tools and virtually every aspect of economic life. In principle, well-managed woodland is a self-sustaining resource, but predictably it tended to fall victim to overcropping and conversion, with the result that wood prices rose faster than those of any other major commodity. Although quite substantial areas of woodland belonged to local communities, the great majority was in the hands of larger landowners – the monarchies, the nobility and the church. Here too, pressure on resources generated a series of conflicts, as alleged customary rights and straight theft were increasingly met by new systems of protection and exclusion. Growing numbers of foresters pursued the delinquents who nibbled away at the margins of their territory; angry scenes, threats and violence resulted from some of their attempts to arrest and fine the offenders. This cannot have been a popular job, and sometimes the resentments created became the basis for witchcraft charges. Some five years before the trial of Laurence Bandesapt, her husband Vincent had cut some wood without permission, so the abbot of Étival instructed the forester Nicolas Arnoulx to collect it. As he was bringing it back on a cart he met Vincent; during the ensuing quarrel the latter said 'that it would be easy for her to overturn the cart and the four horses pulling it', to which Nicolas replied 'she must then be very powerful'. All four horses, worth at least fifty écus each, then died, so he naturally suspected her of causing this.[6] There could be trouble over communal woodland too, where practices akin to stinting were applied, often by naming days on which a specified amount of wood could be cut under supervision. Meanwhile the poor, including many of those older women who could rarely find paid work, pilfered fuel wherever they could, raiding hedges and unattended piles of firewood. This furtive, anti-social behaviour was just the sort of thing irritated neighbours would have expected from those whose marginal status included reputations as witches.

Timber was perhaps an extreme case of a commodity whose supply could hardly have been increased very much or very quickly. There is a wider question about the apparent failure to expand agricultural production, when yields were so poor overall. Technological limitations are not the whole answer here, since there are cases where the fourteenth century outputs had actually been higher, quite apart from regional variations which cannot be explained by relative natural endowment. Peasants themselves were shrewd and knowledgeable about local conditions, not at all the passive, ignorant boobies they are still too often conceived as having been. Productivity on their own small plots was probably very high; since it was almost wholly for their own consumption this has left little trace in the records. Traditional agriculture could achieve good results in terms of yields per acre, but at a high cost in labour, so that there was a strong tendency for per capita production to decline in an inverse relationship to intensive cultivation practices. Nevertheless, there seems to have been a fair amount of underemployment in the local economy, so even such marginal gains would have been well worth securing. Failure to do so is most plausibly explained in terms of landholding and tenurial systems, which imposed certain structural patterns on the rural world.

Larger landowners, whether they were nobles, ecclesiastical corporations or royal officials, did not run their estates in person. They relied on subordinates and intermediaries, who let out the land and managed the revenues; although elaborate accounting procedures had been developed to maintain some degree of control, these still had many inadequacies. In most parts of Europe the result was inefficient management, with all parties preferring the status quo as the safest way of retaining their individual niches in the system. Since the best way of investing in land was to buy up more, rather than improving the productivity of existing holdings, there was a tendency towards concentration of land in the hands of the rich. For the most part it was then rather poorly farmed, either by tenants who lacked sufficient capital, or by the miserable sharecroppers found in much of southern Europe. Agrarian capitalism was a very sickly growth in this environment; the market generally functioned too feebly to be a dynamic force generating expansion. Even where significant changes did occur, in parts of north-west Europe, the trend was often to improve profitability by minimizing the amount of labour used, a process that was only socially tolerable where alternative commercial and industrial employment developed. In England at least this was only accomplished after a painful, protracted transition period, involving a good deal of social dislocation. The process effectively destroyed the English peasantry, as the countryside was reorganized into the familiar structure of landlords, tenant farmers and landless labourers that would endure into the modern age.

European peasantries generally survived much better than their English counterparts as a social class, even in most parts of the Low Countries, where there was a comparable development of the market. Their success in retaining small plots of land, with the associated communal rights, was only a very relative matter, however. Everywhere the large majority were effectively being pauperized, as rural society split into two increasingly antithetical elements. Medium-sized holdings tended to disappear, as land was concentrated in the hands of outside landlords and a small group of relatively wealthy peasant oligarchs. The way this process worked is instructive. Every time that a harvest crisis brought dearth and high prices many families could only survive by borrowing or by disposing of assets. Those who had grain in reserve held the whip hand, and were able to impose very unequal contracts; sales at low prices, loans at extortionate rates of interest or with heavy penalties for failure to repay on time. Such arrangements also operated in more normal times, of course, when a particular family suffered individual misfortune and had to raise money. Apart from the actual transfer of land, a complex structure of debt was built up, layer upon layer, much of it in the form of annual payments to town-dwellers. A sequence of harvest crises was likely to trigger off not just fresh indebtedness, but a wave of foreclosures on the land of those already weakened by previous borrowings. Even such vital forms of property as houses and gardens were caught up in the process, which could often leave people as mere tenants of property they had previously owned. Share-cropping contracts for animals also became more common; this was another way in which the economic balance was tilted against the poor.

Some of the political consequences of these long-term movements are considered as part of the next chapter. The relevance of the economic shifts themselves to witchcraft beliefs and persecution should however be obvious. The position of most peasants was that of people trying to cling to a sharply inclined sandhill, whose loose surface was always liable to give way and carry them downwards. This could only produce a deep sense of insecurity, exacerbating all the extant tensions between relatives, neighbours and interest groups. The 'moral credit' economy of village society was placed under such intense strain that it was bound to suffer at least partial breakdown. This created just the kind of confusion over mutual obligations which bred resentment and irreconcilable disputes, leaving all parties feeling aggrieved. In social terms the sharpest conflict was between the peasant oligarchs and those who were increasingly dependent on them for work, charity and protection. Such antagonisms must have been sharpened by the way members of this dominant group tended to control the local operation of surplus extraction through rents, feudal dues, taxation and tithes. The generally more overt nature of this hostility, however, may actually have operated as something of a barrier to witchcraft suspicions. Most historians have found that these arose much more often between individuals or families who were fairly close in economic terms; if it was more likely that the witch would be slightly poorer than the victim, this was by no means always the case. The syndrome seems to have found routine expression among those who interacted regularly on relatively equal terms, people who should have been friendly and co-operative towards one another, but readily believed one another to be guilty of secret treachery. Witchcraft was primarily the idiom of conflict between closely matched rivals, rather than between those at opposite ends of the spectrum of wealth and power, although as usual this was a tendency rather than a firm rule. One may suspect that this reflected certain central features of the belief itself, which went some way to dictate those situations in which it would be thought applicable. There is of course a classic 'chicken and egg' puzzle here, since the belief was also shaped by the social context, but this particular feature is sufficiently widespread to appear something of a cross-cultural constant. As Evans-Pritchard noted of the Azande:

> A man quarrels with and is jealous of his social equals . . . It is among householders of roughly equal status who come into close daily relations with one another that there is the greatest opportunity for squabbles, and it is these people who most frequently place one another's names before the oracles when they or members of their families are sick.[7]

The stagnation which increasingly afflicted the agricultural sector had serious knock-on effects elsewhere. Many country-dwellers were at least partially employed in ancillary occupations, ranging from smiths, wheelwrights and cobblers, through millers and carters, to builders and other craftsmen. While elite requirements for some such services may have risen, the overall demand trend was probably downwards, with falling incomes driving most consumers to economize on these services wherever possible. At the same time competition between those engaged in these sectors meant lower returns, so it is no surprise to find a significant number of such rivalries behind witchcraft accusations. These might be between millers disputing leases, smiths arguing over a new forge, or any comparable individuals in similar situations. The miller Demenge Demengeon found himself the target for several accusations relating to past conflicts of this kind, including one from Nicolas le Conte who claimed that when he took the lease of the mill at Dompierre, Demenge had been angry, 'saying that he would have been wiser not to compete with him in this way, that he would make hardly any profit and not be long at the mill in question, adding that he had worked it for forty-five years continuously'. Over the next three years he and his son had so many difficulties with the mill breaking down that they had to reassign the lease to Demenge, whom they blamed for their problems, in view of his long reputation. By Demenge's own account he had warned them they would make a loss because they were paying too much rent.[8] Meanwhile industrial activity was stagnating or declining in most areas, as market demand suffered from the problems in the dominant agricultural sector. Much textile production was already dispersed in the countryside, taking advantage of surplus labour and the lack of guild or other restrictions; these workers, who were simply engaged on piecework, had no security at all. Many urban workers found themselves in a similar position, for the guild structures which had offered some protection were now decaying fast. Here too there was a polarization between the established families of the masters, perpetuating themselves from generation to generation, and the journeymen and apprentices, few of whom now had any chance of rising above their initial status. For reasons which remain obscure, the urban milieu does not seem to have generated many witchcraft cases in most parts of Europe. The obvious exceptions are the pandemics which afflicted some German towns and the more routine persecution found in parts of the southern Netherlands, the latter an exceptionally urbanized region suffering from severe economic dislocation. It may be that elsewhere even these relatively small urban populations were just sufficiently mobile and anonymous to discourage the long build-up of hostility characteristic of witchcraft accusations in tight-knit rural societies. The much more random and explosive quality of the spectacular urban witch-hunts does suggest that a strikingly different dynamic was at work here. Certainly one cannot assume that living standards or job opportunities were any better than in the countryside, for those not born to at least a modest degree of affluence.

Disease and warfare

By the early seventeenth century, European population growth had declined to very modest levels, just as there were signs of limited economic recovery in some areas. These last may have owed more to favourable weather and a brief period of peace than to deep structural features. If the population stabilized, this resulted from a combination of low birth rates – themselves connected to late age of marriage for women – and high mortality, particularly among infants and children. Ultimately it is impossible to determine the precise importance of the various factors; malnutrition and poor living conditions opened the way for disease, but epidemics had their own 'microbic history', and often struck in random fashion. Although the bubonic plague never repeated the general devastation caused by its first and most virulent outbreak, it remained the greatest terror. Some other diseases, such as influenza, also came in waves, while there were those such as typhus, dysentery and smallpox which tended to appear in intense local outbreaks. Syphilis and other venereal diseases attracted a good deal of comment, probably rather out of proportion to their fairly marginal significance for the population as a whole. There is not the slightest sign, however, of specific connections with witchcraft accusations, whether one takes the trial records or the writings of demonologists. While the history of malaria is still too little known, there are reasons to think that a more virulent strain affected the wetlands in this period, becoming an endemic phenomenon which debilitated people as often as it actually killed them. Malarial fevers, with their pattern of crises and remissions, probably lent themselves rather well to diagnosis as witchcraft, not least because the doctors had no idea about their cause. On the other hand their localization meant that they, like plague, tended to be explained as the result of bad air and other environmental factors.

At the time, a rare specific link made between epidemic disease and witchcraft came in the form of the occasional claims that 'engraisseurs' had spread the plague, found repeatedly in Geneva (1530, 1545, 1567–8, 1571, 1615), in neighbouring Savoy and in Milan in 1630.[9] There appear to be few other instances of such accusations, despite the range and urgency of reactions to plague across the Continent. In the intense debate about the causes of plague, doctors and divines asserted various theories which tried to balance between infection and divine punishment. However dubious their premises and their logic, these arguments finally led to some quite sensible measures of public health and quarantine that probably did quite a lot to contain the disease. Popular behaviour and official doctrines certainly agreed in treating it as highly contagious, so that at the level of 'second causes', diabolical intervention was a rather redundant explanation. It was a good deal more convincing to blame other communities which were known to have had it earlier, the bad air caused by tradesmen such as butchers and tanners, or the usual vagabonds and beggars. Of course pestilence, like the other great afflictions, might always be interpreted as a sign of divine anger at wickedness among men, reinforcing the desire to enforce moral order and punish deviants, but there is little sign that witches were brought into the equation specifically. Although the great persecutions in south-western Germany between 1627 and 1631 are certainly linked to a group of militant counter-Reformation prince-bishops, the causal links are complex and indirect. Moreover, these episodes must also be seen against a background of plague, runaway inflation and harvest crises, all related to the Thirty Years' War. It was just the areas most seriously affected by these linked misfortunes which experienced the worst witchcraft panics. On the other hand, there was nothing automatic about these responses, because when viewed at the microscopic level the persecutions still appear very erratically distributed. It is also plain that there was a kind of cross-infection between the towns and regions affected, which operated in a similarly unpredictable manner. Here too infectious disease appears as one of several factors which combined to intensify fear and anxiety, yet there is no direct link to witchcraft; indeed, far the worst outbreaks of plague came between 1633 and 1636, just as witchcraft trials virtually ceased across the region.

It was the period after 1631 which also saw military operations reach their most destructive peak in most of Germany, so that here too no simple relationship can be postulated. Warfare was certainly the worst of all the routine scourges of early modern society, less through direct killing and maiming than through widespread disruption of ordinary life. Troops seized livestock, cut down standing corn, ransomed communities and carried off anything they could find. Even relatively orderly billeting for winter quarters could have devastating effects. Armies also played a major role in spreading infectious disease, with some of the worst early modern epidemics travelling along their lines of march. It would be rash to claim that military operations were necessarily more destructive in this period than earlier. The Hundred Years' War had already shown that late medieval warfare could make a good attempt at ruining a flourishing kingdom. Nevertheless, the scale and extent of damage between 1560 and 1660 was exceptional, particularly in connection with the Revolt of the Netherlands, the French Wars of Religion, the Thirty Years' War and the Franco-Spanish war of 1635–59. In what might be thought a rather paradoxical fashion, there appears to have been an inverse relationship between really intensive military activity and witchcraft persecution. The explanation here is probably a very prosaic one. The human agents of disaster were all too easily identified, while the survivors were driven together in a manner which overcame all normal rivalries or hostilities. Communities which lost half or more of their population must have been so changed that the slow processes whereby suspicions normally crystallized would have been completely disrupted. Something of this kind happened in Lorraine, where within a few years of the first appearance of French and Imperial troops in 1632 the population of the whole duchy may have declined by 60 per cent. Witchcraft trials, which had for decades been proceeding routinely at a fairly steady rate, abruptly came to an almost complete halt, never to resume in any numbers.

When outbursts of witchcraft persecution can be related to warfare, it is usually on the fringes of conflict or when its impact was less overwhelming. The German cases already discussed may well fit this pattern, belonging to a period when the fear of war was intense, but people were suffering serious indirect repercussions rather than full-scale devastation. There are parallels here with the events in Burgundy and Champagne in 1644 or Matthew Hopkins's crusade the following year in East Anglia. So long as local communities remained more or less intact, perceived unfairness in billeting, information given to the troops and similar issues might form the raw material of quarrels and accusations. In a much more general sense, war brought high taxation, which could also exacerbate local hostilities. Across Europe the various tax systems were riddled with manipulation, fraud, evasion and exploitation. A pervasive sense of grievance was engendered among the less well-off, whose most spectacular expression took the form of tax revolts. Much of the ill-will was very local, however, directed against the collectors themselves; it was just as likely to be sparked off by attempts at greater fairness, if these meant changing established routines or rates of tax. It is predictable that both witches and their supposed victims should be found explaining malevolence against particular individuals in this way. Mongeon Bourard explained that the previous summer, when he had been the deputy of the commune charged with collecting the taxes, he had added two blancs to Jean Marion's payment because he believed him to be able to pay this, while reducing some other payments. An angry confrontation followed, as Marion claimed he had overcharged him, at which moment his four-year old son, who was beside him eating berries out of a hat, told him he was ill. For five weeks the child was unable to stand, until Bourard put it about the village that Marion had bewitched him, even telling the mayor – then he recovered within a few days.[10]

Historical demographers have demonstrated that falling living standards affected marriage patterns, albeit with something of a time-lag. Away from the Mediterranean regions, with their very different customs, women in particular married later, and might even find it difficult to marry at all. Parents were slower to come up with dowries, while girls in service found that it took longer to accumulate the modest collection of household objects regarded as the minimum equipment for a bride. Long delays increased the chances that contracts would be broken off, perhaps creating serious resentments in the process. The worst possible scenario, from the family angle at least, was that which left the girl pregnant but abandoned by her fiancé or seducer. In fact the statistics do not suggest that this was very common, for rates of illegitimacy and premarital pregnancy actually seem to have fallen in the relevant period. The causes of such trends remain mysterious; did individuals react to hard times by behaving more cautiously, or were moral campaigns by religious reformers surprisingly effective? Whatever was happening in these respects, marriage negotiations and arrangements must have taken on a heightened significance, in that the stakes were raised for all parties. Jennon Napnel had a long and complex history of relations with a neighbouring family, that of Jacot Girard Pechey; originally they must have been close allies, since they had acted as godparents for one another's children. When she was first accused of witchcraft around 1598, however, he had testified against her. Despite this he wanted to marry her later, when they were both widowed, to be indignantly refused and asked if he did not realize the dishonour he had done her. At her second trial Jacot's daughter Claudatte, aged twenty-five, explained that she had been seduced by Jennon's son Claude under promise of marriage, and had a child still living by him. The previous year her brother had quarrelled with Claude at a marriage feast, and she was afraid they might renew their quarrel at the subsequent dance, so went to watch. On the way back, Jennon came up without provocation and said that a whore should not go and see the dances; the witness replied 'that it was as much her business as that of her whoremaster of a son, and if she meant to say that she had prostituted herself to anyone else than her son, she had lied like a witch'. Jennon later said that there had been a long lawsuit over Claudatte's demand that Claude should marry her.[11] One has to suppose that the potential tensions and conflicts discussed in previous chapters risked being sharpened in such situations; here too a 'strain-gauge' theory might well be appropriate. At the most basic level, women running households could hardly help feeling torn between obligations to husbands and children when resources were simply inadequate.

Hidden agendas: the Salem witches

The links between socio-economic trends and witchcraft anxieties are by their very nature bound to remain tenuous. All too rarely does the evidence permit anything more than plausible guesswork, while as usual there is nothing predictable about the outcome of any particular combination of circumstances. The most convincing example of how such processes might work themselves out is to be found in a rather unlikely setting – none other than the famous Salem Village crisis of 1692.[12] The greatest 'betterment migration' of the seventeenth century was that from Britain to North America, and in most respects the colonists enjoyed a much higher standard of living than their stay-at-home relatives. The extraordinarily rich records for early New England, however, allow us to see that prosperity was not universal, with individuals and communities still liable to decline and crisis. Salem Village was just such a case, so that the dramatic events there cannot be fully explained without an understanding of their wider context. That context is not just economic, of course, and has much to do with the type of power relations to be studied in the next chapter; the present discussion will indeed provide a bridge between these and other related themes. We must also bear in mind the earlier history of witchcraft in New England, a territory to which the colonists had imported more in the way of Old World beliefs than Puritanism alone. Although the number of court cases was small, and convictions much rarer still, there is no doubt that ideas of black and white witchcraft were commonplace among the settlers. On the whole, magistrates, ministers and juries had treated the occasional accusations with sensible caution, often allowing the balance of doubt to determine an acquittal. This official clemency did not stop some of the accused becoming virtual outcasts, living in isolation on the fringe of the community. Perhaps the powerful feelings evident in ostracism of this kind needed to come to a head, so that New England could confront the implications of its contradictory belief systems.[13]

While there may be some ultimate sense in which the Puritan ministers created a peculiar ambience, saturated with ideas of divine punishment and diabolical power, their official position on witchcraft was as equivocal as that of Perkins and his colleagues some generations earlier. Cotton Mather himself, whose fascination with the supernatural was ultimately to cause him so much trouble and embarrassment, was atypical only in the rather naive way he drew attention to the whole issue. There was something of a gap between the rhetoric through which the ministers made everything into evidence of the cosmic struggle between good and evil, and the scrupulous manner in which they usually tried to weigh individual cases. Their loss of control and limited complicity, in the first months of the 1692 outbreak, probably had a special cause, the presence of the ex-village minister George Burroughs as a key suspect. By this date Burroughs had moved to a radical sectarian position which more conservative ministers could only interpret as a deadly threat to the religious orthodoxy of the colony. To them he must indeed have seemed an agent of the Devil, whose elimination was so important that it overrode their normal caution. Whatever one may think of the behaviour of the current Salem Village minister Samuel Parris and a few of his more credulous colleagues, however, it is a travesty of the facts to see the clerics as the driving force behind the persecution as a whole, when their influence was decisive in bringing it to an end. Nor were the trials instigated by a dominant oligarchy of local rulers; their main supporters were declining and even embittered figures, who were making a half-understood last stand against inexorable forces of change. Since this was part of the great transition from Puritan to Yankee, there was a sense in which the values espoused by the ministers more generally were at stake, but at the time none of them seems to have been aware of this. The nightmare which afflicted the village was blamed on the 'restless frame of spirit' of its inhabitants, with no recognition of the structural reasons which rendered them so quarrelsome.

Salem Village was not really a community at all, for it possessed neither the institutions nor the cohesion which would have entitled it to that name. In all essentials it was just the rural area attached to the thriving mercantile port of Salem Town, and having seen other parts of their original hinterland achieve separate township status, the town rulers had no intention of surrendering this final section. By the later seventeenth century the town was ruled by wealthy merchants whose lifestyle had more in common with Restoration England than with the homespun values of the early settlers. Meanwhile many of the farmers and labourers of the village were finding life hard, in the face of problems all too familiar to their ancestors in England. This must have been particularly hard for many to bear, because the social origins of early New Englanders were not evenly spread. A high proportion came from better-off English families, so for these the experience of impoverishment carried a painful sense of degradation. As land was subdivided among the heirs of the second and third generations, what had been comfortable holdings were becoming inadequate; much of the land was poor, with no access to navigable water. The usual operation of commerce, inheritance and sheer chance saw some families improve their lot, while others plunged into poverty and want. There was a crucial division between those whose property lay near the town and the waterways to the south-east of the village, and those cut off in the more distant sectors. Not only did the first profit from better land and communications, they also tended to be involved in the more diverse economy of the town, where their primary loyalties lay. This basic division of interest became entangled with two highly divisive issues. At the public level, there was the long struggle to establish a separate church for the village; this carried the implication of possible separation from the town at a later date, since a church was the crucial institution of an independent community. At a private level, relations between the two most powerful landholding families of the early settlement, the Putnams and the Porters, became soured by an acrimonious inheritance dispute.

A group of the villagers had been trying to set up an independent church since 1666. Between 1672 and 1688 three ministers had been engaged, although there was as yet only a meeting house, not a properly constituted church with its own separate membership. All three eventually got into such difficulties with one or another group among their quarrelsome flock that they gave up and left. With the appointment of Samuel Parris in 1689 the church was finally established in proper form, but a simultaneous move for greater political independence from Salem Town failed. Apart from the church, the only formal body in the village was a five-man committee, appointed by a general meeting of the householders, whose duty was to meet the minister's salary by taxing the community. This was not an easy task, since the constables appointed by the town refused to enforce payment, and arrears quickly mounted. In the autumn of 1691, a few months before the witchcraft troubles began, a new committee entirely composed of men hostile to Parris was elected; it was plain from the start that they were determined to stop any taxation, so that his salary would disappear. This was a deadly threat to Parris, a man already embittered by a series of disappointments. The younger son of a wealthy London merchant, he had received little from his father's estate, then failed as a merchant in Boston. For him the ministry and the idealized community of the church stood in opposition to the treacherous world of commerce. It would be all too easy for him to convert this into the language of sermons which saw dark threats and devilry threatening the beleaguered group of God's elect. His values and his anxieties must have struck deep chords with many of his hearers, for they articulated a whole range of very real fears they could all share.

Parris seems to have come to Salem Village as the nominee of the Putnam family, whose leading members would (with one significant exception) support him to the end. Thomas Putnam, the oldest and best-provided-for son of the original settler, had died in 1686, leaving two sons and four daughters from his first marriage. Crucially, however, he had married again, and was survived by his second wife and their only son Joseph. Thomas Putnam Jr, already established on his own farm, would have expected further bequests at this point, but found that all the remaining property went to his stepmother and half-brother. A vain attempt to break the will was followed by Joseph's marriage in 1690 to

Elizabeth, daughter of Israel Porter, the richest and most influential man in the village. In effect, Joseph Putnam, already well connected in Salem Town through his mother, had now joined ranks with the rival influence group led by the Porters, whose business interests straddled the commercial and agricultural sectors. The other Putnams, whose lands lay further from the town, found themselves limited to purely rural concerns, as their relative status and wealth fell. Joseph was already considerably richer than the much older Thomas Jr, while the latter had already been involved in another expensive and futile lawsuit when his wife's mother and elder brothers contrived to keep the family property in their own hands. These classic inheritance disputes, involving siblings and half-siblings as well as rival families, clearly created much bitterness. When the witchcraft accusations began, they would come from the circle around Parris and the Putnams, and be directed against people who had links with, or could be thought to represent, their personal and political enemies.

The colony was in a tense state at this time, for the 1688–9 revolution had brought about the overthrow of the royal governor, Sir Edmund Andros, leaving a vacuum in the central government until his successor arrived with a new charter in 1692. In addition, in late 1691 there seems to have been something of a craze for fortune telling; in Salem Village it was groups of young girls wanting to foretell their marriages, those vital indices of status. Significantly, it was in the household of Samuel Parris himself that these activities turned into strange behaviour and fits, the signs of the Devil at work, early in 1692. As contemporaries observed, however, the centre of the accusations lay in the household of Thomas Putnam Jr., where his wife joined three other girls in naming the witches they could see in their fits. There might have been a cathartic effect of a normal type had it been possible to get the first cases to court quickly, with a few trials proving sufficient to clear the air, but the special court established by the new governor only started sitting in June 1692. By then the afflicted women and girls were in full spate; an atmosphere of hysteria had been created which drove them on unstoppably. It is not necessary to believe that they acted from deliberate malice, although some may well have done so, and individuals had moments of lucidity in which they tried to pull back. Such episodes generate enormous psychic forces within the affected group, and although the choice of victims has meaning it is readily operated at the level of the unconscious. Those the Putnams chose seem to have been surrogates for the traitors within their own family, for they could not actually bring themselves to name Joseph and his mother. Unless they had managed this final step, the displacement on to others was bound to remain provisional, and the accusations were likely to continue until outside force stopped them. Parris also had to be reckoned with. Where other ministers would have been very cautious, he drove the outbreak forward in sermons which implied that the witches were themselves devils, and insisted that there could be no neutrals in the struggle between God and the Devil. In consequence, nineteen people were hanged and another pressed to death for refusing to plead, while over a hundred more were arrested as the panic spread to the neighbouring townships.

As the trials began, the accusations also spread upwards socially, with several members of the wealthy ruling elite in Salem Town and even Boston being named. None was brought to trial, but some had to flee or bribe their way out of prison. Here one may surely suspect the resentments of the country cousins, for these individuals were plainly known to their accusers only by name, and stood for the 'corruption' of that nearby yet unknown world of mercantile capitalism. Opposition and disquiet grew, until the ministers of Massachusetts (with Burroughs now safely dead) intervened to denounce the use of 'spectral evidence' on grounds which included the familiar point that the Devil could never be trusted. They may also have come to see the accusers as possessed rather than bewitched, a reclassification which made their revelations inadmissible as legal evidence.[14] Once the bubble had been pricked the hysteria subsided as quickly as it had begun, the prisons were rather shamefacedly emptied and the people of the colony turned to repentance for the shedding of innocent blood. For some this would be long and bitter. Parris did not become a pariah in the village, for a majority of the inhabitants still supported him as minister, but in the end his position proved intolerable, and he resigned in 1696, to continue his descent into genteel poverty. When Thomas Putnam Jr. died three years later his estate was heavily encumbered with debt; his heirs sold up and left the neighbourhood. In the struggle for a place in the sun they had been decisively worsted. The witchcraft trials had been a brief, destructive protest on behalf of a group and a way of life which were already on the defensive, whose decline they had only hastened. Economic difficulties were not the only cause, yet without them one can hardly envisage events of such ferocity, which mobilized similar forces across numerous communities. If it is hard to trace similar factionalism in European villages, usually because we simply lack the necessary information, there is every reason to suspect it was present just below the surface of many accusations. In one or two Fenland villages, for example, there are hints that parties formed for and against the drainage operations which destroyed the old (more egalitarian) local economy, and that these tensions spilled over into witchcraft charges.[15]

It is fascinating to see how the socio-economic development of New England constituted almost a speeded-up replay of the changes which had created much more intense hardship in the Europe the colonists had abandoned. In the case of Salem Village, relative rather than absolute deprivation had been enough to engender hostilities which tore a community apart. There were other cross-currents, of course; some of the accused (as in other New England trials earlier) were themselves people who had sunk into poverty from more affluent beginnings, resented it deeply and behaved in a thoroughly obnoxious fashion even to those who helped them. We should also note the oddity that only those who would not confess were condemned to death, the reverse of the normal pattern in European trials. That so many of the accused refused to purchase their lives by a false confession is one of the most remarkable features of the Salem affair, reminding us that Massachusetts Puritanism must not be underestimated, just as it must have reinforced the doubts of the ministers and other critics. Another aspect is the ambiguity of the possessed girls' position, for they had dabbled in forbidden magic themselves, while their fits could just as easily have been interpreted as signs of their own enslavement to the Devil. Accusations against others surely represented a way of displacing guilt and responsibility, while inverting the ill-will which proceeded from within themselves. These factors interacted to produce a lethal cocktail that exploded into one of the most dramatic and famous, as well as the most misunderstood, episodes in American history.

CHAPTER IX

THE WEB OF POWER

Secret powers for good and ill

TO DESCRIBE WITCHCRAFT as being about power is at once true and rather unhelpful. Power is a slippery concept, precisely because of its universality as a central element of all social forms and relationships. Witches allegedly dealt in forbidden power, while suspects certainly suffered at the hands of others more powerful than themselves. In making links with the subject matter of the last chapter, another truism must be invoked, that power and resources are inseparable. Those who possess more resources normally enjoy greater power in consequence, and vice versa. One of the many conceptual inversions which formed part of early modern ideas about witchcraft was to think of it as the weapon of the weak and powerless, those left vulnerable through poverty, isolation, or gender. Although others might succumb to the Devil's wiles through excessive greed or ambition, his natural followers were those at the bottom of the heap, whose resentment and spite were empowered by his aid. In this connection it is interesting to note an apparent coincidence, in at least some areas, between the decline of witchcraft persecution and an increase in charges of arson; setting fire to ricks or barns was another form of secret revenge for the poor, even if there was nothing supernatural about it. Interestingly, such fires (extending to the destruction of whole towns) also seem to have been particularly widespread in Germany between the 1520s and the 1570s, a period when there were few witchcraft trials.[1] Arson, like witchcraft, had a certain utility to beggars and their like, who might need to employ such risky threats to survive at all. In both cases a natural reaction to misfortune was to think of those neighbours or recent vagrants who might bear one a grudge. The mechanism of projected guilt, which has already appeared in several guises, inevitably reinforced the tendency to blame social inferiors in such situations. At the opposite extreme, witchcraft could be invoked to explain success, although this was much rarer in early modern Europe than in some other cultures, or more recent times. Men who boasted of doing better than their neighbours were occasionally accused of being witches, as were women who made too much butter or cheese. What one cannot really tell is whether the occasional trials of this type indicate much more extensive beliefs. It is unlikely that many peasants or artisans would have taken the risk of making open charges against stronger enemies, so it is easy to imagine such rumours circulating widely under cover, but surfacing very rarely.

In some respects witchcraft was conceived of as a form of raw power, which might be dangerous to the user. The witch was often thought, at least by implication, to direct it rather than cause it; the diabolical powders, familiars and similar agencies can all be interpreted this way. Many varieties of counter-magic were supposed to work on the mirror principle, reflecting the evil force back to its source, in the expectation that it might inflict serious harm or even death. Others seemed to envisage that some part of the witch's own essence was involved, so that to trap or attack this would have physical results. Various operations on the bodily waste products of the sufferer might, according to this line of thought, cause acute discomfort, often forcing the witch to appear in person. Here was a network of hidden supernatural connections, along which hostile forces might be transmitted in both directions, the magical counterpart of the everyday social world. Such modes of thought have insidious effects; they allow a kind of translation or exchange between the outer and the inner worlds, in which fantasy is always liable to get the upper hand over fact. Reginald Scot rightly sensed that witchcraft beliefs as a whole were vulnerable to a demonstration of the illusory nature of magic; his *Discoverie of Witchcraft* devoted much of its (considerable) length to exposing the fraudulent tricks of professional magicians, conjurors and Popish priests. Scot went to the extreme of denying that the spirit world inhabited by angels and devils could have any physical effect on material objects or creatures of flesh and blood, drawing a radical divide between matter and spirit. He also reported how some well-known cunning men and women admitted – perhaps on their deathbeds – that they had never been anything but cheats, exploiting the gullibility of their clients. Since they were the key players in the 'magical exchange' model, as operators of the counter-magic which identified and damaged witches, this attack was also shrewdly aimed.

We need not suppose that all those who resorted to the cunning folk were convinced of their powers; many may well have been adopting a 'belt and braces' approach, willing to try anything in the cause of self-protection, on the basis that it could do no harm. The same was no doubt true of the use of sacramentals and other forms of permitted religious magic. The implied vision of the world as permeated by secret forces, some of which at least might only be accessible through forbidden knowledge, was at once widespread and nebulous, capable of great flexibility. Among the forms it took was the notion that women had special abilities within their own sphere, perhaps even connected with the different constitution of their bodies. Although no area of magical power was totally or consistently gendered, large parts of folk medicine and (not surprisingly) love magic tended to become feminine specialities. One can detect signs of a general belief that women possessed a greater sensitivity to many natural processes; the theory of elements and humours provided a convenient way of rationalizing such ideas. This whole way of thinking carried the implication that profitable, dangerous and ambivalent power was potentially available to almost anyone who was prepared to take certain risks. It is easy to see how a diabolical interpretation could be superimposed, but some caution is necessary here. The baffled replies of many of the accused in witchcraft trials leave a strong impression that the normal reaction – even among most members of the elites – was to see such powers as natural and useful. They were only reinterpreted in an unfavourable light when there were particular reasons to suspect the users, which could of course include a failure to produce the promised relief.

State and church, law and order

Political, social and religious power found their highest organized expression through the twin agencies of state and church. Highly traditional in most respects, these were nevertheless undergoing dramatic and far-reaching changes in the age of the great witchcraft trials, so that historians have naturally sought to explain persecution as at least partly resulting from such developments. Grand theories of this type are particularly difficult to handle, because the boundaries are so fluid that the evolution of the state can become virtually synonymous with the historical process as a whole. There may well be a sense in which everything ultimately has some influence on everything else, and society is an aggregate of all the multifarious local phenomena taking place over a certain time-scale. The mere fact that phenomena occur simultaneously, however, does not establish any significant causal patterns. For example, the idea that aggressive, expanding political regimes use the persecution of deviants – witches, heretics, or criminals more generally – to reinforce their authority has considerable plausibility. Yet the historical record shows that there is nothing inevitable about such policies, and that very often governments of this type have proved to be restraining influences on the persecution of specific groups. Local variations are in fact so great that the selective use of evidence can seem to justify almost any theory; only a rigorously comparative approach reveals the flaws in the more sweeping claims.

These variations begin with the relations between states and local societies. Europe had a bewildering variety of political regimes; there were large states with virtually no control over their constituent parts (the Holy Roman Empire), strong monarchies with extensive police powers (Castile), urban oligarchies with well-defended privileges (the Netherlands). In the early sixteenth century all those named were ruled by the same man, Emperor Charles V, with predictably unhappy results. It would be possible to list scores of different patterns, even within a relatively coherent state such as France. While this diversity was very significant, as will emerge in the course of further discussion, a number of generalizations do hold more widely. After a period in the later Middle Ages when city states and smaller principalities had flourished, larger nation states were coming to dominate much of the continent and its affairs. The so-called 'new monarchies' of Spain, France and England set the pace in the sixteenth century. The contemporary statesman and essayist Francis Bacon, in a brilliantly perceptive analysis of factors for change, identified three crucial inventions which had altered the face of the world – gunpowder, printing, and the magnetic compass.[2] Their impact on warfare, administration, ideology, empire and trade was little short of revolutionary, going far to create a new Europe in which state power was both more dynamic and more dangerous than for centuries past. One does not have to accept the relatively crude causality implied here to recognize the deft way Bacon symbolized the forces which were threatening to tear the old world apart. In truth even the greater states of early modern Europe were distinctly ramshackle constructions, whose ambitions far exceeded their real capacities. On the whole they were very bad news for ordinary people, who had to pay oppressive taxation, provide winter quarter for troops, or even be forcibly recruited into their ranks. In France and Spain, at least, the fiscal operations of the state could have disastrous effects on the social and economic life of its subjects, as the rulers obstinately pursued dynastic ambitions they could never realize, while costs spiralled inexorably upwards. Smaller, more local political groupings were usually less oppressive, but also very vulnerable to invasion and exploitation by stronger neighbours.

Despite the new techniques they sometimes adopted, European monarchies were essentially agrarian societies whose internal structures and ideologies remained highly traditional. Kings had to rule through the twin oligarchies of military aristocracies and the church, whose support was always conditional on the bestowing of patronage and the maintenance of privilege. It was a system of self-reinforcing hegemonies, very remote from anything resembling bureaucratic line management. The picture was complicated by the emergence of a powerful group of lawyer-administrators, often purchasers of venal offices, whose dependence on the state did make them valuable agents in extending its power, but they too rapidly became entrenched interest groups with their own priorities. Political thought was dominated by theories of natural order, posited on the basic assumption that stability and hierarchy were the normal, God-given state of affairs. In reality, of course, factionalism and instability were much more typical; these were routinely explained in terms of ambition, envy and treason on the part of individuals or groups, rather than as inevitable features of political life. The parallel with the identification of witches as traitors to the godly commonwealth is obvious, and there must have been some cross-influence here. Monarchs reacted to threats against their authority by further developing a multi-layered and highly symbolic style of rule; the king as God's anointed, military leader, dispenser of justice and cultural exemplar. Lawmaking and law enforcement offered a particularly attractive opportunity to assert their pre-eminence, while pandering to the interests and prejudices of the ruling classes. Faced with a real or imaginary danger of popular insurrection and crime, fuelled by the trends described in the last chapter, governments could reinforce their position by identifying and punishing deviants. Although policing of both cities and countryside remained highly inefficient and unreliable, they did employ a range of ferocious legislation and punishments to make examples of some unlucky individuals. As has already been suggested, across much of Europe capital sentences probably reached an all-time peak in the sixteenth century, aided by a relatively new style of inquisitorial justice in secular courts, until less extreme attitudes gradually developed among lawyers and magistrates.

Witchcraft persecution was plainly an important part of this law-and-order drive, although this does not mean that rulers ever took a deliberate decision to make it so. The whole process was much less conscious, more a case of various interests and ideas coinciding in a complex give-and-take at every level from the national to the local. One reason for tighter law enforcement was anxiety about religious dissidence. The profound impact of the Reformation imposed enormous additional strains on the state as well as the church, going up to the point of full-scale civil war. The programme of religious reform, on both sides of the Protestant-Catholic divide, also helped create visions of a godly state, in which moral and spiritual order was an indispensable part of any successful polity. Persecutions and massacres of heretics were the unpleasant downside of this age of faith, as militant Calvinism clashed with the Catholic counter-Reformation in many parts of Europe. Once again the fears of the 'fifth column', the secret deviants within, were reinforced. New definitions of true Christianity and superstition took root, encouraging campaigns against long established popular forms of religion. Missionaries came to assert that the superstitious and illiterate masses were no better than pagans, harder to convert than the Indians of the New World. Changing attitudes and new legal practices came together to facilitate the prosecution of offenders for victimless crimes. While most witches were supposed to have victims, and indeed were accused by them, the idea that deserting God for the Devil was a capital offence on its own had a role to play in mass trials, based on denunciation of accomplices seen at the sabbat.

It is dangerously easy to build up a 'functionalist' explanation of witchcraft persecution along these lines, in which the state becomes the dynamic agency, labelling and punishing deviants as part of a ruthless drive to enhance its power. After all, many of the supposed witches were ideal scapegoats: isolated, widely disliked and often unproductive figures on the margins of society. When church and state were united in reinforcing hierarchical values, promoting the authority of natural rulers throughout society, down to the basic level of the father within the family, this group of largely female outsiders made an ideal target. The legal pursuit of witches could stand for the general purification of society, while for the local elites who participated it symbolized their membership of the ruling classes, and their rejection of traditional superstition. This kind of logic has an added plausibility, as a historical explanation, because it does offer reasons why different social groups might reasonably have sunk their differences in pursuit of a common enemy. The pattern of self-definition at the expense of 'the other' is a well-attested one, identifiable behind many episodes of persecution in human history. Nevertheless, the facts do not support a general thesis of this kind about the origins and nature of witch-hunting; it appears to be far too simplified and monothematic to do justice to the immense complexity of the local situations. Only in a small minority of cases, and on a very temporary basis, did alliances of this kind develop as the basis for intense persecution. Apart from any other factors, one must doubt whether the necessary degree of ideological uniformity ever existed. However much people wrote and talked about hierarchy and authority, in practice they used such ideas when it suited them and evaded them when it did not. Abstractions of this kind do not in reality have much motivating force. Religious faith was a very different matter, but the demanding new versions of Christianity tended to be highly divisive; for them, in any case, the enemy without primarily took the forms of the heretic and the worldly.

None of the stronger, more centralized states of the early modern period ever undertook a major nationally organized campaign against witches. Spain, France and England all displayed persistently low rates of persecution, both absolutely and in proportion to their populations. Jurists and clerics in all these countries plainly disagreed over the scale and nature of the danger, so that the efforts of relatively isolated zealots to launch purges were routinely frustrated by more sceptical colleagues. None of the monarchs revealed any enthusiasm for such activities, with the somewhat limited exception of James VI and I during the first period of his effective rule in Scotland; his later metamorphosis into a sceptical detector of fraud makes his case even more ambivalent. In these states the overriding concern of the rulers was apparently with the disciplining of lesser jurisdictions, so that procedural irregularities of the kind always associated with witchcraft trials attracted repeated sanctions. It is possible to claim that one of the best signs of a strong monarchy is close control over witchcraft cases, not their use as an ideological prop. For examples of persecution directed from above one has to look at smaller territories. Perhaps the clearest instance is that of Denmark between 1617 and 1625, when King Christian IV took a personal interest in the encouragement of prosecutions under a new ordinance, as part of a more general drive to enforce moral codes. In Jutland at least some 60 per cent of all known cases were concentrated in these few years, although absolute numbers were still in hundreds rather than thousands. The king was apparently influenced by trials in the town of Køge in 1612–13, which saw eleven women put to death; he had one of the accused taken to Copenhagen for further questioning and, like his brother-in-law James VI twenty years earlier, was alarmed by whatever he heard. The appointment of the rigorist Lutheran Hans Poulsen Resen as bishop of Sealand in 1615 was another contributory factor in this brief if intense persecution, although some of the parish clergy seem to have been less enthusiastic.[3]

There are signs that some of the close counsellors of Maximilian I of Bavaria, a devout Catholic prince with ascetic leanings, were keen to step up action against witches in the years around 1600. The duke's father, William V, had already shown the way, reacting to a group of trials beginning in 1587 with an instruction in 1590 to the ducal officials that ordered the use of torture on a wider scale. This was in order 'to save the honour of God, of His beloved saints, and the most venerable sacraments, as well as to avert all manner of temporal hurt and mischief that was visited by this accursed vice, not only upon the bodily well-being of men, but also upon the cherished fruits of our fields'.[4] In 1600 a casual denunciation by a convicted thief was the catalyst for a new assault on witches as the embodiment of vice and delinquency, through the grue-some 'show trial' of the Pappenheimer family, in which the ferocious use of torture produced some spectacular confessions. The brutal elimination of these tinkers and some of their associates, however, proved less than a total success for the persecutors on the ducal council. In part this may have been because the confessions raised great expectations that corroborative evidence would be found, for the accused admitted killing hundreds of people, yet physical traces of these crimes, or even lesser confirmation of them, proved completely elusive.[5] Moreover, Maximilian may have been a bigot, but he was a conscientious bigot, who listened to the advice of his spiritual mentors, and of councillors who were more cautious about the problems of trying suspected witches. Among the former was the leading Jesuit intellectual Adam Tanner, one of several members of his order who were to play a leading part in exposing the cruelty and logical frailty of the trials. For a number of years the duke hesitated, seeming to favour first one policy then another. Across the duchy as a whole, meanwhile, the local elites seem to have blocked any widespread persecution; this may have had more to do with preserving their independent judicial rights than with any hesitation about witchcraft as such. A sustained campaign would have implied such innovations as special ducal commissions, highly unwelcome precedents for wider intervention in local affairs.[6] In such instances it is important to remember that proponents and opponents of persecution almost certainly did not act in a cynical or calculating spirit, whatever their unconscious motivation may have been. Witchcraft was not an isolated phenomenon, and decisions about how to treat it were inextricably mixed up with an intricate set of power relationships.

In contrast to the very low rates of persecution in the Spanish and Italian territories of the Habsburgs, the old Burgundian regions still ruled by the Spanish monarchy experienced several episodes of witchhunting with official support. One reason, ironic in view of popular views of the Inquisition, was that in these regions north of the Alps the Holy Office could not easily override secular courts, so that its relatively enlightened view of the matter was far less influential. Another was that in practice, authority had to be delegated to viceroys or other substitutes who might have views of their own, and would certainly have to reckon with those of the local elites. This affected the Inquisition too, which had difficulty in maintaining authority over individual agents like Father Symard in the Franche-Comté; it was only after some three years that his abusive procedures led to his dismissal in 1660. In the Spanish Netherlands and Luxembourg the semi-independent government of the Archdukes Albert and Isabella was responsible for issuing the ordinances of 1592, 1595 and 1606, whose general tendency was to bring witchcraft within the ambit of a broader counter-Reformation offensive, directed against immorality, superstition and disorder. The Council of State in Brussels did show periodic concern over procedural irregularities, however, and there is no clear evidence that the number of trials increased markedly as a direct result of the ordinances. Local variations over small distances are so great that the most important factor was probably the attitudes of a few key office-holders within each jurisdiction. Another interesting feature of this region was that individual urban trials were more common than elsewhere, carried out as far as can be seen by the town rulers on their own initiative, responding to popular demands. In an area marked by powerful local privileges, and whose loyalty was so crucial, the Council of State was bound to proceed cautiously; the government could be authoritarian, but only when absolutely compelled to such dangerous courses. Only if over-zealous persecution threatened more general disorder was this likely to happen, as it did over the possession scandals of the 1610s. Here it is significant that convents patronized by influential families were involved, which enabled highly-placed opponents to invoke the danger that an epidemic would spread through all religious houses as a reason for greater caution and scepticism.

Any map of the relative intensity of persecution would show a dark ribbon stretching some fifty to one-hundred miles on each side of the Rhine, running from Switzerland to the Spanish Netherlands, in which over half the known trials took place. This corridor was well-known to early modern statesmen for other reasons; it was an unstable region of small states, the source of numerous wars and international crises, and the site of the so-called 'Spanish Road'. The vital artery of Habsburg power, the overland route running between the Alpine passes and the Netherlands, played a key role in the conflicts between the 1560s and the 1630s, exactly coterminous with the peak decades of witchcraft persecution. The temptation to see a direct link between these phenomena is great, but probably ought to be resisted. It was precisely because the states and territories between the scattered Habsburg possessions were weak that the game of protection, threats and bribery was played out with such intensity there by bigger European rivals. The region was a chaotic patchwork of divided sovereignties, where frontiers rarely had a clear meaning and small enclaves were more the rule than the exception. Religious division was also the order of the day, with Protestants often ruling Catholics and vice versa, but this too may not have been as important as one would expect. Only in the 1620s, as the imperial armies advanced northwards and Catholic reconquest briefly seemed a real possibility, did confessionalism play a leading role in any but isolated cases. The prince-bishops who earned themselves permanent obloquy by sponsoring intensive torture-based witch-hunts were enthusiasts for the militant counter-Reformation; plainly they had been drawn into a policy of exterminating witches as part of a more general drive against heresy. Yet the majority of ecclesiastical rulers who shared this general religious and political attitude failed to follow their lead, so there was no necessary association here; it appears to be a latent tendency which was only activated in some cases. The underlying intellectual basis may well have been a reaction against the official Lutheran position, with its emphasis on the overweening power of divine providence, and consequent picture

of witches as merely deluded believers in the power they supposed themselves to possess. The notion that Protestants were soft on witchcraft,
combined with a desire to defend more traditional views of the relationship between man and God, would account for a trend towards greater
harshness in handling witchcraft accusations on the part of some
Catholics.

The end of the great trials of 1627–31 in this region has often been
attributed to a particularly direct intervention of state power, in the form
of the advance of the Swedish armies under King Gustav Adolf. On
closer examination this proves to be substantially false. In most cases the
trials stopped well before the Swedes arrived, through a familiar process
which saw local doubts build up until the persecution suffered a kind of
internal collapse. Nevertheless, the great victory at Breitenfeld (September 1631) totally reversed the previous trend of the Thirty Years'
War, driving most of the Catholic rulers out of the Rhineland and
neighbouring territories. The terrible hardships which followed were all
too plainly the result of war and military occupation to be plausibly
blamed on the Devil and his witches. Although there were ways, as
we shall see, in which these circumstances could be incorporated into
witchcraft charges, continued mass persecutions were probably rendered
virtually impossible by the events of the wars. In a similar fashion, French
occupation of Lorraine and parts of Alsace has often been credited with
ending the widespread if more diffuse trials previously found in these
territories. Here too the evidence is highly ambiguous; persecution seems
to have been slackening already in the 1620s, and total disruption of
ordinary life from the early 1630s is likely to have been the most important factor in accelerating the decline. There is no sign of a coherent or
conscious attitude on the part of the occupying power, which relied
heavily on local collaborators in any case.[7] Here as elsewhere the mechanisms of the state were potentially available to individuals or groups who
wanted action in relation to witchcraft, but such possibilities were not
often realized on a general scale. Groups or individuals did on occasion
exploit them, to push for either the extermination of witches or tight
control on the local abuses perpetrated by witch-hunters. Until the
late seventeenth century, when the latter attitude came to prevail
widely, neither policy was applied more than sporadically – and often
ineffectively.

This was connected with the embarrassing fact that the grandiose
claims made for royal justice were often nothing but a sham. No early

modern state could afford the expense necessary for a truly effective centralized system of law enforcement, which would in any event have been completely foreign to the received ideas of the time. The best that could be achieved was an arrangement of checks and balances, in which sophisticated royal judges oversaw the operation of local courts, through such devices as obligatory consultations or an appeal system for serious offences. In their different ways the major states had taken this process unusually far, which does much to explain the modest rates of persecution they experienced. Over much of Europe, courts were largely staffed by lay judges, men who sat there because of their political standing in the community but possessed no legal training as such. In smaller towns and rural communities many of them may have been illiterate. Until the late Middle Ages, justice had essentially been adversarial, the hearing of disputes between two parties, so that crimes were only taken to court at the behest of the victims or their families. Since the aim was to maintain the peace, settlement rather than punishment was the rule, and the parties normally came to an agreement mediated by the court. This tradition of arbitration remained immensely strong, but was being overlaid by the development of what was generally known as inquisitorial procedure. Certain types of case were now taken over by official prosecutors, even when there was a complainant; witnesses and the accused were questioned, and if a *prima facie* case was made out torture could be employed. Very often the lay judges seem to have done nothing more than rubber-stamp the actions of the prosecutors. This untidy combination of old and new styles opened the way to the very harsh criminal justice of the sixteenth century, which was backed up by new law codes such as the German *Carolina* (1532) or the French ordinance of Villers-Cotterets (1539). A whole range of crimes was now reclassified in terms of offences against the social order and the state; since imprisonment was hardly practicable, death, whipping, or banishment were the standard punishments. Fortunately the practice was a good deal less severe than the theory; implementation was predictably sporadic and variable, not least because the prosecutors soon felt themselves to be underpaid and overworked. Much of the time it amounted to little more than the random making of examples, often separated by periods of inactivity. The absence of effective police forces made this virtually inevitable; it also ensured that the courts would spend much of their time regulating what amounted to a vigilante system, with all its sinister implications. Awareness of such dangers was a major factor in determining the everyday handling of criminal cases by the higher courts, whose judges were in general more intelligent and fair-minded than later critics have allowed.

Courts and judges

As usual, a favourable assessment like this one needs to be balanced against a multiplicity of contrary examples. Judges were quirky and unreliable; the same court or legal faculty would appear to change its attitudes unpredictably from one case to the next. There are plenty of modern examples to remind us that the legal process is always liable to the most bizarre irrationality and disregard for its own proclaimed rules. A strong impression from many trials is of the insouciance and careless-ness displayed by the persecutors, who twisted arguments to suit their whim. The dangers of judicial torture were well known, so there was a standard requirement for free reiteration of confessions later, yet attempts to recant at this stage were routinely brushed aside. Although those who employed sleep deprivation apparently knew about its hallucinatory effects, rambling accounts obtained in this fashion often became the basis for convictions. There was also a fundamental internal absurdity; torture was meant to elicit confessions of details which only the true criminal could know and which might then be verified. Since witches confessed to secret dealings which could hardly ever be checked, while everyone knew what they were supposed to do, standard rules of proof had to be disregarded in their case. This was the basis for the classification of witchcraft as a *Crimen Exceptum*, so that uncorroborated confessions were enough for a capital sentence, while normally ineligible witnesses might be heard.[8] It is hard to avoid the sense that many judges, as well-educated members of the social elite, felt a certain contempt for the humble folk they were dealing with. At the insistence of the two judges concerned, their clerk Thomas Potts wrote a lengthy account of the Lancaster trials of 1612. Sir Edward Bromley told five of the accused who had been acquitted by the jury:

> presume no further of your Innocence than you have just cause: for although it pleased God out of his Mercy, to spare you at this time, yet without question there are amongst you, that are as deep in this Action, as any of them that are condemned to die for their offences: The time is

now for you to forsake the Devil: Remember how, and in what sort he hath dealt with all of you: make good use of this great mercy and favour: and pray unto God you fall not again: For great is your happiness to have time in this World, to prepare yourselves against the day when you shall appear before the Great Judge of all.[9]

He was evidently happy to see this egregious display of bullying and self-satisfaction preserved in print. Potts, for whom the judge could manifestly do no wrong, made much of his astuteness in detecting the frauds of Grace Sowerbutts, supposedly instigated by 'one Thompson a Seminary Priest', and securing the acquittal of three women she accused:

> But here as his Lordship's care and pains was great to discover the practises of those odious Witches of the Forest of Pendle, and other places, now upon their trial before him: So was he desirous to discover this damnable practise, to accuse these poor Women, and bring their lives in danger, and thereby to deliver the innocent.

To emphasize the point, he ridiculed the flimsiness of the evidence brought in this case, which was precisely the same in character as that regarded as damning against the other accused.[10] It is easy to see why Christina Larner, dealing with similar evidence, pithily described Scottish witch-hunting as 'savage, random, and inefficient.'[11]

Changes in procedure and the severe treatment of deviants clearly reflected external pressures as much as the internal evolution of the legal system. They were in large part a response to the growing social tensions of the sixteenth century, discussed in the previous chapter, as the ruling classes became seriously alarmed about popular unrest and criminality. This is made plain by the parallel trends in England, despite the peculiarity of its legal structures based on common law, circulating assize judges and the various forms of jury. Of course this system ensured massive input from the laity, since nearly all the crucial decisions were taken by juries; it also avoided the need for routinized torture, since convictions could be obtained without a confession. That these very different arrangements produced such similar results to those on the Continent is an important reminder of how flexible the rules tended to be in practice. Law was fashioned by the powerful to suit themselves, a process in which many groups might share, down to the most local level. This opened the way for appalling abuses, but also for unexpected progress. One of the more remarkable developments of the period is in fact that of higher abstract standards, better jurisprudence and a concern for procedural rigour. By the middle decades of the seventeenth century, these trends were actually having a distinctly beneficial effect, in the sense of moderating earlier excesses; they played a very large part in ending large-scale persecution of witches. Even judicial torture was increasingly disfavoured, and much better controlled where it survived. Although justice hardly became above reproach, there was a sense in which the excesses of a period of rapid change were gradually recognized and tamed. In England from the 1620s at least the combined efforts of monarch, privy council, judges and grand juries worked to this end. The French *parlements* had been unusually critical from the start, so that it is odd to find France constantly cited as the scene of extensive witch-hunting; many scholars do not seem to have understood that neither the modern department of the Nord, nor the large regions of Lorraine and Franche-Comté, were within the kingdom of France at the relevant dates. In New England it is standard form from the start to find local juries presenting charges, only to have them dismissed by the magistrates and ministers. In the case of Mercy Disborough of Fairfield, Connecticut, convicted by a jury in 1692 only to be cleared by a special committee of magistrates, there was a remarkable declaration of elite scepticism. The committee pointed out that there was no confession, nor testimony showing the accused to have done anything impossible without help from the Devil. What was left was merely 'the common things of spectral evidence, ill events after quarrels and threats, teats, water trials, and the like, with suspicious words – all of which are discarded, and some of them abominated, by the most judicious as to be convictive of witchcraft'. The blunt conclusion was 'Those that will make witchcraft of such things will make hanging work apace'.[12]

A good deal of the activity of local courts was below the notice of any professional; minor actions for breaches of economic regulations, petty theft, boundary disputes and so forth. Small fines, restitution and agreed settlements were the normal outcome. On occasion it is possible to link such cases with witchcraft, when they reveal a back history of conflict which illuminates later accusations. By far the most important connection is through the numerous slander cases, for these predictably show that 'witch' was one of the commonest insults thrown against women. Offenders normally got off with a retraction and a small fine, but of course the crucial aspect was the public acknowledgement that the charge was false. Court records do bear out the claim by some accused witches that poverty discouraged them from seeking formal redress in this way; those who could not prove their case usually had to pay the standard fine themselves, and it was not easy to find witnesses prepared to testify. There is little doubt that official records of this kind are merely the tip of an iceberg, for there are many references to less formal methods through which similar arbitration was sought, and courts were just part of a much wider range of agencies whose aim was to maintain communal harmony. To judge from the number of occasions when offenders reappeared on similar charges this was something of a vain hope, but one should not underestimate the extent to which animosities were kept within bounds. At the same time there is no mistaking the manner in which matters were class-biased, for courts had little real power to enforce their decisions on the dominant members of the community, while informal arbitration was non-binding almost by definition. Richer peasants and bourgeoisie, the men who usually ran these petty jurisdictions, were fairly evidently predisposed in favour of their own group against the poor. One Lorraine witch, Zabel de Sambois of Moriviller, who was suspected by the village mayor, agreed to a formal reconciliation and request for his pardon. This was at the persuasion of the *curé*, who told her bluntly 'that the poor should give way to the rich'. When on trial she burst out with a denunciation of the false charges against her, 'all of it through envy and ill will, for the poor people are always treated like this, and if all the doings of the mayor Galand were known he would not be much better thought of than she was'.[13] Unfairness of this type was inevitable, and just as obvious in decisions taken by higher courts on matters affecting landlords and tenants, for example; it is no surprise that peasants routinely expressed hatred for lawyers as greedy agents of oppression. Slander cases had another aspect, for it was always possible for the defendant to claim fair comment, so that a certain (admittedly small) proportion of witchcraft trials actually began in this way, when the attempt to deter an accuser backfired disastrously.

The atypical case of England excepted, no European state had progressed far towards full-scale replacement of older jurisdictions, whether feudal or not. Such control as was achieved was by the superimposition of additional layers on what was already a dauntingly complex mosaic of interlocking, often disputed rights. The process was most successful where litigants themselves saw advantages in royal justice, or where (as with some aspects of criminal justice) the lords found independent rights more of a nuisance and expense than they were worth. This shift was aided by the new law codes, with their demands for costly procedural innovations and tighter supervision by superior courts. Various models were available for altering the relations between levels of the system. The most far-reaching, adopted in France, restricted the hearing of certain crimes to higher courts, while imposing extensive rights of appeal. Disquiet about procedural irregularities in witchcraft trials led to an intensification of the appeal regulations in this specific instance. As early as 1588 the Paris *parlement* considered instituting an *automatic* appeal procedure, under which all those convicted of witchcraft were sent to Paris for a second hearing, and this was finally installed in 1624, soon to be imitated by several regional *parlements*. The hanging of three local judges for the murder of a suspect in 1641 was only the most spectacular of many disciplinary measures against local abuses. The danger of punishment for illegal procedure, the expense of sending suspects to Paris and the regularity with which sentences were annulled or reduced must all have contributed to a sharp decline in the activities of lesser courts. The motivating force behind this policy had nothing to do with the royal government as such; it derived from the existence of a proud and self-assertive group of venal office-holders, who associated their own prestige with the imposition of rationality and order on ignorant, superstitious provincials. By 1640, thirty years before the crown decided to enforce such rules nationally, this attitude had created a situation in which, for half the French population at least, it was impossible to be legally sentenced to death as a witch. The Parisian judges did not deny the possibility of witchcraft; they had simply concluded that satisfactory proof of such crimes was impossible, and that most accusations were malicious. Where the evidence seemed unusually strong they resorted to banishment, which had the incidental advantage of preventing the lynchings that were still a real danger.[14] Of course this centralized system could work the other way if a *parlement* – like that of Rouen – displayed an obstinate determination to convict witches. This must have encouraged the outbreak of prosecutions in Normandy in 1670–2, which led Louis XIV and his minister Colbert to enforce the Parisian jurisprudence on a national scale.[15] It should also be noted that Denmark had brought in the automatic appeal system as early as 1576; this evidently helped to discourage persecution in general, and may have limited the number of convictions even when Christian IV launched his campaign after 1617.[16]

In Spain and parts of Italy the Inquisition played a similar role to the French royal courts, maintaining continual pressure on other jurisdictions, and claiming an effective monopoly over witchcraft trials. While this was not always successful, the overall effect was clearly to inhibit local abuses and discourage large-scale persecution. Instead of an appeal system, this was an assertion of the right to control proceedings from start to finish. Within the inquisitorial structure, however, the *Suprema* in Madrid was able to exercise fairly effective discipline over the local tribunals, as the famous Logroño affair in the Basque country demonstrated. Elsewhere in Europe, weaker central authorities found it impossible – or at least unwise – to take such a tough line with their subjects. A typical middle way can be seen in Lorraine, where from 1569 the dukes had managed a rather timid degree of standardization, by requiring all local courts to consult the central tribunal in Nancy in serious cases. At each stage of the procedure the documents were sent up to the capital for approval, so that arrest, torture and final sentence were all separately overseen by the experienced ducal lawyers. Occasional reprimands were handed down, and orders to release suspects or treat them leniently were usually followed, yet when the courts of first instance disregarded the advice given (always in the direction of greater severity) nothing effective was ever done. In the Holy Roman Empire generally, the *Carolina* was only approved by the German princes and cities with a saving clause giving priority to local custom, so that it was consultative rather than compulsory. However, its final section (article 219) was enormously influential in establishing what became an accepted rule, that lay courts should seek expert advice, preferably from a university law faculty. The resulting *consilia* played a vital role in mediating the application of the law. They were of course very diverse, reflecting the differing opinions between faculties, and among their individual members. After about 1650 a clear trend did finally become apparent, as a new generation of German legists displayed much greater caution and scepticism; this confirmed the simultaneous shift of opinion perceptible among princes and city rulers.

The potential for manipulating the system of consultation can be illustrated from numerous cases. The small Protestant city of Esslingen in south-west Germany had known only a handful of cases, most of them resulting in acquittals, until a belated persecution between 1662 and 1665, largely concentrated in two rural communities, produced seventy-two trials and thirty-seven executions. The moving spirit was undoubtedly the young town advocate, Daniel Hauff, whose premature death brought about the end of the trials. At the outset a consultation of his own university of Tübingen dismissed the confessions of the key suspect as melancholic delusions; Hauff then turned to Strasbourg, to obtain an opinion which allowed him to execute the youth concerned. When a subsequent request for torture was rejected by the Strasbourg jurists, their colleagues in the rather obscure faculty of Altdorf proved more obliging. Even so, Hauff's dubious tactics were not totally successful, for resistance mounted in the case of some children who had confessed, so that a combination of local opposition and unfavourable *consilia* imposed a more merciful attitude. By this stage it was only the advocate's obstinacy which kept the trials going at all, in a case which shows yet again how a well-placed individual could turn personal obsessions (in this instance homosexuality, bestiality and adolescent sexuality more generally) into a persecution most of his compatriots evidently distrusted from the start.[17] It was in such instances that the indirect approach taken by many among the elites revealed its weakness. So long as the theoretical basis of witchcraft charges went unchallenged, greater procedural rigour was only a partial barrier to persecution, and an individual zealot who was also a skilled legal operator might prove very difficult to stop. A rather different scenario prevailed in another town in the same region, Balingen, after a devastating fire in 1672. The people blamed three witches, and the magistrates were dismayed when Tübingen ruled that the suspects could not be tortured, fearing they would be lynched and the magistrates themselves would be in danger. They begged the Stuttgart Superior Council 'in order that we might give the vulgar a sop and silence their mouths', that they be allowed 'to consult a different faculty, like Strasbourg, since it is well known the legal faculty of Tübingen is much too lenient in criminal matters and especially in *delictis occultis* and are always inclined to the more gentle'. The request was granted, but the chief suspect would not confess under torture, and was killed by stoning when on her way to banishment.[18] Rather similar events in Calw in 1683 caused the Stuttgart authorities to send in troops to keep order.[19] One should be careful not to assume a linear progress towards enlightenment, however, since in the early eighteenth century the Tübingen faculty actually seems to have hardened its attitude towards the isolated cases which still came before it.[20]

Local communities at the heart of persecution

From these examples, and much else that has been said, it will be evident that justice was not simply imposed from above. There was a complex process of negotiation, involving virtually all social levels, which allowed a great deal of power to those lower down the scale. However ferocious a drive towards social control the state and its lawyers tried to mount (if there ever was a clear intent of this kind), it was almost wholly dependent on ordinary people for the denunciations without which it would be completely toothless. There was a very real sense in which the system was demand-led, so that official measures against witchcraft often prove to have been responses to pressure from below. In so far as the expansion of justice was a means for the state to increase its power, this could only be achieved by offering something more attractive to the users than the alternatives available from lords and other holders of intermediate rights. It is also crucial to realize that while efficient bureaucracy was still in its infancy, local government was in most respects the dominant feature in ordinary people's lives. Village communities, in particular, were complex structures which retained some remarkably democratic features; across much of Europe many crucial decisions were vested in the general meetings of householders which were the fundamental expression of communality. These assemblies, which regulated multiple details of social and economic life and elected to various posts, were not however composed of equals. Beneath a surface appearance of democracy there was an oligarchic deep structure, which reflected the economic dominance of the small minority of rich peasants. Their monopoly of crucial positions as agents of the state, the church and the lords further entrenched their power, allowing them to manipulate the collection of taxes, rents and tithes, and manage property on behalf of absentee landlords. Many smaller peasants depended on wealthier neighbours for credit, and for the paid work which was essential to their survival. As was explained in the last chapter, in many regions the sixteenth century saw a drastic widening of the gap between this peasant elite and the rest, so that movement into the ruling group became rare and difficult as it hardened into a hereditary class. The effect on village meetings was predictable; under normal circumstances the dependent majority no longer dared to challenge the oligarchy, and many lesser peasants did not even bother to attend.

Dominant families employed quite elaborate strategies for ensuring their long-term survival. Informal understandings between themselves prevented too much competition for leases, so that the lords were unable to force up rents. Younger sons normally moved sideways, into trade or office in the towns, or into comfortable positions in the church. These processes helped to integrate the upper peasantry into the ruling classes more generally, building up political and cultural ties between members of the key groups at the interface where privilege, wealth and education met various forms of deprivation. If there was to be a general reinforcement of patriarchal authority through the imposition of economic, social and religious discipline, then the heads of such households would have a vital role to play. Local implementation was unthinkable without their co-operation, which must require not just advantages for them, but the development of new attitudes on their part. Some historians have seen the more personalized, morally demanding religion, arguably propagated by Catholic reformers as much as by Protestants, as the ideological counterpart of the state's demand for order. Both allegedly formed part of a process of acculturation, a cultural offensive designed to impose the values of the ruling minorities throughout society, while destroying the diverse local practices of village culture. These latter were now associated with popular ignorance, superstition and rebellion. The peasant oligarchs were drawn into aping their social superiors, displaying an exaggerated hostility to older beliefs, partly at least because they felt guilt at their own ambivalence towards these. When they managed the prosecutions of poorer neighbours as witches, or appeared as witnesses against them, they were underlining their own allegiance to a new set of values.[21]

This is an interesting hypothesis, which would explain rising concern with witchcraft as one expression of a fundamental social change. There are certainly some cases in which motivations of this kind seem to have played a large part, so that they must be reckoned among the numerous elements which might either spark or sustain a persecution. Overall, however, the evidence does not give much support to a broad-brush theory of this nature. Social and political changes across Europe were a good deal more diverse and localized than would be necessary to sustain such claims. While the mass of the peasantry throughout most of the continent were indeed pauperized, no uniform pattern of domination resulted. In some areas the lords, or townsmen acting as their agents, took control; in England and parts of the Netherlands there was a transition towards recognizably modern forms of tenant farming. The decisive objection, however, is that close analysis of witchcraft trials simply does not bear out the claim that the wealthy peasants routinely exercised decisive influence over them. Their participation appears far too patchy and sporadic, and while one cannot rule out the possibility of hidden power struggles, these need not conform to the scheme of dominance being reinforced. The rare example of Salem Village, where exceptionally good information (and great historical ingenuity) does allow us to decode such a struggle, is a case in point. Here it was families in decline who resorted to witchcraft accusations, in what finally proved a vain attempt to defy the forces of social change. This does seem far more psychologically convincing than the idea that the winners should manipulate trials in order to buttress a position which was hardly in danger. They might feel threatened as individuals, of course, when aware of the resentment and ill-will of their inferiors, so that a specific misfortune might easily be attributed to witchcraft – but in so doing it was traditional beliefs which were being invoked, rather than new ones. More generally one can accept that some representation of the ruling groups in local society among those hostile to the suspect was an important factor in bringing about a formal trial, but this is merely a predictable reflection of the power structure as a whole.

Village committees and witch-hunters; the Saarland and Germany

Another fascinating example of how local political structures could inter-act with witchcraft persecution is to be found along the western fringes of Germany, in and around the Saarland. Some parts of the region were ruled by the duke of Lorraine, but for the most part it was under the rather distant and ineffective suzerainty of the ecclesiastical Electors of Mainz and Trier, or a variety of other absentee overlords. The complexities of shared local jurisdiction, which were always liable to generate disputes between lords, added to their difficulties in imposing control. Much of the time the rulers or their local agents seem to have gone along with the tide of local opinion, merely trying to canalize it through the formal legal procedures. This was a region with strong traditions of local self-government; it was also one undergoing the typical processes of concentration of land and wealth, but in which these had not yet eliminated middling peasants. Wine-producing areas usually tended to be less socially stratified in any case, and it was in the villages around Trier that a very potent form of village organization made its strength felt during the major persecution of 1587–94, which claimed at least 500 victims. This was the special village committee, elected at a general meeting of the community to take charge of action against suspected witches. A long sequence of bad harvests in the 1580s and 1590s provided the crucial spur for such action; shared disasters of this kind whipped up general feeling, and the mythology of the sabbat made it easy to blame them on a diabolical conspiracy of witches. Once the committees had emerged to such effect they were rapidly imitated in surrounding territories, where demands for their institution became widespread. These were not always welcome to the rulers, but only the dukes of Lorraine – who were quite willing to sanction persecution provided it was through orthodox channels – seem to have been consistently able to prevent them taking charge of matters.[22]

Village committees of this type – which had made occasional appearances at least as early as the 1550s – naturally claimed to represent communal solidarity, with everyone united in demanding persecution. The meetings at which they were set up seem often to have been excited affairs, where it would have been very hard for anyone to stand up against popular feeling; this was sometimes expressed by making the new committee members swear an oath on a knife.[23] Although the local elite participated, and up to a point continued to dominate as members of the committees, the situation was potentially dangerous for them. Membership of the committee gave some protection against accusation, but this was far from absolute. The process allowed men just below the top rank, those who were not court jurors or similar office-holders, to assert themselves. In some cases there are signs of political tensions beneath the surface, as one might expect. Whereas in the earlier trials, most of the accused seem to have conformed to the normal pattern (individuals with long reputations drawn from the poorer groups), by the 1630s wealthier peasants were coming to make up a significant element among the victims. While they were still a small minority, in proportion to their numbers they were actually now more at risk than others. It looks as if the mechanism was taking on a new significance and a life of its own, as a way of settling local scores, and for some individuals to displace others in terms of wealth, status and power. In 1592 the distinguished theologian Cornelius Loos, an eyewitness of the

Trier persecution, had written of his fears that 'innocent lives are taken, and by a new alchemy gold and silver coined from human blood.' Loos himself had his manuscript seized, was forced into a public recantation of his critical views, then exiled.[24] He was certainly right to identify economic factors as an important element in the trials, although this does not mean that they were primarily driven by a desire for gain. It was more a case of opportunities for profiteering and personal advancement riding on the back of a typical persecution, initially motivated by fear, then encouraged by an amalgam of popular and elite beliefs.

Money can never have been far from the minds of those involved, because costs were often very high in this region. The effects of this were ambiguous, because villages were liable for the costs if confiscations from those convicted were inadequate to meet them; a witch-hunting spree might create debts which would burden a community for decades. Lorraine was again a contrast here, because the ducal authorities managed to keep costs far lower – perhaps only a third of the typical rate elsewhere in the Saarland – yet the rate of persecution was very similar. Overall there is no reason to suppose that legal profiteering was *the* explanation for persecution. On the other hand, it must take its place among those factors which could facilitate trials, helping to break down normal restraints and encouraging certain individuals. While it is possible to formulate a purely cynical and materialistic interpretation, this is not really plausible; even greedy witch-hunters probably convinced themselves that they were doing holy work, producing a typical amalgam of idealism and self-interest. Committees had an important role in relation to costs, because they could effectively become a taxing device for funding trials. They also put constant pressure on the authorities to change the basis on which confiscations were operated, taking advantage of the loopholes whereby local custom might modify the rules laid down in the *Carolina*. Those acquitted might still be required to pay costs, spouses be made liable for one another's costs, or the rich surcharged to make up the shortfall incurred in cases involving the poor – this last a kind of inverted communal solidarity applied to the imagined diabolical community. Gradually a system developed under which trials might be self-financing, leading to the confiscation of large assets. Over time the position of the accused was steadily eroded, particularly in the period of the Thirty Years' War, when the lords virtually surrendered control to the localities. In practice this does not seem to have produced more trials; the impact of the war more generally may have been a factor here, together with the legacy of previous actions that had proved very expensive to the villagers, and the success of the local elites in keeping control in most places.

Where the committees did operate, however, they proved highly dangerous. They were very efficient in spreading rumours, collecting witnesses and manipulating denunciations. Frequently they also established an effective alliance with local officials, another way of evading central control by appropriating its own agencies. While shared beliefs and family ties are probably more significant reasons for this complicity than direct economic motives, events such as the lavish dinners held to mark the end of trials – in part a celebration of supposedly restored local harmony – helped cement these links. Many other people gained something from the bustle of activity surrounding trials and executions; those who provided facilities such as transport and valuations, the clergy who officiated and so on. They also provided handsome pickings for local innkeepers, a group with considerable potential influence where rumour and gossip were concerned. Committee members themselves were the most potent operators of all, for they, their associates and their relatives went out seeking additional testimony. Poorer people were recruited to make statements about typical sequences of quarrels followed by losses of animals, illnesses and so forth. Those who had overheard quarrels were sometimes coerced into making unwilling statements about them – their reluctance is enshrined in the court records. The families of those already accused or executed were also put under pressure to demonstrate their own innocence and good behaviour by participating. There was an obvious danger that anyone who stood out against the trials would be a target for accusations, as the committees reshaped the structures of power in the villages. It became impossible, or at least highly dangerous, to bring slander cases, while censures against irresponsible witch-hunters by priests and pastors became ineffective.

These processes never became general, even in the Saarland; moreover, they carried the seeds of their own eventual destruction. The threat to the authority of the lords was too evident, and likely to provoke a reaction once circumstances changed. Committees and local officials were all too prone to perpetrate abuses, using excessive torture, denying legal rights, or manipulating confessions and accusations, for example. A growing body of legal and clerical opinion stigmatized such irregularities, and found increasing sympathy among the rulers themselves. Richer peasants who found themselves or their relatives accused were liable to put up a stern fight, making their grievances known to outside authority.[25] In the end, witchcraft accusations, for all their terrifying potential as agencies of ambition and revenge, were open to challenge on too many fronts to sustain such a high profile as agencies of social conflict. Nevertheless, there are some individual cases which demonstrate how matters could go in favourable circumstances. Between 1640 and 1660 the village of Winningen was virtually torn apart by a sequence of trials and threats, whose outcome radically changed the internal balance of power. Here nine of the twenty-four accused came from the top level of local society, and another four were related to them – most of these were very prosperous. It is apparent that the hegemony of the richer peasants, who held office as jurors, was being assailed by a group of younger men of only middling fortunes; the reasons for this are clearly of the greatest interest.

The climax of the first wave of trials in 1642–3 saw three wives of jurors executed. One of the husbands, Dietrich Siegbert, expressed his hostility to the committee through complaints to the authorities. There are signs that the persecutors were frightened, and sought to obtain accusations against Siegbert and the Mölich family (his relatives by marriage), partly by suborning those who confessed to name them as accomplices. This proved a slow business, for they only dared move formally when they had enough evidence to ensure the ability to torture suspects. Hans Wilhelm Mölich was finally brought to trial in 1652, forced into confessing, and executed. At an early stage the local Protestant curate had defended him in a sermon against the witch-hunters; there were threats that the curate's wife would be accused, but he had influential protectors who moved him elsewhere. When Friedrich Mölich was tried in 1659 he resisted the torture, then appealed to outside authorities for rehabilitation and a reduction in the costs charged. Although his apparent victory was largely negated by procedural difficulties, the heavy costs and intense legal battle not only discouraged his opponents, they also stimulated a successful drive to reassert central control. Winningen also saw a conflict between the different lines of the Kröber family; those descended from Peter Kröber had been much more successful in economic and political terms than the brothers Hans and Thonges Kröber, who were struggling to remain on the margins of the elite. Hans became a committee member, while Thonges was a frequent witness; it was the latter who, in October 1640, blamed damage to the vines on Catherina Knebel, whom he called a witch in public. It was this attempt to find a scapegoat for a communal misfortune which led to the formation of a committee. Between 1642 and 1653 all the four children of Peter Kröber had their partners (three wives, one husband) executed as witches, alongside some other relatives by marriage. As at Salem, it looks as if family hostilities were displaced on to surrogates; there was a tendency for wives to become involved in their husbands' quarrels, with potentially disastrous results. Hans Kröber was resentful towards others as well. His younger colleague on the first witchcraft committee, Hans Richard Münden, became a juror before Kröber, only to find that their previous alliance was broken, and to see his wife and mother-in-law executed. The pattern which emerges generally is that of a struggle between the old elite and a group of younger men in their thirties, the latter, initially at least, with good reason to feel insecure about their futures. Another source of resentment may have been the fact that many jurors were also church elders, whose claim to exert moral control over the lives of others could easily cause anger, tempting those they criticized to seek revenge by describing them and their wives as witches.[26]

Interpretations of this type are bound to remain conjectural to some extent. Apart from one or two statements by threatened members of the elite, who expressed fears that they were being victimized through envy, direct proof is naturally lacking. The most that can be said is that there does seem to be a coherent pattern to the accusations that suggests that the identification of witches was stage-managed on occasions, and that those concerned had plausible motives for such conduct. There was particular disquiet about the way those who had already confessed might be pressurized into naming others allegedly seen at the sabbat, which could well imply a degree of complicity between gaolers, executioners and committees. One of the most dangerous features of the situation was the way highly flexible beliefs in witchcraft enabled those involved to project their own resentments and hatreds into their victims. In their own self-image the persecution could then become a godly enterprise, aimed at the elimination of evil people and the rescue of their souls from the Devil. One might almost think of the accusers as sleep-walking their way through their odious conduct, largely unaware of their own motivation, and sustained by a shared rhetoric. This might extend to quite unfounded claims that everyone was united in the demand for persecution, when no such communal solidarity truly existed. Once trials and executions had taken place, those who had manipulated the process needed to protect themselves against relatives or other families that had become mortal enemies; such behaviour was not necessarily cynical, given popular beliefs and the way resentment was expected to work. As so often, there was a typical mixture of idealistic and materialistic motivation in evidence. The existence of such committees also allowed those whose attempts at magical cures failed to try the alternative method of seeking relief through justice.

Another feature of the Winningen trials is the slowness with which the tragedy unfolded, little groups of trials being followed by quieter periods during which rumours accumulated. There were some structural reasons for this; a blanket proscription of the ruling elite would have been practically and psychologically almost impossible. Both the participants and outside authorities would have been brought face-to-face with the underlying reality, which might be either ignored or concealed so long as only a few examples were made in each round. Moreover the victims would have been driven into determined collective action in their own defence, whereas as matters stood they were tempted to isolate themselves from the selected individuals. Some of the complexities emerge from an incident in 1649, when there was an attempt to renew the prosecution of the wife of Martin Schop, first accused in 1644. The family had since moved to Coblenz, and Schop reacted by threatening legal action against their persecutors. The local Amtmann, apparently fearing a scandal, chose to slow the procedure down until it died a natural death.[27] Reopening this case was plainly not a functional action, since the suspected family has already been forced out of the village, so it was easier to halt it in this way. On the other hand, that it was made at all suggests that witchcraft itself was experienced as a very real danger; individuals were feared as witches, not just as economic or social rivals. It was in selecting the suspects that these other factors operated, and when the more prosperous were often the targets there are grounds for identifying the same conflict between individualism and traditional solidarities as can be detected in England and her American colonies.

How exceptional was Winningen? Until comparable village studies have been made on a wider scale it is hard to say for sure, but current evidence would suggest that it was an extreme case. Attention has already been drawn to the numbers of richer peasants among the men accused in the Saarland, and the signs that this was a trend towards the 1640s, which suggest that had central control not been restored there would have been more such episodes when members of the elite were accused. On the other hand, the absolute figures are quite small, and the vast majority of those tried throughout the period were relatively or absolutely poor. In one nearby village, Kastellaun, there is also evidence for social divisions; here the persecutors have been identified as a group of immigrant artisans – smiths, coopers and the like – who felt disadvantaged by local rules favouring established families. Here, there was a further alarming threat to use stories from children about adults they had seen at the sabbat, which produced strong reactions from the accused and their families and seems to have been headed off.[28] The experiences of the war years may also have sharpened resentment of the elites, when some members tried to evade communal duties such as keeping watch, while others were accused of collaborating with the soldiers.[29] Whether rich or poor were identified as witches, of course, some of the polarities were still the same; the conflict between individualism and traditional solidarities could manifest itself in many different forms. Another perennial tension was that between centre and periphery, with the implicit threat to the authority of the rulers from the committees and their allies. Already in 1591 the Elector of Trier, while still bent on the persecution of witches in general, had responded to complaints about the heavy costs of such activities by seeking to abolish independent committees and ensure that proper legal advice was taken.[30] In the 1650s the danger to central power was becoming so obvious that the authorities, now unimpeded by wartime disruption, began a general clampdown on procedure. Various scandals came to light, and in one case led to the execution of a notary who had doctored both the evidence and the accounts.[31] A much more critical group of urban lawyers now took a leading role, men who had defended some of the accused and been influenced by Spee.[32] By the 1660s the committees had virtually disappeared, while policies of repopulation brought widespread immigration, so that old communal solidarities – and hatreds – were heavily diluted.

Witchcraft fears and persecutions in this area represented a complex fusion of popular and elite elements, so that every small territory has its own individuality. Similar themes combined in subtly different fashions, as popular ideas about *maleficium* and the official doctrines about the satanic conspiracy interacted. The severe persecution which took place under Prince-Archbishop Johann von Schönenburg of Trier seems to have found its intellectual drive from his suffragan Peter Binsfeld, author of a treatise about the confessions of witches. This work was not responsible for the elaborate stories told about the sabbat, however, which had become commonplace in the area over the two years before its publication in 1589 – Binsfeld simply recorded what he had heard. He was particularly concerned with a sensational trial which had just taken place, that of Dr Dietrich Flade, vice-governor of Trier. Over the past few years a conflict had been developing between Flade, whose court had taken a moderate line over accusations, and the enthusiastic witch-hunters. After 1584 one of these, Johann Zandt von Marll, had become governor; he was responsible for over a hundred executions in his own jurisdiction of Pfalzel in 1587, and was clearly determined to get rid of the obstructive Flade. The evidence strongly suggests that confessions were manipulated to this end. The first charge was cunningly circumstantial; a boy aged fifteen told how an unknown witch at the sabbat had boasted of administering poison to the Elector himself, taking advantage of the fact that he held a high position in his service. The ruler had also forgotten to wear a protective waxen *Agnus Dei* round his neck as he normally did, but there was not enough poison to kill him, only to make him ill. The boy had later identified Flade when he saw him at a flogging; that same summer of 1587 the pressure was stepped up when an old woman who was condemned at Pfalzel made a very public accusation against the judge on her way to the stake. After this it was only to be expected that others would pick up the story, as duly happened.

By April 1588 another old woman on trial in Zandt's court, Margarethe of Euren, produced a florid confession, according to which Flade had arrived at the sabbat in a golden waggon to urge the destruction of all the crops. When the poor objected she joined in their protests, only for the judge to strike her with his stick saying that the people of Trier had enough yet. On other occasions he and his followers had brought on a terrible hail-storm that killed forty-six cows, by standing in a brook and pouring water over their heads in the name of a thousand devils, and aimed to destroy both the Pfalzel and the Euren woods so that no more stakes could be made for the burning of witches. He had also created the snails which had harmed the crops, by means of which he could tell if he was questioned. Others had joined with him to dig up the body of a baby from the churchyard at Euren, so that its heart could be baked in a fritter and shared among the witches to make it impossible for them to confess; if this had not prevented her doing so, that was because she had only eaten a little. Even after this it took another year for Flade to be put on trial, after the Elector was persuaded to appoint a commission of investigation. A certain unease is betrayed in his letter to the theology faculty, in which he stresses that twenty-three convicted witches have identified the accused, but concedes that 'among scholars there are current all sorts of objections as to the confessions that this one or that has been seen at the witch-sabbat'. This was an important point, for Flade himself based his defence on the claim that the Devil must have assumed his form; when the torture forced him to admit his guilt, he continued to qualify his identifications of others with the formula 'but whether it was himself in person or only the Evil One in his form, I cannot say'. Binsfeld avowedly made this issue the central one in his treatise, denying that the Devil could perform such impersonations. He may well have been referring to Flade when he claimed that a 'certain jurist' had told him 'that he cared naught for a thousand denunciations'. The case was picked up by the demonologist Del Rio, for whom Flade was the perfect example of the secret witch in high places, using his position to protect lesser servants of the Devil. From the publicity given to his case one must conclude that what appears in modern eyes as a blatant misuse of power, directed against a conscientious judge, looked quite different to contemporaries caught up in the passions of a witch-hunt. The fate of Flade – strangled and burned in September 1589 – and the persecution experienced by Loos, shows just how dangerous opposition to the ruler might be in these small states, where much the safest option was to join in the campaign. Another point concerns the hidden operations of second-rank officials, for the sinister personage of Peter Ormsdorf, notary of the ecclesiastical court at Trier and in other courts where witches were tried, can be detected behind the Flade case and many others. He was reported to have taken bribes from an accuser to suggest the names of accomplices to those making confessions, while he kept a register in which he recorded thousands of accusations made by more than three hundred of those convicted.[33]

The coercion of opponents operated in a similar, though not identical fashion in the territories of another prince-archbishop, the Elector of Cologne. In the first decades of the seventeenth century the courts here had been cautious and moderate, to the extent that at the end of the 1620s complaints that witches from elsewhere were taking shelter in his lands gave the bigoted archbishop Ferdinand von Wittelsbach (brother of Maximilian of Bavaria) the excuse to intervene. Through the 1630s he sponsored one of the most severe persecutions ever seen in Europe; there may well have been 2000 executions among a population of perhaps 220,000. There is little sign of widespread local enthusiasm behind this drastic purge, although it must have drawn on the usual suspicions and enmities. It was operated by a group of special commissioners, notably

Dr Franz Buirmann, Dr Johann Möden, Dr Heinrich von Schultheiss and Lic. Kaspar Reinhard. We know of Buirmann's methods from the account given by Hermann Löher, one of the assessors in the court at Rheinbach (near Bonn). Löher had tried to oppose the commissioner, but saw his danger and fled to Amsterdam with his family just in time. A number of other members of the elites, or their wives, were convicted as a way of breaking down resistance to the arbitrary proceedings of the commissioners. These included the predictable range of abuses; indiscriminate use of torture, manipulation of confessions and failure to consult outside legal authorities. Other courts tried to hinder them, only to find that the archbishop frustrated their efforts.[34] Men like this established a reputation as specialists, so that there was a constant risk they would be called into neighbouring territories, where they would spread further persecution. They were extreme examples of the possibilities that jurists could make careers out of witchcraft, of which there are numerous lesser examples – terrible evidence for Loos's bitter vision of a 'new alchemy' turning blood into gold. It is still not entirely clear why attitudes among these men underwent something of a sea change in the 1650s and 1660s; awareness of abuses cannot be a wholly satisfactory explanation on its own, since these had been so evident to men like Loos and Spee in previous generations. It is certainly arguable that Spee's book, which appeared in numerous editions and translations, was peculiarly effective through its concentration on procedural questions, which avoided most of the problems which arose in any attempt to challenge witchcraft beliefs directly. One may even suspect a generation gap, with younger lawyers seeking to distance themselves from the extremism of their predecessors in a world where certain kinds of explanation – and confessionalism itself – had gone out of fashion. For whatever reason, power struggles at every level were no longer mediated through witchcraft charges, although a trickle of cases continued in various regions of Germany well into the next century.

An even trickier problem arises in relation to many parts of Germany which saw relatively little persecution. They were subjected to the same socio-economic pressures as their neighbours, and experienced similar religious changes. Here too the wage-price scissors, and rising population, played havoc with social systems based on a presumption of rough equality between peasant cultivators, leading to bitter complaints about the emergence of an 'unchristian economy'. This was associated with the extension of a wider market economy, for agricultural as well as craft products, across areas of central Europe which had previously been relatively isolated. On the face of it, the experience of these regions appears to constitute a counter-example, a strong challenge to any version of the 'strain-gauge' theory as a general explanation for rising concern about witchcraft. A possible answer lies in the special character of the middling-sized princely state that encouraged the development of very particular power structures. A new type of *Herrschaft* (lordship) evolved in response to the specific difficulties of the later sixteenth and early seventeenth centuries. This was indeed patriarchal, in that it was based on tighter control over both marriages and inheritance systems; these moves were generally welcomed by the peasant elite, who shared the princes' interest in maintaining stability and deference. Reinforced by impartible inheritance and much stronger marital discipline, the household tended to displace the wider community as the fundamental social unit. The process certainly generated intense strains *within* families, of the kind that could easily lead to witchcraft accusations; second marriages, half-siblings and widows were all particularly liable to be involved. On the other hand, the fact that (as in New England) these matters tended to be firmly handled by local courts may have helped defuse such situations, however brutal the results for the losers. The wider problem of the poor and landless was met to some extent by paternalistic means. *Ad hoc* reductions in taxation, and distributions of grain in bad years, were the rulers' way of preventing rebellion and disorder. Expanded administrative structures and better records helped to reinforce the multiple strands of dependence between princes and subjects, which operated through a series of implicit bargains. The quest for order and stability in an insecure, changing world vastly strengthened the capacity of the powerful to dominate their inferiors; in the process it created a new subservience, even perhaps a culture of dependence. It is at least arguable that where power relations of this kind were relatively quickly established, witchcraft was less likely to become a major issue than where they only came about slowly and painfully. A great deal may therefore have depended on the skill and energy of the rulers, and the extent to which circumstances or past history allowed them to assume a dominant role in their territories. It is striking that in the Saarland such developments seem to have come rather late, when the persecution was already in sharp decline.[35]

Salzburg and its beggars: the Zaubererjackl trials

On the whole the authorities were fairly successful in averting social rebellion (as opposed to the widespread resistance to taxation), but there was another more insidious form of disorder which largely defied their efforts. The landless poor were too numerous, and often too desperate, to be kept wholly in place by edicts or exemplary punishments. Although true vagrants only made up a tiny proportion of the population, they were highly visible evidence of hard times and individual misfortune, increasingly feared and marginalized. In the archbishopric of Salzburg, between 1675 and 1690, this group became the target of a particularly vicious and belated persecution, known as the Zaubererjackl trials, which claimed at least two hundred lives.[36] In some senses this was the ultimate development of the powerful/powerless dichotomy which was always so strong in witchcraft. The victims were the most deprived, isolated and defenceless people in the whole society; the majority were boys and young men still in their teens, many of them illegitimate or orphans. Jakob Koller himself, the 'Jacob the magician' who gave his name to the whole episode, was the teenage son of typical aggressive beggars, literally born into a career of vagrancy, theft, and deceit. Not only did he claim fantastic powers for himself, other beggars continued to elaborate on these, turning him into a mythical figure capable of making himself invisible and avenging their wrongs. One beggarwoman told those who refused her alms that when the 'Jäggl' came he would teach them to be properly generous, a daredevil strategy which proved fatal. Such threats were the last resort of the weak in tit-for-tat arguments; they were effective but very dangerous, given the general belief in powers of magical revenge. The logic of demonology and underlying social factors interacted, as the beggars reacted to humiliation with displays of malice that encouraged the rest of the population to join in the action against them. There was a tendency for the authorities to attack indiscriminate almsgiving, and to drive a wedge between the settled population and the vagabonds; this had been evident much earlier in the larger states, but the trials marked a sharp move away from the milder policies previously followed in Salzburg. New ideas about begging raised questions about the legitimacy and truthfulness of requests for alms, intensified the distinction between the deserving and undeserving poor and required individual decisions about whether or not to give.

The beggars were routinely associated with magical practices (even when this was really unfair), and also with the lack of religious instruction and belief, so that they constituted an obstacle to the programme of Catholic reform. Priests might make them scapegoats for their own difficulties in converting their flocks, blaming them for spreading heretical books or maintaining popular superstitions. When the missionary enterprise failed it was tempting to identify the powers of darkness at work. The beggars did not realize the growing danger associated with magical practices, when these were only a minor part of their life. They normally gave the most realistic version of magic they could, and rarely claimed to have seen the 'Jackl' who could make himself invisible. The tendency was to produce adolescent fantasies rather than plausible evidence of fearful magical powers for the judges. When these fantasies were of revenge they only expressed their real powerlessness and poverty. The testimonies also reveal abundant evidence of harsh and unfriendly treatment by the general population, with insults and humiliation as routine experiences. The attempt to use harmful magic was not a sign of some profoundly magical world view, but of the social situation. Often the beggars produced florid self-accusations when questioned, which might revolve around fantasy compensations for their actual position. Since clothing was one sign of deprivation that marked them off from other people, their dreams of respectability might be expressed in terms of clothes. The weather magic practised at the sabbat represented another fantasy, this time of collective action to avenge themselves against whole communities which treated them badly. Behind it one may detect an anxiety to remember occasions when they were treated with more respect, coupled with resentment at their exclusion from occasions of communal festivity. Fantasies of unlimited power were related to this, while even stories of the sabbat can be seen as compensatory, allowing membership of a community, however disreputable.

As one would expect from patterns elsewhere, there was a hard core of persistent beggars – although even these took seasonal work when possible – and a much wider group who passed in and out of employment. The practice of hiring servants by the year meant there was a batch of new beggars every year, but a chance for others to find positions. The social disintegration of beggar families, which saw children separate off once they became useless as a claim for sympathy, was unwilling; families reverted to established patterns wherever they could. Nor was there much sign of truly organized groups among them, only temporary alliances between individuals – and also a good deal of rivalry and violence, with the kind of disorderly conduct usually expected of bodies of adolescents. Structures of communication between them were also much weaker than people thought, giving no justification for elite fears of possible rebellion; like the rest of their behaviour these were just strategies for survival. There was a tendency for a stylized vision of the beggars to emerge, because in their brief contacts with potential donors they presented themselves in such ways, playing up to expectations. To the extent that they had to rely on lies and clumsy deceitful tricks to obtain alms, moreover, these must ultimately have affected their self-image and sense of truth. As a result, when they came before the judges they did not share the same rational approach to reconstructing past events; their truth functioned on several levels and was adjustable to current circumstances. It proved all too easy to extract damning confessions from them. The purge of these pitiful and defenceless people, many of them mere children, by the Salzburg courts seems unusually horrible even by the dismal standards of other persecutions. Perhaps this is because they were victims twice over, reduced to desperate poverty by factors quite outside their control, then mercilessly exterminated for trying to survive at all. For them, the web of power was deadly indeed.

The crucial balance: threats and conflict within the community

Unless a wave of persecution was launched, bringing any witch to trial was almost bound to be a tense, protracted business. Very few individuals were prepared to initiate legal action without knowing that a significant group of neighbours were prepared to back them, yet it was hard to get such assurances without making one's intentions public, thereby running a risk of a pre-emptive strike by the witch. There was also the problem of ill-will from the relatives, particularly dangerous if they too were suspected. This emerged in the successive trials of Mengette and Jean Cachette. During the first, Sebille Belat claimed she had not known good health since her husband accused Mengette's mother Laurence, who had been imprisoned but released; over the past seven weeks this had become worse, so that she had been unable to work and earn her living. Sebille believed that if Mengette was a witch as reputed then this was her doing in revenge for their action against her mother – it was in their house that one of Mengette's daughters had told incriminating stories about her grandmother. By the time Jean was tried, a year after his wife, Dieudonnée Vannier appeared to assert that he had killed her husband, because at the time of his wife's trial they had said they could only depose against the pair of them. Jean had reputedly said there were only two men in the village he hated, and one was already dead, after which word had gone around that this was her husband, who had blamed him during his illness.[37] A related danger was that the witch might be acquitted, then take revenge personally. Mongeon Valentin had been the plaintiff against Jean Lallemant at his first trial, then when Lallemant was accused again his brother explained that Mongeon had fallen strangely ill after the first trial, to die believing himself bewitched.[38] Fear of suffering in such ways may be one reason why would-be accusers often seem to have thought better of it. Another was the danger of being unable to pay the costs if the trial proved unsuccessful, or the witch was too poor for confiscation to meet them. Jean Marlier had intended to have Libaire Bouchier arrested and tried, 'but since he did not have the means to carry this through he changed his opinion on the advice of his friends, hoping that in due course there would be a charge brought against her'.[39] When Catherine Courier, who was a widow, believed her illness resulted from bewitchment by Jennon Ramaixe, she asked the *prévôt* of Blamont to arrest her, but he advised her that she was too poor to meet the costs and would do better to seek a cure from Jennon. The latter was finally persuaded through intermediaries to offer her a drink of water from the well, after which she quickly recovered.[40]

There were other dangers for those who decided to initiate legal proceedings. In many jurisdictions it was still normal practice to imprison plaintiff as well as accused; it is true that it seems to have been normal to release the plaintiff on bail once the initial depositions had been taken, while conditions of imprisonment are unlikely to have been equally harsh, the prospect could hardly have been an enticing one. In earlier times there had been a far more extreme principle of reciprocity in operation, the *lex talionis*, which, in the event of a prosecution failing, rendered the plaintiff liable to the same penalties as the accused would have suffered if it succeeded. In one Dutch case of 1515 this was actually applied. Hadewich Barniers of Kempen accused Heyle Schoenmakers of witchcraft, after a test in which milk was boiled in a pan together with some needles – when the milk would not boil over this was supposed to demonstrate that it was bewitched. Both women were imprisoned and tortured, but Heyle would not confess, then died in prison, after which her relatives successfully demanded that her accuser be put to death.[41] Had this harsh system been maintained more widely (there does seem to have been a second Dutch case in 1553) it would have had a dramatic effect on witchcraft persecution, and indeed on law enforcement in general, but it was plainly incompatible with the broad evolution towards new styles of criminal justice.[42] Lesser constraints were still surprisingly effective, if we can judge from the complaints of Jean Magnien, schoolmaster at Azelot. He alleged that over the previous year the mayor Gergonne Roussel had been offering several men money in return for becoming plaintiffs against Catherine Claude, with little success, until he saw his chance on an evening when Magnien had dined rather too well. After he was offered an assurance that his costs would be covered, as well as the promise of a new overcoat, the schoolmaster rashly agreed to take on the task. When the mayor denied the whole account Magnien had to recognize that it was one man's word against another and proceed, although he now said he merely knew of Catherine's reputation, rather than having any charge to bring against her. He was lucky that despite her denials of witchcraft she was convicted and banished for superstitious healing, with the costs realized against her property – a decidedly partial verdict perhaps by the local court.[43]

One would certainly expect that powerful individuals might feel greater freedom to move from suspicion to action, yet even here the record is often ambiguous. In the case of Senelle Hanns of Insming, the local *prévôt* and his wife testified to their belief that she was responsible for the death of their small son about three years earlier, when the diagnosis of witchcraft had been supported by the local *curé*. Yet they appear to have taken no action against a widely suspected local witch, on the face of it an extraordinary failure to exploit their power.[44] This is the kind of mystery which defies any reliable solution, and is quite common when the cases are studied in detail. Perhaps the best explanations are that people were very reluctant to seek the death of others, while their suspicions were often much more tentative than later testimony given in court suggested, but these do not seem wholly adequate. Another expectation that was not regularly fulfilled was for suspects who became isolated, notably childless widows, to be picked off as easy targets whom no-one would defend. While there was a statistical trend here, it was far from being quick or automatic, with many individuals surviving for years in this dangerous situation. In most places they ran greater risks of being beaten, insulted and called witch than of actual prosecution; it took a rather mysterious rise in the emotional temperature of the community for latent hostility to come to a head and produce decisive action. Where we can get the odd glimpse below the surface of local society, wariness and reluctance to take the lead appear to be the dominant characteristics of early modern peasants and artisans. They showed little reticence in making threats, but great caution following them up. The typical relationship between a witch and his or her enemies may have been like that of Catherine Claude and her neighbour Jean Bertrand. He often called her witch when he had been drinking, and suspected her of causing the deaths of several animals, so he eventually threatened to have her put on trial. She retorted 'that she would have his fingers bitten to the bone', after which he suffered more losses; since he had a 'fantasy' that she was the cause, he 'sometimes had thoughts of exterminating her himself when he met her in a lonely place, if he had not judged that it would be better to achieve this through the expedient of justice'. In the end her trial seems to have been precipitated by a denunciation from a convicted male witch, rather than any initiative from the twenty-seven witnesses against her.[45]

Survival was one thing – and as we have seen, a bad reputation may have had its uses in stimulating charity. The moral and psychological cost of such an existence is another matter. Even those who did not have to confront suspicious neighbours daily as part of their struggle to keep alive, but who knew of their own reputations, must have lived in the shadow of a constant fear that their turn would eventually come. Their unwise propensity to make threats may be evidence for the corrosive effects of this situation, more than an explanation for how it arose in the first place. Whenever a trial began in the vicinity some individuals knew themselves to be at great risk, for two related reasons; the dangers of imitative behaviour and of specific denunciations. It was hard to keep a cool head in such situations, as can be seen from the behaviour reported by numerous witnesses. After Claude Pieton had fled, Babillon Girard remarked to his son, 'Bastien, I am very glad your father has gone away, so that he will accuse no-one', then when he was on trial she told his wife he should not accuse good people.[46] Catherine Charpentier expected to be named by Jean Claude Colin, so had her son watching to bring her news; seeing him approaching, she said to her sister-in-law, 'that wicked man is sure to have accused me, and if he has once spoken my name, then I will be fried'. She then took to the fields and seems to have absented herself from the village for two or three years, behaviour she herself later recognized to have been highly unwise.[47]

Others made hostile comments about trials; when Bastienne Mathieu gave evidence against a miller who was on trial, her neighbour Margueritte le Charpentier remarked that many were damning themselves, then the next day Bastienne fell ill after eating in Marguerite's house.[48] It is plain that many suspects drew attention to themselves in such ways, as they might also do if they believed an individual had finally decided to bring charges. Jean Gerardin was frightened that Pierron Gerdolle might do this, because of threats Jean had rashly made to him, so took Beniste Renouard into his confidence. When she told him that Gerdolle was pursuing the matter,

> he begged her and her husband affectionately to be on his side, and another time he came to her house to talk of the same subject, throwing himself down on a bench and striking his stomach with his fists, declaring that he had something in his heart telling him 'kill yourself, kill yourself', to which she replied that he should not do this because he would damn himself, adding that it was the Devil who suggested it. He replied that on the contrary it was God, then wearied by his continual demands to know whether Gerdolle was persisting in his complaints, she told him he was not, but was renouncing them, at which news the accused was greatly cheered, and became more confident than before.[49]

Another compromising statement was made by Claudatte Parmentier, who told her sister-in-law that if she were to confess, her goods would be confiscated, leaving nothing for her children, while 'she knew for certain that Jacotte Haulte Rue of le Viel Marché had eaten the heart of a child, which was the reason she had confessed nothing under torture, and been released from prison'.[50] Like remarks by other suspects, this horrible fantasy (which we have already met in the Flade case) must reflect the fears of torture and the rumours which circulated about what happened in that secret other world of the torture chamber.

The sense of being abandoned by God was mentioned by several suspects, like Jeanne Petiotte, who told a neighbour who warned her that she was under investigation, 'the devil should carry off her body if she was not a good woman, and that she had prayed so much to God and the good saints, despite which they had deserted her'.[51] Dion Remy was complaining that she was about to be arrested; when Babon Charles said she must have patience and trust in God she replied 'she had been praying to him for more than seven years and he had done nothing for her, so she saw clearly that he did not want to preserve her, in the place where she had to go, and that she would not pardon people, that she did not care for her part, and that the judges were wicked people'.[52] Those who thought like this were surely preparing the way for their subsequent collapse under interrogation and torture, when they would accept the verdict of their neighbours, declaring themselves to have served the Devil in place of that God who had proved so unhelpful. Others tried to shore up their position through promises, even outright bribes. Valentin Girard was threatening to accuse Jennon Girard (it is not clear if they were related), so Jennon's husband offered to remit a debt of twenty *écus*, then add twenty francs he was owed by another, if he would withdraw. She was another who was finally arrested after a denunciation; she seems to have fled to a nearby village for some days, then hidden in her house or the surrounding fields, until caught in bed at night.[53] When Jean Vosgien was on trial he named both Didier Mobille and Humbert Marchal as accomplices, after which Mobille fled and was hidden for several weeks by Humbert, who allegedly asked him not to accuse him if he were taken and forced to confess, promising to feed his children and offer all the help he could. When Mobille was arrested Marchal bribed the sergeant who was guarding him, so that he finally named all those already identified by Vosgien, with the sole exception of Marchal.[54] The idea of pacts made at the sabbat not to name one another surfaced in a fair number of confessions, a ghastly parody of the real-life situations in which suspects found themselves.

An alternative to bribery was to offer threats. Marguitte le Cueffre, who blamed her alarming five-year illness on Marion le Masson, was called to the house of Marion's neighbour Jacquin Martin as rumours of her imminent arrest spread, for him to tell her she should keep quiet. Marion herself then appeared with another woman, the latter telling Marguitte

that she had used evil words against the said Marion when she said she had made her ill, that this should be put under foot and not spoken of again, and that for the honour of God she should ask Marion's pardon. When she refused to do this Marion herself told her off roundly, saying she would speak to the mayor Jean de Sarrux and to Ferry Ferry, her nephews, in order to have her arrested, when it would either cost her a hundred francs or she would make her prove her claims. Since the witness was alone among these people who were persuading her with either prayers or threats to beg Marion's pardon, and she feared Marion might cause her another even greater misfortune, she did beg her pardon, nevertheless this was under compulsion and in fear, so she persisted in her belief that Marion had given her the sickness – which she still had – in the said bowl of soup.[55]

Marion was clearly a woman of a certain status, with good connections, who hoped to outface accusers who might normally be expected to defer to her. She was shown to have a long reputation, stretching back thirty years by some accounts, while there were stories that she had poisoned another convicted witch in prison some years earlier, the implication being that this was to prevent a denunciation. One is led to wonder whether the relatively recent death of her husband had left her more exposed to the tide of local rumour – and to what proved a fatal accusation from yet another local witch. Direct threats seem to have been rather rare, but generalized statements of ill-will were relatively common. Jean Blanchar claimed that Odile Claude had told him, 'they say I am a witch, I would like to be a complete devil, when I would do so much that some would repent for a long time', while Mengeatte Jacques told Claudon Vannier 'she wished she could be a witch for two hours to do as she wanted', adding that this was in order that she might harm those who called her witch.[56]

Imaginary diabolical power, as invoked by these suspects, was a real enough threat for those who believed in it. This was one line of self-defence which might well prove quite effective, at least for a while. Another was the fear that friends or relatives might seek revenge, even perhaps launching counter-accusations against vulnerable members of families involved in the persecution. This could be two-edged, since there are occasional signs that individuals felt under pressure to testify precisely because they themselves had a reputation that they hoped to belie in this fashion. The really crucial threat in this respect, however, lay in the terrible power the whole system bestowed on confessing witches themselves. When they were invited to name their accomplices, those whom they had been able to identify at the sabbat or with whom they had carried out acts of malevolence, they were handed a potent weapon no-one else could wholly control. Lawyers and demonologists were evidently worried about the dangers; indeed, there seems to have been widespread agreement that these denunciations were insufficient on their own. It was therefore impossible, in most cases, for the accused to derail the whole process by naming their enemies, or the judges themselves, as witches. Such claims would have been quite readily detected for what they were, and have had no real impact. The partial exceptions are found in some of the German urban persecutions, where denunciations were exploited in a very incautious fashion, so that there are instances where naming rulers, magistrates or judges had a salutary effect in bringing a degree of sanity into the proceedings. These episodes also provide some examples where the system was manipulated, with names being suggested in order to build up suspicion against particular individuals, as seems to have happened with Flade at Trier. This was the kind of malpractice it was all too easy to conceal, or indeed to justify to oneself. In the more normal, small-scale operations found across the villages and small towns of rural Europe, the accused generally appear to have responded by naming those neighbours who did have reputations; they may well have believed that these people really were witches.

Those who knew themselves to be in danger of arrest were not slow to draw the consequences, or to see the chance of deterring others from proceeding. There are quite a number of telling statements preserved in the Lorraine trial records. Georgeatte Grand Didier was heard saying on her way back from church that if she was arrested 'she would accuse others whether they were good women or not'.[57] Georgeatte Herteman complained to a group of other women about the way she had been insulted, and how some wanted to bring her to trial, then said that if she was imprisoned she would claim that all the women in the neighbourhood were the same as her, even if she were quartered.[58] Mengeotte Lausson was heard to say that if she was burned as a witch she would denounce her husband's sister Toussaince as one too, while if she was taken many others would be as well; on another occasion she remarked that she was very glad her husband was the same as her, since otherwise his sisters would act against her.[59] Chrestaille Wathot claimed that if she was arrested, 'I would accuse such important people of witchcraft that they would release me for love of them'.[60] When Nicolas George was on trial, Colin Rembault testified about an exchange he had overheard in the vineyard twenty years earlier between Nicolas and his wife. Speaking of Didier Jacquat and his wife, she told him, 'those wicked people have spoken angrily to me, threatening to have us arrested, saying that we are witches and have caused the deaths of their animals', to which he replied, 'we must let them do as they wish, but say that if they have us taken, we will cause others to be taken as well'.[61] There is no doubt that this strategy was quite widely employed and may well have been extremely effective in many instances, although it is impossible to make any definite judgement on this point. The danger that such remarks might finally become part of the prosecution case has to be balanced against the evidence that witchcraft trials had many villagers terrified lest they might be drawn into the pool of suspects, or have existing suspicions turned into legal action. It certainly becomes easier to understand the reluctance to initiate prosecutions once one recognizes the complex interplay of checks and balances just below the surface of village society. To overcome these restraints it was usually necessary for several families or individuals to pool their grievances and suspicions, perhaps egging one another on in the process – but it was hard to manage this secretly. One of the most striking aspects of the procedure was its jerkiness, with matters seeming to stick at a certain point, often for many years, until an invisible threshold was passed, with a sufficient number of neighbours committed to action on what now became an all-or-nothing principle.

Some of the complexities emerge from the proceedings against Claudon de Benamenil. In the spring of the year before his arrest, a roofer was working on the next house when a hailcloud approached, so he took shelter and started a conversation with Claudon. The latter remarked

that there were many evil persons who caused such things, to which he replied that they were being removed little by little, then Claudon started to talk about the late Petit Noel, saying that he had been accused so many times, and if once he were summoned to depose against Noel he would say what he knew about him. Nevertheless he later heard, when the inhabitants of the village were returning from watching Noel's execution, they were saying that Claudon had testified to far less than he had talked of beforehand. He had also heard something of his ill fame, although this was mostly since Noel's execution. For his part he had never suspected him of this crime, adding that one day when he met Claudon after Noel's execution he told him he had suffered many adversities since they last met, and that Noel had accused him in hatred because he deposed against him.[62]

In fact, the testimony against Claudon was relatively weak, in terms of clear instances of supposed bewitchment; there was some disagreement about how much torture should be applied, and the judges carefully recorded their moderation in this respect, which may be one reason he resisted and was released – the outcome witnesses must have feared the most. Huguette Couroyeur accused three other women, although she seemed rather uncertain and changeable, then on the day of her execution two priests admonished her about the need for truth, at which she said all her accusations had been false. The executioner later claimed that her last words reinstated the charges against two of the women, but since no-one else had heard this they were released.[63] Courts that at other times showed scant regard for the rights of the accused were quite capable of sensible pragmatism in such ways. This was one of the numerous respects in which early modern justice was distinctly unpredictable, not to say capricious; intermittent rationality was one of its most striking character-istics, setting up curious oscillations between shrewdness and credulity. Officials and judges also responded to the mood around them, as their counterparts are still liable to do today. A famous instance of this relates to a very late English trial, at Exeter in 1682, when Lord Chief Justice North offered a rather embarrassed justification to one of the Secretaries of State after three old women had been sentenced to death:

> The evidence against them was very full and fanciful, but their own confessions exceeded it. They appeared not only weary of their lives, but to have a great deal of skill to convict themselves. Their descriptions of the sucking devils with saucer-eyes were so natural that the jury could not choose but believe them. Sir, I find the country so fully possessed against them that, though some of the virtuosi may think these things the effects of confederacy, melancholy, or delusion and that young folks are altogether as quicksighted, as they who are old and infirm, yet we cannot reprieve them without appearing to deny the very being of witches, which, as it is contrary to law, so I think it would be ill for his Majesty's service, for it may give the faction occasion to set afoot the old trade of witch finding that may cost many innocent persons their lives, which this justice will prevent.[64]

These lame rationalizations seem to do no more than invoke public feeling and entirely speculative repercussions (of a very improbable kind) as an excuse for judicial pusillanimity.

Attitudes among the richest and most powerful members of local communities, which must have been important, are hard to trace with any certainty. In the mass of surviving trials there is little to suggest any standard pattern, such as might see the local elite joining together to manage the trials as a way of controlling their inferiors. Some support at this level was clearly helpful in mounting a prosecution, but there are plenty of cases – probably a majority – in which the real impetus seems to have come from people of only middling status. Local power-holders might even obstruct legal action, like the mayor of Moyement; Claudatte Girard reported that during her husband's fatal sickness he several times asked the mayor to arrest Ulriot Colas Ulriot, whom he blamed for his state, promising to become the *partie formelle* against him and pay the costs, yet because the mayor was on Ulriot's side he would take no notice. Things seem to have changed after a new mayor took office, since Ulriot asked why so many people had assembled outside the mayor's house. When he was told it was to ask the chapter to take steps against the witches he said he did not think there were any in the village, to receive the disconcerting answer that he would probably be one of the first against whom evidence was sought.[65] It was often at this upper level of local society that fraud was alleged to have taken place, or conspiracies to have been hatched. In the case of Mengeon Clement Thiriat it soon became evident that the moving spirit in bringing the prosecution against this fairly wealthy, elderly peasant was the mayor Noel Gerardin, whose charges included the claim that Mengeon had caused the possession of his niece. Mengeon complained to the duchess of Lorraine, by which means he succeeded in having over thirty of his own witnesses heard; some of them testified how Gerardin had coached witnesses, reminding them of incidents they had forgotten, also holding secret councils with two other men. A background of grievances over land sales and other matters, with threats made by Gerardin, was also revealed. Although the suspect was finally put to the torture, it was under unusually strict supervision, so it is not wholly surprising that he held out to be released.[66] Another complaint to the top, this time to the duke, was by the tradesman Claude des Fours, who had been named by the convicted witch Nicolas Fontaine. The authorities in Nancy were evidently convinced there had been a deliberate manipulation by the *prévôt* and court at Einville, with Fontaine being prompted to make a whole series of charges. While he did make limited admissions which supported this theory, they seem to have been content to let the matter drop once he withdrew all his accusations.[67]

A rather similar case from the Franche-Comté is that of Pierre Recurdey and his father, who had been the target of a systematic campaign by their enemy Pierre Genévois. In this instance, where rather different procedural rules applied, the younger Recurdey was sentenced to banishment and a heavy fine in the local court (the aged father having died in prison). An appeal to the *parlement* of Dôle was supported by extensive testimony pointing up the numerous weaknesses in the prosecution case; again many witnesses appeared for the defendant, who eventually escaped with a fine for blasphemy.[68] Identifying the malpractices and their authors might not be enough, however, as in the case of George Durand of Clemecey, who made a successful appeal to the council of the duke of Lorraine in 1622. His enemies Humbert Jardelle and Nicolas Jean du Vic were convicted of conspiracy and suborning witnesses, being obliged to pay a fine and make a humiliating public confession of their guilt in the presence of their victim and persons chosen by him, while recognizing he was innocent of witchcraft. This does not seem to have produced the desired results from Durand's point of view, because a brief mention in another document reveals that in 1623 he was tried again and convicted.[69] What several of these cases do emphasize is that local opinion could be sharply divided on whether or not specific persons were witches, so that if the accused got the chance to defend themselves a considerable amount of support might be forthcoming. This is probably only the tip of the iceberg, and one may reasonably think that in many cases there was a hidden group of sympathizers who remained silent not just from prudence or fear, but because the legal proceedings were structured to exclude them. Jim Sharpe has unearthed some Yorkshire petitions in support of accused or convicted witches, one of them signed by around 200 people. A very poignant instance comes from the village of Denby in 1674, when a teenage girl had made accusations against Joseph and Susan Hinchcliffe. Fifty of their neighbours signed a petition in their favour, while the local justices were trying to manage the case sympathetically. Unfortunately Joseph was so upset that he hanged himself in the woods; before his body was found his wife had died in her bed, praying in the most edifying manner for the enemies who had falsely accused her.[70]

Where accusations of conspiracy were made, they usually involved families from the 'middling sort', not the humble people who dominated numerically as both witches and witnesses. This may partly represent differential ability to exploit the legal possibilities of making such a defence, since families of this status were more likely to have the allies and the funds necessary to take such steps. On the other hand, it was also true that most of the evidence about feuds more generally would support the notion that these were far more endemic and bitter among kin groups at this level, who had so much more to lose, and were precariously poised at the edge of respectability. Members of this minor local elite, who were not often charged with witchcraft, also seem to have defended themselves with unusual vigour, betraying a certain sense of their own consequence. Some of them plainly thought that there was a social slur involved, since witchcraft was not an appropriate charge to bring against any but the poor. In England the Court of Star Chamber was peculiarly well adapted to hearing the kind of follow-up litigation involved, so that the study of its records by C. L. Ewen produced several excellent examples. There was the 1623 case of the Ipswich grocer Thomas Methwolde, who had married an apothecary's widow against the wishes of their kin, then found himself before the Quarter Sessions charged with bewitching his wife's three-year-old niece. At Heacham in Norfolk there was a feud between the Stockdales and the Cremers, which saw Nicholas Stockdale accused in 1600 of bewitching twelve sheep which 'became so black that they were cast upon the dunghill and lost'; the Cremers must have been disconcerted when it emerged that they had overeaten when put on fresh barley stubble, but recovered after prompt treatment by the shepherd. Nothing daunted, his enemies had Stockdale tried in 1602 for causing the deaths of three persons, only for him to be acquitted and to win £40 in damages for conspiracy. There was a long-running Cambridge feud between Margaret Cotton, wife of a pewterer, and Dorcas Swetton, wife of an apothecary, that seems to have begun with a lawsuit over pew rights which the Cottons lost, allegedly at a cost of a hundred pounds. Threats and slander suits followed, then Margaret was tried at the Cambridge assizes in 1603 for bewitching the Swettons' infant son to death. After further lawsuits she had to face a second trial in 1609 for bewitching three other people, which led to another acquittal, while several witnesses stated they had been offered money to appear, providing the basis for the subsequent Star Chamber suit in which the Cottons alleged conspiracy.[71]

Fascinating though cases of this type undoubtedly are, too much should not be read into them. For a start, we must recognize that those involved may have been largely unaware of the motivation which looks so obvious in retrospect. The Swettons may have been absolutely convinced that Margaret Cotton, who had certainly uttered violent threats against them, had bewitched their baby; a deep sense of injustice after she was acquitted would then have encouraged them to interpret later events as showing they had been right all along, and to take unwise steps to ensure she would not escape a second time. On a wider basis, the vast majority of known trial records contain no hint at all of such themes, beyond the usual lists of petty quarrels and the last-minute mobilization of local opinion. Continental judicial systems included specific provisions for the accused to challenge witnesses, with personal enmity as the prime ground for doing so, yet only a minuscule number of the accused took advantage of this. When they did attack the *bona fides* of witnesses, it was almost always on the basis that they had behaved dishonestly in the past (usually this meant petty theft), in line with standard village ideas about personal worth. The fact that a handful did allege conspiracy, with no sign that they felt inhibited about it, gives all the more reason to believe that when others did not this was because it had not even occurred to them. While abuses of power were commonplace at many levels in the identification and prosecution of witches, they were rarely so overt, except as practised by those highly-placed witch-hunters who could afford to disregard normal rules – at least for a time. Power in the local community was not easily mobilized in such ways, so that its effects were usually ambiguous, matching the perpetual threat to those under suspicion as witches with features which gave them a degree of protection.

CHAPTER X

INTERNAL AND
EXTERNAL WORLDS

Self-awareness and modernity

AGAIN AND AGAIN the historian studying witchcraft is brought up against the question of how individual human beings in the past related to the world around them. How far can we hope to get beneath the skins of our ancestors, to understand how they thought about themselves, their neighbours and their environment? Such questions lead into the difficult topics of subjectivity and personal identity, which have been much discussed in recent work on early modern culture and society. As with theories of gender – which have themselves been central to the debate – the tendency has been strongly towards different versions of social and linguistic constructionism. In effect, those who argue in this way tell us that people can only think of themselves as far as their limited conceptual equipment permits; language therefore determines not only thought but even self-awareness. In the works of such writers as the late Michel Foucault, the stress is on the arbitrary and selective nature of all interpretative frameworks, while other post-modern theorists have effectively set out to demolish any notion of objective truth. The results can be rather startling; intellectual changes, for example, become attempts to impose new hegemonic systems in the interests of specific groups. Such terms as 'deconstruction' and 'the linguistic turn' have come into use to describe a major change in methods of interpretation that is supposed to go far beyond the naive positivism of earlier historians and critics. The ultimate outcome is a totally relativistic picture, in which there is no final authority, so that all solutions are provisional. This has proved a powerful and seductive vision, which has brought some real gains, forcing us to look much harder at the hidden agendas behind 'rational' thinking, and to beware of facile anachronisms. Greater sensitivity to the differences between periods and cultures is rightly combined with an awareness that all forms of identity are necessarily shaped by their contexts.

Many historians and social scientists, however, consider that when these theories are taken to extremes they result in a kind of paradoxical absurdity. Witchcraft is something of a test case, as a prime example of a belief which possesses a powerful internal logic, but which few would wish to defend as a guide to practical conduct. When Paul Feyerabend praised the *Malleus Maleficarum* one must presume he did not actually intend anyone to start a new persecution – yet it is not at all clear how such a line can be drawn.[1] Feyerabend advanced the curious proposition that the *Malleus* presented alternative arguments fairly, then adopted the best solutions in the light of current knowledge. This appears to be a basic misunderstanding of the scholastic method adopted by the book, whose style was far more loaded in favour of a predetermined result than he recognized. His purpose was to contrast this supposedly fair-minded approach with that of modern scientists who dismissed astrology without bothering to understand its claims. If the desire to shock is very obvious here, so too is a certain intellectual frivolity. Relativism is a vital part of the modern Western tradition and surely one of its healthiest features, yet it can become strangely destructive when turned into a dogma. One well-known paradox is that full-blown relativism obliges the holder to allow free expression to the views of extremists who would themselves obliterate freedom of thought the moment they took power. Where witchcraft is concerned, respect for the ideas of others raises analogous difficulties. Who, from the standpoint of a strict cultural relativist, can argue effectively with the Headmen of Botswana, who used the Chiefs' Workshop of 1995 to attack the 1927 Witchcraft Act, because it proclaimed that there was no such thing as witchcraft, and made the accusers liable to defamation proceedings? The Headmen argued that the Act was the work of 'the colonial masters' who failed to take 'the culture of the indigenous people' into account, and that trials for witchcraft should be allowed to resume.[2] We may even have to admit that it would be better to allow legal action against supposed witches, if the alternative is the brutal murder of suspects in the fashion recently reported from South Africa, where scores (and probably hundreds) of people have been victims of mob justice, using burning car tyres as a method of execution. This was very much the calculation made by many educated judges in the early modern period, who thought it was wiser to channel and control popular feelings through formal trials.

Witchcraft may well be seen as the ultimate constructed crime, whose credibility depends on certain highly stylized ways of interpreting both events and feelings. This would seem to result inexorably from that crucial void at the centre, where real and imaginary, physical and spiritual, are alleged to meet through the agency of witch and devil. These fictitious transactions were indeed maintained through a particular kind of discourse, only finally losing credibility when it was replaced. At the level of theology and jurisprudence the 'intellectual framework' approach is clearly the right one to adopt, particularly since there were always major differences of opinion. Where witchcraft beliefs are concerned, on the other hand, it can equally be contended that these are so widespread across a huge range of societies, and share so many basic characteristics, that they provide good evidence for the existence of universals which transcend contextual differences. Their persistence at many levels in our own time, in the face of attacks from all sides, adds strength to this view. In this area, at least, some cautious rehabilitation of the idea of a common human nature seems to be in order. This chapter will explore some aspects of human psychology as they emerge from the witchcraft material, to show that convincing and worthwhile results can be obtained in this way. One implication must be that the human mind, far from being infinitely malleable, tends to impose certain inbuilt patterns on experience. This claim can be supported from the general findings of social anthropologists, for despite their surface variability, known human societies operate within a very restricted range when compared with the theoretical possibilities.

No sensible historian can doubt that the particular ways in which people thought about witchcraft were powerfully influenced, at any given time or place, by an outer world of language and ideas. This interface between individuals and received ideas was where much of the crucial action took place, so that it must be a central subject for study. What is unacceptable is the further claim that is sometimes made, that the *only* legitimate approach is through the beliefs current at that moment in time. While the warning against anachronism must always be heeded, in other respects such an attitude is absurdly restrictive. In the case in point, too much insistence on the difference, even the ultimate opacity, of individual sensibilities in the past can block off important avenues of interpretation. Most of the enduring power and fascination of witchcraft lies precisely in its capacity to express vital aspects of the inner world, those dark fantasies and passions lurking within the self. The relationship between one's inner life and the external world has always been one of interaction, not the exclusive domination of one or the other. It is essential to balance the understanding that individuals can never be fully understood out of context and that identities are contingent, against a sense of shared biological and psychological heritage. This is not a purely historical point, for aggressively constructionist theories of the self commonly proceed from an interpretation of the past to make claims about the present and the future. Their hidden or overt implication is that we are free to construct ourselves as we wish, while all supposed constraints are merely self-serving inventions. My own belief is that the evidence points firmly in the other direction, although I am equally hostile to the reactionary or racist doctrines which have at times been built around dubious theories of human nature. The fact that witchcraft beliefs are something nearly all cultures share, combined with their primitive and elemental power, places them somewhere near the heart of these debates.

This very centrality provides another reason to challenge some of the restrictive stances which have been adopted towards any psychological analysis of such topics. To take a particularly well-known example, one of the most impressive and influential 'new historicist' literary critics (or cultural historians), Stephen Greenblatt, has written a striking essay arguing that Freudian psychoanalysis is a misfit as applied to the Renaissance, and should itself be historicized.[3] The central suggestion is that psychoanalysis is dependent on a sense of selfhood which was largely the creation of the early modern period, therefore psychoanalytic interpretation is crippled until 'proprietary rights to the self have been secured'. This is far too complex a topic to be discussed properly here, since a formal attempt to refute or modify Greenblatt's views would completely unbalance this chapter; my doubts can only be expressed briefly. The fact that communal influences were far greater, possibly to the extent of inhibiting full adult individuality, does not have to imply that childhood experience was radically different; how far have familial and peer group pressures at this stage really changed? Furthermore, what is being challenged is actually one specific style of interpretation among many possible ones, and one which is unusually vulnerable to these particular criticisms. One is not likely to get very far in understanding early modern mentalities by referring only to Freud and a related school of American ego psychoanalysis which concentrates almost exclusively on the verbal. Greenblatt appears completely unaware of a massive psychoanalytic literature, most of it non-Freudian, referring to the formation of the self; to ignore the phenomenon of projective identification in reference to either the case of Martin Guerre or the exchange of identities in the drama is simply perverse.

There is also an obvious circularity in employing literary sources from the period itself as a way of defining Renaissance selfhood, then claiming that later ideas do not fit. In itself such circularity is perhaps inevitable, but it becomes a more serious objection when other relevant evidence is excluded. There was an extensive formal psychology of the period, based on a full-blown theory of the passions, reason and the will, that appears to rely on a far more distinct sense of the self, and can also be found in much moral theology.[4] The general notion of instinctual drives which must be controlled by higher faculties was fundamental to such thinking, which once again operated in terms of polarized categories. The whole question was highlighted by Christian apologetics, in such formulations as original sin, grace and election, however controversial these might be. Individual responsibility and the need for self-knowledge were constantly emphasized, while the examination of conscience was almost an obsession of the early modern period. While these doctrines may have been ignored by many ordinary people, the very stylized world of imaginative literature is also a poor guide to their ways of thought. By far the best evidence for actual subjectivities, in a largely oral culture, comes in the form of depositions and statements made before courts. While these certainly raise great problems of interpretation, they frequently invite just the type of psychological discussion which is being declared inappropriate.

It is curious that the one real-life instance Greenblatt employs, the famous impersonation case of Martin Guerre, involves both witchcraft beliefs and convincing psychoanalytic elements.[5] Martin was a mid-sixteenth century Pyrenean peasant who abandoned his wife and child to go off as a soldier. Some years later another man returned claiming to be the absentee, lived with his wife for a period and was only convicted and hanged as an impostor after a dramatic reappearance by the genuine husband. The real Martin seems to have experienced great difficulty in establishing his own manhood, to the extent of remaining impotent for eight years after his marriage at the age of fourteen. He was only cured when an external agency was identified – witchcraft – and countered by ritual means. The disappearance which gave the impostor his chance followed a classic oedipal conflict, in which Martin tried to steal grain from his father and was threatened with disinheritance. Greenblatt explains this background, with its stress on questions of personal development and identity, excellently, then rather curiously seeks to deny its importance through a discussion of the trial, which stresses that the identity of the two claimants was judged from external signs alone. As he admits, this was not a very surprising attitude for a lawcourt to take. Moreover, the case is only known from the polished, ironic account by the Toulouse judge Jean de Coras, and a briefer report by another lawyer; the loss of the court records means that we are deprived of the participants' own voices. The great contemporary student of the self, Michel de Montaigne, makes a passing reference to Martin Guerre in his essay 'On Cripples', the same piece where he also raises fundamental questions about evidence against witches. This does not validate Greenblatt's description of him as 'the canniest Renaissance observer of the case', however, because he specifically states that he can only remember one thing about it – his own feeling that Coras was unable to provide convincing reasons for the court's decision about the true identities of the two men. In such difficult cases, Montaigne thought, it would be preferable to avoid a judgement altogether.[6]

Historians faced with the problem of defining past sensibilities might well be tempted to follow the same option. It can hardly be a realistic one, however, for a book whose purpose is to contextualize witchcraft, when this can well be seen as a language for describing things that did not really happen, or which only took place on some boundary between real experience and fantasy. We cannot hope to understand how this all worked without a sense of how contemporaries perceived such matters. Many of the problems do seem to become more manageable if we start from a rather different position to that taken by many recent scholars. My fundamental assumption is that feelings and passions have not themselves changed in any essential respect over known human history; love and hatred, fear and hope, greed and generosity, these and their like are recognizable as far back as our sources stretch. This position does fit in with the recent findings of evolutionary psychology, which suggest strongly that our minds do not at all resemble the *tabula rasa* model favoured by some philosophers, powerful computers with no inbuilt software. On the contrary, we can only manage the world at all because we enter it equipped with multiple frames or grids which structure our responses, and include complex modes of interaction with other people.[7] If evolutionary psychology is basically correct then the more doctrinaire post-modernist theories which attribute an entirely contingent nature to both individuals and society are fundamentally, irrevocably mistaken. There is a common human nature, and much of our behaviour is determined by natural selection, not imposed by the specific culture into which we happen to have been born. Although these patterns are the result of evolution over countless generations, their rate of change is of course far too slow to make any difference over a few millennia. The very large range of variations between cultures must therefore be explained in terms of context, which remains crucially important, but as part of a permanent interaction. Genetic inheritance has endowed human beings with such complex perceptions and desires that their detailed behaviour is extraordinarily malleable; they are also capable of deliberate attempts to change and control it. The interplay between inherited traits and contingent cultural forms is virtually identical with the historical process itself and is, therefore, in constant flux. One area in which there have been great changes is the interpretation and valuation of feelings, and this must in turn have affected how people actually behave. When self-fulfilment is seen as lying in the familial sphere, for example, and that message is reinforced on numerous cultural levels, attitudes to spouses and children will change overall. This is likely to be a shift along a spectrum; many more people will now behave as a minority used to do, while conduct which was once normal may come to be stigmatized as aberrant. Whereas romantic love was once seen as dangerous and irrational, a threat to the stability of both family and individual, in the West it has now become the internal oracle which tests the suitability of a prospective mate. Instead of seeking to repress sexual attraction, culture encourages and celebrates it. Meanwhile the idea that parents should discipline children, by physical means if necessary, has fallen into disrepute in many quarters. These are merely a few examples of many drastic shifts which together comprise the birth of modernity.

The disenchantment of the world

This picture needs to be brought into line with Durkheim's brilliant insights into the binding power of concepts continuously reinforced by ritual, in which collective excitement functions as a means of imprinting. Like so many sociological notions, this one would appear to be better at explaining continuity than change. How on earth did a world with such a strong ritual endowment, in which virtually everyone seems to have participated with some enthusiasm, come to undergo a conceptual revolution? This mystery has so far defied adequate historical explanation, but no-one should underestimate the importance of what happened.

Between the sixteenth and the eighteenth centuries, ways of thinking hitherto common to mankind were not merely altered; in some vital respects they were reversed. Traditional boundaries between external and internal came under intense challenge, as older visions of the world order started to crumble. Another great founding father of sociology, Max Weber, coined the phrase 'the disenchantment of the world' in relation to the process; unfortunately he never produced a systematic account of his thinking on the question. Weber's phrase, which might also be translated as 'the exclusion of magic from the world', gives poetic expression to the idea of a profound shift in consciousness. He was surely also right to associate it closely with the Protestant Reformation, although the relationship between cause and effect remains both elusive and highly contested in this case.

The traditional world view was one in which Man was the central figure in an ordered cosmos, all of whose parts interacted constantly. Macrocosm and microcosm, great and small worlds, were linked by an intricate web of correspondences and powers. The world of magic, as then understood, was not some kind of technically incompetent forerunner of modern science, because its fundamental concepts were inimical to scientific thinking in the modern sense. Powers were actually believed to be inherent to particular substances and verbal formulae, requiring no further explanation. If Weyer identified witches as melancholic, this was not a statement about their inner mental condition as we would understand it, but about the imbalance of humours in their bodies, which left them with an excess of black bile. This substance did not act on their constitution as a chemical might; it simply *was* melancholy, since that was its essential nature, while its presence allowed the Devil to implant delusions in his victims. Such ideas were part of a comfortable, almost instinctual way of thinking which placed social coherence far above logic or referential accuracy. Ernest Gellner has convincingly described this in terms of multi-stranded meanings, bundled together in a fashion which made it impossible to disentangle them, or to apply with any consistency that divisive logic which is the basis of modern analytical thought. He also employs the ingenious image of a 'multi-periscope submarine' to clarify the point.[8] The implication is that a remarkably homogeneous, yet largely erroneous, world-view is possible in pre-modern societies because much of it is not in contact with observed reality at all. Where such contact is made it is in discrete areas, which are not regarded as having any necessary interconnection, so that certain types of data can be filtered out if they threaten the coherence of the system as a whole. This fits very well with a situation in which very considerable practical skills are operated by craftsmen and agriculturalists, yet largely ignored by the elites who frame the general theories. It is we who are peculiar, in having at least partly (and rather unwillingly) adopted an opposing posture that sees separate and equal facts operating within a single logical space. Our world is unified by the manner in which we apprehend it, not by socially determined presuppositions about its meaning. Magic and the sacred have in consequence lost their old functional place, so that they become inviting escape routes for those in search of a spiritual dimension, instead of socially approved ways of thinking from which hardly anyone can escape. There remains a strong possibility, even a probability, that they are still natural or innate to our mental processes, so that we revert easily to them at the first opportunity. Certainly we need some explanation for the renewed interest in magic and the irrational, which has assumed such a large place in the supposedly 'rational' modern subjectivity.

While religion was crucial in maintaining the pre-modern world view, it also appears to have played a vital part in destroying it. The Protestant reformers (followed by many Catholic counterparts) rejected magic long before science undermined its whole rationale. It may well be significant that this was associated with an enormous vogue for that pioneer of introspective Christianity, St Augustine, and a lesser but important one for neo-stoic ideas of self-mastery; both implied that the human agent was capable of remaking himself, even if in many versions this was only through total subjugation to God. For a complex of reasons the older assimilative style of faith, absorbing a whole range of techniques for controlling the world, and allowing the deity wide latitude to intervene in everyday life, suffered a profound internal collapse. There are grounds to think that this was strongly connected with a slightly earlier, partly overlapping trend in the other direction, towards emphasizing the super-natural aspects of religion, which stressed the whole system to the point where a powerful reaction was generated. The endless ways of propitiating God were now condemned as no better than a protection racket, insti-tutionalized bribery and corruption in both the spiritual and the worldly spheres. The true deity was orderly and severe, unappeasable by any such means. Occult forces might still exist, but to invoke them through magic was the worst kind of blasphemy, for it saw man intruding on a sphere of power reserved to God. Protestants extended this argument to the

Catholic sacraments, whose alleged power to alter the state of the participants was held to be diabolical if it existed at all. These moves also
tended to induce, even if they did not absolutely require, the creation of
a new boundary between the psychic and the physical, which cut right
across traditional views of magic.

The formulation of the mind-body antithesis by Descartes in the early
seventeenth century gave clear expression to the implications of these
changes for subjectivity. Ideas had once been inherent to the cosmos, the
very basis of reality, and individuals had functioned more or less well in
so far as they had aligned themselves to them. Now ideas were within
the mind, applied to external objects, so that they could be modified or
rejected by the individual subject in search of a better fit against the
external world. For a self of this kind to be trapped within a tangle of
magical forces was to suffer a loss of autonomy which was very threatening, and could easily be represented in terms of an invasion or possession
by hostile forces. Heightened anxiety about witchcraft among the elites
can very plausibly be related to just this transition; although it is certainly
not an overall explanation for either witchcraft persecution or its subsequent decline, one can hardly doubt that it contributed significantly
to both.[9] Over the century or so when trials were at their height it is
also relevant that a profound divide was being created between the
educated minority and the masses, as their world views polarized to
the point where vast areas of what had once been common belief were
stigmatized as superstition. Of course these descriptions are 'ideal types',
which exaggerate the internal coherence and consistency of beliefs in the
real world, but the trends which lead towards the eighteenth-century
Enlightenment are unmistakable much earlier. Popular and elite views
of witchcraft had always differed, notably over specifically diabolic power,
which never had the same importance for ordinary people as it did for
judges or clerics; this is just the fault-line one would expect in the light
of the observations above. Villagers thought the malevolence proceeded
from the witch, part of his or her essence, and would have been baffled
by claims that the Devil deluded his servants into a false belief about
their own powers. They had no problem with the idea that the Devil
played a part – indeed they obviously believed this – but saw the operation
as essentially a joint one. On the other hand, they were perfectly capable
of making the common-sense observation that the sabbat might be a
dream-experience, since in the absence of a clear boundary between
the psychic and the physical it was quite plausible that the witches

and the Devil should pool their evil wishes through the corporate imagination.

Collusive fantasies and persecuting figures

Many African belief systems distinguish between night witches, who embody evil in a general, symbolic sense (often they are described in quite fantastic terms), and the day witches who are enemies responsible for individual misfortunes. Although European beliefs are often said to have merged the two, this may in fact be something of an oversimplification. On closer investigation there are many signs of a similar split, which is not simply between popular and elite views since folk beliefs made their own vital contribution to the myth of the sabbat. Although demonology might pretend to unite the two conceptions, this was always a rather clumsy conjunction. As we have already seen, there was a good deal of uncertainty about the relationship between the night-time meetings and the practical misdeeds attributed to witches. Only a tiny proportion of the natural disasters which the mythology associated with the sabbat – storms and crop-failure being the principal ones – seem to have given rise to direct accusations. Suspicions about weather magic do appear in the trials, but usually in a secondary role. The major witch-hunt in eastern France in 1643–4 is probably the most notable case where they played a dominant part. A much more local instance occurred in the German town of Esslingen in August 1562, when a great storm saw the sky as black as night and the crops devastated by hail. Here, however, the arrest and (unsuccessful) torture of three suspects seems to have been inspired by the preaching of the sectarian Protestant Thomas Naogeorgus, a great hater of women and denouncer of witches, so popular feelings were manipulated to some extent.[10] A handful of Lorraine cases reveal communal anxiety about similar storms, or about epidemic disease killing animals. The efforts by such clerics as the Lutheran Johann Brenz to show that such misfortunes came from God, and must be borne with patience, also suggest a strong awareness of such tendencies.[11] Nevertheless, attempts to portray the sabbat as a place where acts of *maleficium* were plotted generally remained very half-hearted. Even the witches of German-speaking Lorraine, who claimed to carry out attacks on their enemies in small groups, balanced this by separating off larger meetings where the typical inverted ceremonies took place, assemblies whose purpose was ritual and communal.

These instances also relate to a rather different interaction between the inner and outer world that was more social than psychological. The small towns and villages of Europe were inward-looking, largely self-contained communities, deeply suspicious of their neighbours and of outsiders in general. These attitudes have proved remarkably durable, still apparent for example to modern ethnographers in search of witch-craft, who are routinely told that although no-one in this village is so benighted, such things do go on at nearby places. Folklore studies also reveal a bewildering range of detailed variations within the broader regional patterns. This strongly cellular structure of local belief and custom, together with the great range of social organization found in Europe, could in theory form the basis for a much more diversified set of witchcraft beliefs than actually seems to have existed. The comparison with Africa has led most observers to see the relative uniformity of the European beliefs as powerful evidence for the influence of clerics and judges, the elites responsible for imposing ideas about the Devil and his machinations.[12] The *Malleus Maleficarum* and its successors assembled an untidy mass of stories and superstitions that were pulled together within a theological and legal framework to form a fairly coherent pattern. The printing press, the courts and officials, and the churches then combined to spread the information across the continent, in a form that could readily absorb any further variants. A flexible amalgam of popular tradition and general theory provided the basis for the innumerable negotiations which turned personal or communal suspicions into legal action. The inner world of the community was brought into an effective relationship with the outside powers, to make both demonology and persecution possible.

This account is plausible, and must be substantially correct. European witchcraft was peculiar in its location within what was already a highly complex society, whose political and intellectual organization operated on such a wide scale; literacy had a crucial part to play here. Church and state could penetrate the world of the peasants, even if the messages they handed down were always liable to be adapted to suit the recipients. The overall tendency can only have been to homogenize the various levels of belief, and smooth out local particularities. Every trial, every public reading of the confessions made by the accused, must have reinforced the symbiosis, providing more material to be recycled in the future. This was emphatically not a case of judges simply imposing their own views, however. There is very little in the evidence to support the idea that a combination of leading questions and torture can account for most confessions, with the suspects as hardly more than puppets. Admittedly there are some lists of standard questions to be put, while court records cannot be seen as reliable verbatim accounts of all that happened. Nevertheless, long and detailed confessions rarely appear to be merely stereotyped. Where collusion is obvious, this is usually among suspects or witnesses who had been kept together, notably the children involved in the Basque and Swedish trials. That there were many subtler forms of collusion between judges, gaolers, executioners and their victims cannot of course be doubted; confessions normally emerged slowly through relentless pressure on the accused. In most cases, however, this was restrained by a simple fact which we find it hard to accept, that these horrible proceedings were carried out in good faith. Witchcraft offered multiple possibilities for the persecutors to align their own inner worlds with the behaviour of the accused, as much as for the opposite process. This is one of several ways in which it may be helpful to think in terms of the standardized nightmares of society.

The permeability of the boundary between real and imaginary worlds was a crucial element behind what can easily appear as the most cynical manipulation. There is a constant temptation to portray accused witches as oppressed victims, caught up in a labelling process; this in turn is readily explained in terms of the social and psychological forces which drove people to seek scapegoats. In its own terms this is perfectly correct, but only gives a partial account of a complex situation. It is vital to recognize the extent to which individuals collaborated in their own downfall, while confirming a world view that virtually all of them shared with their persecutors. Nor were all the accused wholly guiltless. The general belief in magic led many to employ it to secure advantages for themselves; often this was in ways which must implicitly damage others. Since economic life was normally perceived in zero-sum terms, one person's gain was expected to be another's loss. Similar ideas applied in the case of counter-magic, which explicitly sought to harm hidden enemies, while at other times people must surely have tried to avenge themselves for more routine wrongs. Occult powers were also a direct means to threaten or coerce others, so that reputations were used to exact favours and payments. More subtly, they might further provide ways for individuals to seek vengeance for deeply felt grievances by asserting themselves against family members or neighbours associated with persecuting figures from their own past. Suspects who displayed aggressive and almost suicidal behaviour often seem to fit this pattern. The tendency to strike out against the persecutors who filled their internal world did not have to be public, however; it might be confined to the mind, only to be expressed in their confessions of imaginary wrongdoing, the raw material from which much of the mythology of witchcraft was elaborated. One can readily imagine a similar mechanism at work on the part of accusers and judges, with deadly effect, but here the sources are less helpful. Printed treatises are elaborate documents, far less reliable as guides to their authors' state of mind than the ingenuous statements found in court records. All one can say is that the *tone* of certain demonologists – Sprenger and Krämer, Binsfeld, Bodin, de Lancre all come to mind – carries the impression of deep inner tensions, finding their outlet in the construction of nightmarish universes where diabolical power ran riot.

Perversity and punishment

There is nothing very surprising about this, for the witchcraft narratives dealt in materials with profound capacities to disturb. They portrayed a series of distorted or perverse relationships that had to do with fundamental human experiences and anxieties, and dramatized these vividly. Two areas stand out above all. Maternal feelings, nourishment and succour were routinely parodied or denied, as witches attacked infants, nursing mothers, crops, or animals. Oedipal tensions between fathers and children were equally invoked as the normal relations of authority were inverted, legitimate power rejected and perverse sexuality exhibited. The vulgar assumption that any psychoanalytic interpretation must be primarily concerned with sexual themes risks being particularly misleading here. It is hardly necessary to be a doctrinaire Kleinian to grasp the profound formative role played by infantile attachment to the mother, with all its ambiguities and its ferocious interplay of love and hate. Birth and motherhood were of course also intense, deeply disturbing experiences for the adult women concerned. In an age when both subsistence and survival itself were so precarious, the associated tensions must have been constantly reinforced in ways hard to imagine from within the pampered societies of the modern West. Hunger, pain, and the dread of an isolated, miserable death were everyday companions, not remote fears which could be pushed below the surface of consciousness. It is interesting to note that some modern psychoanalysts have described how hunger calls up unconscious sexual impulses of a primitive kind, often of an oral-sadistic nature. The folklore of the day compensated with visions of a land of Cockaigne where food, drink and warmth were abundant; in contrast, sexuality has a very muted part in such imaginings. The sexual element is more obvious in fantasies of the witches' sabbat, yet with rare exceptions it is curiously unspecific. Generalized terms such as sodomy were employed to evoke some unspecified range of perversities, while artists such as Hans Baldung Grien, despite their manifestly erotic intentions, remained very naive in their depiction of feminine sexuality. As has already been emphasized, the routine sexual possession of witches by the Devil at the moment of apostasy was almost exclusively an expression of power, involving pain rather than pleasure.

The Devil's identification with a sadistic and punitive father-figure is so complete that virtually every action attributed to him can be seen in these terms; he is truly the alter ego of God the Father, the other self on which the inadmissible evil side of the divine being can be projected, once it has been split off and denied. One can well argue that a magnification of his role was a necessary part of the more intense, demanding religious sensibility of the early modern period. Protestant stress on the total power and knowledge of God, now stripped of all the old intercessors, made it inevitable that rebellious or wicked thought or actions should be attributed to this antagonistic, corrupting figure. For Catholics the situation was rather different. Since they were bound to stand out against the Protestant determination to weaken the links between the physical and the divine, they positively welcomed opportunities to show that the Devil was a physically active presence in the world, one who could be combated with ritual and sacred objects. In their different ways both creeds dramatized the world in terms of a perpetual conflict between good and bad fathers. On the Catholic side, this was balanced by a huge upsurge in the devotion to Mary as the epitome of the caring mother, accessible to the believer in an intimate fashion no purely male deity could ever be. It may not be too fanciful to see Protestant ideas about the holy household and the nature of the marriage bond as some kind of counterpart, although on a symbolic level the reformed churches were fatally handicapped by their concentration on an abstract, masculine

God. Whichever precise form it took, the religious universe of the period provided a series of powerful images with which believers were naturally drawn to people their own inner worlds.[13] Much of their force derived precisely from their status as projections, of course, as any survey of the abundant religious literature of the period reveals.

Theatres of the mind

Individual inner worlds have been appropriately described as theatres of the mind, private stages on which dramas of deep personal significance are repeatedly played out.[14] The characters are projections or fantasies whose nature reflects the traumas and conflicts of one's formative years. Personal identity as it is really experienced is not something stable and absolute; it is better understood as an unstable composite of the multiple identities secreted in this inner space. Understood in these terms, such an identity is constructed against the forbidden and the impossible. The first of these crucial boundaries involves libidinal or violent longings – incest and murder being the most extreme – which are rigorously prohibited by social convention. The second concerns our narcissistic wishes for unlimited power, knowledge and immunity to pain or death. In fantasy we are all omnipotent, bisexual and immortal, but maturity requires us to renounce these false goals and replace them with more modest and realistic ones. The degree of integration achieved by individuals varies enormously, in terms of both fantasy and adaptation to the real world, with those who have been less successful in this respect displaying various neurotic symptoms. Among the most interesting of these is the tendency to repeat unsatisfactory relationships, casting other people into predetermined roles, which can largely be understood as projections of hidden, rejected aspects of the self. These might be described as addictive relationships, whose script is written by their creator in a preordained pattern. This structure has significant implications for witchcraft cases. Although perfectly predictable, it is still rather startling how many of the central themes of the forbidden and the impossible are also of crucial importance in the fantasies of witchcraft. Unnatural or incestuous sexuality, the killing of enemies, siblings, husbands and children, a kind of omnipotence in which wishes become deeds – these all confirm yet again, if it were necessary, how these imaginings spring from the very core of the human psyche. In their more elaborated, written forms they may be located in the 'transitional space' between fantasy and reality, the place of cultural and creative activity where they still flourish in modern culture.

The idea of addictive relationships might lead us to ask how far suspects chose themselves, rather than being selected by mere chance. Michelet's old idea of the rebellion of the oppressed, untenable if applied literally, becomes far more plausible when recast in psychic terms. There is likely to have been a considerable overlap between poorly integrated personalities and inability to prosper in small communities. Those who felt themselves to be repeatedly disadvantaged, while routinely provoking antagonisms, would also have been unusually bad at disguising their hostile fantasies, so that a self-reinforcing pattern would have been established. Everyone would have found it easy to slip recognized witches into their inner theatres, as classic persecuting figures, probably finding comfort in displacing hatreds they could not readily admit on to these more acceptable substitutes. In these and other ways witches and their victims may often have been drawn together by unacknowledged complicities. These are forms of causality the historian can scarcely hope to bring into full view, given the limitations of the sources, but they are not to be discounted for all that. A purely mechanistic view of the highly personal relations evident in most cases, which would explain everything in terms of general economic, social, or political forces, can hardly be seriously credited. Any account of these matters which ignores the power of fantasy and the inner workings of the mind flies in the face of both the evidence and everything we ought to recognize about the wellsprings of human interaction. At various points in previous chapters, moreover, we have seen how the occasional, well-documented case virtually demands attention for its psychological subtext. It is unfortunate that most surviving interrogations are too brief and schematic to reveal much at this level; the exceptions are often urban trials, where judges might be prepared to question suspects repeatedly. In the case of a man like Hauff at Esslingen this probably reflected his own obsessive interest in details about the personal depravity of the accused, alongside his need to convince both wavering public opinion and sceptical jurists that he was right. The wealth of detail found in some North American trials may well have rather similar origins, for here the courts were very reluctant to convict, while Puritan observers were eager to learn more about the wiles of the Devil. Instances of demonic possession also tend to be very revealing, because they allowed the afflicted quite exceptional liberty to express forbidden thoughts.

Exorcism, acting out and confessions

These cases of demonic possession also involved disturbing transactions across forbidden boundaries, but with significant differences. Here the age bias was very obvious, with a massive concentration among the young. The Devil was normally represented by the sufferers as having entered their bodies against their will, often with the supposed assistance of a witch; this exonerated them from blame for behaviour which could have been interpreted as evidence of their own depravity. It has often been noted that such symptoms were associated with intense religious backgrounds, which strongly implies that those involved found an outlet for their repressed feelings and desires by splitting them off, then projecting them into the evil spirits. However wilful and deceptive such behaviour may have been, it was also addictive and self-destructive, the more so when it was rewarded by attention from a circle of fascinated adults. Young women incarcerated in convents were of course an extreme case, for their situation was at once an incitement to such forms of protest and a perfect opportunity for it. The acting out of shared fears and obsessions in this fashion might get completely out of hand, as it did at Loudun, where the possessed nuns kept up their performances for several years in the presence of great crowds. Over this period several of the exorcists themselves became deranged, helplessly caught up in a psychic whirlwind they had rashly joined in creating. Public exorcisms were also horribly dangerous because they tended to get linked up with religious and political controversies, which the more naive participants were quite incapable of separating from the personal aspects. This was a notable feature in France, but was often true in Germany, the Spanish Netherlands and England as well. There was a curious tension here between the need to cure the sufferer, as evidence that the exorcist enjoyed divine support, and the desire to keep the performance going as a propagandist exercise. One may suspect that the star performers read the unconscious wishes of their spiritual managers correctly when they found a series of ingenious compromises. Periodically one devil would be driven out with great display, only to be succeeded by another, or to slip back in overnight.

In some cases the only answer was to isolate the possessed, thus cutting off the oxygen supply of publicity which kept the fire alight.

Whatever the more zealous or credulous exorcists might wish, their activities never commanded general support among the elites. The manipulation was frequently too obvious, and fraud too often detected, while medical opinion – although always divided – tended towards naturalistic explanations. One of the reasons for these sceptical attitudes was the manner in which the possessed subverted normal power relations, using the diabolical personae to mock their interlocutors, claiming special knowledge, and of course denouncing others as witches. Their use to support particular causes was also bound to provoke opponents. Mobilizing the Devil within as a mode of influencing the external world was therefore a dubious proposition in most circumstances, all too likely to prove counter-productive in the longer term. Until well into the seventeenth century there was a predictable division along religious lines, for the mainline Protestants, with their rejection of traditional views about the permeability of the physical and supernatural worlds, were generally hostile to the practice of exorcism. As time passed a number of sectarian groups, drawing on the biblical precedents for casting out devils, developed their own versions of these practices, but it was the Catholics who initially saw possession as an ideal opening to demonstrate that the heavenly force was with them. The corporeal power of relics, holy words, consecrated hosts and their like, exemplified in these dramatic circumstances, was to be a living refutation of Protestant claims that these were mere shams. There were some unseemly contests in places where both confessions had a foothold, with the possessed becoming the centre of competitive diagnosis and therapy; on the whole, the Catholics probably had the better of it on a case by case level. Protestant allegations that the whole business merely emphasized the extent to which their opponents were in league with the Devil, however ingenious, lacked the same force on any but the purely intellectual plane. After this initial enthusiasm, however, Catholic attitudes gradually changed as the Tridentine reforms took effect. They brought with them a slow transition to a more austere, rational and controlled religious universe, one in which leading clerics often seemed to agree with their Protestant counterparts that the age of miracles was past. While many aspects of belief and practice maintained traditional ideas that divine influence could be mobilized for immediate earthly purposes, they were now accompanied by a fierce determination to maintain an iron grip over anything which threatened good order and discipline. Spectacular public exorcisms gave voice to just those kinds of wild, uncontrolled, largely feminine religiosity which the hierarchy instinctively mistrusted; after a period of hesitation the authorities moved decisively to suppress them. This was made easier because confessional boundaries had effectively stabilized, so that Protestantism no longer seemed a mortal threat and the controversial aspect lost its edge.

There is little doubt that both the possessed and witches under repeated interrogation engaged in a peculiar kind of dialogue with their interlocutors, adapting their responses to meet expectations. The making of false confessions, once seen as a great problem, becomes much easier to understand in the light of more recent findings about the dynamics of such interchanges. Sustained questioning routinely brings about a situation in which the accused seeks to meet the expectations of the interrogator. Witchcraft suspects, already demoralized by the hostility of their neighbours or relatives, appalling prison conditions and the threat (or reality) of torture, were also particularly vulnerable to such pressure in at least two other respects. Their judges could pose with perfect sincerity as intermediaries whose aim was to purge them of their apostasy, thus reconciling them with God and the Christian community, even if this required their death. Secondly, it was all too easy for them to turn their own life experiences into the kind of stories required, translating them into the language of the diabolic, and describing their repressed wishes as if they had been murderously effective in reality. In most accounts the sabbat has strongly theatrical characteristics, with the use of masks and false appearances placing it in the borders between reality and fantasy. The sexual activity described in the more lurid confessions merges into a phantasmagoria of perversity and death, in which the witches themselves were brutalized and humiliated in a thoroughly sado-masochistic fashion. These imaginings expose a primitive state of mental distress, in which boundaries seem to have collapsed and evil forces have burst out in the most destructive fashion. In a similar fashion the original seduction and sexual surrender to the Devil represented a failure to contain evil, as the feeble defences of an isolated individual were overwhelmed. This is usually represented as a fatal lapse at a moment when emotion – anger or despair – had made the subject vulnerable. It can be associated with images of both the individual and the family as frail containers, constantly menaced by the vices within them, whose release implied a loss of control leading to anarchy.

The confessions were structured as narratives, around the banal succession of temptation, diabolical pact, sabbat and harm done to neighbours. At each stage the witch reaffirmed the negative, antisocial position from which he or she now supposedly wished to be liberated, albeit at the cost of life itself. The sequence was one in which forbidden boundaries were repeatedly crossed, with the moral community being abandoned for its negation in the fantastic anti-world ruled by the Devil. The individual who made this transition became something akin to the humanoids beloved of science fiction, as a being from another world concealed within a human exterior, who was then reinserted in the everyday world equipped with lethal powers. The idea of the flight to and from the sabbat was partly a symbolic expression of this passage between contradictory modes of existence, breaking the normal rules of human capacity. The ability of the accused to offer these more or less standardized images reflects their double origin, as products of both the inner theatre of the mind, as a hidden set of common experiences between all participants, and of the public sphere of popular culture. Specific witchcraft beliefs were cultural artefacts at this second level, maintained and subtly inflected through various agencies of transmission now largely lost to us, except in folklore collections from more recent times. What this residue suggests, as one might expect, is that storytellers and others were very reticent in providing detailed information about the diabolical; the sabbat was largely absent from their repertoire, except as a shadowy presence in the background. This may help to explain an interesting feature of the confessions. A high proportion of the more elaborate accounts were given by the rather exceptional group of young suspects, most notably by adolescents; this is particularly striking because there were so few of them in proportion to the mass of witches well past the prime of life. The vivid imaginings associated with the Basque and Swedish witch-hunts must be related to the exceptional prominence of children and adolescents among the accused. The other groups most inclined to produce stories of this kind were the well-educated elite victims and the cunning folk. It seems as if the typical accused – older members of the oral culture – were far more likely to offer the most banal and standardized version, the minimum necessary to satisfy their questioners. It is possible that many of the younger witches fell into the putative 'self-selected' group, whereas the identification of older suspects (apart from the cunning folk) usually had more to do with socio-economic factors. There are good reasons to believe that young people, still making the crucial transition to full independence, have an exceptional capacity to generate intense fantasies about domination, sexuality and magical powers, in just the style found in their confessions.

Witchcraft and evolutionary psychology

The centrality of these conflicts between the desired and the permitted in any discussion of both human societies and human personality makes their analogous position in connection with witchcraft very significant. When this is coupled with the presence of strikingly similar witchcraft beliefs in most known societies, questions are raised about the relationship between witchcraft and those 'human universals' posited by evolutionary psychology. It is even worth asking the apparently strange question whether human beings are born with a specific inherited mechanism for detecting witches, although to date I have not found a convincing reason why our Pleistocene ancestors would have needed such an instinct. It is much easier to believe that among the set of programmed social skills, developed by evolution to meet our basic needs for survival and reproduction, there are some which might incidentally predispose us to identify other people as malevolent secret enemies. The underlying premise is that

> human architectures are 'pre-equipped' (that is, reliably develop) specialized mechanisms that 'know' many things about humans, social relations, emotions and facial expressions, the meaning of situations to others, the underlying organization of contingent social actions such as threats and exchanges, language, motivation, and so on.[15]

Such capabilities enable us to achieve a wide range of essential goals, from selecting mates and detecting aggression to avoiding unnecessary conflicts. Among these mechanisms is one which interprets the conduct of other people in terms of invisible internal entities – beliefs and desires – and emerges very early in children. This is part of a broader group of instincts helping us to evaluate the behaviour of the people around us, specific capacities that in combination can tackle very general problems. We are skilled at deceiving other people, but also in detecting such deception or manipulation. A further suggestion is that much of human intelligence is social intelligence, the product of selection for success in social competition: There is little doubt that we were selected for the ability to predict and influence the behavior of potential rivals for resources, present and potential allies, possible mates, and of course, close kin. Presumably, this predictive ability implies the development of elaborate internal representations of others.[16]

This is what the world of gossip and rumour helps us to do, with particular reference to those people in our immediate environment whose behaviour is most important to us.

A series of putative links do suggest themselves here. The propensity to detect witches may be enhanced in periods of stress, because one of the prices people have to pay for good social relationships is repression, normally coupled with splitting and projection. This prevents the immediate expression of hostile, unfriendly and conflictive feelings, attitudes and intentions – but at a very dangerous cost. As Blake's brilliantly intuitive poem 'The Poison Tree' puts it,

> I was angry with my friend:
> I told my wrath, my wrath did end.
> I was angry with my foe:
> I told it not, my wrath did grow.

Telling your anger is an act between friends; it digests the stress then permits reconciliation, while *not* telling it stokes up murderous consequences. Another interesting phenomenon is that peaks of hostility towards a specific enemy, usually quite disproportionate to the offence, generate an equally unrealistic feeling of goodwill towards all other neighbours. This suggests a further hypothesis about the behaviour of a community under chronic or unusual stress, such as shortages, disease, mass migrations, war, or frightening and uncontrollable changes in weather. In such circumstances it may only be possible to maintain superficially congenial relationships among the majority in a band or community if somebody or something is identified as the source of the problem, which can then be dealt with magically or practically. This would have obvious relevance to Pleistocene bands coping in a big and dangerous world, and may therefore be a universal substratum or grid in the human mind, employing the mechanisms of splitting and projective identification at both individual and group level. We should also note than in hunter-gatherer societies, human aggression is a constant threat to the cohesiveness of groups, operating to force periodic division. Members of such bands respond by spending enormous amounts of time talking out their relationship problems, especially at night around the fire, just as early modern peasants did at their winter fireside assemblies.

These are just some of the reasons to think that witchcraft beliefs might at least partly be explained as accidental yet powerful by-products of the systems by which human beings orient themselves in the social world. Our instinctual antennae are highly sensitive to subtly coded messages, quick to detect possible antagonism or deceit on the part of others. In this light, projecting our own feelings into others is part of a constant process whereby we try to assess relationships and relative standing. When false notes are struck, our bodies react in ways beyond our conscious control, which can extend to hostile gestures or outright aggression. As a case in point, it is worth reflecting on how we react to that classic witchcraft situation, an unwelcome demand from a beggar. Common responses include real physical discomfort, barely repressed impulses to violence and fantasies about possible retribution. This is a paradigm for many other situations in which we seem quite unable to detach ourselves from an invasive social world, because our instincts hook us into it despite ourselves. A banal but plausible conclusion would be that the social equipment evolved to meet the needs of small bands of hunter-gatherers remains relevant and functional in large complex societies, but sometimes operates in ways outside observers consider cruel and unjust. Although human beings are so adaptable that they create new ways of managing these problems, stress lines are bound to appear, and beliefs in the malevolence of others are a predictable indicator of such tensions. Witchcraft may therefore be a phenomenon we are predisposed to suspect, a psychic potential we cannot help carrying round within ourselves as part of our long-term inheritance.

CONCLUSION

THE READER WHO HAS come this far will certainly appreciate that European witchcraft was a massively complex phenomenon that poses a major challenge to historians. The wide range of analyses and explanations offered in this book may have appeared confusing or indecisive to some. Surely, they may think, after all the research undertaken into the subject, it must be possible to come up with some clear, unequivocal conclusions. There are indeed historians who claim that there is something illegitimate about offering multiple explanations for simultaneous occurrences of a general kind, although this argument has never wholly convinced me. In any case, witchcraft would probably escape such causal logic, because on closer inspection there is no single thing to be explained. The existence of witchcraft beliefs across European society is significantly different from the legal persecution of witches, while of course not unrelated. The beliefs are in essentials ancient, tenacious and still observable today in modified forms; the persecution was relatively brief, patchy and contingent. There is always a danger that the two will be conflated, since it is only through the trials that we can gain access to the beliefs, yet it was the latter which were the one absolute prior necessity if there were to be trials at all. In this sense the explanation for persecution is disarmingly simple. People believed in witches, and laws were passed which enabled suspects to be taken to court effectively. The puzzle is less why this should have happened than why it did not occur earlier. Many people are still understandably confused about the temporal sequence, so that one often sees claims that 'in the Middle Ages such a person would have been burned as a witch'. In fact it was only at the very end of the medieval period, in the fifteenth century, that there was any such risk; until then the relative scepticism of the ruling elites, together with the nature of the legal system, excluded the possibility.

The reasons for the relative, limited and localized breakdown of that scepticism from the fourteenth century onwards have not formed part of the subject matter of this book. Many historians have already discussed them at length, while the subject is likely to be revitalized by Stuart Clark's forthcoming study of demonological theory.[1] Once this (admittedly vital) intellectual aspect has been put to one side, my own interpretation of the nature of the persecution, as a social and political phenomenon, is very straightforward. Village and small town witchcraft was the basic type, the everyday reality around which everything else was built. The more exotic variants which so often confuse our understanding – possession cases, intense short-term persecutions, witchfinding, lycanthropy, vampirism – were secondary elaborations. It is suggestive that most of the really good examples in these genres come from the last phase of persecution, when, alongside such other developments as the growing prominence of children, they helped to strengthen elite doubts about the whole process. The longer persecution continued, the more florid such epiphenomena tended to become. Full-blown diabolical theatre, in the styles of Würzburg, Loudun, or Salem, was usually the coda, not the overture, to extensive activity against witches. These famous episodes brought together many strands which were found individually in humdrum trials of peasants and artisans, but almost never combined so extensively in a single case. Witchcraft was about envy, ill-will and the power to harm others, exercised in small face-to-face communities which, although they could often contain such feelings, found it almost impossible to disperse them. Those involved relied heavily on the cunning folk and their counter-magic, alongside a range of social and familial pressures, to deal with suspect neighbours. Only at a few brief and limited points in time and space did they think of eradicating them completely. Witches were people you lived with, however unhappily, until they goaded someone past endurance.

It is therefore a misconception to see persecution as essentially directed and managed from above, a mere adjunct to state-building, religious conflict and social hostility. In this vision it is readily portrayed as an oppressive technique, serving selfish ends, exploited by bigoted or cynical ruling groups. While there are traces of such behaviour in individual episodes, I hope to have shown that it is totally inadequate to account for events on a more general basis. We must downgrade support by the rulers to being a necessary condition for widespread persecution, not its fundamental cause. Although it is certainly true that many members of the elites showed a new willingness to identify and punish witches, this was far from being a complete surrender to demands for ruthless campaigns against them. In most of Europe, belief in the reality of witchcraft, and the need to provide legal means to repress it, was combined with cautious scepticism about individual cases. Very few of the jurists, clerics and doctors who debated the issue failed to recognize that there were serious difficulties about proof, that admissions under torture were unreliable, or that it was hard to draw boundaries between real and imaginary worlds. This did not, of course, prevent a good many judges from behaving in thoroughly abusive ways, as a number of cases described earlier demonstrate. For some at least, the trials provided a perfect opportunity to indulge their own sadism free of guilt. When one considers the overall record, however, it is plain that such instances are rare and localized. Europe as a whole did not surrender in panic to a wave of witch-hunting, not least because such episodes provoked increasingly critical reactions, which helped create a situation where persecution largely ceased before the supporting belief structure had been abandoned.

The multiple local variations resulted from a complex and unpredictable interaction between popular and elite ideas about witchcraft. These were of course far from being wholly distinct; at every stage it is vital to remember that such distinctions are an interpretative convenience. The innumerable ways in which particular themes were shared, challenged, or evolved make it very hard to perceive the underlying structures correctly. One might well argue that loose endings and fuzzy logic were an integral part of the situation, something any serious analysis must take into account. Over recent decades such analyses have proliferated. A very large body of explanations has been mobilized to account for witchcraft persecution, most of them portraying it in functionalist terms as an outgrowth of social, religious, economic and political tensions. Few of these arguments are wholly worthless, although quite a number only apply to exceptional or isolated cases. This creates a curious problem, for when they are aggregated it becomes hard to understand why persecution was not far more intense than the records show it to have been. Wild claims that nine million witches were executed may completely distort the true picture, but it is easy to see why they gain currency, since the logic of recent interpretations points to a much more impressive figure than the meagre 40,000 or so which sober research can actually justify. I do not mean to minimize the unpleasantness of the phenomenon; anyone who has read hundreds of interrogations under torture, as I have, can only feel sickened by the horrors they contain. Nevertheless, across at least 75 per cent of Europe the persecution was minimal in numerical terms, so that a substantial majority of towns and villages did not experience a single trial, successful or otherwise, over the whole period. We should not assume that these communities were unaware or unconcerned; their inhabitants almost certainly believed some of their neighbours to be witches, and took what they thought were appropriate steps in self-defence. These just did not include trying to compass another person's death through the criminal law.

While there might seem to be a certain perversity in setting out to explain why the persecution was a relative failure, which only gained momentum in relatively few exceptional instances, a good case can be made out for this view. The demonologists who wrote demanding much greater action by the rulers repeatedly attacked the indifference or outright scepticism of their contemporaries. Far from assuming they were the mouthpieces of orthodoxy, they often chose to present themselves as isolated campaigners, Cassandras to whom few would listen. Their passionate and partisan arguments are not evidence for consensus among the elites, but the reverse. There are obvious difficulties in building a satisfactory model which can incorporate all the elements in such an elaborate nexus of cause and effect. On the one hand we have the multiple reasons to interpret witchcraft as an attractive vector for numerous underlying strains or conflicts, many of which should already have become clear. The socio-economic 'scissors' of the sixteenth century, the development of inquisitorial process and criminal justice, religious division, gender relations, printing; these are just the most obvious areas to which we must look to see forces working for change. To understand why these were not more effective, on the other hand, it is necessary to include another set of factors which may account for the 'stickiness' of the phenomenon as a whole. Understanding how witchcraft worked in detail may not constitute an explanation in itself; it does, however, set certain limits on the kinds of interpretation we can accept. In particular, a better conception of the restraints which operated to minimize persecution in most places most of the time is crucial on at least two levels. We need to know why most places escaped so lightly, and we can only hope to discover why these controls broke down in specific cases if we can identify them properly.

In many areas, witchcraft charges seemed to offer an outstandingly good prospect of success for the accuser. The combination of communal pressure and torture made short work of all but the toughest among the accused. Yet the internal evidence of the trials themselves reveals a singular reluctance to employ such weapons, since the typical suspect had a reputation stretching back over many years, while witnesses usually spoke of deaths and losses of the most serious kind covering the whole period. Numerous factors arising from kinship and communal relations have already been suggested to account for these enormous delays. Their effect on persecution is obvious; since the criminal justice system relied on denunciations, the supply of victims was largely regulated by the population at large. The one important way round this was through the identification of accomplices by those convicted, and most of the intense local persecutions by zealous judges exploited this loophole. Very often, however, such charges did not lead to immediate prosecutions, probably because local officials usually wanted to be sure there was communal support before they undertook these expensive and time-consuming activities. Popular reluctance to use the courts becomes much more comprehensible in the context of the more general functioning of the legal system. In most jurisdictions very few cases of theft, personal violence and similar misdemeanours ever came to a verdict. Starting court proceedings was normally just a ploy, whose purpose was to secure a settlement through less formal modes of arbitration. Witchcraft was different; once a trial began, there was little hope of retreat, while the case might well have to be argued in front of strangers with whom all parties felt uncomfortable. Whenever these were educated professionals applying stringent standards of proof, as in France, the sense of alienation became a major deterrent. It is noticeable that most areas of persistent village-inspired trials, such as Lorraine, Luxembourg and the Saarland, used very local courts staffed by lay judges. Peasants were most likely to engage in enthusiastic persecution if they could take control of the whole system, as with the village committees in the Saarland, or rely on the kind of swift and highly manipulable justice provided by itinerant witch-finders like Matthew Hopkins, *le petit prophète*, or the henchmen of the Elector of Cologne. Even in these instances it is doubtful whether the very high levels of persecution could have been maintained once the initial supply of suspects was exhausted.

One objection to the indiscriminate use of the term 'witch-craze' to describe the persecution as a whole is precisely that it should be saved for these exceptional cases. Much of the confusion in general discussions of the subject arises from a failure to grasp their very particular character, and their complex relationship to the wider phenomenon. There are very important distinctions and contrasts between endemic local persecution

– by far the dominant mode – and epidemic witch-hunting. The latter never lasted very long in any specific place, and was very restricted geographically. Although they accounted for a significant proportion of all known victims (perhaps 10–20 per cent depending on one's definition), genuine witch-crazes only touched the lives of a tiny fraction of Europeans. Virtually all the significant examples are located between the 1590s and the 1640s. A few earlier cases did see groups of up to thirty or so fall victim to brief local panics; one of these, the Vauderie of Arras (1459–62) was such an obvious frame-up that those convicted were posthumously rehabilitated by the Paris *parlement* in 1491. The handful of witch-hunts which claimed victims in their hundreds are therefore a very late development, and in many ways a parasitic one, which emerged from the background of limited local persecution. Even within this group there is a distinction between officially sponsored movements and the activities of popular witch-finders, although this is not a clear frontier. In part this was a contrast between urban and rural, but the former also tended to place far greater emphasis on conspiratorial fantasies of the sabbat, and strike at unexpected targets. In a number of cases, including Scotland, Trier and Cologne, major hunts mixed the two; as one would expect, this was a particularly dangerous combination, and these episodes tended to last longer than usual. Popular witch-finders could themselves only operate successfully if they enjoyed support from local authorities, as the Hopkins and Stearne crusade illustrates. It is of course impossible to draw any clear line between large and small persecutions, which might share some features, yet the latter do have a very different feel. Some combination of zealous local judges and popular feeling is the standard background to these small chains of accusation, linking up accusations by convicted witches and long-standing reputations. It was rare for them to involve more than a dozen suspects, or to extend beyond the known group of local witches. Despite their small scale, they were so numerous that they may well account for the majority of European witch trials.

If these very dangerous possibilities did not develop into a truly European witch-craze, this had a good deal to do with the attitudes of the lawyers. The misfit between formal legal proceedings and local attitudes, which often deterred peasants from using the courts, also operated in the opposite direction. Sophisticated judges were likely to react critically to the evidence deployed, sensing the danger that they might be recruited into the world of peasant feuds and superstition. Since the moment when the literati, the crucial class of trained administrators, had first appeared on the scene in numbers during the high Middle Ages, part of their self-definition had been to establish their distance from this alternative universe. This may well be one of the fundamental reasons for the relative scepticism about witchcraft typified by the *Canon Episcopi* and such leading medieval intellectuals as St Thomas Aquinas. Attitudes of this kind could only be reinforced, in the eyes of early modern lawyers, by the spectacle of popular witch-hunting, breaking the rules in every possible fashion. They were also associated with a long-running battle between professional and lay judges, in which procedural irregularities in the lower courts provided justification for restricting or even removing their powers, bringing them under much tighter control. While these factors did not prevent particular courts or individuals from engaging in enthusiastic witch-hunting, their overall effect was to create openings for doubt and disagreement. As we have seen, similar ambiguities are apparent in the case of the other professionals most often involved, the clerics and doctors; for every enthusiastic persecutor one can find a determined sceptic, and probably several doubters. There was also the insouciance and lack of logic often found in day-to-day practice, with individuals liable to apply quite different standards from one case to another.

The previous chapter suggested some of the psychological factors which make it so tempting to manufacture scapegoats. It is also a sociological commonplace that persecution has the apparently paradoxical effect of strengthening social bonds, by a similar process which unites other groups against scapegoats who are blamed for a range of ills. As an outstanding recent book by Bob Moore has shown, this process first appeared on a large scale in Europe around the eleventh and twelfth centuries (one must assume it has always been widespread at the communal level). It was associated with the great development of religious and secular power structures, built around those literati just mentioned, the men who took the lead in organizing persecution. The targets were not witches, however, but three other groups identified as deviants; heretics, lepers and Jews. In each case the mode and the motivation was subtly different, but a similar mythology of sexual depravity and anti-social conspiracy was used to justify violent repression. While numerous agencies collaborated in these activities, their classic expression in institutional terms was through the Inquisition, with its new procedural style and its concern to punish 'victimless' crimes damaging to society at large.[2] Historians have rightly associated these earlier trends with the subsequent criminalization of witches. One can hardly doubt that techniques and ideas were transferred, so that there are causal as well as generic links between the various persecutions. On the other hand, there are strong objections to the over-mechanical views once advanced, which envisaged spare repressive capacity, released by the elimination of other deviants, seeking out new victims in the form of witches. This could be associated with the notion that scapegoats had become some kind of functional social need, so that as one group was eliminated another was forced into the role.

These arguments gained plausibility until twenty years ago, through two bizarre historical frauds. The more significant of the two involved an early nineteenth-century writer of pulp fiction, Étienne Lamothe-Langon, who filled large sections of his largely imaginary history of the Toulouse Inquisition with fourteenth-century witchcraft trials of his own invention. When these materials were absorbed into standard German collections later in the nineteenth century, they seemed to show that the Inquisitors in southern France had moved smoothly from condemning Cathar heretics to punishing witches; the missing link between different types of deviant was neatly provided. A secondary deception, giving a similar picture for northern Italy, arose from sixteenth-century printed editions of the fourteenth-century jurist Bartolus of Sassoferrato, which included a group of fictitious interpolated witchcraft trials.[3] Once these non-existent cases are removed, it becomes evident that there was far too long a chronological gap between the major heresy trials and those for witchcraft for anyone to sustain the idea that the Inquisition had to manufacture new categories of deviance simply in order to maintain its throughput (and its income). There were admittedly some obsessive Inquisitors around the fringes of the Alps, at a rather later date, who pursued both heretics and witches; in this sense there was some genuine cross-influence. We must note, however, that these trials did not set off an immediate reaction elsewhere in Europe, for after the first surge of persecution in the late fifteenth century, the level of activity dropped back sharply until the second and much greater wave which began in the 1570s and 1580s.

Compared with the earlier persecutions then, that of witches was astonishingly slow to take off, with something like 150 years separating the appearance of the recognizable stereotype from the beginnings of widespread action across much of Europe. Yet we must suppose that there was always a potential supply of suspects, since they were readily found wherever they were actively sought, so this picture adds force to the idea that persecution was not as attractive as it might seem to the casual eye. One problem was identification; witches were much harder to detect than even heretics, from a legal standpoint. Perhaps more significant was the difficulty of presenting them as a really serious social menace, outside the most local context. For all the ingenuity of the demonologists, claims that Satan and his minions were on the brink of destroying the Christian commonwealth were deeply unconvincing; even at the theoretical level their alleged efforts in this direction hardly rose above the trivial. The most plausible of them was the charge, by Puritans in the Perkins mould, that a combination of witches and cunning folk was undermining true religion, but as we have seen this ran too much against the grain of popular belief to work as a basis for persecution. In truth, witches were almost completely eclipsed by the two great fears which haunted the ruling classes in the sixteenth century – religious division and popular revolt. These were real and immediate threats, whose potential had been repeatedly demonstrated. At times they coalesced, as happened with the German Peasants' War of 1525, the Anabaptist excesses in Munster in 1534, the Pilgrimage of Grace in 1536 and the Netherlands crisis of 1565–6. In England, the revolts of 1549 left a long memory, while urban and rural uprisings were a repeated feature of French experience for most of the early modern period. The traumatic effects of religious conflict were visible everywhere, giving rise to intense struggles which threatened to tear European societies apart. Perhaps the most vicious of all were the Wars of Religion in France, which raged intermittently for nearly four decades after 1560. It is a sobering fact that the massacres perpetrated by French Catholics (and to a lesser extent Protestants) probably claimed as many lives as witchcraft trials in all of Europe, without taking into account those killed in the associated wars. In 1572 the Parisian massacre of St Bartholomew's Day, and its provincial imitations, led to thousands of deaths within a couple of weeks, with men, women and children slaughtered simply because of their religion. Montaigne thought the barbarity of his countrymen surpassed that of the cannibals, not least because their cruelties were perpetrated 'not among ancient enemies, but among neighbours and fellow citizens, and what is worse, on the pretext of piety and religion'.[4]

It is surely relevant to note that witchcraft did echo these dominating fears on its own mythical stage. At the imaginary level witches were the ultimate heretics and the most extreme social rebels, engaged in a conspiracy whose aim was the utter subversion of religious and social order. This is further evidence for the pervasiveness of the fears, and it must have contributed to the 'confessional' witch-hunting discussed at various points in this book. In general, however, witchcraft rated a poor third behind the great overt threats, for which there was so much compelling evidence in the everyday world. The rulers had far stronger motives for responding to these direct challenges than to the obscure personal grievances of peasants against neighbours whom they blamed for what outsiders must have regarded as the trivial misfortunes of village life (to rulers, but not of course to those involved). Relatively brief experience of actual trials was often enough for such charges to be regarded as a source of disorder and conflict themselves, tiresome evidence for the backwardness and ignorance of the lower orders. Such scornful, dismissive attitudes took many decades to establish themselves across the continent, with many local fluctuations, but by the later seventeenth century the trend was unmistakable in western Europe. This polite disdain largely coincided with a growing confidence in the stability of the social and religious order, rumours of whose demise had proved to be much exaggerated. Since witchcraft had always been a parallel in fantasy to the direct fears, its grip on the imagination of the ruling elites faded with them. In the England of Queen Anne there were still a few Tory propagandists who thought there was some mileage in identifying their Whig opponents as being soft on witchcraft, but neither they nor their Presbyterian counterparts in Scotland found much response to such claims.

It was certainly fortunate that most European rulers and their more powerful servants took such a hesitant and ultimately sceptical line. The exceptional cases in which restraint was abandoned – Scotland and Trier in the 1590s, Denmark, Würzburg, Bamberg and Cologne in the 1620s and 1630s, alongside numerous smaller towns and states – provide chilling warnings of how persecution by an alliance of rulers and people could spiral out of control. It is true that none of the really intense persecutions lasted more than a few years, suggesting that there was some kind of self-righting mechanism which would eventually come into operation. On the other hand, we are not really entitled to take the comfortable view that things were more or less bound to turn out as they did. There is no obvious reason why, given a slightly different shake of the historical dice, the levels of persecution found in the Rhineland corridor should not have prevailed much more widely. The local balances between higher and lower authority, credulity and scepticism, restraint and ferocity, were distinctly fragile. In this situation it actually mattered what line individuals took, and I do not think historical relativism need extend to excusing zealots for persecution on the grounds that they were merely typical of their age. The evidence actually suggests that they were not, and that they went far beyond what most of their educated contemporaries thought reasonable. Men like Hauff were sadistic and manipulative, misusing their positions to pervert the course of justice even as it was understood in their own time; whatever unrecognized inner demons drove them on, they do not seem sufficiently insane to escape responsibility for the very real horrors they inflicted. Jean Bodin was a particularly troubling case, for he was a great political thinker, and his position on witchcraft formed an integral part of his vision of the world. This is not to say that he was obliged to structure his arguments in the way he did, of course, and one near-contemporary observer was scathing about the result. The adventurous French free-thinker Gabriel Naudé remarked sarcastically in 1625 that as a result of Bodin's other writings, 'he might perhaps have been mistaken for a man, and we would certainly have thought him highly intelligent, if he had not left marks and traces of his humanity in that *Démonomanie*'.[5] Even if we find intellectual reasons that make Bodin's position comprehensible, it remains true that his *Démonomanie* is an odious production, full of shabby intellectual dishonesty, and endorsing gruesome cruelties on the grounds that the end justifies the means. This was a book quite specifically written with the aim to kill; if it was less successful than the author hoped, both the intent and the effect would still merit a place in one of the lower circles of hell. The best of the critics – Scot, Loos, Spee – stand out in contrast for courage, intelligence and compassion, as does the astonishingly perceptive Inquisitor, Salazar.

A degree of relativism does seem more appropriate when we consider local judges who merely responded to insistent popular demands for action, directed against individuals who had shown manifest ill-will. It is fair to recognize that the evidence often has an intensely compelling quality; when reading the witness depositions hundreds of years later it can still take a conscious effort not to be drawn into the frame of mind that would convict the witch. One can, however, detect degrees of fairness in the conduct of the trials that do not necessarily go in the ways one would expect. There are good reasons, for example, to believe that the Puritan exorcist John Darrell did not get a fair hearing before the High Commission, although it is hard to disagree with the verdict. We must be tempted to take an even more tolerant view of illiterate peasants and artisans, who passionately believed that they or their children were suffering from the malevolence of a witch. Most of this book has been devoted to explaining how deeply rooted such notions were, to the point where they could hardly be challenged from within the belief system which sustained them. When, in addition, they were given formal support by the rulers, and individuals were regularly made examples of, grass-roots scepticism scarcely seems a possibility. This may in fact be too condescending a view of popular *mentalités*, because the trial documents do contain evidence for more varied attitudes than one might expect. While there are no heroic village theorists unpicking the whole doctrine, more limited and immediate doubts about witchcraft as an explanation for misfortune are commonplace. There was nothing automatic about the diagnosis of witchcraft; it needed to be supported by chains of reasoning and evidence that may have been defective, but were certainly not absurd. Ordinary people seem to have felt the need for multiple confirmations before they took violent action against their neighbours in the belief they were witches. Very often their primary interest was in securing a cure, for when witchcraft was blamed this opened up possibilities for counter-magic, or for healing by the witch in person.

Witchcraft beliefs were so deeply embedded in early modern social structures and ways of thought that they inevitably tended to become domesticated. This was the natural counterbalance to a destructive potential that, had the beliefs been interpreted in a literal or mechanical manner, would have proved utterly ruinous. A society which took such thinking to its limits would have autodestructed in a frenzy of mutual accusations and killing. In practice people usually lived with witches and their malice as they did with all the other risks of an unpredictable environment. There were many techniques for limiting one's personal exposure, and for controlling the suspect's behaviour. Negotiation rather than confrontation was the preferred mode, often used with some subtlety. The exceptional cases where intense persecution took over are misleading as a guide to everyday attitudes, although they too were rooted in popular belief and represent a hideous warning of the dangers when the rulers gave unwise encouragement to its more violent side. Excessive concentration on these episodes can distort our understanding of the wider scene. The facile condescension which portrays our ancestors as barbaric and deluded in their attitudes to witchcraft is really rather objectionable; it is usually based on a mixture of ignorance and dubious

self-satisfaction. Modern scepticism does appear to be something exceptional in human history when we look at other cultures, but it had its
origins in the very period when persecution was at its height. It is
essentially the product of the intellectual and scientific revolution which
culminated in the Enlightenment and the creation of industrial society.
When we consider the ease with which we slip back into earlier ways of
thinking, and the modern appetite for *ersatz* occultism, it remains an open
question whether most people do not retain a not-so-secret preference for
magical rather than logical ideas. Perhaps certain kinds of analytical
thought really do not come naturally to us, or have such unpalatable
consequences that we are always looking for escape routes from them.

In many respects witchcraft thinking provided intuitively attractive
ways of evading logic. Precisely because it was an imaginary crime, the
'hole in the middle' where unseen or impossible things were alleged to
happen could act as a focal point for many different transactions. In other
words, the gap is one we now perceive, because we know that the causal
links were essentially fictitious ones, built around the belief that other
people's malevolence could hurt through various diabolical or magical
agencies, which were supposed to be employed deliberately. The very
existence of these beliefs was enough to empower social and psychological
structures that did – to some extent – produce genuine results that
confirmed the false presumptions. Despite its illusory nature, therefore,
witchcraft mobilized real power to cause suffering. The central void was
indeed a 'transactional space'; rich in possibilities, it was an area in which
a great deal of psychological and social work could be done. Across this
gap the deepest and wildest fantasies could meet basic, visceral fears;
ill-will was transmuted into pain and death. Words, rituals and magical
operations supposedly brought about physical effects, inflicting harm,
returning it, or warding it off. The other world controlled by the Devil
was brought into effective contact with the everyday world, sometimes
in the form of diabolic possession. On a more theoretical level, uneasy
alliances were established between popular and elite conceptions of witchcraft, with a convenient blurring of vital boundaries. This process was
dangerous to all those round it. We may think of rulers drawn into sadism
and the destruction of trust, exorcists who went mad, communities or
families divided, those who fell ill or died because they believed themselves bewitched, and of course the witches themselves. The flexibility
of this nexus of ideas was a great tactical advantage, which allowed
connections to be made across the gap with insidious ease and encouraged

a process of reinforcement which was more symbolic than logical. This was also an ultimate weakness, however, because there was no reliable way of limiting such thinking, which was always liable to spiral away out of control. The emotional power generated for those within the immediate vicinity led them to excesses they saw as perfectly justified, but to which those on the outside responded with anger, ridicule, or contempt.

Understanding witchcraft therefore involves understanding ourselves and our past in a very deep sense. The subject raises questions about human personality, social structures, religious beliefs and a host of other fundamental topics. If there is one thing this book should have demonstrated, it is the way witchcraft interacted with innumerable other features of early modern European society. The contemporary relevance of this kind of study should be obvious. At the cultural level, witchcraft and magic seem to become ever more fashionable; those who exploit these themes may not 'believe' in them, yet use the 'transitional space' of the creative imagination to renew their subliminal appeal. The enormous popularity of the witch in fictional form might tempt one to think that just as rabbits have a 'hawk detector' in their retina, so human beings have a 'witch detector' somewhere in their consciousness, and derive excitement from having it activated. A more direct and disturbing parallel, of a very obvious kind, can be seen in the recent spate of claims about satanic ritual abuse. The problem of the sexual abuse of children is a real and troubling one, although it raises great difficulties about proof; the idea that it is committed by powerful conspiratorial groups of satanists is another matter. Although the link with witchcraft is explicitly made by critics, the obvious questions which follow seem to bounce off the armour-plated minds of self-appointed 'experts', who never trouble to answer them. The descriptions of rituals are like identikit pictures, slightly varied combinations of precisely the same elements found in the charges against heretics, Jews, witches and other scapegoats in the past. To anyone who recognizes their antecedents it is incredible that this tawdry collection of recycled fantasies can be mistaken for anything but inventions. Murdered babies, excrement as food and perverse group sex were the stock in trade of extorted confessions long before the Marquis de Sade turned them into the ultimate degenerate thrill; the torture, of course, was for real. Ideas of this kind are truly dangerous, because they turn into shrill demands for punishment, yet another case of splitting and projection. Real people in our own world have their children taken away, and are sometimes convicted, on this flimsy basis. How long will it be, one wonders, before the renewed enthusiasm for the death penalty in the United States leads to someone being executed for, in all but name, being a witch? Those who jump on this band-wagon are taking a terrible responsibility on themselves, for like Bodin's writings their words threaten to destroy other people. While roasting alive is no longer a literal threat, Montaigne's warning remains as strong as ever once it is revised to read: 'it is putting a very high price on one's conjectures to have a man's life wrecked because of them'.

No amount of rational argument will ever put a stop to such misguided and dangerous thinking; the rational study of witchcraft provides all too many reasons for believing that the irrational is here to stay. It also illustrates the invulnerability of conspiracy theories, which can answer any criticism by including the maker within the conspiracy, as a number of early critics found to their cost. No doubt we should see it as in part a cautionary tale, although not I hope a warning to the curious. M. R. James used that title for a classic ghost story, an early version of a theme which has become hackneyed, with a researcher falling victim to the occult mysteries he set out to study. Historical witchcraft was really more humdrum than occult, however, an integral part of everyday life. As a result, we need to understand witchcraft in order to understand early modern Europe, while it is only the wide context that makes the beliefs themselves comprehensible. At the same time, the subject compels us to probe the inner depths of consciousness. The witch may be the other, but witchcraft beliefs are in ourselves.

Notes

These source notes have been kept as brief as possible and are intended to provide references for specific examples and points made in the text. Many general statements have been left unsupported, although background for most of them will be found in the 'Further Reading' section. The Lorraine material is largely drawn from the archives of the Meurthe-et-Moselle department, which are held at Nancy; these appear as ADMM. A few cases indicated as AD Vosges come from the archives of that department at Epinal. Place names for the trials are omitted in the notes when they are clear from the main text. Full citations and information are given only for first citations of published works; short titles are used thereafter.

CHAPTER 1

1 ADMM B4077 no 1
2 R. Scot, *The Discoverie of Witchcraft* (London, 1584), IV, iv (62). Page references to Scot are to the only reliable modern edition, by B. Nicholson (London, 1886)
3 Ibid, Epistle, xiii
4 J. Widdowson, 'The Witch as a Frightening and Threatening Figure', in V. Newall (ed), *The Witch Figure* (London, 1973), 208
5 Scot, *Discoverie of Witchcraft*, I, iii (5)
6 G. B. Harrison (ed), *The Trial of the Lancaster Witches*, 1612 (London, 1929), 33
7 J. Gaule, *Select Cases of Conscience touching Witches and Witchcraft* (London, 1646), 4–5
8 Remy, *Demonolatry*, I, xiv, III, v (trans. E. Ashwin, London, 1930, 53, 159)
9 Ibid, I, xvi, xviii (Ashwin, 58–9, 62–3)

10 R. Mandrou, *Magistrats et sorciers* (Paris, 1968), 198–210; A. Lottin, *Lille: citadelle de la contre-réforme?* (1598–1668) (Dunkirk, 1984), 170–4
11 ADMM B8678 no 2, St Dié, 1596
12 ADMM B8700 no 1, le Vic, 1607
13 ADMM B8708 no 3, Brehimont, 1611
14 ADMM B3358, Nutting, 1621; B3804 no 3, Fontenay, 1620; B3813, Grandvillers, 1625
15 ADMM B8682 no 9, Claudatte Parmentier, Ste Marguerite, 1598
16 ADMM B8691 no 13, Remémont, 1603
17 ADMM B4094 no 1, Essegney, 1608
18 ADMM B8704 no 1, la Neuveville les Raon, 1610
19 ADMM B8941 no 1, St Nicolas, 1577
20 ADMM B8721 no 8, 1618
21 B. Rosen, *Witchcraft* (London, 1969), 73–4

22 Ibid, 78

23 Ibid, 186–7

24 Harrison, *Lancaster Witches*, 18–19, 21–2, 39

25 P. de Lancre, *Le Tableau de L'Inconstance des Mauvais Anges et Demons* (Paris, 1613), sig. û i. See also M. M. McGowan, 'Pierre de Lancre's Tableau de L'Inconstance des Mauvais Anges et Demons: the Sabbat Sensationalized', in S. Anglo (ed), *The Damned Art: Essays in the Literature of Witchcraft* (London, 1977), 182–201

26 R. Kieckhefer, *European Witch Trials* (London, 1976), 20–1, 73–4; N. Cohn, *Europe's Inner Demons* (London, 1975), 225–30

27 Ginzburg, *Ecstasies: Deciphering the Witches' Sabbath* (London, 1990), 69–73

28 Ibid, 68–9

29 Kieckhefer, *European Witch Trials*, 20–1, 73–4; N. Cohn, *Europe's Inner Demons*, 225–30

30 Bodin, *Démonomanie des Sorciers* (Paris, 1580), II, iii–iv (f. 79r–94r)

31 ADMM B7301, Jarville, 1591

32 G. Henningsen, *The Witches' Advocate* (Reno, Nevada, 1980), 316

33 Montaigne, *Complete Works*, trans. D. Frame (Stanford, 1948), 788, 790 (*Essays* III, 11)

34 Lottin, *Lille, citadelle de la contre-réforme?*, 185

35 Ginzburg, *Ecstasies*, passim

36 M. A. Murray, *The Witch-Cult in Western Europe* (Oxford, 1921) and *The God of the Witches* (London, 1933). The definitive refutation in that by N. Cohn, *Europe's Inner Demons*, 107–25

37 S. Clark, 'Inversion, Misrule and the Meaning of Witchcraft', *Past and Present* 87, 1980, 98–127, and 'Le sabbat comme système symbolique: significations stables et instables', in N. Jacques-Chaquin and M. Préaud, *Le Sabbat des sorciers* (Grenoble, 1993), 63–74

38 ADMM B2512, Seuche, 1594

39 ADMM B4444, Rebeuville, 1553

40 AD Vosges, G706, Badonviller, 1561

41 ADMM B2192 no 2, Salonnes, 1612

42 ADMM B8691 no 13, Remémont, 1603

43 ADMM B8712 no 1, Pajaille, 1614

44 ADMM B8682 no 5, Ste Marguerite, 1598

45 ADMM B5354 no 2, Assenoncourt, 1613

46 ADMM B8677 no 12, St Blaise, 1596

47 ADMM B2199 no 1, le Bourget d'Amance, 1616

48 ADMM B8677 no 1, Haillieulle, 1592

49 ADMM B8947, St Nicolas, 1584

50 ADMM B9573, Ste Croix, 1604

51 ADMM B4093, Charmes, 1607

52 ADMM B8677 no 10, Mandray, 1596

53 ADMM B3327 no 4, Reillon, 1604

54 ADMM B8700 no 2, Vacqueville, 1606

55 ADMM B2583 no 1, l'Estraye, 1624

56 ADMM B2583 nos 4 and 6, l'Estraye, 1624

57 M. Kunze, *Highroad to the Stake* (Chicago and London, 1987), 181–5

58 See also E. Biesel, 'Les descriptions du sabbat dans les confessions des inculpés lorrains et trévirois', in Jacques-Chaquin and Préaud, *Le Sabbat des sorciers*, 183–97

59 Henningsen, *Witches' Advocate*, 87–8

60 ADMM B8959 no 1, St Nicolas, 1598

61 ADMM B8678 no 2, St Dié, 1596

62 ADMM B4077 no 2, Charmes, 1596

63 ADMM B8680 no 8, Sarupt, 1597

64 ADMM B4077 no 3, Charmes, 1596

65 ADMM B8684 no 2, Sauceray, 1599

66 ADMM B7316, la Neufville de Nancy, 1597

67 ADMM B8667 no 3, Ste Marguerite, 1592

68 L-F. Sauvé, *Le Folk-lore des Hautes-Vosges* (Paris, 1889), 168–86, 288–90

69 B. Ankarloo, 'Sweden: The Mass Burnings (1668–1676)', in B. Ankarloo and G. Henningsen, *Early Modern European Witchcraft* (Oxford, 1990), 285–317, and 'Blåkulla, ou le procès des sorciers scandinaves', in Jacques-Chaquin and Préaud, *Le Sabbat des sorciers*, 251–8

70 C. L. Ewen, *Witchcraft in the Star Chamber* (n.p., 1938), 44–54

71 J. C. V. Johansen, 'Denmark: The Sociology of Accusations', in Ankarloo and Henningsen, *Early Modern European Witchcraft*, 339–65, esp. 358–65

72 C. Larner, *Enemies of God* (London, 1981), 151–6; *Witchcraft and Religion* (Oxford, 1984), 3–22

73 C. Ginzburg, *The Night Battles* (London, 1983), passim

74 M. Meurger, 'Plantes à illusion: l'interprétation pharmacologique du sabbat', in Jacques-Chaquin and Préaud, *Le Sabbat des sorciers*, 369–82

75 M. Del Rio, *Disquisitionum Magicarum Libri Sex* (Louvain, 1599)

76 C. H. Firth (ed), *The Life of William Cavendish, Duke of Newcastle* (London, 1886), 198, cited by K. V. Thomas, *Religion and the Decline of Magic* (London, 1971), 518–9

77 ADMM B8677 no 7, Entre-deux-Eaux, 1596

CHAPTER II

1 E. E. Evans-Pritchard, *Witchcraft, Oracles and Magic among the Azande* (Oxford, 1937), 26–9, 70–78, 111, 388–9, 540–44

2 S. Bradwell, 'Mary Glover's Late Woeful Case', 5–6, 19, in M. MacDonald, *Witchcraft and Hysteria in Elizabethan London* (London, 1991)

3 W. B. Cannon, 'Voodoo death', *American Anthropologist*, new ser. 44, 1942, 169–81

4 J. Favret-Saada, *Deadly Words: Witchcraft in the Bocage* (Cambridge, 1980), 78–91

5 ADMM B7134 no 2, Ambacourt, 1624

6 ADMM B5312 no 5, Bisping, 1594

7 ADMM B4077 no 2, Charmes, 1596

8 ADMM B3789 no 2, Brouvelieures, 1615

9 ADMM B8713 no 1, Benifosse, 1614

10 ADMM B3323 no 9, Leintrey, 1602

11 Heywood, *Diaries*, iv, 53–4, quoted by Thomas, *Religion and the Decline of Magic*, 497.

12 *The most wonderfull and true storie, of a certaine witch named Alse Gooderidge of Stapenhill* (London, 1597), 1–4. Summaries and extracts from the pamphlet in Ewen, *Witchcraft and*

Demonianism, 176–81, and Harrison, *Lancaster Witches*, xxxiv-viii.

13 ADMM B8687 nos 4 and 6, La Rochatte, 1601

14 ADMM B3335 no 1, Leintrey, 1608

15 Harrison, *Lancaster Witches*, 138–45

16 ADMM B8678 no 3, Remomeix, 1596

17 ADMM B6723 no 1, Flin, 1602

18 ADMM B8684 no 8, Sarupt, 1600

19 Muchembled, *La Sorcière au village*, 164 (Bazuel, 1601)

20 ADMM B4500 no 2, La Neuveville-sous-Châtenois, 1586

21 P. de Lancre, *Tableau de l'inconstance*, 356

22 Larner, *Enemies of God*, 141

23 ADMM B4103 no 1, Gripport, 1615

24 ADMM B2199 no 1, le Bourget d'Amance, 1616

25 ADMM B8707 no 1, la Bolle, 1610

26 ADMM B8919 no 3, Raon, 1617

27 D. Harley, 'Historians as demonologists: the myth of the midwife-witch', *Social History of Medicine* 3, 1990, 1–26

28 ADMM B8702 no 2, Raon, 1609

29 L. Roper, 'Witchcraft and fantasy in early modern Germany', in *Oedipus and the Devil* (London, 1994), 199–225

30 E. A. Wrigley and R. S. Schofield, *The Population History of England 1541–1871: A Reconstruction* (London, 1981), 215–9, 528–9

31 ADMM B4094 no 1, Charmes, 1608

32 ADMM B8713 no 4, Pajaille, 1614

33 ADMM B8682 no 3, Moriviller, 1598

34 ADMM B8693 no 3, Entre-deux-Eaux, 1604

35 ADMM B3323 no 3, Leintrey, 1602

36 ADMM B4576, Neufchâteau, 1611

37 For these distinctions, see D. Harley, 'Explaining Salem: Calvinist Psychology and the Diagnosis of Possession', *American Historical Review* (forthcoming).

38 M. MacDonald, *Mystical Bedlam: Madness, anxiety and healing in seventeenth-century England* (Cambridge, 1981), esp. 107–10, 210–2.

39 ADMM B3327 no 1, Domjevin, 1603

40 ADMM B8691 no 11, St Blaise, 1603

41 ADMM B8717 no 3, la Grandfosse, 1616

42 ADMM B8699, Lubine, 1606

43 AD Vosges 3C 239, Badonviller, 1645

44 ADMM B3317 no 1, Blamont, 1599

45 ADMM B7137 no 1, Villoncourt, 1625

46 E. Le Roy Ladurie, 'L'aiguillette', in *Le territoire de l'historien*, II (Paris, 1978), 136–49

47 De Lancre, *Incredulité*, 324–5

48 ADMM B8673 no 1, Lubine, 1593

49 ADMM B8708 no 3, Brehimont, 1611

50 Ewen, *Witchcraft and Demonianism*, 90–1

51 ADMM B4103 no 1, Gripport, 1615

52 Muchembled, *Sorcière*, 192–6

53 ADMM B5344 no 2, Wirming, 1608

54 ADMM B8715 no 3, Vic, 1615

55 ADMM B6723 no 2, Flin, 1603

56 ADMM B7134 no 2, Ambacourt, 1624

57 ADMM B3755, Brouramont, 1602

58 Boguet, *Discours des sorciers* (3rd ed, Lyon, 1610), 361–2

59 C. F. Oates, 'Trials of Werewolves in the Franche-Comté in the early modern period' (Ph.D. thesis, London, 1993), 150–1

60 ADMM B8712 no 6, le Vivier, 1614

61 ADMM B8712 no 2, 1614

62 ADMM B3329, 1605

63 ADMM B2192 no 1, 1612

64 ADMM B8691 no 12, la Neuveville-les-Raon, 1603

65 ADMM B8724 no 5, Raon, 1619

66 ADMM B2199 no 3, Laitre-sous-Amance, 1615

67 ADMM B8719 no 1, 1617

68 ADMM B3335 no 2, Blamont, 1606

69 ADMM B5344 no 4, 1608

70 ADMM B8669, Ginfosse, 1592

71 B. Capp, *Cromwell's Navy* (Oxford, 1989), 326–7

72 Ewen, *Witchcraft and Demonianism*, 194

73 H. de Waardt, 'Prosecution or Defense: Procedural possibilities following a witchcraft accusation in the Province of Holland before 1800', in Gijswijt-Hofstra and Frijhoff (eds), *Witchcraft in the Netherlands from the fourteenth to the twentieth century* (Rotterdam, 1991), 83

74 Muchembled, *Sorcière*, 170

75 ADMM B8667 no 5, La Bolle, 1592

76 ADMM B8281 no 1, Villers-sous-Preny, 1599

77 ADMM B8689 no 3, Moyemont, 1602

78 ADMM B2521, Xenennay, 1598

79 H. Pohl, *Hexenglaube und Hexenverfolgung im Kurfürstentum Mainz. Ein Beitrag zur Hexenfrage im 16. und beginnenden 17. Jahrhundert* (Stuttgart, 1988), 67

80 ADMM B8669 no 2, St Dié, 1593

81 Rosen, *Witchcraft*, 97

CHAPTER III

1 C. Mather, *The Wonders of the Invisible World: Being an account of the trials of several witches lately executed in New England* (London, 1862), 80 (first ed. Boston, 1693)

2 For these topics see, inter alia, Thomas, *Religion and the Decline of Magic*, J. Bossy, *Christianity in the West, 1400–1700* (Oxford, 1985), K. von Greyerz (ed), *Religion and Society in Early Modern Europe, 1500–1800* (London, 1984), P. Burke, *Popular Culture in Early Modern Europe* (London, 1978), R. W. Scribner, *Popular Culture and Popular Movements in Reformation Germany* (London, 1987). For the Ten Commandments and their implications see J. Bossy, 'Moral Arithmetic: Seven Sins into Ten Commandments', in E. Leites (ed), *Conscience and Casuistry in Early Modern Europe* (Cambridge, 1988), 214–34, esp. 229–32. Also M. Aston, *England's Iconoclasts 1: Laws Against Images* (Oxford, 1988), chapter 7, 'The Sin of Idolatry: the teaching of the Decalogue', 343–479

3 Scribner, *Popular Culture*, 12, 40, 261–2

4 ADMM B8667 no 9, Ste Marguerite, 1592

5 ADMM B3335 no 3, Blamont, 1608

6 ADMM B8680 no 3, Mandray, 1597

7 ADMM B8702 no 4, Raon, 1609

8 ADMM B8715 no 1, la Neufville-les-Raon, 1615

9 G. Gifford, *A Briefe Discourse wherein is declared the subtil practise of devils by witches and sorcerers* (London, 1587) sig F4 r-v

10 ADMM B8677 no 9, Mandray, 1596

11 ADMM B8691 no 10, St Blaise, 1603

12 ADMM B8689 no 1, Moriviller, 1601

13 ADMM B5344 no 1, Insming, 1608

14 ADMM B8708 no 5, St Remy, 1611

15 ADMM B2192 no 2, Salonnes, 1612

16 ADMM B3789 no 3, Bruyères, 1615

17 ADMM B8712 no 1, Pajaille, 1614

18 ADMM B8684 nos 2 and 5, Sauceray, 1599–1600

19 ADMM B8677 no 7, Entre-deux-Eaux, 1596

20 ADMM B8721 no 6, le Paire, 1618

21 ADMM B7134 no 1, Hymont, 1624

22 ADMM B8682 no 9, Ste Marguerite, 1598

23 ADMM B3327 no 3, Reillon, 1604

24 ADMM B4500 no 2, la-Neuveville-sous-Châtenois, 1586

25 Henningsen, *Witches' Advocate*, 165

26 Ibid, 297–300

27 ADMM B8702 no 2, Raon, 1609

28 ADMM B3753, Bruyères, 1601

29 ADMM B3323, Leintrey, 1602

30 ADMM B7316, la Neufville de Nancy, 1597

31 Thomas, *Religion and the Decline of Magic*, 523

32 ADMM B8687 no 4, la Rochatte, 1601

33 J. A. Sharpe, *Witchcraft in Seventeenth-Century Yorkshire: Accusations and Counter-Accusations*, Borthwick Papers 81 (York, 1992), 9

34 ADMM B8677 no 9, Mandray, 1596

35 ADMM B8702 no 11, la Vacherie, 1609

36 Rosen, *Witchcraft*, 115

37 Monter, *Witchcraft in France and Switzerland*, 44–5, 47–9, 115–8

38 I owe this point to Yves-Marie Bercé

39 ADMM B8704 no 5, Raon, 1609

40 ADMM B4094 no 1, Essegney, 1607

41 ADMM B6760, Rehainviller, 1624

42 Sharpe, *Witchcraft in Seventeenth-Century Yorkshire*, 14

43 ADMM B5757, Einville, 1606

44 ADMM B8678 no 1, Ste Marguerite, 1596

45 Sharpe, *Witchcraft in Seventeenth-Century Yorkshire*, 16

46 Ibid, 17

47 Rosen, *Witchcraft*, 89

48 ADMM B8260, Vilcey-sur-Trey, 1584

49 ADMM B7137 no 1, Villoncourt, 1625

50 ADMM B8979 no 5, St Nicolas, 1609

51 ADMM B6723 no 1, Flin, 1602

52 ADMM B8986 no 2, St Nicolas, 1613

53 ADMM B8687 no 1, St Blaise, 1601

54 ADMM B3323 nos 1 and 4, 1601–2

55 MacDonald, *Mystical Bedlam*, passim

56 Gifford, *A Briefe Discourse*, sig G1 v

57 G. Klaniczay, 'Hungary: The Accusations and the Universe of

Popular Magic', in Ankarloo and Henningsen, *Early Modern European Witchcraft*, 219–55, esp. 253–5, and 'Witch-Hunting in Hungary: Social or Cultural Tensions?', in Klaniczay, *The Uses of Supernatural Power* (Oxford, 1990), 151–67

58 Klaniczay, 'The Decline of Witches and the Rise of Vampires under the Eighteenth-Century Habsburg Monarchy', in *The Uses of Supernatural Power*, 168–88.

59 R. Martin, *Witchcraft and the Inquisition in Venice, 1550–1650* (Oxford, 1989); G. Ruggiero, *Binding Passions: Tales of Magic, Marriage, and Power at the End of the Renaissance* (New York and Oxford, 1993)

60 J. Tedeschi, 'Inquisitorial Law and the Witch', G. Henningsen, 'The Ladies from Outside: An Archaic Pattern of the Witches' Sabbat', and F. Bethencourt, 'Portugal: A Scrupulous Inquisition', in Ankarloo and Henningsen, *Early Modern European Witchcraft*, 81–118, 191–215, 403–22. Also J. Caro Baroja, *Vidas mágicas e Inquisición* (2 vols, Madrid, 1967); J. P. Paiva, *Práticas e crenças mágicas: o medo e a necessidade dos mágicos na Diocese de Coimbra (1650–1740)*, (Coimbra, 1992); M. O'Neil, 'Magical Healing, Love Magic and the Inquisition in Late Sixteenth-century Modena', and J. P. DeDieu, 'The Inquisition and Popular Culture in New Castile', in S. Haliczer (ed), *Inquisition and Society in Early Modern Europe* (Beckenham, 1987), 88–114, 129–46; E. W. Monter, *Frontiers of Heresy: The Spanish Inquisition from the Basque Lands to Sicily* (Cambridge, 1990); D. Gentilcore, *From Bishop to Witch: the system of the sacred in early modern Terra d'Otranto* (Manchester, 1992).

61 Larner, *Enemies of God*, 180–1

62 ADMM B3323 nos 1, 2 and 4, 1601–2

63 Perkins, *Works* (Cambridge, 1609), iii, 638

64 Scot, *Discoverie of Witchcraft*, Epistle, xviii and I, ii (3)

65 Gifford, *Dialogue*, sig. M3v.

66 Remy, *Demonolatry*, III ii-iii (Ashwin, 142–54)

67 ADMM B8684 no 4, Sauceray, 1599–1600

68 J-F. de Reims, *Le Directeur pacifique des consciences* (4th ed, Paris, 1645), 304–5

69 *Statuts synodaux pour le diocèse de Saint-Malo* (Paris, 1619), cited in F. Lebrun, 'La religion de l'évêque de Saint-Malo et ses diocésains au début du 17e siècle, à travers les statuts synodaux de 1619', *La Religion populaire* (CNRS, Paris, 1979), 45–51

70 ADMM B8947, St Nicolas, 1584

71 ADMM B8667 no 8, le Viel Marché, 1592

72 M. de Certeau, *La possession de Loudun* (Paris, 1970), 60–1, 136–40

73 D. P. Walker, *Unclean Spirits: Possession and exorcism in France and England in the late sixteenth and early seventeenth centuries* (London, 1981), 77–84

74 Mandrou, *Magistrats et sorciers*, 163–79; Walker, *Unclean Spirits*, 33–42

75 MacDonald, *Witchcraft and Hysteria*, xlviii-lv, G. L. Kittredge, *Witchcraft in Old and New England*

(Cambridge Mass., 1929), 276–
328, Walker, *Unclean Spirits*, 77–
84.

76 Mandrou, *Magistrats et sorciers*,
197–312, M. de Certeau, *La
Possession de Loudun* (Paris, 1970),
M. Carmona, *Les Diables de Loudun:
sorcellerie et politique sous Richelieu*
(Paris, 1988)

CHAPTER IV

1 Boguet, *Discours des Sorciers*, 140
2 Rosen, *Witchcraft*, 88
3 ADMM B8712 no 2, Grattain,
1614
4 ADMM B3327 no 4, 1604
5 Scot, *Discoverie*, I, iii
6 Ady, *A Candle in the Dark* (London,
1656), 114–5
7 *Tableau de l'inconstance*, 541
8 *Démonomanie des Sorciers* (Paris,
1580), f. 124 r-v
9 *Demonolatry*, III, v (Ashwin, 159)
10 ADMM B8719 no 2, le Menil,
1617
11 ADMM B8702 no 1, 1609
12 ADMM B8678 no 2, St Dié, 1596
13 ADMM B3327 no 1, Domjevin,
1603–4
14 A. Gregory, 'Witchcraft, Politics
and "Good Neighbourhood"
in early seventeenth-century
Rye', *Past and Present* 133,
1991, 61
15 ADMM B9573, Ste Croix, 1604
16 ADMM B2192 no 2, Salonnes,
1612
17 Rosen, *Witchcraft*, 130–1
18 ADMM B8712 no 2, Grattain,
1614
19 ADMM B8708 no 8, la Voivrelle
1611
20 ADMM B2521, Xennenay, 1598
21 ADMM B8721 no 2, Giriviller,
1618

22 ADMM B8667 no 4, le Paire
d'Avould, 1592
23 ADMM B8707 no 3, Sachemont,
1610–11
24 ADMM B8721 no 8, Chastay, 1618
25 ADMM B8689 no 2, Moyemont,
1602
26 ADMM B8715 no 6, Raon, 1615
27 ADMM B8717 no 4, la Salle, 1616
28 ADMM B8535 no 2, Rosières,
1603
29 ADMM B4077 no 2, Charmes,
1596
30 ADMM B8684 no 1, Hurbache,
1599
31 ADMM B8691 no 12, Raon, 1603
32 Sharpe, *Witchcraft in
Seventeenth-Century Yorkshire*, 8
33 AD Vosges G563, Giriviller, 1594
34 ADMM B4998, Condé, 1626
35 ADMM B3792 no 4, Dompierre,
1615–6
36 ADMM B8735 no 6, Raon,
1624–5
37 ADMM B8961, 1599
38 ADMM B4500 no 1, St Prancher,
1586
39 ADMM B8735 no 6, Raon,
1624–5
40 ADMM B3789 no 3, Bruyères,
1615
41 ADMM B3804 no 3, Fontenay,
1620
42 ADMM B3325 no 3, Domjevin,
1603
43 Muchembled, *Les derniers bûchers*,
16–20
44 ADMM B3323 no 4, Leintrey,
1602
45 ADMM B8682 nos 3 and 4,
Moriviller, 1598
46 ADMM B8677 no 7,
Entre-deux-Eaux, 1596
47 G. Gifford, *A Discourse of the Subtil
Practises of Devilles by Witches and*

Sorcerers (London, 1587), sigs. G4-G4v

48 Larner, *Enemies of God*, 98–9

49 Gifford, *A Dialogue concerning Witches and Witchcraftes* (London, 1593), sig. M2

50 J. Favret-Saada, *Deadly Words* (Cambridge, 1984); P. Gaboriau, *La Pensée ensorcelée: la sorcellerie actuelle en Anjou et en Vendée* (Paris, 1987)

51 ADMM B2521, Xennenay, 1598

52 ADMM B4094 no 1, Essegney, 1607

53 ADMM B8667 no 5, la Bolle, 1592

CHAPTER V

1 ADMM B7301, Jarville, 1591

2 Scot, *Discoverie*, XVI, ii (398–9)

3 Ibid, XII, xvi (209–10)

4 Ibid, VIII, i (126)

5 ADMM B3327 no 1, Domjevin, 1603–4

6 ADMM B8715 no 2, Sachemont, 1615

7 ADMM B3728, le Void de Belmont, 1591

8 ADMM B3753, Bruyères, 1601

9 ADMM B2584, Arches, 1624

10 Remy, *Demonolatry*, III, iii (Ashwin, 150)

11 ADMM B7309 no 1, Nancy, 1593

12 ADMM B3327 no 2, Domjevin, 1603–4

13 ADMM B7279, Azelot, 1583

14 ADMM B8682 no 2, Colroy, 1598

15 ADMM B8260, Hillevix Magister, Vilcey-sur-Trey, 1584

16 ADMM B8272, Pargny, 1594

17 ADMM B4103 no 3, Gripport, 1615

18 ADMM B5312 no 1, 1594

19 W. de Blécourt and F. Pereboom, 'Insult and admonition: Witchcraft in the Land of Vollenhove, seventeenth century', in M. Gijswijt-Hofstra and W. Frijhoff (eds), *Witchcraft in the Netherlands from the fourteenth to the twentieth century* (Rotterdam, 1991), 123

20 Macfarlane, *Witchcraft in Tudor and Stuart England*, 125

21 C. F. Oates, 'Trials of Werewolves in the Franche-Comté in the early modern period' (Ph.D. thesis, London, 1993), Appendix 11, *arrêt* of the parlement of Dole, 1629, 300

22 G. Jerouschek, *Die Hexen und ihr Prozess: die Hexenverfolgung in der Reichsstadt Esslingen* (Sigmaringen, 1992), 98–106, 153

23 Midelfort, *Witch Hunting in Southwestern Germany, 1562–1684*, 101–2

24 De Lancre, *Incredulité*, 774–85

25 H. de Waardt, 'At bottom a family affair: feuds and witchcraft in Nijkirk in 1550', in Gijswijt-Hofstra and Frijhoff (eds), *Witchcraft in the Netherlands from the fourteenth to the twentieth century*, 139

26 K-S. Kramer, 'Schaden und Gegenzauber in Alltagsleben des 16.–18. Jahrhunderts nach archivalisten Quellen aus Holstein', in C. Degn, H. Lehmann and D. Unverhau, *Hexenprozesse: Deutsche und skandinavische Beiträge* (Neumünster, 1983), 227

27 Ewen, *Witchcraft and Demonianism*, 364

28 ADMM B3345, Autrepierre, 1613

29 ADMM B8691 no 13, Remémont, 1603

30 Perkins, *Discourse*, 644

31 Gifford, *Dialogue*, sig. A3

32 E. Olivier, *Médecine et santé dans les pays de Vaud* (2 vols, Lausanne, 1962), II, 645–6

33 H. de Waardt and W. de Blécourt, 'It is no sin to put an evil person

to death', in Gijswijt-Hofstra and Frijhoff (eds), *Witchcraft in the Netherlands from the fourteenth to the twentieth century*, 70

34 W. Frijhoff, 'Witchcraft and its changing representations in Eastern Gelderland, from the sixteenth to twentieth centuries', in Gijswijt-Hofstra and Frijhoff (eds), *Witchcraft in the Netherlands from the fourteenth to the twentieth century*, 170

35 H. de Waardt, 'At bottom a family affair: feuds and witchcraft in Nijkirk in 1550', ibid, 132–48

36 Rosen, *Witchcraft*, 103–57

37 C. A. Holmes. 'Women, Witnesses and Witches', *Past and Present* 140, 1993.

38 J. Glanvill, *Saducismus Triumphatus* (London, 1681), II, 126–7

39 E. W. Monter, *Witchcraft in France and Switzerland*, 77–8, 81–7; F. Bavoux, *Hantises et diableries dans la terre abbatiale de Luxueil* (Monaco, 1956), 71–182

40 Muchembled, *Sorcières, justice et société*, 207–26

41 Midelfort, *Witch Hunting*, 132–4

42 W. Behringer, *Hexenverfolgung in Bayern. Volksmagie, Glaubenseifer und Staatsräson in der Frühen Neuzeit* (Munich, 1987)

43 Henningsen, *The Witches' Advocate*, passim

44 Monter, *Frontiers of Heresy*, 265–7, 274–5; H. Kamen, *The Phoenix and the Flame: Catalonia and the Counter Reformation* (New Haven and London, 1993), 237–45

45 Larner, *Enemies of God*, 69–72, *Witchcraft and Religion*, 7–17

46 Ewen, *Witchcraft and Demonianism*, 254–303, *Witch-Hunting*, 291–313

47 C. M. A. Caspers, 'Witchcraft trials in Peelland, 1595', in Gijswijt-Hofstra and Frijhoff (eds), *Witchcraft in the Netherlands*, 91–102

48 D. Crouzet, *Les Guerriers de Dieu: la violence au temps des troubles de religion* (vers 1525 – vers 1610) (2 vols, Paris, 1990), esp. ii, 287–425.

49 Bodin, *Démonomanie*, 137–8 and 166–7.

50 A. Soman, *Sorcellerie et Justice Criminelle* (Ashgate, 1992), XIV, 23–8

51 R. Mousnier (ed), *Lettres et mémoires adressées au chancelier Séguier* (1633–1649) (2 vols, Paris, 1964), 636–7

52 Mandrou, *Magistrats et sorciers*, 371–81, 385–94

53 Ibid, 392

54 J. d'Autun, *L'incrédulité Savant et la crédulité ignorante au sujet des Magiciens et sorciers* (Lyon, 1671), preface.

55 Mandrou, *Magistrats et sorciers*, 388–90

56 J. d'Autun, *L'incrédulité Savante*, 920

57 Mandrou, *Magistrats et sorciers*, 439–66

58 Labouvie, *Zauberei und Hexenwerk*, 55–6; E. Biesel, 'Les descriptions du sabbat dans les confessions des inculpés lorrains et trévirois', in Jacques-Chaquin and Préaud, *Le Sabbat des sorciers*, 183–97

59 R. S. Walinski-Kiel, '"Godly States", Confessional Conflict and Witch-Hunting in Early Modern Germany', *Mentalities-Mentalités*, 5, 2, 1988, 13–24, and 'La chasse aux sorcières et le sabbat dans les évêchés de Bamberg et Würzburg', in Jacques-Chaquin and Préaud, *Le Sabbat des sorciers*, 213–25

60 Midelfort, *Witch Hunting*, 121–54

61 W. Behringer, 'Allemagne, "mère de tant de sorcières" au coeur des persécutions', in R. Muchembled (ed), *Magie et Sorcellerie en Europe* (Paris, 1994), 73–7

62 J. C. V. Johansen, 'Denmark: The Sociology of Accusations', in Ankarloo and Henningsen, *Early Modern European Witchcraft*, 339–65, esp. 341–9

63 B. Ankarloo, 'Sweden: The Mass Burnings (1668–1676)', ibid, 285–317

64 Midelfort, *Witch Hunting*, 36–61

65 ADMM B3333, Domjevin, 1607

66 de Certeau, *La Possession de Loudun*, 312

67 Bérulle, *Correspondance* (J. Dagens (ed), 3 vols, Paris and Louvain, 1937–9), III, 613–4

68 L. Tronson, *Correspondance* (L. Bertrand (ed), 3 vols, Paris, 1904), III, 292

69 G. Levi, *Inheriting Power: The Story of an Exorcist* (trans. L. Cochrane, Chicago and London, 1988)

70 Thomas, *Religion and the Decline of Magic*, 483–6; Walker, *Unclean Spirits*, 61–73; MacDonald, *Witchcraft and Hysteria*, xx-xxii.

71 D. Harley, 'Mental Illness, Magical Medicine and the Devil in Northern England, 1650–1700', in R. French and A. Wear (eds), *The Medical Revolution of the Seventeenth Century* (Cambridge, 1989)

72 Larner, *Enemies of God*, 166

73 Ibid, 70–1

74 Ibid, 110–2

75 Muchembled, *Les derniers bûchers*, 197

76 Muchembled, *Sorcières, justice et société*, 150.

77 ADMM B7134 no 3, Bettoncourt, 1624

78 AD Vosges G710, Vomécourt, 1631

79 De Lancre, *L'incrédulité*, 358

80 C. Pfister, *Histoire de Nancy* (3 vols, Nancy 1902–9), III, 964–8; E. Delcambre and J. Lhermitte, *Un cas énigmatique de possession diabolique en Lorraine au XVIIe siècle* (Nancy, 1956), 57–64

81 Scot, *Discoverie*, I, iii

82 Ady, *A Candle in the Dark*, 115

83 Rosen, *Witchcraft*, 242–3

84 Ewen, *Witchcraft and Demonianism*, 348–52

85 J. Cotta, *A Short Discoverie of the Unobserved Dangers of Severall Sorts of ignorant and unconsiderate Practisers of Physicke in England* (London, 1612), 58–9

86 Ady, *A Candle in the Dark*, 169

87 B. Rosen, *Witchcraft*, 141.

88 MacDonald, *Witchcraft and Hysteria*, passim

89 Ibid, xlviii-li; Larner, *Witchcraft and Religion*, 3–22; S. Clark, 'King James's Daemonologie: Witchcraft and Kingship', in S. Anglo (ed), *The Damned Art* (London, 1977), 156–81; C. L. Ewen, *Witchcraft in the Star Chamber* (n.p., 1938), 28–36; also chapter 3, note 68

90 G. Keynes, *The Life of William Harvey* (Oxford, 1966), 206–16.

91 P. Pigray, *Epitome des preceptes de medicine et chirurchie* (Rouen 1649), 516–20

92 M. Marescot, *Discours veritable sur le faict de Marthe Brossier de Romorantin, pretendue demoniaque* (Paris, 1599), 30

93 Mandrou, *Magistrats et sorciers*, 163–4; Walker, *Unclean Spirits*, 33–42

94 Walker, *Unclean Spirits*, 65–6

95 Mandrou, *Magistrats et sorciers*, 282

96 de Certeau, *La Possession de Loudun*, 164

97 Ibid, 200

98 P. Yvelin, *Examen de la possession des religieuses de Louviers* (Paris, 1643)

99 Dupont-Bouchat, *Prophètes et sorciers*, 115; ADMM B86, 1614

100 Soman, *Sorcellerie et Justice Criminelle*, II, 40, XII, 195, XV, 15

101 J. A. Sharpe, 'Women, witchcraft and the legal process', in J. Kermode and G. Walker (eds), *Women, Crime and the Courts in Early Modern England* (London, 1994), 110

CHAPTER VI

1 ADMM B8687 no 9, la Vacherie, 1601

2 ADMM B9573, Ste Croix, 1604

3 ADMM B8667 no 8, le Viel Marché, 1592

4 ADMM B8680 no 5, Saulcy-sur-Meurthe, 1597

5 M. Gaskill, 'Witchcraft and power in early modern England: the case of Margaret Moore', in Kermode and Walker, *Women, Crime and the Courts in early modern England*, 125–45

6 ADMM B8719 no 1, Moyenmoutier, 1617

7 ADMM B8713 no 1, Benifosse, 1614

8 ADMM B4535 no 2, Neufchâteau, 1596–8

9 Henningsen, *Witches' Advocate*, 66

10 ADMM B8689 no 2, Moyemont, 1602

11 ADMM B6723 nos 1 and 2, Flin, 1602–3

12 ADMM B2199 no 2, le Bourget d'Amance, 1615–6

13 ADMM B8693 no 2, le Vivier d'Étival, 1604

14 ADMM B4093, Charmes, 1607

15 ADMM B8708 no 3, Brehimont, 1611

16 ADMM B8700 no 3, Raon, 1608

17 Muchembled, *Sorcière au village*, 34–5

18 ADMM B8682 no 1, les Trois Maisons, 1596–8

19 ADMM B8682 no 8, Laygoutte, 1598

20 ADMM B8669 no 4, Develine, 1593

21 ADMM B4535 no 1, Neufchâteau, 1598

22 ADMM B8678 no 1, le Faing, 1596

23 AD Vosges G708, Remémont, 1601

24 Ewen, *Witchcraft in the Star Chamber*, 55–6

25 ADMM B8680 no 7, la Ruelle de Saulcy, 1597

26 ADMM B3755, Brouramont, 1602

27 Rosen, *Witchcraft*, 109–10

28 Gifford, *A Briefe Discourse*, sig G 4v

29 Muchembled, *Sorcières, justice et société*, 211

30 ADMM B2583 no 4, l'Estraye, 1624

31 ADMM B8717 no 4, la Salle, 1617

32 ADMM B2583 no 4, l'Estraye, 1624

33 ADMM B3792 no 4, Dompierre, 1615

34 ADMM B8682 no 3, Moriviller, 1598

35 ADMM B8945, St Nicolas, 1582

36 ADMM B8691 no 1, St Nicolas, 1599

37 ADMM B4077 no 3, Charmes, 1596

38 ADMM B3323 no 5, Leintrey, 1602

39 MacDonald, *Witchcraft and Hysteria*, passim

40 ADMM B7134 no 1, Hymont, 1624

41 ADMM B3343, Leintrey, 1607

42 ADMM B8713 no 2, la Chapelle, 1614

43 ADMM B4094 no 2, Charmes, 1608

44 ADMM B3804 no 2, Dompierre, 1620

45 ADMM B6723 no 2, Flin, 1603

46 ADMM B8667 no 4, le Paire d'Avould, 1592

47 ADMM B8682 no 4, Moriviller, 1598

48 ADMM B8687 nos 7 and 9, la Vacherie, 1601

49 G. Jerouschek, *Die Hexen und ihr Prozess: die Hexenverfolgung in der Reichsstadt Esslingen* (Sigmaringen, 1992), 136–40, 152, 154–60.

50 E. Labouvie, *Zauberei und Hexenwerk: Ländlicher Hexenglaube in der frühen Neuzeit* (Frankfurt am Main, 1991), 212

51 ADMM B3792 no 2, Dompierre, 1615

52 ADMM B8693 no 2, le Vivier d'Étival, 1604

53 ADMM B3317 no 1, Blamont, 1599

54 ADMM B3345, Autrepierre, 1613

55 Labouvie, *Zauberei und Hexenwerk*, 155–62

56 D. Unverhau, *Von "Toverschen" und "Kunstfruwen" in Schleswig 1548–1557: Quellen und Interpretationen zur Geschichte des Zaubern und Hexenwesens* (Schleswig, 1980), 22–6

57 ADMM B8682 no 1, les Trois Maisons, 1596–8

58 Muchembled, *Sorcière au village*, 176–7

59 ADMM B4077 no 2, Charmes, 1596

CHAPTER VII

1 de Lancre, *Tableau de l'inconstance*, 291

2 Bodin, *Démonomanie*, fo 225r

3 Soman, *Sorcellerie et Justice Criminelle*, passim

4 Midelfort, *Witch Hunting*, 179–82; Monter, *Witchcraft in France and Switzerland*, 119–21

5 Muchembled, *Sorcières, justice, et société*, 107

6 Eva Labouvie, *Zauberei und Hexenwerk: Ländlicher Hexenglaube in der frühen Neuzeit* (Frankfurt am Main, 1991), 68–9; Dupont-Bouchat, Frijhoff and Muchembled, *Prophètes et sorciers*, 127

7 Ankarloo and Henningsen, *Early Modern European Witchcraft*, passim

8 J. Favret-Saada, *Deadly Words* (Cambridge, 1984); P. Gaboriau, *La Pensée ensorcelée: la sorcellerie actuelle en Anjou et en Vendée* (Paris, 1987)

9 J. P. Demos, *Entertaining Satan: Witchcraft and the Culture of Early New England* (New York and Oxford, 1982), 68

10 Holmes, 'Women, witnesses and witches', 47–9

11 Clark, 'The "Gendering" of Witchcraft in French Demonology: Misogyny or Polarity?', *French History* v, 1991, 426–8

12 ADMM B8678 no 2, St Dié, 1596

13 ADMM B3789 no 1, Docelles, 1615

14 ADMM B3317 no 2, Blamont, 1599

15 S. D. Amussen, *An Ordered Society: Gender and Class in Early Modern England* (Oxford, 1988), 42–7, 16–70, 119–21, 182–3

16 ADMM B8717 no 6, Fouchifol, 1616

17 ADMM B8717 no 3, la Grandfosse, 1616

18 D. E. Underdown, *Revel, Riot and Rebellion: popular politics and culture in England, 1603–60* (Oxford, 1985), 99–103

19 ADMM B3323 no 3, Leintrey, 1602

20 Thomas, *Religion and the Decline of Magic*, 489

21 Holmes, 'Women, witnesses and witches', 65

22 Ibid, 57–60, 62–5, 76–7

23 Karlsen, *The Devil in the Shape of a Woman*, 77–116 (quote 116)

24 ADMM B3789 no 1, Docelles, 1615

25 ADMM B8667 no 9, Sainte Marguerite, 1592

26 ADMM B2512, Seuche, 1594

27 Demos, *Entertaining Satan*, 250–6

28 ADMM B8691 no 16, St Dié, 1603

29 ADMM B8947, St Nicolas, 1584

30 ADMM B8986 no 2, St Nicolas, 1613

31 ADMM B5312 no 1, Bassing, 1594

32 ADMM B8682 no 8, Laygoutte, 1598

33 D. Harley, 'Historians as demonologists: the myth of the midwife-witch', *Social History of Medicine* 3, 1990, 1–26

34 ADMM B8712 no 4, Mazelay, 1614

35 ADMM B8702 no 3, Raon, 1609

36 Holmes, 'Women, witnesses and witches', 65–75; Sharpe, 'Women, witchcraft and the legal process', 108–12

37 Ewen, *Witchcraft and Demonianism*, 244–51

38 Larner, *Enemies of God*, 111

39 Roper, *Oedipus and the Devil*, 199–225

40 Clark, 'The "Gendering" of witchcraft in French demonology: misogyny or polarity?'

CHAPTER VIII

1 H. Smith, 'The Poor Man's Tears', in *Sermons* (T. Fuller (ed), 2 vols, London, 1867), II, 48

2 A. Borst, 'Anfänge des Hexenwahns in den Alpen', in A. Blauert (ed), *Ketzer, Zauberer, Hexen. Die Anfänge der europäischen Hexenverfolgung* (Frankfort-am-Main, 1990), 43–67; 'The Origins of the Witch-craze in the Alps', in Borst, *Medieval Worlds: Barbarians, Heretics and Artists in the Middle Ages* (Cambridge, 1991), 101–22

3 Klaniczay, *The Sources of Supernatural Power*, 151–88

4 Ankarloo and Henningsen, *Early Modern European Witchcraft*, passim

5 ADMM B8717 no 5, Entre-deux-Eaux, 1616

6 ADMM B8708 no 9, Pajaille, 1611

7 Evans-Pritchard, *Witchcraft, Oracles and Magic among the Azande*, 7–5

8 ADMM B3804 no 2, Dompierre, 1620

9 Monter, *Witchcraft in France and Switzerland*, 44–9, 94–5

10 ADMM B8691 no 10, St Blaise, 1603

11 ADMM B8702 no 6, Raves, 1609

12 P. Boyer and S. Nissenbaum, *Salem Possessed* (Cambridge Mass., 1974), and B. Rosenthal, *Salem Story: Reading the Witch Trials of 1692* (Cambridge, 1993) are the two outstanding modern accounts of

the famous trials and their
background

13 Demos, *Entertaining Satan:
Witchcraft and the Culture of Early
New England*, R. Weisman,
*Witchcraft, Magic, and Religion in
Seventeenth-Century Massachusetts*
(Amherst Mass., 1984), C. F.
Karlsen, *The Devil in the Shape of a
Woman: Witchcraft in Colonial New
England* (New York and London,
1987), and R. Godbeer, *The Devil's
Dominion: Magic and Religion in
Early New England* (Cambridge,
1992) are outstanding recent
studies

14 D. Harley, 'Explaining Salem:
Calvinist Psychology and the
Diagnosis of Possession', *American
Historical Review*, forthcoming

15 M. Gaskill, 'Witchcraft and power
in early modern England: the case
of Margaret Moore', in Kermode
and Walker, *Women, Crime and the
Courts in early modern England*,
131–2

CHAPTER IX

1 R. W. Scribner, 'The Mordbrenner
Fear in Sixteenth-century
Germany: Political Paranoia or the
Revenge of the Outcast?', in R. J.
Evans (ed), *The German Underworld:
Deviants and Outcasts in German
History* (London, 1988), 29–56

2 Bacon, *Novum Organum* I, cxxix, in
Works, Life and Letters (J. Spedding,
H. L. Ellis and D. D. Heath (eds),
London, 1857–74), iv, 114

3 J. C. V. Johansen, 'Denmark: The
Sociology of Accusations', in
Ankarloo and Henningsen, *Early
Modern European Witchcraft*, 339–
65, and *Da Djaevelen var ude . . .
Trolldom i der 17 århundredes*

Danmark (Odense, 1990), 308–9
(French summary).

4 M. Kunze, *Highroad to the Stake*
(Chicago and London, 1987), 203–
5

5 Ibid, passim (for the case in
general), and 321–70 (the search
for corroborative proof)

6 W. Behringer, *Hexenverfolgung in
Bayern. Volksmagie, Glaubenseifer
und Staatsräson in der Frühen Neuzeit*
(Munich, 1987), passim, and 241–
58 for the hesitations after 1600.
For Tanner, see Behringer, 'Zur
Haltung Adam Tanners in der
Hexenfrage. Die Entstehung einer
Argumentationsstrategie in ihrem
gesellschaftlichen Kontext', in
Hartmut Lehmann and Otto
Ulbricht, *Von Unfug des
Hexen-Processes: Gegner der
Hexenverfolgung von Johann Weyer bis
Friedrich Spee* (Wiesbaden, 1992),
161–85

7 J. Klaits, 'Witchcraft trials and
absolute monarchy in Alsace', in
R. M. Golden (ed), *Church, State and
Society under the Bourbon Kings of
France* (Lawrence, Kan, 1982),
148–72

8 Larner, ' "Crimen Exceptum"? The
Crime of Witchcraft in Europe', in
Witchcraft and Religion, 35–67;
Midelfort, *Witch Hunting in
Southwestern Germany*, 118

9 *The Trial of the Lancaster Witches*,
167

10 Ibid, 83–107, quote 100

11 *Enemies of God*, 116

12 Demos, *Entertaining Satan*, 287

13 ADMM B8667 no 5, 1592

14 Soman, *Sorcellerie et Justice
Criminelle*, passim

15 Mandrou, *Magistrats et sorciers*,
397–8, 439–58, 478–86

16 Johansen, 'Denmark: The Sociology of Accusations', 340–44

17 G. Jerouschek, *Die Hexen und ihr Prozess: die Hexenverfolgung in der Reichsstadt Esslingen* (Sigmaringen, 1992), 136–295

18 Midelfort, *Witch Hunting in Southwestern Germany*, 190–91

19 Ibid, 158–63

20 Ibid, 54, 191

21 Muchembled, *Sorcières, justice et société*, and *Le Roi et la sorcière* (Paris, 1993)

22 E. Labouvie, *Zauberei und Hexenwerk: Ländlicher Hexenglaube in der frühen Neuzeit* (Frankfurt am Main, 1991), esp. 55–69, 82–102, 135–54; W. Rummel, *Bauern, Herren und Hexen. Studien zur Sozialgeschichte sponheimischer und kurtrierische Hexenprozesse 1574–1664* (Göttingen, 1991), esp. 26–87, 237–51, 276–94, 298–301

23 Rummel, *Bauern, Herren und Hexen*, 38

24 E. Zens, 'Cornelius Loos – ein Vorläufer Friedrich Spees im Kampf gegen den Hexenwahn', *Kurtrierisches Jahrbuch* 2, 1962, 41–69, and P. C. van der Eerden, 'Cornelius Loos und die magia falsa', in Lehmann and Ulbricht, *Von Unfug des Hexen-Processes*, 139–60

25 Labouvie, *Zauberei und Hexenwerk*, and Rummel, *Bauern, Herren und Hexen*, passim

26 Rummel, *Bauern, Herren und Hexen*, 226–97

27 Ibid, 226–37

28 Ibid, 222–6, 297–8

29 Ibid, 308–15

30 Labouvie, *Zauberei und Hexenwerk*, 55–6

31 Rummel, *Bauern, Herren und Hexen*, 237–9

32 Ibid, 254–8

33 G. L. Burr, 'The Fate of Dietrich Flade', in L. O. Gibbons (ed), *George Lincoln Burr: His Life and Selections from his Writings* (Ithaca and N.Y., 1943), 190–233

34 G. Schormann, *Der Krieg gegen die Hexen: das Ausrottungsprogramm des Kurfürsten von Köln* (Göttingen, 1991), passim

35 T. W. Robisheaux, *Rural Society and the Search for Order in Early Modern Germany* (Cambridge, 1989), passim

36 N. Schindler, 'Die Enstehung der Unbarmherzigkeit: Zur Kultur und Lebensweise der Salzburger Bettler am ende des 17. Jahrhunderts', in *Widerspenstige Leute: Studien zur Volkskultur in der Frühen Neuzeit* (Frankfurt, 1992), 258–314

37 ADMM B6723 nos 1 and 2, Flin, 1602–3

38 ADMM B8684 no 7, St Lienard, 1600

39 ADMM B8678 no 4, St Dié, 1596

40 ADMM B3317 no 2, Blamont, 1599

41 H. de Waardt and W. de Blécourt, 'It is no sin to put an evil person to death', in Gijswijt-Hofstra and Frijhoff (eds), *Witchcraft in the Netherlands from the fourteenth to the twentieth century*, 72–3

42 M. Gijswijt-Hofstra, 'Six centuries of witchcraft in the Netherlands: Themes, outlines, and interpretations', ibid, 28

43 ADMM B7279, Azelot, 1583

44 ADMM B5344 no 3, Insming, 1608

45 ADMM B8721 no 3, Wisembach, 1618

46 ADMM B5679, Bathelemont-les-Bauzemont, 1610

47 ADMM B8691 no 13, Remémont, 1603

48 ADMM B8726 no 1, la Bourgonce, 1620

49 ADMM B8707 no 4, la Voivrelle, 1611

50 ADMM B8682 no 9, Ste Marguerite, 1598

51 ADMM B8986 no 1, St Nicolas, 1613

52 ADMM B8719 no 3, Raon, 1617

53 ADMM B8708 no 5, St Remy, 1611

54 ADMM B8724 no 1, Coincourt, 1619

55 ADMM B8678 no 2, St Dié, 1596

56 ADMM B5327 no 2, Assenoncourt, 1599–1600, and B6760, Rehainviller, 1624

57 ADMM B8687 no 7, la Vacherie, 1601

58 ADMM B3789, Brouvelieures, 1615

59 ADMM B3804 no 3, Fontenay, 1620

60 ADMM B8275 no 1, Preny, 1597

61 ADMM B4103 no 3, Gripport, 1615

62 ADMM B3325 no 1, Gondrexon, 1602–3

63 ADMM B4569 no 1, Neufchâteau, 1609

64 Ewen, *Witchcraft and Demonianism*, 372–3

65 ADMM B8689 no 2, Moyemont, 1602

66 ADMM B3813, Grandvillers, 1625–6

67 ADMM B7309 no 2, Einville, 1593

68 C. F. Oates, 'Trials of Werewolves in the Franche-Comté in the early modern period' (Ph.D. thesis, London, 1993), 183–6 and 290–302

69 AD Vosges G710; ADMM B8731

70 Sharpe, *Witchcraft in Seventeenth-Century Yorkshire*, 21–3

71 Ewen, *Witchcraft in the Star Chamber*, 12, 20–2, 37–41

CHAPTER X

1 P. Feyerabend, *Science in a Free Society* (London, 1978), 92

2 *New Scientist*, no. 1998, 7 October 1995, 63, citing the *Okavanga Observer*

3 S. Greenblatt, 'Psychoanalysis and Renaissance Culture', in *Learning to Curse: Essays in Early Modern Culture* (New York and London, 1990), 131–45

4 A. Levi, *French Moralists: the Theory of the Passions, 1585 to 1649* (Oxford, 1964)

5 N. Z. Davis, *The Return of Martin Guerre* (Cambridge Mass. and London, 1983)

6 Montaigne, *Essays* III, xi, in *Works*, trans D. Frame, 788

7 J. H. Barkow, L. Cosmides, and J. Tooby, *The Adapted Mind: Evolutionary Psychology and the Generation of Culture* (New York and London, 1992)

8 E. Gellner, *Plough, Sword and Book: The Structure of Human History* (London, 1988), 51–3 and 39–144, passim

9 C. Taylor, *Sources of the Self: The Making of the Modern Identity* (Cambridge Mass., 1989), 192 and 143–98 passim

10 G. Jerouschek, *Die Hexen und ihr Prozess: die Hexenverfolgung in der Reichsstadt Esslingen* (Sigmaringen, 1992), 73–97

11 Midelfort, *Witch Hunting in Southwestern Germany*, 36–61

12 R. Rowland, '"Fantasticall and Devilishe Persons": European Witch-beliefs in comparative perspective', in Ankarloo and Henningsen, *Early Modern European Witchcraft*, 161–90

13 Roper, *Oedipus and the Devil*, passim

14 J. McDougall, *Theatres of the Mind: Illusion and truth on the psychoanalytic stage* (New York, 1985)

15 J. Tooby and L. Cosmides, 'The Psychological Foundations of Culture', in Barkow *et al*, *The Adapted Mind*, 89

16 J. H. Barkow, 'Beneath New Culture is Old Psychology: Gossip and Social Stratification', in ibid, 628

CONCLUSION

1 S. Clark, *Thinking With Demons* (Oxford, forthcoming)

2 R. I. Moore, *The Formation of a Persecuting Society: Power and Deviance in Western Europe, 950–1250* (Oxford, 1987)

3 Cohn, *Europe's Inner Demons*, 126–46

4 Montaigne, 'Of Cannibals', Essays I xxxi, in *Works*, trans. Frame, 155

5 G. Naudé, *Apologie pour tous les grands personnages qui ont esté faussement soupçonnez de Magie* (The Hague, 1653), 127 (first ed. Paris, 1625)

Further Reading

There is an immense literature on witchcraft, of very variable quality. This selective bibliography makes no pretension to cover the field properly; I have omitted books and articles on various grounds. Some I have not read, others I think erroneous or misguided, while more again are buried in specialist journals accessible to very few people. Essentially this is a personal selection of writings I have found helpful, even when I do not wholly agree with their conclusions. The most recent attempt at a more comprehensive bibliography is H. C. E. Midelfort, 'Witchcraft, Magic and the occult', in S. E. Ozment (ed), *Reformation Europe: A Guide to Research* (St Louis, 1982).

There is no really satisfactory book on European witchcraft persecution and belief as a whole. The most reliable summary in English is B. P. Levack, *The Witch-Hunt in Early Modern Europe* (London, 1987, 2nd ed., 1995), a competent but rather unadventurous book. G. P. Quaife, *Godly Zeal and Furious Rage: the Witch in Early Modern Europe* (London, 1987), is in some ways livelier, but lacks critical acumen and is fatally damaged by the author's seemingly exclusive reliance on literature in English. J. Klaits, *Servants of Satan: the Age of the Witch-hunts* (Bloomington, 1985), is really no more than a long essay. The older books by J. Caro Baroja, *The World of the Witches* (London, 1965), and H. R. Trevor-Roper, *The European Witch-Craze of the Sixteenth and Seventeenth Centuries* (Harmondsworth, 1969), predate the major research effort of the last three decades. Both were distinguished contributions in their time and, like many other scholars, I owe them a major debt. Unfortunately, so many of the factual statements made by Trevor-Roper (in particular), have now been disproved that his beautifully-written and elegant essay, while still valuable, can easily mislead the unwary. R. H. Robbins, *The Encyclopedia of Witchcraft and Demonology* (New York, 1959), is also now outdated, while the author's general stance is often simplistic. Nevertheless this remains a very useful collection of information and older bibliography.

In French, a recent collective volume edited by R. Muchembled, *Magie et Sorcellerie en Europe* (Paris, 1994) contains excellent chapters by specialists on different regions, but is inevitably less good as a general interpretation. An older book with a similar title is Y. Castan, *Magie et Sorcellerie à l'époque moderne* (Paris, 1979), which although not an easy read is subtle and thoughtful. Perhaps closest to my own approach is R. Muchembled, *La sorcière au village (XVe-XVIIIe siècle)* (Paris, 1979), a mixture of texts and commentary which works very well, but is largely confined to French-speaking regions. His more recent *Le roi et la sorcière: l'Europe des bûchers XVe-XVIIIe siècle* (Paris, 1993) has a broader coverage, and is very well-informed about recent scholarship. On the other hand, the author presents a bold interpretation linking witchcraft to broad political and social changes, with which I find myself in some (friendly) disagreement, because I think that many of the alleged links are much weaker than he supposes.

For the Middle Ages, there is much interesting work with a bearing on witchcraft. V. Flint, *The Rise of Magic in Early Medieval Europe* (Princeton and Oxford, 1991), is rather controversial; R. Kieckhefer, *Magic in the Middle Ages* (Cambridge, 1990), tackles the later period more cautiously. R. I. Moore, *The Formation of a Persecuting Society: Power and Deviance in Western Europe, 950-1250* (Oxford, 1987) is important and thought-provoking. Although J. B. Russell, *Witchcraft in the Middle Ages* (Ithaca and London, 1972) provides a useful survey of source material, I often find his interpretations strained or misguided. Like most other earlier writers, he was misled by the forgeries identified by N. Cohn, *Europe's Inner Demons: An Enquiry Inspired by the Great Witch-Hunt* (London, 1975) and R. Kieckhefer, *European Witch Trials: Their Foundations in Popular and Learned Culture, 1300-1500* (London, 1976); these two books are now essential reading for the early phase of persecution. C. Ginzburg, *Ecstasies: Deciphering the Witches' Sabbath* (London, 1990) also concentrates on this early period. To me this is a *tour de force* of learning and ingenuity that ends up as a heroic failure, and has less to say about witchcraft than one would expect. A useful collection of articles in German is A. Blauert (ed), *Ketzer, Zauberer, Hexen. Die Anfänge der europäischen Hexenverfolgung* (Frankfort-am-Main, 1990); the editor has also written a book entitled *Frühe Hexenverfolgungen. Ketzer-, Zauberei- und Hexenprozesse des 15. Jahrhunderts* (Hamburg, 1989). One of the best essays in the collection is available in English in A. Borst, *Medieval Worlds: Barbarians, Heretics and Artists in the Middle Ages* (Cambridge, 1991). A new study of early trials in Dauphiné can be found in P. Paravy, *De la Chrétienté Romaine à la Réforme en Dauphiné. Evêques, fidèles et déviants (vers 1340 – vers 1530)* (2 vols, Rome 1993).

Moving into the early modern period, an outstanding collection of essays is that edited by B. Ankarloo and G. Henningsen, *Early Modern European Witchcraft: Centres and Peripheries* (Oxford, 1990), which makes available in English recent work on many less well-known parts of northern, central and southern Europe. Important in a different way is L. Roper, *Oedipus and the Devil: Witchcraft, sexuality and religion in early modern Europe* (London, 1994), which offers striking new insights into some German cases. On demonology there are the rather uneven pieces edited by S. Anglo, *The Damned Art: Essays in the Literature of Witchcraft* (London, 1977). We keenly await the major study by S. Clark,

Thinking With Demons (Oxford, forthcoming). For a taste of his approach see his classic essay 'Inversion, Misrule and the Meaning of Witchcraft', *Past and Present* 87, 1980, and more recently 'The rational witch-finder: conscience, demonological naturalism and popular superstitions', in S. Pumphrey, P. L. Rossi and M. Slawinski (eds), *Science, Culture and Popular Belief in Renaissance Europe* (Manchester, 1991). Another general collection of essays will appear shortly as J. Barry, M. Hester and G. Roberts (eds), *Witchcraft in Early Modern Europe: Studies in Culture and Belief* (Cambridge, forthcoming). A more specialized volume is N. Jacques-Chaquin and M. Préaud (eds), *Le Sabbat des sorciers* (Grenoble, 1993). There is a stimulating recent article by W. de Blécourt, 'Witch doctors, soothsayers and priests. On cunning folk in European historiography and tradition', *Social History* 19, 1994. The posthumously published essays of C. Larner, *Witchcraft and Religion* (Oxford, 1984), contain many good things, although I do not agree with her general interpretation of European (as opposed to Scottish) witchcraft (see notes).

Collections of source material include those by A. C. Kors and E. Peters, *Witchcraft in Europe 1100–1700: a Documentary History* (Philadelphia, 1972) and E. W. Monter, *European Witchcraft* (New York, 1969). Monter's *Ritual, Myth and Magic in Early Modern Europe* (Hassocks, 1983) provides useful background, as does another volume in the same series, M. R. Weisser, *Crime and punishment in early modern Europe* (Hassocks, 1979). S. Haliczer (ed), *Inquisition and Society in Early Modern Europe* (Beckenham, 1987) and G. Henningsen and J. Tedeschi (eds), *The Inquisition in Early Modern Europe: Studies on Sources and Methods* (Dekalb, 1986) both contain some excellent essays, while there is another book by Monter, *Frontiers of Heresy: The Spanish Inquisition from the Basque Lands to Sicily* (Cambridge, 1990).

No-one has written a straightforward account of English witchcraft in general since W. Notestein, *A History of Witchcraft in England* (Washington, 1911). This was usefully supplemented by G. L. Kittredge, *Witchcraft in Old and New England* (Cambridge Mass., 1929). Jim Sharpe is now writing a new general study. Modern literature on the subject is dominated by two major books. K. V. Thomas, *Religion and the Decline of Magic* (London, 1971), is a magisterial work with a long section devoted specifically to witchcraft. A. D. J. Macfarlane, *Witchcraft in Tudor and Stuart England: a regional and comparative study* (London, 1970) uses anthropological methods to great effect alongside more traditional historical ones to examine the extensive materials from Essex. A good deal of oblique light is thrown on the subject by Michael MacDonald, *Mystical Bedlam: Madness, anxiety and healing in seventeenth-century England* (Cambridge, 1981), while he has made a valuable direct contribution through an edition of texts with a long introduction, *Witchcraft and Hysteria in Elizabethan London: Edward Jorden and the Mary Glover Case* (London, 1991). Interesting articles include two by C. A. Holmes, 'Women, Witnesses and Witches', *Past and Present* 140,

1993, and 'Popular Culture? Witches, magistrates and divines in early modern England', in S. L. Kaplan (ed), *Understanding popular culture: Europe from the middle ages to the nineteenth century* (Berlin, 1984), as well as A. Gregory, 'Witchcraft, Politics and "Good Neighbourhood" in early seventeenth-century Rye', *Past and Present* 133, 1991. There is a valuable pamphlet by J. A. Sharpe, *Witchcraft in Seventeenth-Century Yorkshire: Accusations and Counter-Accusations*, Borthwick Papers 81 (York, 1992), and an article by him on 'Witchcraft and women in seventeenth-century England: some northern evidence' in *Continuity and Change* 6, 1991, while there are articles by Sharpe and M. Gaskill in J. Kermode and G. Walker (eds), *Women, Crime and the Courts in early modern England* (London, 1994). More specialized studies include J. L. Teall, 'Witchcraft and Calvinism in Elizabethan England: divine power and human agency', *Journal of the History of Ideas* 23, 1962, A. Pollock, 'Social and economic characteristics of witchcraft accusations in sixteenth and seventeenth-century Kent', *Archaeologia Cantiana* 95, 1979, R. C. Sawyer, ' "Strangely handled in all her lyms": witch-craft and healing in Jacobean England', *Journal of Social History* 22, 1989, and D. Harley, 'Mental Illness, Magical Medicine and the Devil in Northern England, 1650–1700', in R. French and A. Wear (eds), *The Medical Revolution of the Seventeenth Century* (Cambridge, 1989).

Many of the sources for English witchcraft have been published, notably by C. L. Ewen in *Witch-Hunting and Witch Trials* (London, 1929), *Witchcraft and Demonianism* (London, 1933) and *Witchcraft in the Star Chamber* (n.p., 1938). Another useful source publication is G. B. Harrison (ed), *The Trial of the Lancaster Witches, 1612* (London, 1929). A good selection of pamphlets and other materials is reprinted by B. Rosen, *Witchcraft* (London, 1969). The essential book by R. Scot, *The Discoverie of Witchcraft* (London, 1584) should be read in the only reliable modern edition, that by B. Nicholson (London, 1886), which was reprinted in 1973. The important tracts by G. Gifford, *A Briefe Discourse wherein is declared the subtil practise of devils by witches and sorcerers* (London, 1587) and *A Dialogue concerning Witches and Witchcraftes* (London, 1593) have also been reprinted. Other works like T. Ady, *A Candle in the Dark* (London, 1656) are likely to prove harder to find. The witch-hunter John Stearne's *A Confirmation and Discovery of Witchcraft* (London, 1648), on the other hand, was reprinted at Exeter in 1973. K. M. Briggs, *Pale Hecate's Team* (London, 1962) is an attractive survey of literary and folkloric materials. Most fictional works about witchcraft are dismally bad, so it is worth noting an exception in Leslie Wilson's sensitive novel *Malefice* (London, 1992); here is a writer who has taken the trouble to read the historians carefully.

For Scotland, few will feel much need to go beyond C. Larner, *Enemies of God: the Witch-hunt in Scotland* (London, 1981), one of the best of all national studies. She had previously edited, with C. H. Lee and H. V. McLachlan, *A Source-Book of Scottish Witchcraft* (Glasgow, 1977). There is also E. Cowan, 'The darker vision of the Scottish Renaissance', in I. B. Cowan and D. Shaw (eds), *The Renaissance and Reformation in Scotland* (Edinburgh, 1983), and B. P. Levack, 'The great Scottish witch hunt of 1661–1662', *Journal of British Studies* 20, 1980. King James VI and I's *Daemonologie* was edited by G. B. Harrison (London, 1924). For the king's own attitudes there are very helpful new ideas in J. Wormald, 'The Witches, the Devil and the King', in T. Brotherstone and D. Ditchburn (eds), *Scotland: The History of the Medieval Nation: Essays presented to Grant G. Simpson* (Edinburgh, 1995).

Witchcraft beliefs among the English settlers in North America have been the subject of some outstanding recent work. Much of this has inevitably been on Salem, notably P. Boyer and S. Nissenbaum, *Salem Possessed: The Social Origins of Witchcraft* (Cambridge Mass., 1974) and the same authors' *Salem-Village Witchcraft: A Documentary Record of Local Conflict in Colonial New England* (Belmont Calif., 1972; new ed., Boston 1993). The most extensive reconsideration of the trials themselves is that by B. Rosenthal, *Salem Story: Reading the Witch Trials of 1692* (Cambridge, 1993). Some important points are raised by D. Harley, 'Explaining Salem: Calvinist Psychology and the Diagnosis of Possession', *American Historical Review* (forthcoming). On New England more generally, important books include J. P. Demos, *Entertaining Satan: Witchcraft and the Culture of Early New England* (New York and Oxford, 1982), R. Weisman, *Witchcraft, Magic, and Religion in Seventeenth-Century Massachusetts* (Amherst Mass., 1984), and R. Godbeer, *The Devil's Dominion: Magic and Religion in Early New England* (Cambridge, 1992). C. F. Karlsen, *The Devil in the Shape of a Woman: Witchcraft in Colonial New England* (New York and London, 1987), proposes a socio-economic explanation for the choice of certain women as suspects. D. D. Hall, *Worlds of Wonder, Days of Judgment: Popular Religious Beliefs in Early New England* (New York, 1989) is also helpful, while Hall has edited *Witch-Hunting in Seventeenth-Century New England: A Documentary History 1638–1692* (Boston, 1991). There is also the much older collection edited by G. L. Burr, *Narratives of the Witchcraft Cases 1648–1706* (New York, 1914).

Perhaps the most active centre of recent research has been Germany, which is appropriate in view of the scale of persecution in the German lands and the richness of surviving archives. The best study available in English is still H. C. E. Midelfort, *Witch Hunting in Southwestern Germany, 1562–1684* (Stanford, 1972), but this should soon be joined by a translation of W. Behringer's excellent *Hexenverfolgung in Bayern. Volksmagie, Glaubenseifer und Staatsräson in der Frühen Neuzeit* (Munich, 1987). M. Kunze, *Highroad to the Stake* (Chicago and London, 1987), offers a very readable account of the Pappenheimer trials of 1602. Two very important books give a vivid picture of events in the Saarland and nearby territories; these are E. Labouvie, *Zauberei und Hexenwerk: Ländlicher Hexenglaube in der frühen Neuzeit* (Frankfurt am Main, 1991) and W. Rummel, *Bauern, Herren und Hexen. Studien zur Sozialgeschichte sponheimischer und kurtrierische Hexenprozesse*

1574–1664 (Göttingen, 1991). To these may be added H. Pohl, *Hexenglaube und Hexenverfolgung im Kurfürstentum Mainz. Ein Beitrag zur Hexenfrage im 16. und beginnenden 17. Jahrhundert* (Stuttgart, 1988) and G. Schormann, *Der Krieg gegen die Hexen: das Ausrottungsprogramm des Kurfürsten von Köln* (Göttingen, 1991), although it has been suggested that the latter exaggerates the role of the Elector and his officials.

For those who do not read German there is less to offer, apart from the book by Lyndal Roper already cited. There is a good article by R. S. Walinski-Kiel, ' "Godly States", Confessional Conflict and Witch-Hunting in Early Modern Germany', *Mentalities-Mentalités* 5, 2, 1988, and the admirable old study by G. L. Burr, 'The Fate of Dietrich Flade', in L. O. Gibbons (ed), *George Lincoln Burr: His Life and Selections from his Writings* (Ithaca and New York, 1943). Midelfort has written interestingly on 'Johann Weyer and the Transformation of the Insanity Defence' in R. Po-Chia Hsia (ed), *The German People and the Reformation* (Ithaca and London, 1988). Among other recent German monographs and collections some of the more interesting are D. Unverhau, *Von "Toverschen" und "Kunstfruwen" in Schleswig 1548–1557: Quellen und Interpretationen zur Geschichte des Zaubern und Hexenwesens* (Schleswig, 1980), C. Degn, H. Lehmann and D. Unverhau (eds), *Hexenprozesse: Deutsche und skandinavische Beiträge* (Neumünster, 1983), G. Jerouschek, *Die Hexen und ihr Prozess: die Hexenverfolgung in der Reichsstadt Esslingen* (Sigmaringen, 1992), H. H. Kunstmann, *Zauberwahn und Hexenprozess in der Reichsstadt Nürnberg* (Nuremberg, 1970), H. Lehmann and O. Ulbricht (eds), *Von Unfug des Hexen-Processes: Gegner der Hexenverfolgung von Johann Weyer bis Friedrich Spee* (Wiesbaden, 1992), and R. van Dülmen (ed), *Hexenwelten: Magie und Imagination* (Frankfurt am Main, 1987).

A group of recent German studies I did not see in time to incorporate their findings includes R. Walz, *Hexenglaube und magische Kommunikation im Dorf der Frühen Neuzeit: Die Verfolgungen in der Grafschaft Lippe* (Paderborn, 1993), I. Arendt-Schulte, *Weise Frauen – böse Wieber: Die Geschichte der Hexen in der Frühen Neuzeit* (Freiburg, 1994), S. Lorenz (ed), *Hexen und Hexenverfolgung im deutschen Südwesten* (Karlsruhe, 1994), G. Wilbertz, G. Schwerhoff and J. Scheffler (eds), *Hexenverfolgung und Regionalgeschichte: Die Grafschaft Lippe im Vergleich* (Bielefeld, 1994), and G. Franz and F. Irsigler (eds), *Hexenglaube und Hexenprozesse im Raum Rhein-Mosel-Saar* (Trier, 1995). I greatly admire the essay on the *Zaubererjackl* persecution by N. Schindler, 'Die Enstehung der Unbarmherzigkeit: Zur Kultur und Lebensweise der Salzburger Bettler am ende des 17. Jahrhunderts', in his *Widerspenstige Leute: Studien zur Volkskultur in der Frühen Neuzeit* (Frankfurt, 1992). There is a book on the early classic of demonology by P. Segl, *Der Hexenhammer: Entstehung und Umfeld des Malleus Maleficarum von 1487* (Cologne, 1988), while Weyer has recently been edited and translated by G. Mora, *Witches, Devils and Doctors in the Renaissance: Johann Weyer's De Praestigiis Daemonum*

(Binghampton, 1991). For the Austrian lands the standard work is still F. Byloff, *Hexenglaube und Hexenverfolgung in den österreichischen Alpenländern* (Berlin and Leipzig, 1934).

Some intensive research is now under way on the rich Hungarian archives; preliminary results of great interest are reported by G. Klaniczay in his contribution to the Ankarloo and Henningsen volume and in some of the essays in his *The Uses of Supernatural Power: The Transformation of Popular Religion in Medieval and Early-Modern Europe* (Oxford, 1990). For German Switzerland there is G. Bader, *Die Hexenprozesse in der Schweiz* (Affolteren, 1945), for French-speaking areas and the Jura, E. W. Monter's *Witchcraft in France and Switzerland: The Borderlands during the Reformation* (Ithaca and London, 1976) provides both an excellent overview and some detailed analyses. More recently there is C. Broye, *Sorcellerie et superstitions à Genève (XVIe-XVIIIe siècles)* (Geneva, 1990). Four relatively early trials are the subject of a good monograph by P-H. Choffat, *La Sorcellerie comme exutoire. Tensions et conflits locaux: Dommartin 1524–1528* (Lausanne, 1989), while the quantitative approach is well represented by P. Kamber, 'La chasse aux sorciers et aux sorcières dans le Pays de Vaud. Aspects quantitatifs (1581–1620)', *Revue historique vaudoise* 90, 1982. There is an article by S. Burghartz on 'The Equation of Women and Witches: A Case Study of Witchcraft Trials in Lucerne and Lausanne in the Fifteenth and Sixteenth Centuries' in R. J. Evans (ed), *The German Underworld: Deviants and Outcasts in German History* (London, 1988). Although Savoy still awaits a full scholarly study, an idea of the potential interest of its archives is given by M. Brocard-Plaut, *Diableries et sorcellerie en Savoie* (Le Côteau, 1986).

Moving into northern Italy, there is the fascinating book by C. Ginzburg, *The Night Battles: Witchcraft and Agrarian Cults in the Sixteenth and Seventeenth Centuries* (Baltimore, 1983); a short pendant is his article 'Witchcraft and Popular Piety: Notes on a Modenese Trial of 1519', in *Myths, Emblems, Clues* (London, 1990). Another outstanding work is that by G. Levi, *Inheriting Power: The Story of an Exorcist* (Chicago and London, 1988). Complementary views of the Venetian situation are given by R. Martin, *Witchcraft and the Inquisition in Venice, 1550–1650* (Oxford, 1989) and G. Ruggiero, *Binding Passions: Tales of Magic, Marriage, and Power at the End of the Renaissance* (New York and Oxford, 1993). Further south, local beliefs are examined by D. Gentilcore, *From Bishop to Witch: the system of the sacred in early modern Terra d'Otranto* (Manchester, 1992), and by J-M. Sallmann, *Chercheurs de trésors et jeteuses de sorts: la quête du surnaturel à Naples au XVIe siècle* (Paris, 1986). There are good articles in the collections on the Inquisition by Haliczer and Henningsen and Tedeschi mentioned above.

These collections also contain material on Spain, while for Portugal there is an excellent article by F. Bethencourt in the Ankarloo and Henningsen volume. The outstanding book on witchcraft in Spain is G. Henningsen, *The Witches' Advocate: Basque Witchcraft and the Spanish Inquisition, 1609–1614* (Reno,

Nevada 1980); there is also material on Aragon in Monter's *Frontiers of Heresy*. An important earlier book is J. Caro Baroja, *Vidas mágicas e Inquisición* (2 v., Madrid, 1967), while popular beliefs in Portugal are illuminated by J.P. Paiva, *Práticas e crenças mágicas: o medo e a necessidade dos mágicos na Diocese de Coimbra (1650–1740)* (Coimbra, 1992). Developments across the Atlantic are admirably treated by F. Cervantes, *The Devil in the New World: The Impact of Diabolism in New Spain* (New Haven and London, 1994).

The smaller territories between Germany and France, the scene of a good deal of persecution, have attracted numerous historians. For the Franche-Comté, apart from Monter's *Witchcraft in France and Switzerland*, there are two rich local studies by F. Bavoux, *La Sorcellerie au Pays de Quingey* (Monaco, 1954) and *Hantises et diableries dans la terre abbatiale de Luxueil* (Monaco, 1956). I have also been able to benefit from the unpublished work of C. F. Oates, 'Trials of Werewolves in the Franche-Comté in the early modern period' (Ph.D. thesis, London, 1993). There has been less recent work on Alsace, but there is a useful article by J. Klaits, 'Witchcraft trials and absolute monarchy in Alsace', in R. M. Golden (ed), *Church, State and Society under the Bourbon Kings of France* (Lawrence Kan., 1982). On Lorraine the most extensive work to date is E. Delcambre, *Le concept de la sorcellerie dans le duché de Lorraine au XVIe et au XVIIe siècle* (3 vols, Nancy, 1948–51), to which can be added two articles by myself in *Communities of Belief: Cultural and Social Tensions in Early Modern France* (Oxford, 1989). A more specialized monograph is E. Delcambre and J. Lhermitte, *Un cas énigmatique de possession diabolique en Lorraine au XVIIe siècle* (Nancy, 1956). For Luxembourg see M-S. Dupont-Bouchat, 'La répresssion de la sorcellerie dans le duché de Luxembourg aux XVIe et XVIIe siècles', in the volume by herself, R. Muchembled and W. Frijhoff, *Prophètes et sorciers dans les Pays-Bas, XVIe-XVIIIe siècle* (Paris, 1978).

The northern Netherlands have been admirably treated in a collective work, M. Gijswijt-Hofstra and W. Frijhoff (eds), *Witchcraft in the Netherlands from the fourteenth to the twentieth century* (Rotterdam, 1991). For the then Spanish Netherlands, further to the south, there are a number of important studies by R. Muchembled, most of them collected in *Sorcières, justice et société aux XVIe et XVIIe siècles* (Paris, 1987), but also including a substantial monograph, *Les derniers bûchers: Un village de Flandre et ses sorcières sous Louis XIV* (Paris, 1981). The possession cases are subtly discussed by A. Lottin, *Lille: citadelle de la contre-réforme?* (1598–1668) (Dunkirk, 1984), and in the same author's 'La "déplorable tragédie" de l'Abbaye du Verger en Artois (1613–1619)', in J. de Viguerie (ed), *Histoire des faits de la sorcellerie* (Angers, 1985).

That collection also contains several useful articles on French witchcraft, while I have attempted an overview in an essay in *Communities of Belief*. The two most important works on French witchcraft are R. Mandrou, *Magistrats et sorciers en France au XVIIe siècle* (Paris, 1968) and the collected articles (some in

English) of A. Soman, *Sorcellerie et Justice Criminelle: le Parlement de Paris (16e–18e siècles)* (Ashgate, 1992). Mandrou also edited a valuable selection of texts, *Possession et sorcellerie au XVIIe siècle: textes inédits* (Paris, 1979). D. P. Walker, *Unclean Spirits: Possession and exorcism in France and England in the late sixteenth and early seventeenth centuries* (London, 1981), is a lively if unduly brief book, while the Loudun case is superbly analysed by M. de Certeau, *La possession de Loudun* (Paris, 1970), and more conventionally presented by M. Carmona, *Les Diables de Loudun: sorcellerie et politique sous Richelieu* (Paris, 1988). A lightly fictionalized treatment in English is A. Huxley, *The Devils of Loudun* (London, 1952), the basis for John Whiting's outstanding play *The Devils* (London, 1961). An important long article, with extensive examples, is J-F. Le Nail, 'Procédures contre les sorcières de Seix en 1562', *Société ariégoise: sciences, lettres et arts* 31, 1976, while another interesting local study is J-F. Détrée, *Sorciers et possédés en Cotentin* (Coutances, 1975). Survival of the beliefs into later periods can be followed in E. Le Roy Ladurie, *Jasmin's Witch* (Aldershot, 1987), B. Traimond, *Le pouvoir de la maladie: Magie et politique dans les Landes de Gascogne 1750–1826* (Bordeaux, 1980), and J. Devlin, *The Superstitious Mind: French Peasants and the Supernatural in the Nineteenth Century* (New Haven and London, 1987). For the present-day situation, see J. Favret-Saada, *Deadly Words* (Cambridge, 1984), and by the same author with J. Contreras, *Corps pour corps: Enquête sur la sorcellerie dans le Bocage* (Paris, 1981); see also P. Gaboriau, *La Pensée ensorcelée: la sorcellerie actuelle en Anjou et en Vendée* (Paris, 1987).

On the vexed question of gender and witchcraft there is a very level-headed summary in chapter 7 of M. E. Wiesner, *Women and Gender in Early Modern Europe* (Cambridge, 1993), with a good selective bibliography. A persistent misconception on this subject is admirably demolished by D. Harley, 'Historians as demonologists: the myth of the midwife-witch', *Social History of Medicine* 3, 1990. There are some useful essays in J. R. Brink, A. P. Coudert and M. C. Horowitz (eds), *The Politics of Gender in Early Modern Europe*, Sixteenth Century Essays and Studies 12 (Kirksville Miss., 1989), and pieces by myself, 'Women as victims? Witches, judges, and the community', and S. Clark, 'The "Gendering" of Witchcraft in French Demonology: Misogyny or Polarity?', in *French History* 5, 1991. On a different form of putative discrimination there is E. Bever, 'Old age and witchcraft in early modern Europe', in P. Stearns (ed), *Old Age in Preindustrial Society* (New York, 1982).

This is not the place for a full bibliography of anthropological studies relating to the topic, but no-one should ignore the brilliant book by E. E. Evans-Pritchard, *Witchcraft, Oracles and Magic among the Azande* (Oxford, 1937, abridged ed., 1976), which set the agenda for so much of the best work on the subject. The best survey of the literature is still L. Mair, *Witchcraft* (London, 1969), while a good collection of articles is that edited by M. Douglas, *Witchcraft Confessions and Accusations* (London, 1970). There is a selection of readings edited by M. Marwick, *Witchcraft and Sorcery* (Harmondsworth, 1970). A fine recent book on an Indian village case is F. G. Bailey, *The Witch-Hunt; or, The Triumph of Morality* (Ithaca and London, 1994). On modern witchcraft in Britain, see T. M. Luhrmann, *Persuasions of the Witch's Craft: Ritual Magic and Witchcraft in Present-day England* (Oxford, 1989). Rather less satisfactory works on the American scene are M. Adler, *Drawing Down the Moon* (Boston, 1986), and G. G. Scott, *Cult and Countercult: A Study of a Spiritual Growth Group and a Witchcraft Order* (San Francisco, 1980), and *The Magicians: A Study of the Uses of Power in a Black Magic Group* (New York, 1982). An interesting collection of folklore studies was edited by V. Newall, *The Witch Figure* (London, 1973).

Index

FOR THE BEST IN PAPERBACKS, LOOK FOR THE

In every corner of the world, on every subject under the sun, Penguin represents quality and variety—the very best in publishing today.

For complete information about books available from Penguin—including Puffins, Penguin Classics, and Arkana—and how to order them, write to us at the appropriate address below. Please note that for copyright reasons the selection of books varies from country to country.

In the United Kingdom: Please write to *Dept. JC, Penguin Books Ltd, FREEPOST, West Drayton, Middlesex UB7 0BR.*

If you have any difficulty in obtaining a title, please send your order with the correct money, plus ten percent for postage and packaging, to *P.O. Box No. 11, West Drayton, Middlesex UB7 0BR*

In the United States: Please write to *Consumer Sales, Penguin USA, P.O. Box 999, Dept. 17109, Bergenfield, New Jersey 07621-0120.* VISA and MasterCard holders call 1-800-253-6476 to order all Penguin titles

In Canada: Please write to *Penguin Books Canada Ltd, 10 Alcorn Avenue, Suite 300, Toronto, Ontario M4V 3B2*

In Australia: Please write to *Penguin Books Australia Ltd, P.O. Box 257, Ringwood, Victoria 3134*

In New Zealand: Please write to *Penguin Books (NZ) Ltd, Private Bag 102902, North Shore Mail Centre, Auckland 10*

In India: Please write to *Penguin Books India Pvt Ltd, 706 Eros Apartments, 56 Nehru Place, New Delhi 110 019*

In the Netherlands: Please write to *Penguin Books Netherlands bv, Postbus 3507, NL-1001 AH Amsterdam*

In Germany: Please write to *Penguin Books Deutschland GmbH, Metzlerstrasse 26, 60594 Frankfurt am Main*

In Spain: Please write to *Penguin Books S. A., Bravo Murillo 19, 1° B, 28015 Madrid*

In Italy: Please write to *Penguin Italia s.r.l., Via Felice Casati 20, I-20124 Milano*

In France: Please write to *Penguin France S. A., 17 rue Lejeune, F–31000 Toulouse*

In Japan: Please write to *Penguin Books Japan, Ishikiribashi Building, 2–5–4, Suido, Bunkyo-ku, Tokyo 112*

In Greece: Please write to *Penguin Hellas Ltd, Dimocritou 3, GR–106 71 Athens*

In South Africa: Please write to *Longman Penguin Southern Africa (Pty) Ltd, Private Bag X08, Bertsham 2013*